MEDITERRANEAN SECURITY INTO THE COMING MILLENNIUM

Edited by
Stephen J. Blank

1999

*****

The views expressed in this report are those of the authors and do not necessarily reflect the official policy or position of the Department of the Army, the Department of Defense, or the U.S. Government. This report is cleared for public release; distribution is unlimited.

*****

Comments pertaining to this report are invited and should be forwarded to: Director, Strategic Studies Institute, U.S. Army War College, 122 Forbes Ave., Carlisle, PA 17013-5244. Copies of this report may be obtained from the Publications and Production Office by calling commercial (717) 245-4133, FAX (717) 245-3820, or via the Internet at rummelr@awc.carlisle.army.mil

*****

Most 1993, 1994, and all later Strategic Studies Institute (SSI) monographs are available on the Strategic Studies Institute Homepage for electronic dissemination. SSI's Homepage address is: http://carlisle-www.army.mil/usassi/welcome.htm

*****

The Strategic Studies Institute publishes a monthly e-mail newsletter to update the national security community on the research of our analysts, recent and forthcoming publications, and upcoming conferences sponsored by the Institute. Each newsletter also provides a strategic commentary by one of our research analysts. If you are interested in receiving this newsletter, please let us know by e-mail at outreach@awc.carlisle.army.mil or by calling (717) 245-3133.

ISBN 1-58487-003-6

CONTENTS

Foreword. v

1. Introduction
   Stephen J. Blank 1

2. Transnational Security Challenges
   in the Mediterranean
   Alessandro Politi 35

3. Regional Security Challenges
   in the Mediterranean
   Stephen Calleya 93

4. NATO in the Mediterranean
   Mario Zucconi 111

5. European Union Security Perceptions and Policies Towards
   the Mediterranean
   Roberto Aliboni. 125

6. Arab Perceptions of the European Union's
   Euro-Mediterranean Projects
   Mohammad El-Sayed Selim. 143

7. The Security Challenge in Kosovo:
   Toward A Region-Stabilizing Solution
   Steven L. Burg 159

8. The Cultural Scope of Balkan Security
   Stefano Bianchini 193

9. South-Eastern Europe at the Brink of the New Century:
   The Security Aspect
   Valeri Ratchev 221

10. Turkish Challenge and European Opportunity:
    Greek Foreign Policy Priorities in a Post-Cold War Setting
    Theodore A. Couloumbis. 249

11. Turkish Security Challenges in the 1990s
    Duygu Bazoglu Sezer. 261

12. Greek-Turkish Rivalry and the Mediterranean Security Dilemma
   R. Craig Nation 279

13. The Stalled Peace Process: Israeli-Syrian Track
   Sami G. Hajjar........................... 315

14. Israeli Security in a Changing Environment: Challenges and Responses
   Gerald M. Steinberg 347

15. American Policy Toward the Middle East in Clinton's Second Term
   Robert O. Freedman 371

16. Europe, the Mediterranean and the Middle East
   Rodolfo Ragionieri........................ 417

17. The Spirit of Eternal Negation: Russia's Hour in the Middle East
   Stephen J. Blank.......................... 443

About the Authors 515

FOREWORD

As Kosovo demonstrates, the United States is and will continue to be deeply engaged in the security of the Mediterranean Basin. Moreover, we will participate in shaping benevolent outcomes there with our allies and partners. Indeed, the United States cannot do otherwise since the multiple challenges to regional security in that area are so diverse and numerous. For these reasons, we must engage our allies and partners in an ongoing dialogue over the nature of security challenges, their perceptions of them, and the most effective ways to address them.

The papers included in this volume represent just such an effort to lay a firmer foundation for this continuing dialogue and to bring together different points of view. In October 1998, the Strategic Studies Institute, assisted by Pepperdine University, assembled a distinguished group of analysts from the United States, Europe, and the Middle East, in Florence, Italy. At a conference titled "Mediterranean Security into the Coming Millennium," the task of the participants was to address current regional security issues in the Balkans, Middle East, and the Aegean, as well as the perceptions of the individual states, the relevant security organizations, NATO and the European Union, and the players and major external actors like the United States and Russia. These papers cover the many areas discussed at the conference and should advance the debate on Mediterranean security both in the United States and abroad.

The Strategic Studies Institute is pleased to publish this compendium as a contribution to the international dialogue on these issues.

LARRY M. WORTZEL
Colonel, U.S. Army
Director, Strategic Studies Institute

CHAPTER 1

INTRODUCTION

Stephen J. Blank

At present, U.S. air, naval, and ground forces stand guard across the Mediterranean and perform multiple missions. The North Atlantic Treaty Organization's Kosovo operation is only the largest and most prominent of these combat or combat-related missions. However, the scope of American civil and military engagement in the Mediterranean basin is enormous and growing. And as the Kosovo operation increasingly appears to encompass a wholesale restructuring of the Balkan sub-regional security system, that scope will only expand further. Therefore, across the Mediterranean the number of troops on active deployment and their missions will probably increase.

This growth in U.S. engagement clearly pertains to our NATO allies as well, and not just in Kosovo. Even before that operation, they had forces in Bosnia due to the Dayton treaty. Both NATO and the European Union (EU) had begun systematic programs of security dialogues with other Mediterranean states in North Africa and the Middle East because of multiple challenges to the security of those organizations' member states. While those challenges are not strictly or even primarily military ones, many member states regard them as the fundamental blocks to regional security. If a lasting structure of peace is to evolve in the Mediterranean basin as a whole, Europe must engage those governments across a wide-ranging agenda of economic, social, political, military, and ecological issues. For these reasons, Mediterranean missions play an enormous role in current U.S. defense and foreign policies and will continue to be essential for our armed forces for some time.

However, even after the Kosovo operation began, the range and extent of the issues that we and our allies and partners must grapple with remain poorly understood and little known. Second, it is clear that so extensive a security agenda requires multilateral efforts and therefore continuing dialogue among all the players if cooperative and mutually beneficial solutions are to emerge. Most, if not all, security problems there, as Brigadier General John Batiste (USA) of AFSOUTH's Policy and Plans Division observed, are not military ones but economic and political.[1] Civilian and military professionals must also share their insights and experience through such dialogues to clarify and publicize the issues and the interrelationships among them. Apart from "trans-Mediterranean" issues, e.g., economic relations among Europe, the Middle East, and North Africa, we find many instances of intra-state security where states are at risk, and far too many cases of sub-regional and transnational challenges to security. For example, the regional agenda goes from Algeria's civil strife or Turkey's Kurdish insurgency to include Lebanon, the peace process, Israel's overall relations with its Arab neighbors, the whole Balkan cauldron, pervasive economic backwardness throughout most of the former Ottoman empire, the use of the Middle East and Balkans as an area of growing transnational crime including narcotics trafficking, proliferation of weapons of mass destruction, and, of course, the activities of the great powers in areas of long-standing rivalry and intervention.

For these reasons, the Strategic Studies Institute and Pepperdine University sponsored an international conference, "Mediterranean Security into the Coming Millennium," attended by civilians and military professionals from the United States, Europe, and the Middle East and held in Florence, Italy, on October 26-27, 1998. Even before international violence erupted in and over Kosovo (i.e., the civil war between the Serbian government and the Kosovo Liberation Army [KLA] was already in progress), it was clear that dialogue was urgently needed. Therefore the conference brought participants together to discuss many of these challenges to security. The papers that follow are some of those that were presented, but the conference agenda was even broader. Besides the papers that follow and a separate monograph on transnational threats such as drugs, terrorism, and proliferation, by Anthony Cordesman, the participants discussed the Arab side of the Israel-Arab relationship; the then recent Wye River Agreement between Israel and the Palestinian National Authority (PNA); and arms control.[2] The discussions were lively, spirited, and probing. Those discussions and the papers provide a basis for further international dialogue and engagement across continents and among civilians and military professionals. A second purpose of the conference was to engage the U.S. Army with regional institutions and experts in an ongoing dialogue on these issues; without such a dialogue the Army's and the West's ability to forge appropriate responses to future challenges will be undermined. That outcome would have a strongly negative impact upon Western security since NATO and the other organizations that provide security in and around Europe are already heavily engaged in the area. As General Klaus Naumann, Chairman of NATO's Military Committee, has written,

> It is in NATO and Europe's interest to keep conflicts at a distance and to cope with new risks which may no longer be the military risks we are accustomed to. It is for this very reason that NATO focuses its attention on the security in the Mediterranean and its periphery together with the Southern Region, which is today NATO's most endangered region.[3]

The need for such dialogues will grow as the engagement of the United States, either alone or with its allies and partners, grows. Without a better insight into the needs, interests, and views of our interlocutors, we are apt to stumble into a morass based on excessive unilateralism and triumphalism. And once so trapped, as in Kosovo, there may be no way out other than through a forceful military operation. This is not merely academic speculation.

Indeed, there are those, like Ambassador Matthew Nimetz, who argue that a U.S.-led Pax NATO is about to descend on the entire region. As Nimetz wrote, a clear U.S. commitment to remaining a military power here will markedly enhance regional security. This is also true for the major NATO powers: France, Germany, Italy, Great Britain, Spain, Greece, and Turkey.[4] To maintain regional security, NATO must not only integrate the entire region into the Western economy and foster the development of "pluralistic institutions," NATO must also grasp the military nettle.

> The Pax NATO is the only logical regime to maintain security in the traditional sense. As NATO maintains its dominant role in the Mediterranean, it must recognize a need for the expansion of its stabilizing influence in adjacent areas, particularly in Southeastern Europe, the Black Sea region (in concert, of course, with the regional powers, primarily Russia, Ukraine, Romania, Bulgaria, and Turkey) and in the Arabian/Persian Gulf. The United States must continue to play the major role in this security system. The Sixth Fleet will be the vehicle to implement this commitment for years to come, although this is something that might be reviewed some time down the road.[5]

However, upon closer examination, the problems of Mediterranean security do not appear to point to so clear-cut a resolution of future issues. And, as Kosovo shows us, NATO was unready to assume this responsibility or shoulder the burden of adequately supervising a regional peace so that war would not again break out. Indeed, challenges to the West as a whole and to the United States in particular may rise in the future beyond our ability to deal with them comprehensively. Kosovo shows the many problems that we now face in trying to execute Nimetz's mandate. And the fact that our engagement in Bosnia will not end anytime soon also will undoubtedly test NATO's staying power.

Mediterranean Security: The Issues.

To discuss Mediterranean security is to enter a conceptual minefield. Nor are these merely academic disputes. Definitional issues are deeply relevant to policy because any definition of the terms "Mediterranean" and "security" shapes the nature of our cognitive and policy responses to local challenges. Nor do these definitional issues pertain solely to U.S. forces. Precisely because the Mediterranean overlaps Asia, Africa, and Europe, our commitments there are often multilateral ones that involve NATO, the Organization for Security and Cooperation in Europe (OSCE), or bilateral partners like Morocco, Egypt, and Israel.

Thus our Mediterranean policies and domestic discussions about them take place in a context of multilateral and international debates and contending approaches to the problems of Mediterranean security. Without a shared understanding of the scope and nature of the issues we are facing, we will find ourselves unable to act alone or in concert with our allies and partners. If the United States or its armed forces disengages from regular concerted dialogues with its prospective regional partners, it will lose much of its standing and ability to shape responses to local security challenges. In that case, dissension rather than consensus will be the order of the day among our allies and partners, not to mention other interested parties. Instead of unity, challengers to local security will find Western disunity and arguments. Quarrels, not common undertakings, will reflect the nature of NATO, OSCE, and EU policy, as in the fiasco of Europe's and Washington's Bosnia policies until 1995 and the Dayton Peace Process or, more recently, Kosovo.

The visible discord among our NATO allies in the Kosovo crisis even after the operation began is very much due to the fact that their concepts of what must be done and what kind of outcomes are desirable diverge sharply from ours. This divergence is one of the primary causes of the difficulties we have faced regarding the Kosovo crisis in 1998-99.[6] A more informed and continuing dialogue among NATO members on Balkan issues in general and this one in particular might have averted this sorry spectacle. Sadly, Kosovo is only the latest in a long list of Mediterranean and Middle Eastern crises where inter-allied discord has hamstrung U.S. policy.[7]

Clearly this lesson must be constantly in our mind because it all too often is not one that sufficiently commands our elite's attention. Europe resents American unilateralism, and the United States is quick to cite Europe's seeming paralysis.[8] But Europe's "paralysis" stems as much from a growing perceptual gap between our allies and ourselves over the nature of security and challenges to it, as from diverging responses to those challenges. Therefore dialogue and discussion, not an arrogant know-it-all posture or self-righteous universalism and excessive faith in the use of long-distance, intense, but short-term military power, is the preferred answer to challenges to *international* security.

At the conference it rapidly became clear that the very terms "Mediterranean" and "security" are problematic and contentious in nature. When we say the word "Mediterranean," do we imply a strict geographical construction to include only those countries whose shores comprise the Mediterranean Sea's coastlines from Portugal and Morocco to Turkey, Syria, Lebanon, Israel, and Egypt? Or do we include whole regions attached to those coastlines, the entire Balkan peninsula, the entire Middle East to the Gulf, and beyond that the Black Sea littoral? After all, as Ambassador Luigi Ferraris observed in his keynote speech, the latter was colonized to some degree by the Greeks, the Romans, and later the Venetians. None of these colonizing peoples' Mediterranean affiliations are open to question.[9] By this standard, and it seems to be materializing before our eyes, Black Sea security issues must already play an important role in any consideration of the Mediterranean's security agenda. Thus definitions of the Mediterranean as a "security space" or "spaces" are subject to political definition as well as historical evolution. And even if we can satisfactorily provide a regional geographical definition so that all security providers agree on the territorial scope of their responsibility to provide security (whatever that means), can we also agree then that there is some overarching generic "Mediterranean" quality to the region?

That is, can we conceptually and thus practically organize our efforts and those of our alliances to create a single regional security system or structure? Or is it rather the case that the diversity of challenges to security across the entire space we have previously defined is so great that any unifying or uniform regional approach is foredoomed to failure and is inherently an absurd undertaking? For instance, Mario Zucconi argues that the Mediterranean space is not a unitary geopolitical realm and that in the absence of the galvanizing Soviet threat, allied interventions throughout the area must now be rationalized on a case-by-case basis.[10] Accordingly, a sub-regional approach that sharply differentiates between the challenges to security in the Balkans and the Arab-Israeli peace process must be the order of the day. Thus the search for a unifying and uniform strategic principle behind our operations in the Mediterranean is as elusive there as it is elsewhere.

And if the heterogeneity of threats to security is what distinguishes the region, can we deal with them through some form of sub-regional organizations? What form would those organizations take and what issues would they address? Furthermore, by what principle would we define the sub-regions and those states who can contribute to the region or sub-region's greater security? Is there a basis for lumping together Israel and Mauritania in the EU's and NATO's ongoing Mediterranean dialogue? Does the limping NATO-Mediterranean dialogue proceed on the same basis and should it do so? Does geography or some other attribute qualify for membership in such debates and fora? And is this a satisfactory way of organizing the Mediterranean littoral for any kind of security challenge? Evidence suggests that Israel, for example, finds such a structuring of the security process to be deeply problematical.[11] And it probably is not alone in doing so although other states will have their own reasons for such dissatisfaction with the Western approach. And these questions are hardly the only such issues of conceptualization and practical organization to bedevil efforts to enhance security. Whether one looks at the EU's Barcelona Initiative directed to the states upon the southern coast of the Mediterranean, or to NATO's Mediterranean dialogue, one finds little progress but continuing mutual suspicion and mistrust between North and South. Observers also discern within these processes mutual mistrust among the southern states, most strikingly, but not exclusively, in fora where Israel and Arab states would logically participate together on an equal basis.[12]

At the same time the Greco-Turkish controversy is heating up, with each side's senior statesmen denouncing the other in highly inflammatory terms as "outlaw states."[13] Professor Duygu Sezer's paper stresses that Turkish policymakers and elites feel surrounded by threats, not just Europe's rejection of Turkey's claim to membership in the EU and thus to an identity as a fully European state.[14] Yet other analysts write about Turkish policy in terms of Turkish high-handedness and confidence in striking truculent poses.[15] Who is right, and how do we square this circle? This too is not an academic point. Getting Turkey right is crucial to consolidating security in many troubled areas of the post-Cold War world. For example, 10 years after the fall of the Berlin Wall, the barriers separating north from south remain deeply entrenched, and the identity of what constitutes Europe remains a matter of intense contention and dispute. Turkey's attempt to enter the EU is a powerful emblem of those barriers and the salience of disputes over Europe's identity.

As Zucconi and many others have observed, NATO may be adapting its military structures, but its governments still cannot reach consensus on how, where, and when to intervene abroad. European governments are not ready to spend money for the proliferating new contingencies in the area that make up the bulk of current U.S. operations. Thus even before Kosovo it was obvious that resources were dwindling while operations tempo (OPTEMPO) and the number of contingencies were increasing.[16] Kosovo's results to date only confirmed many of the problems that will instantly arise due to the underfinancing of an overstretched NATO and U.S. military. Nor are these the only challenges to allied cohesion and comprehension of what must be done in the region. As Zucconi writes,

> And possibly, the main problem is not so much the dwindling budget and reduced force structure, as much as the lack of overall, articulated strategies and of clear determination to be engaged in upholding stability in this area. In fact, there is much improvisation and, in large measure, inability to come into the crisis before the issue becomes an intractable one. In interviews with this author in Brussels in June, 1998, about what to do and when to act in regard to Kosovo, several senior officials and military officers started by warning that the arrival of Christiane Amanpour, the CNN reporter, in Pristina, meant that NATO "had to do something"—needless to say, an indication of [the] lack of overall policies, of strategic planning, and even of well-defined mandates.[17]

And beyond the issues involved in defining and conceptualizing the Mediterranean, we encounter arguments over what security should mean and its definition. And again this is not an academic issue since the definition of security will furnish statesmen with their intellectual guide to policymaking for achieving that condition. Indeed, today the very notion of security itself is deeply contested, and the divisions over its meaning both cause and reflect the Alliance's inner confusion and discord. For NATO as an organization, as U.S. General Batiste made clear, the main sources of challenges and threats to security reside in economic-political structures and their defects.[18] Classical studies on security interpreted security strictly in terms of the defense of the integrity, independence, and sovereignty of a territory and state. The word security applied almost exclusively to military security. That is no longer the case. Security as a concept and as the goal of day-to-day policy is becoming ever more civilianized as are its practitioners. And NATO evidently accepts this trend as legitimate and as an accurate reflection of reality. Security also is increasingly used as a comprehensive term denoting policies across a broad range of governmental and inter-governmental activity that can fairly be described as being of unprecedented scope.[19] In Europe those responsible for security policy and those who contribute to the public discourse on it are increasingly disinclined to see the utility of military force as an answer to problems short of invasion or to fund it as we think they should. The term security now applies to economics, environmental security, societal security (or social but not our old age program) and so forth.[20] But in this context of an expanding definition of security that encompasses virtually all aspects of organized social life, what becomes NATO's role? After all, these kinds of issues are not those for which NATO is most equipped to deal with. But if NATO cannot effectively provide security in these domains and must wait for an explosion before acting, who then can and will provide security in any sense of the term? And can we find mechanisms by which to avert explosions or to anticipate crises? Here Zucconi and Roberto Aliboni seconded General Batiste by highlighting the need for the effective deployment of economic power as a *sine qua non* of any effective Western response to Mediterranean security challenges.[21] Yet at the same time, the EU's rather inhibited dialogues with the Mediterranean countries betrays hesitation, mutual incomprehension, and mutual suspicion as both Aliboni and especially Professor Mohammad El-Selim cogently argued.[22]

Egypt is hardly the only country that has a grievance against the EU. Israel is certainly dissatisfied with the progress of the EU's Barcelona dialogue, and Turkey's anger at its exclusion from the EU has been extensively displayed publicly.[23] Worse yet, as Sezer, Theodore

Couloumbis, and R. Craig Nation all indicated, Turkey's entry into the EU is formally tied to progress on its relationship with Greece and the resolution of the Cyprus issue.[24] Thus the EU's effectiveness as a vehicle for integrating Turkey, and beyond that the Middle East, is severely limited from the start. As Couloumbis stated,

> Greece now openly declares its willingness to lift its objections (given its veto power in the EU) to the building of a close relationship between the EU and Turkey, provided the latter abandons its threats of going to war over the Aegean question and contributes substantively toward a functional and mutually acceptable solution to the Cyprus question permitting the reunification of Cyprus as a federal, bizonal, and bicommunal state that is also a member of the European Union and NATO.[25]

Since even this quite moderate presentation of Greece's position puts or appears to put the onus of action wholly upon Turkey, it is unlikely to provide a satisfactory basis for resolving the issue. Thus the EU's failures and the linkage of Turkish entry to the bilateral political conflict will weaken NATO's cohesion and open the way to mischief makers of all sorts in the area. As R. Craig Nation pointed out, the Cyprus issue is thus tied to other, larger issues of both bilateral and regional security in the Eastern Mediterranean.[26] Already, as Stephen Blank observed, Russia's efforts to sell arms to both Greece and Cyprus are clearly motivated, at least in part, by a desire to fan the conflict's flames and weaken NATO by splitting it.[27]

Thus it would seem from these papers, and from the unhappy Bosnian and Kosovo experiences, that Europe still has not addressed with sufficient seriousness what it itself considers to be the root challenges of security through the EU, the organization most suited to deal with economic security issues. Kosovo may change that as the EU now appears to be moving to create a more comprehensive program of socio-economic reconstruction for the Balkan regional economy which has been devastated by almost 8 years of constant warfare in and around the former

Yugoslavia.[28] And if the EU is somehow remiss in meeting its responsibilities, how can NATO make up the security deficit in places like the Balkans? Or should it even try?

At the same time, the emphasis in Europe on threats stemming from underdeveloped Mediterranean economies' failure to modernize clashes with the U.S. tendency to see threats in more purely military terms and unilateralist approaches. And as we have seen in Bosnia and Kosovo, these differing or clashing perspectives inhibit rapid and unified allied or European response. Those disputes strain our relations with our allies and possibilities for effective coalition building and maintenance. Recently Italian Prime Minister Massimo D'Alema wrote that Italy, by virtue of the threats it faced from uncontrolled migration, drug running, and so on, was a front-line state.[29] While the humanitarian disaster in the wake of the Kosovo operation may increase our understanding of this perspective, his remarks remain jarring or dissonant to American ears since the term "front-line state" clearly denotes a state that is actively threatened in its vital interests by an opposing military force, not migrants fleeing for their lives. And if his analysis is true, NATO cannot do much to prevent these challenges to Italian security.

Until now the EU has been unwilling to act on its own to sponsor the rapid economic integration of Eastern Europe, Southeastern Europe, or the Middle East with Western Europe. As Stephen Calleya warned, there is the danger that European dialogues with the South may come to be seen as an exercise in boundary maintenance—fencing off the South from the North—not integration.[30] By all accounts, the EU's Barcelona process and the EU's Mediterranean Dialogue appear to be marking time. And NATO's parallel dialogue with Mediterranean states does not appear to be flourishing either. As Alberto Bin of NATO's Political Affairs Division and Secretary-General Javier Solana have both stated, the success of this initiative depends on developments in two other fora which are deeply troubled or just marking time, the peace process between

Israel and the Arabs, and the EU's Barcelona Process or Euro-Mediterranean Program.[31]

Meanwhile, the two most acute crisis areas seem to be the Middle East and the Balkans. The Florence conference took place immediately after the Wye River Agreement in Maryland between Israel and the Palestinian Authority in October 1998. Just to get this agreement on paper required a stupendous exertion of American diplomatic activity and appeals from the dying King Hussein of Jordan. Yet, as Robert Freedman and Gerald Steinberg both pointed out, it was not likely that this accord would constitute the decisive impetus to bring the two sides closer to peace. Domestic factors in Israel and the PNA, as well as the intense legacy of suspicion built up over the years, would probably obstruct much more progress. And the subsequent fall of the Israeli government of Prime Minister Netanyahu and the suspension of progress until elections in May 1999 validated their insights.[32] Failure to advance the peace process will likely diminish the U.S. standing in the area, for such a stalemate as well as the depth of the U.S. involvement in the Israeli political process could lead Israel or other states to look for alternatives to the stifling U.S. presence. Not surprisingly, a quite recent rapprochement between Jerusalem and Moscow seems to be emerging, in part for this reason.[33]

Neither do the difficulties of establishing peace in the Middle East end here. Sami Hajjar's discussion of the Lebanon triangle illustrates that fact. As long as the Lebanon issue remains unresolved with Israeli and Syrian forces both exercising an occupation or hegemony over part or all of the country and its government, terrorist attacks by Hizballah against Israeli armed forces in the south with Syrian and Iranian support will continue. But since Syria has no incentive to negotiate Israel's way out of this and accommodate Israel that is taking heavy losses but cannot find any satisfactory way to retreat without endangering its own territory, the conflict will go on. Under those circumstances, it cannot be ruled out that the conflict in

Lebanon could trigger a wider war as almost happened in 1975-76, 1982, and 1996. As Hajjar observed, Israel is now bogged down and trapped in one of the many low intensity or unconventional conflicts now taking place throughout the world. If its leadership cannot find an alternative solution, it may have to withdraw unilaterally, but that may not produce more security for itself or Lebanon either.[34] Thus it is entirely possible that war will go on here for a long time and poison the security environment for all concerned, including the United States. After all, our own recent memories of Lebanon are not happy ones, and it is unlikely we will intervene with force. But is it in American interests or within our capacity to remain aloof or disengaged from this process? On the other hand, if we cannot disengage from the peace process without serious losses to our interests and regional standing, how far should we be engaged? The experience of Israel's 1977 and 1996 elections show that if the United States is perceived as too obviously supporting one Israeli leader or coalition against another, then the U.S.-backed faction is likely to lose.

Obviously the Lebanon war will not come to an end without progress in some fashion between Israel and Lebanon and Syria. Washington's participation is also obviously indispensable. But as no such vista is in sight, the Eastern Mediterranean may not know peace for quite some time. And under such circumstances, as Stephen Blank warned, outside parties with rather different agendas, like Russia, could be tempted to intervene in the area. And indeed Moscow has fished in the turbid Lebanese waters already in 1996 and again at present as its relations with Syria and Israel now illustrate.[35]

The United States and its allies in the Eastern Mediterranean, e.g., Turkey and Israel, face threats beyond these unconventional ones of the Kurds and Lebanon or a renewed Intifada. In the United States the threat of a revived Iraqi weapons of mass destruction (WMD) program or Iran's developing one has become one of the most vital of contemporary defense issues. As missile defense against proliferation takes center stage in the United States, we must also recognize that this is becoming the most dangerous, if not vital, threat perceived by Israel and perhaps by Turkey as well.[36] As Steinberg and Sezer both observed, these missile and WMD threats are also major threats to Israeli and Turkish security and are forcing these governments to contemplate and undertake fundamental changes in thinking about defense strategy, force planning, and overall security policy. In Israel's case, this becomes even more urgent since it is no longer certain that it can achieve conventional superiority and deterrence over its Arab enemies.[37]

The Middle East in general has long since become a place of increased tendencies to long-distance missile warfare. This threat did not begin with Saddam Hussein. Egypt under Nasser had numerous German scientists working on rockets against Israel and Israel's atomic program began in the 1950s. Nor is WMD use a new threat or one that began with Iraq in its war with Iran in 1980-88. Nasser's Egyptian forces in Yemen, in the 1962-67 civil war, used chemical warfare against their Yemeni and Saudi-backed opponents. But what is most dangerous is that Saddam Hussein used chemical war as a strategic operation in the war against Iraq over a decade ago and paid no price for it then or since. The price he has paid is for attacking Kuwait in 1990 and his subsequent defiance of the United Nations Southern Command (UNSCOM) and the United States. Thus, his example is not likely to be the last one, for it succeeded both operationally and politically.[38] For the United States, Israel, and Turkey, proliferation and terrorism, two types of unconventional warfare that are simultaneously arrayed or deployed against them, are real and major threats. For example, Israeli Brigadier General (res.) Aharon Levran, a senior intelligence officer, recently told an interviewer that,

> You don't need heavy weapons to win. When you consider what has happened to us, the Palestinians have succeeded in beating us with the lightest of weapons. Clausewitz defines war as gaining one's goals. And when you consider what the

Palestinians have done—the territory which they have gained— they truly have demonstrated that terror is not only simply a nuisance—**it is in and of itself a strategic threat**. We have already seen how short range light weapons, when used to carry out a campaign of terror, can be just as effective in achieving the Arabs' goals as heavy weapons. After all, terror has achieved something which, traditionally, one side only loses after a crushing defeat—territory.[39] (emphasis author)

However, this is not the case in Europe. Or at least Europe and our major NATO allies do not uniformly see it as such a threat.[40] D'Alema omitted proliferation as a threat.[41] States that do not feel menaced by the same threats will find it difficult to cooperate on the reply to those threats. This is only one source of the difficulties the United States had with devising a new strategic concept for NATO. U.S. allies remain extremely skeptical of our argument that NATO should have the explicit capability and intention to strike at threats that may originate outside of Europe like proliferation.[42] Therefore there is little European urgency about devising effective and unified counterproliferation policies or about arms control regimes in the Middle East.

For instance, a recent article by Francois Gere of the *Fondation pour la Recherche Strategique* argued that a proliferation threat to Europe is highly doubtful as a threat requiring amendment of NATO's new strategic concept, that military ripostes to threats emanating from places like North Korea are taking over NATO's political process, and that there is no reason to believe that NATO would lose its effective deterrent capability *vis-à-vis* Russia if it dissents from Washington's stance on proliferation.[43] Like many European elites, he opposes globalizing the Alliance along lines suggested by the United States and stresses that we are overrating the military threat. Instead, for the Alliance to move forward there must be a strategic convergence of interests between Washington and Europe, and it must be confined to European issues, e.g., the Balkans and the Mediterranean. Therefore Europe must resist the effort to foist a global anti-proliferation posture upon it.[44]

Whether or not his arguments make sense for Europe, it is clear that they are irrelevant at best and dangerous at worst for the Middle East, including Turkey. Sezer has pointed out that Turkey feels surrounded, not least by proliferation of ballistic missiles and WMD.[45] And since such weapons have already been used with impunity in the Middle East, it is unlikely that further instances will not occur. Nor can pro-Western Middle Eastern states necessarily rely on allies and the promises of collective security for,

> In true collective security it should make no difference who commits aggression and who the victim is. But the principles of collective security were ignored even during the Gulf War. [Henry] Kissinger, among others, observed that in its finest hour, the Security Council closed its eyes to that principle when Israel was attacked. . . Tactically the Council's silence made eminent sense, but the implications of this omission are sobering, for they confirm yet again that the Council is governed less by the commitment to respond to unprovoked aggression than by the politics of the situation.[46]

Thus, for these states and for the United States, proliferation is seen as a growing menace. As Stephen Blank pointed out, Russia seems increasingly willing to supply Iran, Iraq, and even Syria with capabilities that can only enhance both their conventional and WMD capabilities.[47] Therefore the threat posed by proliferation of missiles with these capabilities and of conventional ballistic missiles to U.S. allies in the Middle East is rising. Nor do we have effective counters to it. While Russia's interest in obstructing U.S. initiatives is growing and adding another page to the history of the Middle East and Eastern Mediterranean as an area that is constantly and thoroughly penetrated by the great powers' more general rivalries, as Robert Freedman demonstrates, U.S. policy is floundering.[48]

As Freedman shows, the United States has proven to be inconstant in the peace process and unable to forge an Iraqi policy that commands international support. Worse yet,

U.S. attempts to forge a rapprochement with Iran have not yet borne appreciable fruit, and we can expect little progress here as a presidential election draws near. The United States has not succeeded in persuading our allies to invigorate their counterproliferation policies or to join us against Tehran and Baghdad. Instead, we have managed only to draw ourselves into a long-term, low-level war of attrition with Iraq and to commit ourselves to the overthrow of its government, policies and goals that is very unpromising.[49] Despite NATO's rhetorical and organizational commitment to a counterproliferation policy, it is clear that the allies' misgivings about U.S. policy on this issue will frustrate efforts to realize a meaningful strategic commitment.

But this means that the Middle East will remain, not just an arena of ethnic and religious conflict largely populated by authoritarian governments facing increasingly dire socio-economic challenges, but also an area of strategic dissension among our allies.[50] As before in European history, the inability of the powers to agree on the "Eastern Question" has allowed enterprising revisionist powers, today, most notably Russia, to attempt to unhinge the entire status quo using this area's inherent instability as a political crowbar. And we can see similar efforts underway in the Balkans. Russia seeks tactical alliance with powers like France who resent American prominence so that they can both enhance their position at the expense of the United States in Europe as well as in the Middle East.[51] This trend will only further complicate efforts to forge a strategic and operational consensus for NATO's new strategic concept when it comes time to implement it in practice. Therefore in the Middle East, on top of the structural failings in economics and politics that are the main sources of local challenges to internal and external security, we face the abiding tendency of the great powers to use the area as a battleground for their larger global political rivalries.

And the same holds true for the Balkans, Europe's own tinderbox where consensus among the great powers is no less elusive today than in the past. In the Balkans, as in the Middle East, local intrastate conflicts and ethnic rivalries easily spread across borders, threaten existing state borders, and then often, as in the past, generate major international crises. Frequently these crises are intensified because the great European powers approach them from the vantage point of their own interactions. Thus the United States did not intervene decisively in Bosnia until NATO's own cohesion was at stake. So, too, in 1991-92 the Anglo-Franco-German responses to the crackup of Yugoslavia were as much driven by their considerations of their own bilateral and trilateral interactions as they were by efforts to respond to local events and trends.[52]

NATO's new Kosovo operation only confirms and extends this depressing trend. NATO and the EU are now committed to a fundamental and long-term reorganization of the regional status quo and by so doing have decisively worsened relations with Russia. Russian ties to NATO will probably not improve when this war is over, and it already is talking ominously of revising its military doctrine to meet NATO's challenge to its sense of itself as a great power and to its regional security interests.[53] And if NATO fails to achieve its goals, Russia's interest in undermining allied cohesion and capability for doing so will dramatically grow.

While the Balkans may well produce too much history for its own good, that history is inextricable from the larger issues of European security. While nobody writing about the Balkans can just glide over the multiple challenges to security in maladapted political and economic structures, the siren song of exclusivist nationalism, contested borders, and so on, Europe's responses to these problems has been tepid or too little, too late, too often.

As Colonel Valeri Ratchev of Bulgaria makes clear, Romania and Bulgaria are anxiously looking to the West for support and finding encouragement to be in short supply.[54]

Nor is Ratchev's an isolated opinion that calls for a deeper European engagement. Romania's ambassador to the United States recently complained that allied prevarication on the "open door" to NATO is inhibiting foreign investment in her country.[55] That produces a vicious cycle which only impedes Romania's efforts to catch up to NATO and EU membership requirements. The destruction of a substantial part of the regional economy in the wake of the Kosovo operation only adds to this structural problem. Bulgaria may not have made effective use of the first 7 years of post-socialist rule, but it is now striving manfully to make the needed reforms and likewise fears that the doors to Europe will be shut in its face.[56] Perhaps skepticism about the depth of Sofia's or Bucharest's commitments to reform is not unmerited, but we should remember that these are the most pro-Western governments that we can expect in these states. If they fail, what prospect is there for their successors to launch the kind of reforms that will make them more eligible for integration according to Western standards and more secure?

However, the regional picture is not just one of either a total lack of reform or of complaints about the West. In February 1999, Bulgaria and Macedonia signed a treaty to put an end to the "artificial problems between our two countries," namely whether they speak a separate language or not. The two governments renounced national and territorial claims upon each other and refused support to groups who sought to use their territory for purposes hostile the other. Both sides also claimed that they had "found a way to speak in the language of a united Europe." And in March 1999, Romania, Turkey, and Bulgaria announced plans for a free trade zone to begin in 2002. A Balkan peace force made up of local forces is also coming into being.[57] While all these actions are not disinterested ones, they can and do contribute visibly to the possibility for building durable sub-regional or regional security structures in the Balkans that can help move that troubled area to a new and more tranquil place in world politics. These are most welcome developments and should remind us that not all is darkness in the Balkans. But too much still is darkness as Serbian policy daily shows us. The United States and NATO's militaries now realize that the only effective basis for enduring long-term stability in the region is through governments' provision and management of long-term prosperity. As Supreme Allied Commander Europe (SACEUR) General Wesley Clark observed, military force does not bring long-term stability, but prosperity does foster stability.[58] If we are to avoid more Kosovos and Bosnias, this lesson and its implications must forcefully be imprinted upon the official minds of governments who have the capability to help and interests that would otherwise be negatively affected by new conflicts. Therefore as NATO confronts the challenge of restoring a lasting and legitimate order in Kosovo and Bosnia, its challenges are as much political and economic ones as they are military, perhaps more so. And indeed, in 1998, NATO began to rise to the task as Secretary General Javier Solana launched a Balkan economic initiative.[59] Now diplomats, expert analysts, and generals must strive to grasp what policies best promote attaining those goals in Kosovo, Bosnia, and across the Balkans.

Steven Burg provided a detailed and comparative typology of the kinds of solutions that have been tried elsewhere in Europe in analogous conflicts as well as a penetrating analysis of the actual operative facts on the ground in these countries. His conclusions pointed strongly to the need to foster democracy in these areas and for outside democratic players to heavily engage themselves for the long-term in bringing about such a solution. Like Ratchev, Burg insisted that European attention to Balkan trouble spots cannot be intermittent and after the fact. Europe must make its presence and interests felt throughout the political process and not come in at the end with a heavy-handed force for lack of a better alternative or for want of more insight when the conflict could have been prevented or arrested.[60] While preventive diplomacy or conflict resolution, the stuff of many articles and editorials, is not likely, Burg's approach offers us a chance to learn from our past errors or sins of both omission and commission and prevent the deployment of trained soldiers for long periods of time in roles that are ultimately uncongenial to them.

As Burg observed, NATO soldiers cannot be deployed to defend a *status quo* but rather must be instruments of progress towards a better peace. Examination of other precedents, like the Basque one in Catalonia, suggest ways to overcome the conflict in Kosovo and find creative ways to address bitterly contested issues of sovereignty. An indispensable element of any viable solution, as Stefano Bianchini argued, is that the combatants have to get beyond the political culture of nationalism which inflames local passions and get to a new concept of the state which is not coterminous with that of ethnic groups.[61] To the extent that new conceptions of sovereignty and of the state can be implemented in practice and agreed to thereafter, we might be able to overcome the multiple crises, especially in the former Yugoslavia. Bianchini argues that all these crises are intertwined and require an overall solution that builds with neighbors and not against them as nationalism demands. Thus he argues that if NATO alone occupies Kosovo and its autonomy or independence comes about exclusively through the efforts of a military alliance, rather than an international organization like the UN, it will always be seen as an illegitimate outcome.[62] If that is the case, NATO will be trapped there in an increasingly inhospitable and untenable situation. The Balkans, to be secure, must be integrated into the world current of interdependence where alternatives to classical sovereignty have been tried and succeeded.

This consideration returns us to NATO for it is an embodiment of that trend towards the creation of a pluralistic security community where war is unthinkable and where aspects of traditional sovereignty, such as command over national armed forces, have been traded for a broader democratic form of governance. NATO presents this internal harmony of interests among its members because it has formed a true security community, where war among the members and purely unilateral national security policies are inconceivable.[63] NATO's integrated military-political structure subjects current and future members to a rigorous international system of civilian democratic control over the use of armed forces at home and abroad.[64] NATO's 1995 *Study on Enlargement* buttressed this democratic form of control by demanding it as a precondition of membership, and the OSCE's 1994 code of conduct also outlined a politically binding European agenda for such control. NATO staked its claim here to democratize and internationalize controls over governments' defense and security policies.[65] Everyone undergoes democratization and mutual restraint, and becomes more secure.

NATO justified its enlargement simply by requiring democratic civilian control over the armed forces and subjecting all its members to mutual discipline or restraint, as well as internal constitutional restraints that go far in preventing renationalized security policies.[66] This generalized discipline makes NATO a uniquely self-restraining alliance whose inner constitution reassures Europe of peace. Even when Europeans complain about Washington's dictation, they acknowledge that it occurs because Europe cannot overcome its divisions of advocating collective European defense policies, while refusing to spend the money or take the necessary action.[67] NATO works only when it acts in unison, when everyone acts unilaterally, or tries to, the result is failure.[68] When there is European unity, they all say, Washington then does indeed listen to its allies and moderates its position in the interests of allied unity.[69] Even at the height of the Cold War, Washington could not simply dictate to its allies, and it remained exquisitely attentive to their interests and concerns, often being forced to amend its policies to meet those concerns.[70]

NATO thus bridles U.S., French, German, and Russian temptations to unilateralism in Europe. Those who wish to use NATO assets for global crusades and worldwide intervention in the name of collective security or democracy may find this condition irksome. But it is the necessary price we pay for leading this kind of multilateral alliance. We are now learning this lesson again the hard way in Kosovo. But it is essential that NATO again find its way to consensus because it remains the most effective and legitimate security provider in Europe.

As Stephen Calleya pointed out, if NATO fosters the kinds of consensus needed to respond to threats running from economics, through ethnic conflicts, to proliferation, it can achieve a great deal of cohesion and rapprochement among the various conflict zones in the area.[71] The NATO model of an authentic European community holds great potential appeal for non-European and non-member states, and, if successfully developed, it can increase its appeal through successful performance and meeting new challenges to it. The converse is also true so NATO's disarray could unravel some, if not all, of the progress made since 1989. This does not mean NATO should substitute for the OSCE or EU in the Mediterranean, but it should do what it can, if for no other reason than because its abdication or failure will encourage those organizations to evade their responsibilities as well. For this kind of pattern to succeed in promoting peace in the area, NATO and other key states must avoid the perception of or temptation to act according to a scheme which looks like traditional hegemonic power plays. Overcoming security challenges to the area must encompass attention to sub-regional dynamics.[72]

For instance, in the Greco-Turkish rivalry, the issues of EU membership for Cyprus and Turkey, disputed territories in the Aegean, military buildups, etc., must be addressed together as Nation suggests. Nor should Turkey continue to act in a high-handed and threatening manner and make veiled and not so veiled threats against Greece for harboring Kurdish rebels or other sins.[73]

Moreover, to the extent that NATO neglects regional or sub-regional concerns and issues, it will come to be seen as an intrusive interloper that must be resisted or as a power whose true intention is to maintain the boundary between the East and the South. While the West would be a kingdom of integration in this scheme, the East would be the realm of fragmentation and crisis. If states that endeavor to climb up to European levels feel discriminated against or left out of the *status quo*, they will oppose it. And if NATO is not united, it will not be able to reach for solutions like those called for by Burg in the former Yugoslavia or the kinds of long-term engagement Ratchev and Bianchini urged. Then more unilateralist forces, whether in Greece, Turkey, Russia, or the Middle East, will have their day as cooperative multilateralism will have been tried and found wanting.

While there are no easy answers, there are some signs of a rethinking of past postures. Italy's new military policy will devote more attention to rapid reaction forces and to defense against proliferation threats.[74] There are also signs that Germany understands that to safeguard security and its European role, it must move as well towards a broader southern engagement. The St. Malo Agreement between Britain and France in December 1998 gave a new, more vigorous impetus to a European Security and Defense Identity.[75] The aftermath of the Kosovo campaign may also lead to more creative responses to the challenges now on the overall European security agenda. On the other hand, NATO's fractured process over Kosovo in 1998-99 and Russia's determination to frustrate U.S. efforts in Europe and the Middle East, and its occasional success in finding a European partner are very disheartening signs. So is the fact that substantial economic pressures are building up in the United States to reduce its foreign military exposure at the same time as its economic presence in the Mediterranean as a whole is dropping relative to other areas. If there is little discernible profit or return on large investments there as compared to other more clearly strategic areas, the U.S. interest and military commitment in the Mediterranean may well decline over time.[76]

Thus the current Mediterranean situation contains both frustrating and hopeful signs; it is neither sky-blue nor black, but rather something in between, perhaps a more typical, if not wholly satisfactory complexion. But since it is governments that have the power to change the region's weather, they must first try to grasp in what direction all the region's winds are blowing, even if they are seemingly blowing in contradictory directions all at the same time. This may frustrate many, for complexity is not always easily accepted as today's or tomorrow's *status quo*.

Readers may therefore feel somewhat shortchanged that we did not lay out here a blueprint of solutions or a menu from which to choose. However, the more one comes to terms with the entire range of security challenges in the Mediterranean, the more one comes to understand the enormous diversity of those challenges and of perspectives upon them. Hopefully this understanding should serve to help us and governments clarify their thinking and serve as a guide to action. Such clarification through dialogue and mutual engagement is essential. For, as many of the papers that follow imply or even state explicitly, if NATO and the United States fail to understand the dynamics of the challenges to which they are responding, they will fail to extinguish them as sources of conflict. In that case, not only will the forces committed to existing crises and conflicts remain in place, but new forces for new crises will have to be found, and that is a most unappealing prospect.

ENDNOTES - CHAPTER 1

1. Brigadier General John Batiste (USA), "Peacetime Forward Engagement in [the] Southern Region," briefing presented to the SSI-Pepperdine University Conference "Mediterranean Security into the Coming Millennium," Florence, Italy, October 26-27, 1998.

2. Dr. Cordesman's paper was published separately due to its size and comprehensiveness. Anthony Cordesman, *Transnational Threats from the Middle East: Crying Wolf or Crying Havoc?*, Carlisle Barracks, PA: Strategic Studies Institute, U.S. Army War College, 1999.

3. General Klaus Naumann, "The Reshaping of NATO From a Military Perspective," *Royal United Services Institute Journal*, June 1997, p. 7.

4. Ambassador Matthew Nimetz, "Mediterranean Security After the Cold War," *Mediterranean Quarterly*, Vol. VIII, No. 2, Spring, 1997, p. 29.

5. *Ibid.*

6. Fred Hiatt, "Without Muscle in Kosovo," *Washington Post*, March 14, 1999, p. B7; Jonathan Landay, "Bigger NATO; But Deeper Divisions," *Christian Science Monitor*, March 12, 1999, p. 2; Rome, *La Repubblica (Internet Version)*, in Italian, March 14, 1998 *Foreign Broadcast Information Service, Western Europe,* (henceforth *FBIS-WEU*), March 15, 1999, where Vuk Draskovic, Serbian Deputy Prime Minister, confided that a number of EU diplomats "are not playing as a team with the United States."

7. Wayne F. Lesperance, Jr. and Tom Lansford, "Dual Engagement: France and the Persian Gulf," *European Security*, Vol. VII, No. 4, Winter 1998, pp. 137-165. For an examination of the sources of inter-allied discord on issues in the Middle East, see Robert D. Blackwill and Michael Stuermer, eds., *Allies Divided: Transatlantic Policies for the Greater Middle East*, Cambridge MA: MIT University Press, 1997; Jim Anderson, "The European Union: Time for a Place at the Table?," *Middle East Policy*, Vol. VI, No. 3, February 1999, pp. 160-166; Pia Christina Wood, "Chirac's 'New Arab Policy' And Middle East Challenges: The Arab-Israeli Conflict, Iraq, and Iran," *Middle East Journal*, Vol. LII, No. 4, Autumn 1998, pp. 563-580.

8. Michael Brenner, *Terms of Engagement: The United States and the European Security Identity*, Foreword by Jonathan Dean, Washington Papers, No. 176, Westport, CT: Praeger Publishers, 1998.

9. Ambassador Luigi Vittorio Ferraris, "Mediterranean Security Into the Coming Millennium," paper presented to the SSI-Pepperdine University Conference "Challenges to Mediterranean Security," Florence, Italy, October 26-27, 1998.

10. Mario Zucconi, "NATO in the Mediterranean," paper presented to the SSI-Pepperdine University Conference; see also Naumann, p. 7.

11. Alfred Tovias, "Israel and the Barcelona Process;" Eli Oren, "Israeli Views of the Role of NATO and the OSCE Security Model," papers presented to the Conference on the Changing Structure of Euro-Atlantic Security and the Middle East, Begin-Sadat Center, Bar-Ilan University, Ramat Gan, Israel, January 25-27, 1999.

12. The discontent with the EU's role is pervasive. See Tovias; Eberhard Kienle, "Destabilization Through partnership? Euro-Mediterranean Relations After the Barcelona Declaration," *Mediterranean Politics*, Vol. III, No. 2, Autumn 1998, pp. 1-20; Isabel Romero, "The European Union and North Africa: Keeping the Mediterranean Safe for Europe," *Ibid.*, pp. 21-38; Jorg Monar, "Institutional Constraints of the European Union's Mediterranean Policy," *Ibid.*, pp. 39-60; Stephen C. Calleya, "Preface," Stephen C. Calleya, ed., *Economic Diplomacy in the Mediterranean*, Malta: Mediterranean Academy of Diplomatic Studies, University of Malta, 1998; and Eberhard Rhein, "Globalisation of the Economy and Its Meaning for the Mediterranean," *Ibid.*, pp. 27-45; Marc Schade-Poulsen, "The Barcelona Process," *Helsinki Monitor*, Vol. IX, No. 4, 1998, pp. 55-62.

13. See the article by Ilnur Cevik in the *Turkish Daily News* cited by *Turkistan Newsletter*, ISSN-1386-6265. March 9, 1999, at *sota@EURONET.NL*12.

14. Duygu Bazoglu Sezer, "Turkish Security Challenges in the 1990s," paper presented to the SSI-Pepperdine University Conference; *Idem.*, "Turkey's New Security Environment, Nuclear Weapons and Proliferation, *Comparative Strategy*, Vol. XIV, No. 2, 1995, pp. 149-172; see also Ilter Turan, "Mediterranean Security in the Light of Turkish Concerns," *Perspectives*, Vol. III, No. 2, June-August 1998, pp. 16-31.

15. Alan Makovsky, "The New Activism in Turkish Foreign Policy," *SAIS Review*, Vol. XIX, No. 1, Winter-Spring 1999, pp. 93-111.

16. James F. Miskel, "The Future of the US Military Presence in the Mediterranean," *Mediterranean Politics*, III, No. 2, 1998, pp. 93-103.

17. Zucconi.

18. Batiste, "Peacetime Forward Engagement in [the] Southern Region."

19. Barry Buzan, Ole Weaver, Jaap de Wilde, *Security: A New Framework for Analysis*, Boulder, CO: Lynne Rienner Publishers, 1998.

20. *Ibid.*

21. Zucconi; Roberto Aliboni, "European Union Security Policy and Perceptions Toward the Mediterranean," paper presented to the SSI-Pepperdine University Conference.

22. *Ibid.*; Mohammad El-Selim, "Arab Perceptions of the European Union's Euro-Mediterranean Projects," paper presented to the SSI-Pepperdine University Conference.

23. Sezer; Turan, pp. 22-23.

24. Sezer; R.Craig Nation, "Greek-Turkish Rivalry and the Mediterranean Security Dilemma," paper presented to the SSI-Pepperdine University Conference; Theodore Couloumbis, "Turkish Challenge and European Opportunity: Greek Foreign Policy Priorities in a Post-Cold War Setting," paper presented to the SSI-Pepperdine University Conference.

25. Couloumbis.

26. Nation.

27. Stephen Blank, "The Spirit of Eternal Negation: Russia's Hour in the Middle East," paper presented to the SSI-Pepperdine University Conference.

28. Breffni O'Rourke, "EU To Develop Ties with Albania, Macedonia," *Radio Free Europe/Radio Liberty, Newsline*, April 23, 1999.

29. Massimo D'Alema, "Italy, Europe, and the New NATO," *International Herald Tribune*, January 22, 1999, p. 6.

30. Stephen Calleya, "Regional Security Challenges in the Mediterranean," paper presented to the SSI-Pepperdine University Conference.

31. Alberto Bin, "Strengthening Cooperation in the Mediterranean: NATO's Contribution," *NATO Review*, Vol. XLVI, No. 4, Winter 1998, p. 27. Secretary-General Solana similarly passed the buck to the EU

stating that, since the roots of the problems are economic, that organization must take the lead in addressing them; Brussels, *NATO Internet*, November 11, 1997, *Foreign Broadcast Information Service, Western Europe* (henceforth *FBIS-WEU*), 97-316, November 13, 1997.

32. Robert Freedman, "American Policy Toward the Middle East in Clinton's Second Term," paper presented to the SSI-Pepperdine University Conference; Gerald Steinberg, "Israeli Security in a Changing Environment: Challenges and Responses," paper presented to the SSI-Pepperdine University Conference.

33. Hillel Kutler and Danna Harman, "Sharon Scored for Remarks in Kosovo," *Jerusalem Post, North American Edition*, April 16, 1999, pp. 1-2.

34. Sami Hajjar, "The Stalled Peace Process: Israeli-Syrian Track," paper presented to the SSI-Pepperdine University Conference.

35. Blank.

36. For a survey of the regional proliferation problems, see Ian O. Lesser and Ashley Tellis, *Strategic Exposure: Proliferation Problems Around the Mediterranean Area*, Santa Monica, CA: RAND Corporation, 1996; and Cordesman.

37. Steinberg; Efraim Inbar, *Israel's National Security, 1973-96*, Begin-Sadat Center for Strategic Studies, Bar-Ilan University, Ramat Gan, Israel, 1998; reprinted from *The Annals of the American Academy of Political and Social Science*, Vol. 555, January 1998, pp. 72-74; Sezer.

38. Yiftah Shapir, "The Threat Posed by Proliferation of WMD and Ballistic Missiles in the Middle East," paper presented to the Conference on the Changing Structure of Euro-Atlantic Security and the Middle East, Begin-Sadat Center, Bar-Ilan University, Ramat Gan, Israel, January 25-27, 1999; Timothy D. Hoyt, "Diffusion From the Periphery: The Impact of Technological and Conceptual Innovation," paper presented to the 40th Annual Convention of the International Studies Association, Washington, DC, February 18, 1999.

39. Interview of General Aharon Levran by Dr. Aaron Lerner, Director, Independent Media Review and Analysis (IMRA), December 14, 1997, *IMRA@netvision.net.il,* December 15, 1997; see also Allan Castle, *Transnational Organized Crime and International Security*, Working Paper no. 19, Institute of International Relations, University of British Columbia, Vancouver, BC, Canada, 1997, p. 10.

40. Jeffrey A. Larsen, *NATO's Counterproliferation Policy: A Case Study in Alliance Politics*, Colorado Springs, CO: Institute for National Security Studies, U.S. Air Force Academy, Occasional Paper, No. 17, 1997.

41. D'Alema, p. 6.

42. For the most recent statement of the U.S. position, see the speech by Chairman of the Joint Chiefs of Staff, General Hugh Shelton to the NATO at 50 Conference sponsored by the Royal United Services Institute in London, March 9, 1999, "Shelton Remarks on the 'Transatlantic Commitment'," U.S. Mission to NATO, at *http://usa.grmbl.com/s19990309c.html*; Clifford Beal, "NATO: United We Stand?," *Jane's Defence Weekly*, March 3, 1999, pp. 22-23.

43. Francois Gere, "U.S. Hegemony and NATO," *Defense News*, March 8-14, 1999, p. 25.

44. *Ibid*.

45. Sezer.

46. Gidon Gottlieb, *Nation Against State: A New Approach to Ethnic Conflicts and the Decline of Sovereignty*, New York: Council on Foreign Relations Press, 1993, p. 101.

47. Blank; and see more recently, Moscow, *Segodnya*, in Russian, February 17, 1999, *Foreign Broadcast Information Service, Central Eurasia*, (Henceforth *FBIS-SOV*) February 17, 1999, and Moscow, *Izvestiya*, in Russian, February 19, 1999, *FBIS-SOV*, February 19, 1999.

48. Freedman.

49. *Ibid*; Paul Richter, "No End in Sight for U.S. Assault on Iraq," *Los Angeles Times*, March 3, 1999, p. 1.

50. Blackwill and Stuermer, *passim*.

51. Blank.

52. James Gow, *Triumph of the Lack of Will: International Diplomacy and the Yugoslav War*, New York: Columbia University Press, 1997.

53. Colonel Valeri Ratchev, "South-Eastern Europe At the Brink of the New Century: The Security Aspect," paper presented to the SSI-Pepperdine University Conference.

54. Ibid. and Beal, p. 22.

55. Jeffrey Simon, "Bulgaria and NATO: 7 Lost Years," National Defense University, Institute for National Security Studies, *Strategic Forum*, No. 142, 1998; Robert Lyle, "Bulgaria Receives Praise from INF Directors," *Radio Free Europe/Radio Liberty Newsline*, March 11, 1999; Kevin Done, "Still hurdles to Overcome," *Financial Times*, special section on Bulgaria, March 8, 1999.

56. William Pfaff, "Good news From the Balkans: Bulgaria and Macedonia," *International Herald Tribune*, March, 9, 1999, *Turkistan-Economy Bulletin*, ISSN-1386-6265, March 15, 1999, kryopak@WORLD.ATT.NET.

57. "Turkish Moves in the Caucasus, Balkans, Irk Rivals in Region," *Defense News*, August 3-9, 1998, p. 12.

58. Luke Hill, "NATO Chief Embraces New Economic Model for Balkans," *Defense News*, March 15, 1999, p. 18.

59. Speech by Secretary General of NATO, Javier Solana at the Royal United Services Institute, London, March 9, 1999, *www.NATO.int*.

60. Steven L. Burg, "The Security Challenge in Kosovo: Toward a Region-Stabilizing Solution," paper presented to the SSI-Pepperdine University Conference.

61. *Ibid.*; Stefano Bianchini, "The Cultural Scope of Balkan Security," paper presented to the SSI-Pepperdine University Conference.

62. *Ibid.*

63. Karl Wolfgang Deutsch, *et al.*, *Political Community and the North Atlantic Area: International Organization in the Light of Historical Experience*, Princeton, NJ: Princeton University Press, 1957, is the classic statement of this thesis. For a recent restatement of it, see Catherine McArdle Kelleher, *The Future of European Security*, Washington, DC: Brookings Institution Press, 1995.

64. General Klaus Naumann, "NATO Is Changing," *Central European Issues: Romanian Foreign Affairs Review*, Vol. III, No. 1, 1997, pp. 18-28.

65. *NATO Study on Enlargement*, NATO Internet, Brussels, September 28, 1995.

66. *Ibid.*; "The Enlargement of the Alliance," Draft Special Report of the Working Group on NATO Enlargement, November 1994, NATO Internet; David Carment, "NATO and the International Politics of Ethnic Conflict: Perspectives on Theory and Policy," *Contemporary Security Policy*, Vol. XVI, No. 3, December 1995, pp. 364-365.

67. Brussels, *Knack*, in Dutch, July 16-22, 1997, *FBIS-WEU*-97-197, July 16, 1997; Thomas Risse-Kappen, *Cooperation Among Democracies: the European Influence on U.S. Foreign Policy*, Princeton, NJ: Princeton University Press, 1995.

68. *Ibid.*

69. *Ibid.* Vienna, *Die Presse*, in German, July 16, 1997, *FBIS-WEU*-97-197, July 16, 1997.

70. *Ibid.*; Risse-Kappen, *passim.*

71. Calleya.

72. *Ibid.*

73. Cevik; Makovsky, pp. 93-111.

74. Paolo Valpolicini and Richard Bassett, "Defined Lines," *Jane's Defence Weekly*, March 3, 1999, pp. 25-26.

75. Andreas Jacobs and Carlo Masala, "Germany's Mediterranean Challenge," forthcoming in *European Security*; Joseph Fitchett, "Paris Joins London On A Push for Defense," *International Herald Tribune*, December 2, 1998, p. 1; Theresa Hitchens and Christina Mackenzie, "Europe's Big Three Drop Defense Bombshell," *Defense News*, December 7-13, 1998, pp. 3, 40.

76. Miskel, pp. 93-103.

CHAPTER 2

TRANSNATIONAL SECURITY CHALLENGES IN THE MEDITERRANEAN

Alessandro Politi

Executive Summary.

The objectives of this paper are to define the boundaries of the Mediterranean Region, to provide a definition of transnational security challenges, to offer a description of the major risks and their effects on European security, and to describe some policies to cope more effectively with them.

A transnational security challenge is a phenomenon that threatens different areas irrespective of borders or distances. In this paper, we will consider as transnational security challenges mainly three phenomena: transnational organized crime, illegal drug trafficking, and international terrorism. The exclusion of other possible security concerns stems from the observation that either they cannot be faced with forceful means or because they are not necessarily transnational.

In describing a geopolitical map of these challenges, the paper focuses on:

- three centers of gravity, concerning major transnational organized criminal organizations, namely Italy, Russia, and Turkey;

- 21 regional gravitating support areas: Albania, Croatia, Bulgaria, Djibouti, Egypt, Eritrea, France, FRY, FYROM, Georgia, Greece, Israel, Jordan, Lebanon, Morocco, Rumania, Slovenia, Somalia, Spain, Syria, Tunisia;

- two states at risk of failing (Algeria and Russia), and ten having experienced various degrees of failure (Albania, Bosnia-Herzegovina, Croatia, Eritrea, FRY, FYROM, Georgia, Lebanon, Slovenia, Somalia);

- four islands which have relevant grey zones and different degrees of organized crime control/connection (Corsica, Cyprus, Sardinia, and Sicily);

- two major (Morocco and Russia) and two minor drug producers (Lebanon and former Yugoslavia);

- three major drug trafficking routes: Atlantic Route, Balkan Corridor, and Russia;

- three major drug trafficking entry points: Russia, Spain, and Turkey;

- three major people-smuggling sea-routes (Morocco-Spain, Tunisia-Italy, and Albania-Italy) and four land-routes (Sarajevo-Croatia-Slovenia-Italy/Austria; Istanbul-Ukraine- Poland-Germany or Istanbul-Romania-Hungary- Slovakia-Czech Republic; Istanbul-Greece- FYROM-Italy/Austria, Russia-Finland);

- three regional financial offshore centers, i.e., Cyprus, Malta, Monaco;

- the presence of Chinese, Colombian, and Japanese organized criminal groups and the relative absence of North American and Mexican ones;

- the prevalence of drugs such as cannabis, heroin, and ATS, with cocaine increasing;

- 20 countries with internal/endemic/civil war terrorism, inspired by nationalist/ethnic motivations (Spain, Israel, Greece, FRY, FYROM, Turkey, Iran, Iraq, Russia) or by political/religious motivations

(Morocco, Algeria, Tunisia, Libya, Egypt, Israel, Iran, Iraq, Djibouti, Saudi Arabia, Bahrain);

- three countries affected by international terrorism (France, Saudi Arabia, Yemen);

- five countries designated as terrorism supporting states (Libya, Sudan, Syria, Iraq, Iran);

- nine countries seriously violating human rights at various degrees in their counterterrorist actions (Algeria, Libya, Egypt, Israel, Saudi Arabia, Iran, Iraq, Bahrain, Turkey, FRY).

With regard to the possible policies to be adopted, the paper argues that, at an institutional level, the EU is the leading institution in the region. The possible four priorities should be to:

1) continue the gradual integration of the common law enforcement and judicial spaces;

2) prepare to enlarge through policies that enhance formally and informally the cooperation among actors interested in stability and economic development;

3) continue support to Russia; and,

4) devise appropriate policies for the assistance to law enforcement agencies of third countries.

The Boundaries of the Mediterranean Region.

The general use of the word "Mediterranean" may imply that it includes on one hand the countries of the old North Atlantic Treaty Organization (NATO) Southern Flank[1] and on the other the dialogue partners of the Western European Union (WEU) and of NATO.[2] Indeed, for traditional security purposes, this definition would be a reasonable one; although for strategic and political reasons, it should be regarded as a minimalist one.

Personally, I prefer a wider definition, where the European Union (EU)-sponsored Barcelona Process represents a large component (since it represents 27 countries), although not an all-inclusive one, for two main reasons: methodological and political.

Firstly, transnational risks do not conform to international political constellations or mind sets trying somehow to slice a geopolitical area into nice subdivisions. For analytical purposes, one has to see an area as whole, using afterwards the existing political settings or devising new arrangements to implement an appropriate policy.

Secondly, these risks are considered too often in a logic of "us versus them" (i.e., thinking that they come from the external perimeter of our Western "civilised" world), whereas they are as transnational as financial markets with transactions and raids occurring in London, Barcelona, Istanbul, Berlin, Rome, or New York.

It should also be borne in mind that the widespread idea that the Mediterranean is nothing more than a geographic expression, because it is impossible to reconcile very different realities, may reveal three distinct and somewhat politically unhelpful mind sets.

The first one pretends that a region must be somehow homogeneous in order to be considered as a whole. It is very similar to those favouring "unity and purity" within a set geopolitical area.

The second conception, much cherished by simplistic and *pragmatic-by-default* people, tries to exclude as much as possible every complexity, believing that outside a politically correct area the rest is an incoherent, fragmented chaos.

The third mind set derives from the rich, yet limited experience of the last two centuries (19th and 20th centuries), whereby it is nearly impossible to understand realities lacking the relative coherence of nation-states or of great alliances. The problem is that most events challenge political decisionmakers through their diversity, complexity, and more or less substantial disorder.

Now, what will be called in this paper the **Mediterranean Region** can be subdivided into different subregions, but it is impossible to cut apart if one does not want to pay heavy economic, social, political, and strategic prices. Seas create inevitably strong links and to try to use them as bulwarks is an illusion, as two world wars and several migratory waves have demonstrated. The Mediterranean Region is a geopolitical reality connecting willy-nilly the destinies of different countries.

According to these premises, we will consider as the Mediterranean Region the area included by the Straits of Gibraltar, Bosphorus, Kerch, Bab el Mandab, Hormuz, and by the Suez Canal. This means that the Black Sea will be considered as an extension of the Mediterranean, while the Red Sea and the Persian Gulf are not only physically, but also historically and politically linked to the Mediterranean. This area can evidently be subdivided into four smaller subregions: West Europe, Balkan/Black Sea, Middle East/Red Sea, and Maghreb.[3]

During each great historical period, the Mediterranean Region had to face as a whole the great security questions, even if these were considered from different angles in each subregion.

During the Cold War, the subregions of West Europe and of the Balkan/Black Sea were characterised by heavily armed peace, tinged with strong political tensions. The Maghreb, instead, after post-colonial convulsion, was a secondary theatre of confrontation between the two blocks, while in the Middle East/Red Sea subregion war raged.

After the fall of the Berlin Wall, the great Arab-Israeli wars have been superseded by an extremely fragile peace, more marked by internal conflicts (opposing terrorisms, urban guerrillas, social inequalities) than by the great armoured and air battles. Iraq is the only exception, and despite U.N. interventions in the Horn of Africa, the problems of this part of the subregion remain the fights between armed bands and all types of illicit trafficking. Similar plagues affect some Maghreb countries in a more visible (Algeria) or less evident way (Libya).

In several countries of the Balkan/Black Sea subregion, the armed peace has changed into a long civil war, featuring in most cases guerrilla and counterguerrilla operations, conducted by more or less heavily equipped troops. The wars of Yugoslav dissolution, ended in Slovenia, Croatia, Bosnia-Herzegovina, are now continuing in the FRY, Albania, and Macedonia. Yet all the countries in the subregion are affected by the new transnational security challenges (namely drug trafficking, organized crime, and terrorism). In fact, most countries of the Mediterranean Region do not confront a single, classic military threat, but are going back to a multidimensional security.

Defining Transnational Security Challenges.

There have been within the post-1989 Euro-American strategic literature a number of studies trying to redefine in various ways the nature and the scope of changes concerning traditional security.[4] Surely a first bone of contention can be the definition of traditional security itself. If, by traditional security, we understand that political concern and that politically oriented activity that Europe was accustomed to seeing as relevant for the past three centuries in the case of earlier centralised states and for some 150 years for younger states, then we risk missing a wider and much more complex picture. This is particularly true if Western strategic thinking may be still under the unconscious influence of the Cold War.

The fact is that all the security concerns that we pretend are new are stone-age old in other continents and remained pretty much unchanged in other parts of the Mediterranean Region. A cursory glance at history books shows that civil strife and violence, population imbalances and migrations, resource scarcity, environmental degradation, international terrorism, and transnational organized crime are in most cases common during the some four millennia that preceded our age (international terrorism becoming much more frequent in the 19th century due to the evolution of political movements and of technology).[5] This is equally true for many areas that were not directly under the spell of Cold War stabilization, the Middle East being one evident example and the tragic events in Lebanon being almost a paradigm.

Thus, it would be more appropriate and simple to state that we, in the Northern hemisphere, once dominated by the Cold War, are rediscovering traditional security, a security by nature multidimensional, whose concerns might have changed in object and scope when compared to the past.

This return, although justifiable with Vico's theory of the *corsi e ricorsi*[6] (occurrences and recurrences of history), is better explainable with the link that exists between policy and grand strategy. If we take into account major definitions of grand strategy, we shall see that in this realm the old Cold War division between security proper (i.e., external and military interstate security) and internal security or other newer concerns never applied.[7]

An immediate political objection to a wider concept of security is the danger of putting very different things into the same category of security, with the consequence that the policy approach will be less focused on political and social solutions and more in favour of indiscriminately repressive, quasi-military actions. In other words, if potentially everything concerns security, policy responses could be implicitly more and more "militarised." On a more intellectual level, this objection is coupled with the risk of "concept inflation," whereby the progressive widening of security endangers its coherence.

The reply in favour of the return of a of concept of multidimensional security will combine different arguments.

- First, the idea that a broader concept of security should imply a more narrowly focused response is not warranted by itself. On the contrary, a broader concept should allow a flexible, tailored policy where force is only one of the different means employed.

- Secondly, as already shown, the concept of security became singularly "deflated" during the 1948-1989 period in a significant, but not all-encompassing zone of the globe. Conversely, it risks not being inflated when security reacquires its original complexity.

- Thirdly, security has become more visibly multidimensional because attacks on the sovereignty of nation-states can now be carried out more effectively by richer and more powerful non-state actors, and because the complexity of modern societies offers multiple vulnerabilities. Governmental resources, moreover, seem insufficient to control key autonomous components of sovereignty (territorial integrity, strategic control of key areas or resources, financial flows, internal security).

- Finally, security is, and remains, a politically defined concept. One can discuss if the widening of security might be a good or a bad political choice, but security is not intrinsically a self-contained concept, nor can it be related to military affairs only. If the political priorities change, the nature and the means of multidimensional security will inevitably follow and adapt to the different sectors of the political action.[8]

How the political decision on including other concerns within the perimeter of security will respect basic and democratic freedoms does not depend on the concept of security itself, but on the state of actual laws and practices of a given government.

Once one agrees that multidimensional security is a matter of fact, politically and operationally acceptable, it remains still to be seen if all nontraditional risks may be really considered security challenges or not.

In principle, as stated above, once a political leader decides that a specific issue is relevant for security, this should be more than enough, yet this arbitrary element is compounded by some less subjective factors, both practical and conceptual. From a practical point of view, there are some nontraditional concerns that clearly involve the use of violence, allowing easier links to traditional security, such as civil violence and insurrection, international terrorism, transnational organized crime, and illegal drug trafficking.

Environmental degradation, resource scarcity, population growth and migration, all can affect national and international security, but in general they tend to be managed more within higher policy and grand strategy. With regard to these problems, the use of means other than force (economic, political, diplomatic, social, cultural ones) appears to be, in first instance, more cost-effective, even if force may remain the last recourse, as always in politics. In a certain sense, whereas the first four nontraditional security risks are, notwithstanding the causes, manifestations of violence, the remaining ones may be, instead of violence, considered more likely to be stakes for an armed confrontation.

From a more conceptual point of view, grand strategy does work as a bridge between politics and traditional security in both senses. On one hand, as we have seen, it favours the enlargement of the old concept of security, but, on the other, it helps to shift some of the newer security challenges to a domain that is more politically than security-minded.

At this point one can define what a transnational security challenge should be. A security challenge is a phenomenon that threatens the security of a given area, be it defined by geographic, geopolitical, statehood, national, sub-national, or supranational criteria. A transnational security challenge is one that threatens different areas irrespective of borders or distances.[9]

In this paper, we will consider as transnational security challenges mainly three phenomena: transnational organized crime, illegal drug trafficking, and international terrorism. The exclusion of other mentioned security concerns stems from the fact that either they can be considered more the resort in first place of means other than force, as already argued, or because, as such, they are not necessarily transnational. Civil violence and insurrection, for what these somewhat vague terms mean, are characterised in the first place by their localised action and immediate effects, although they sometimes may have transnational aspects either in terms of logistics (sanctuaries) or in terms of terrorist actions. If one takes Algeria as an example, civil violence and insurrection are fairly localised, whereas terrorist actions and political-logistic networks may be transnational.[10]

The delimitation of the analysed transnational security challenges does not exempt us from the equally complicated definition of the three risks themselves. Academics, jurists, and police forces continue to disagree on the definition of transnational organized crime.[11] There are, however, four elements defining organized crime on which a large majority of authors agree: the existence of an organized and stable hierarchy; the acquisition of profits through crime; the use of force and intimidation; and recourse to corruption in order to maintain impunity.

This paper will use the definition adopted in 1993 by the EU's Ad Hoc Group on Organized Crime, then presented to the EU Council:

> Organized crime is present whenever two or more persons are involved in a common criminal project, for a prolonged or unspecified period of time, in order to obtain power and profits and where to the single associates are assigned tasks to carry out within the organization: (1) through business or connected business activities; (2) using violence or intimidation; (3)

influencing politics, media, economy, government or the judiciary, through the control of a determined territory, if necessary, in order to commit the planned crimes that, from a collective or individual point of view, must be considered serious crimes.[12]

Appended to this definition, which is not a common EU definition but represents an important step, was a table of eleven characteristics for use during the preparation of EU reports on organized crime and in pinpointing more easily this phenomenon at international level. They are: (1) collaboration among more than two people; (2) among whom there is a distribution of tasks; (3) who operate for a long or unspecified time; (4) operate under a certain discipline and control; (5) are suspected of serious crimes; (6) operate at international level; (7) use violence and other means of intimidation; (8) use commercial or pseudocommercial structures; (9) launder money; (10) exercise their influence on politics, media, public administration or in the economic field; and (11) seek profit and power. If a criminal group displays at least six of these characteristics, among which are necessarily (1), (5) and (11), it can be considered to be involved in organized crime.[13]

Concerning illegal drug trafficking, for the purposes of the paper it will be called simply drug trafficking. It will not dwell upon the debate on what should be illegal drugs or not or what should be the best strategy to combat this problem. It will consider illegal those drugs considered as such by the majority of EU governments, knowing that some notable exceptions in legal practice or in actual law enforcement priorities in some countries might create political problems and difficulties in implementation, as the Dutch case shows.[14]

International terrorism is no less controversial than the previous two phenomena regarding definitions, despite a marked increase in cooperation during the last 5 years.[15]

Probably the best known definitions are those employed by the U.S. Department of State:[16]

- The term "terrorism" means premeditated, politically motivated violence perpetrated against noncombatant targets by subnational groups or clandestine agents, usually intended to influence an audience.[17]

- The term "international terrorism" means terrorism involving citizens or the territory of more than one country.

- The term "terrorist group" means any group practicing, or that has significant subgroups that practice, international terrorism.

The definition adopted will be that proposed L. R. Beres, which uses the twin criteria of just cause and just means to distinguish between rightful recourse to insurgent force and unlawful terrorism.[18] As has happened also for the Ocalan extradition case from Italy to Germany, the just cause of political violence can always be argued,[19] but the just means are quite clearly defined by international law both for regular and irregular forces. Terrorism is unlawful because the means used fail to satisfy the criterion of just means (i.e., whenever the use of force is indiscriminate, disproportionate, and/or beyond the codified boundaries of military necessity). The group that violates these norms would be guilty of war crimes and possibly even of crimes against humanity.[20]

Further clarification is needed for the term international terrorism. In the wider debate, it is often a fairly imprecise expression that covers actions, differing in degrees of political and moral unacceptability. This paper puts forward seven types of terrorist or terrorist-like situations:

- domestic terrorism, endemic terrorism and civil war;[21]

- international implications of domestic/endemic terrorism and civil war;[22]

- international spillovers of domestic/endemic terrorism/civil war;[23]

- international support to domestic/endemic terrorism/ civil war;[24]

- international state-sponsoring of domestic, endemic terrorism or civil war;[25]

- international terrorism proper. In this case citizens of one country are conducting attacks in countries other than the theatre of civil confrontation and/or against citizens who are neither within the mentioned theatre nor in countries adjacent to it;[26]

- covert operations. Under this denomination are included state-sponsored assassinations of selected individuals whose political or military research activities are considered dangerous or because they are retaliatory targets.[27]

In the international political debate, there is also another category called "state terrorism" and defined as the situation in which a state lends its legitimacy to terrorism or lends its own organs to indulge in acts of terrorism. It appears that this concept, although repeatedly employed, is not particularly helpful in pinpointing the nature of international terrorism. In the case of legitimization of terrorism *per se*, it may be a condemnable political position, but it is not a terrorist act. In the case of using state organs for terrorist operations, it falls mostly either in the category of state-sponsoring or in that of covert operations. It seems that only in the context of a situation of endemic terrorism can one envisage state terrorism as the method by which a government (or a part of it) sets up clandestine groups, whose selected or indiscriminate killings are officially disavowed. In all cases, state terrorism either weakens the rule of law within a given country, or creates in the medium term heavy friction with the rest of the international community.[28]

A Strategic Perspective of New Challenges in the Mediterranean Region.

Transnational organized crime and drug trafficking. The paper will analyse what it considers the two major threats among the transnational security challenges: transnational organized crime and drug trafficking. Both have to be considered together since the drug production and smuggling chain requires criminal organizations. While organized crime can exist without drug trafficking, the reverse is not true. But drugs can be considered a force and a crime multiplier not only for criminal groups, but also for guerrilla and terrorist groups.

Transnational organized crime, and especially its association to drug trafficking, is an outright threat for the governments and societies in the Mediterranean region for the following reasons:

1) The lives killed or maimed by drugs or during criminal confrontations are not only casualties, but represent directly or indirectly an economic gain for dangerous actors, that challenge across the border the authority of the state and of law. Few governments or publics would accept similar levels of casualties in peacekeeping, external attack, and terrorism (at least 16 dead per day in 1996 in Schengen countries, apparently one of the best protected areas).[29] But politicians and citizens at large still entertain the ruinous belief that it is an internal matter, to be fatalistically accepted as car accidents are. The human costs of this dangerous combination are, of course, not the same for the countries in the region, but experience shows that transit countries become in most cases also consumer countries, with all the attendant consequences.

2) The economic resources generated by organized crime and drug trafficking are directly and deliberately used for destabilising the society, the political system, the administration and the economy of the country. Its financial muscle, facilitating the accession to political influence and

power, is far from being understated. Organized crime is a multibillion transnational business: drug trafficking alone, according to the UNDCP *World Drug Report,* yields a $400 billion per year turnover, equal to 8 percent of total global exports.[30] The corresponding effects are: "pax mafiosa," destruction of democratic/liberal values, corruption, money laundering, and business infiltration. Even if in a number of countries the political regimes are not democratic, the undermining effects of parallel power structures should not be underestimated. The case of the Soviet Union shows that organized criminal structures were never fully integrated in the system and that, even then, they produced marked inefficiencies, injustices, and illegal power struggles even within the laws and the logic of the regime.[31] These circumstances could have potentially dangerous effects in the transitions that some regimes in the Balkans, the Middle East, and some states adrift in the Horn of Africa will face at the end of this century.

3) The transnational networks, created and sustained by this combination, attack the territorial integrity both at the borders and within a given country. Whenever organized crime controls an area, transnational organized crime has free access, and law enforcement finds a no-go area or is anyhow ineffective. These areas, also called grey zones, are practically out of state sovereignty. Grey zones are unfortunately also present in many countries of the Mediterranean Region.[32]

4) In addition to the problems experienced by West European countries, many countries in the remainder of the Region risk becoming less reliable international partners because organized crime and drug trafficking undermine them, even if they consider themselves only drug transit countries. In this context, the stability of Russia and Ukraine may be put significantly into question, with evident repercussions at the political and economic level, not the least in the G8 forum, where important political coordination takes place against these risks.[33]

5) The evolution of these phenomena is by no means finished, and it could imply much bigger dangers. Some U.S. analysts believe already that the latest evolution of both phenomena are going towards organized systemic crime (OSC), characterised by increasing alliances between Russian, Chinese, Italian, Japanese, and U.S. criminal organizations, and a fully-fledged narco-industry.[34] Between 1991 and 1993 a number of criminal "summits" have taken place, involving also Cosa Nostra and Russian criminal organizations.

It may be easily overlooked that the Mediterranean region is home to five major transnational organized criminal constellations:

- Italian Camorra, Cosa Nostra, 'Ndrangheta, and Nuova Sacra Corona Unita (SCU);

- Russian and Georgian organized criminal groups;

- Turkish and Kurdish maffia clans.[35]

Moreover, minor, but not less dangerous and virulent organized criminal groups are very active in Albania, Bulgaria, France, Israel, Lebanon, Spain, and former Yugoslavia. To these countries, one should naturally add Malta, Monaco, and Cyprus as centers providing offshore banking facilities and fiscal incentives, a natural magnet for money laundering schemes.

This listing of countries is just an indicator, and one should not concentrate attention only on those geographic areas, because one would miss the formidable interconnections between those groups and the whole of the Mediterranean region, Europe, and the world.

As a first proof that the phenomenon of organized crime must be viewed at a strategic scale, one should take the projected forgery and money laundering operations during the switch to the Euro currency.[36] Naturally, this will not be some Spectre-like secret operation; much worse, it will be the sum of flexible agreements between some sophisticated components of major and minor organized criminal groups, opportunistically exploiting with regional/global capabilities, this great occasion.

The potential damage of gigantic fraud on the public's and market's confidence could be very considerable. One could just imagine if some powerful Russian organized criminal group would have converging interests with aggressive neo-nationalist Russian groups in order to undermine the confidence in future European integration of Central and Eastern European Countries (CEEC). NATO integration would be lamed, proven substantially useless, while politics, societies, and economies would be more infiltrated by diverse criminal organizations. To this risk one could add risks of distortion of the gold trade, because all major criminal organizations are starting to use gold as traceless money laundering means.

The geography of criminal groups is bound of modifying inevitably current geopolitical maps, because in some cases transnational organized crime is capable of modifing the nature of the governmnent. According to the Observatoire Geopolitique des Drogues (OGD), in the Mediterranean Region, Russia, the FSU republics (Georgia, Moldova, Ukraine, in our case), and Turkey are the countries where the dangers of connivance between state organs and criminal groups are greatest.[37]

With the proviso that it is not our intention to substitute the old Soviet enemy with a new Russian one, since Western mafias are absolutely cooperative with Russian *mafiosniky* whenever they settle their power and money feuds, we will point out some relevant strategic implications of Russian and Georgian organized crime before passing to other cases. We will leave the Turkish-Kurdish until the end, when we will treat the mixture of organized crime, drug trafficking, and terrorism.

The end of the Soviet regime marked the mutation of a type of organized crime from the "totalitarian" version towards a "free market" one. While during the Soviet regime organized crime was less visible (and much less relevant) in the Western world, it was nonetheless so present that it undermined significant portions of the Soviet state. Not surprisingly, "mafya" problems already existed in Azerbaijan, Georgia, Kazakhstan, and Uzbekistan in the 1960s-1980s, prompting the Muscovite leadership to replace corrupted and criminal top local party members, who, in turn, complained (not without some reason) that the Moscow bosses led an unfair competition.

With the liberalization of the regime and its ultimate fall, organized crime also became liberalized. The jump in quality of the first generation of former Soviet transnational organized crime is due to these factors:

- strong cohesiveness within the different levels of organized crime and the ethnic groups;

- a higher level of instruction (higher secondary school and university degrees for many bosses);

- the hard training that the first post-*perestroyka* criminal generation received during the Soviet regime;

- the arrival in criminal organizations of well-trained senior military and intelligence officers;

- the long-standing collusions with corrupted sectors of the ruling elite;

- the ongoing collapse of the old police and judicial system;

- the legal and criminal globalization of economy;

- the widespread poverty, hitting also relatively higher classes;

- the slow reconstruction of alternative moral and social values after the vanishing of the old ideology;

- the persistent lack of a transparent and efficient tax collecting, banking and customs system;

- the Western political interest in aiding the development of the Russian economy without questioning too much the destination of funds and the arrival of Russian investments for many years.[38]

This state of affairs has brought important consequences for the stability of the Mediterranean Region and Europe: the existence of criminal regimes in Crimea, Transdnestria, and in other areas affected by civil strife and with high illegal emigration rates (Georgia in our case); the rise of criminal terrorism in Russia and Ukraine; drug production and trafficking in North Caucasus, Black Sea ports, Ukraine, Moscow, St. Petersburg; major smuggling operations in North Caucasus and Ukraine; massive bank frauds and money laundering in the major Russian cities; and substantial economic penetration in the CEEC countries and sizeable investments in the legal economy of West European countries.[39]

Main illegal businesses of these groups are racketeering, smuggling of Western wares and East European antiquities, drug trafficking, arms smuggling, prostitution, and gambling.

A recent disquieting dimension is the export of key proliferating technologies by criminal business and quasi-government entities, which may be outside the direct control of the government, towards sensitive countries like India, Iran, and Syria.[40] This phenomenon is actually much more credible than the dreaded possibility that Russian organized criminal groups might export nuclear weapons or components to proliferating countries. Although the situation does not leave room for complacency, the proliferating pattern by these entities shows that they prefer to do some illegal and lucrative business, instead of risking a dangerous sale with unforeseeable consequences.

The diffusion of these groups is truly on a global scale, since the countries most targeted are France, Germany, Poland, the United Kingdom, and the United States.[41] That said, all CEEC countries are affected at different levels and with them also countries like Austria, Greece, Israel, Italy, Spain, and Turkey.[42] Connections with other major worldwide organized criminal groups have since long taken place.

In this context, Israel is interesting as a country that, besides local criminal organizations that were active in drug trafficking since the 1980s, has particularly experienced the effects of criminal diasporas. The massive immigration of Jewish people from former Soviet Union evidently could not avoid the arrival of elements of the Soviet organized crime. The activities of these groups is suspected of having rapidly influenced the internal political game in the country.

Italy has long been a country synonymous with organized crime, but the evolution in the last decade is fairly different from that of FSU. Also, here the Cold War favoured collusions within a political system that could not enjoy, for strategic reasons, normal competition between governing parties and opposition. Corruption had penetrated a significant number of governmental institutions both at local and at central level, and in several regions organized crime enjoyed substantial impunity.

The end of that period, both in political and judicial terms (generally called *Mani Pulite*—Clean Hands), has opened different scenarios from the previous constant advance of organized crime in southern Italian regions, supported by drug trafficking and white collar crime in the center and north of the peninsula.[43] In this sense, notwithstanding the judicial result, the trial of the former Premier Giulio Andreotti has an enormous political and psychological importance because it is the Nuremberg trial of an era of political-Mafioso liaisons.

Italy, after having experienced an internationalization by the export and the international connections of its Cosa Nostra and Camorra, is now experiencing the globalization in the criminal domain. The most visible event is the eruption of Albanian, Kosovar, former Yugoslav, Turkish, and Russian organized criminal groups in the Italian criminal market. The stream of illegal immigrants and prostitutes from Albania, CEEC, Kurdish areas, North Africa, Nigeria, Philippines, and Turkey, and their social effects have in the first 2 months of 1999 lead to heated political controversy. In the last 8 years the criminal geography of a big city like Milan changed from the coexistence of the old Apulian, Calabrian, Neapolitan, and Sicilian organized criminal groups to the forced entry of six main gangs—five Kosovars and one Croat.[44]

The fight against national organized crime and its evolution continues. On one hand, Cosa Nostra has been severely affected by aggressive investigation techniques, but on the other, if the importance of the Corleonesi "cosca" has been reduced, other families also have reduced their profile in order to continue their business. Especially for what concerns racketeering, the hold of Cosa Nostra appears to be undiminished, and money laundering provides further relevant profits. The relative weakening of Cosa Nostra does favour a certain criminal anarchy which, in turn, creates further problems for law enforcement. Between the cracks of Cosa Nostra's power, organized groups like the Stidda (Star) or smaller "angry young men" gangs have tried to establish with ruthless violence their own influence.

A similar phenomenon of relative disintegration can be observed within the Camorra, which for the first time saw the use of car bombs and antitank rockets in internecine wars.[45]

Much less penetrable is the Calabrian 'Ndrangheta, whose control on the region is particularly strong and whose influence in the shady world of professional kidnapping is remarkable. Only a string of arrests by mid-February in connection with the Sgarella kidnapping has opened a chink in its criminal power.[46]

Finally the Nuova SCU (New SCU) has lost the bosses of the first generation, but has received further impulse by the connections across the Adriatic with Albanian and Kosovar organized criminal groups. It must be taken into account that this group is not alone in the region of Apulia; on the contrary less known, but even more dangerous "Mafias" prosper in the Northern part of the region.[47]

The problem of the deep infiltration of local organized crime within the government and the economy of Turkey is not new (in the 1960s the U.S. Government had pressured Ankara to destroy opium poppy cultivations), but it has acquired a newer international dimension with the fall of the government guided by the premier Mesut Yilmaz and with the Ocalan case.

The fall of that political coalition has highlighted the danger that organized crime poses to the stability of important allies. The warning signals go back to the November 1996 when a car accident in the village of Susurluk revealed to the public that a Mafia boss (working for the Turkish intelligence service), a Kurdish politician, and high official of the police were travelling together in a car full of arms and drugs. A further investigation ordered by the then new premier, Mesut Yilmaz, concluded that organized criminal groups, trafficking in drugs and connected with certain sectors of the government, were responsible for some 2,000 killings.

Revelations that the sale of a major state-owned Turkish bank and of two dailies were tainted by organized crime infiltration, and that both the premier and the minister for economy were aware of the circumstances and that they nevertheless encouraged the deal were the direct cause of the government's fall last November.

This discomforting state of affairs was confirmed a month later by the explosive declarations of a successful top anti-drug police official that detailed how the chief of the Istanbul police, his deputy, and the chief of the Turkish police had been corrupted. In addition to the traditional arms smuggling and drug trafficking businesses, Turkish-Kurdish groups are very active in human trafficking. Ironically, Albanian-Kosovar organized criminal groups might have replaced the Turkish ones in substantial shares of the drug trafficking market.[48]

The Ocalan case adds a further dimension to the international importance of transnational organized crime, but it will be considered further when the paper examines the transformation of terrorism and its links with drug trafficking.

To recapitulate the strategic picture drawn until now in terms of major organized criminal constellations, the Mediterranean Region is characterised by three centers of gravity located in Italy, Russia, and Turkey.

The fact that some of them are NATO members is fairly irrelevant for the effects that this may have on the quality of governance and the prevention/repression of organized crime. This point should be kept in mind, especially now that NATO will enlarge and celebrate its 50th-year anniversary: the argument made by CEEC politicians in favour of NATO membership as a means to "Westernise" their countries is purely political and is not valid beyond that realm. EU enlargement might provide much more help against these plagues, but, precisely because it has higher requirements and standards, it does not have for the time being the needed political push.

All three centers of gravity have remarkable transnational reach: Cosa Nostra for 70 years at least, Turkish-Kurdish groups at least for 30. The Russian-Georgian groups are younger on the international scene, but displayed *Blitzkrieg* quality in their diffusion, thanks to the active cooperation of other local organized criminal groups or gangs. The patterns of drug trafficking will show the complexity of the web of opportunistic alliances and collaborations.

In the meantime, it is useful to recall briefly some of the international connections among major transnational organized criminal groups.[49]

The Colombian cartels are using Europe as an important money laundering area, especially in the tourist, entertaininent, and gambling industries. Spain is used as a main transit point towards Germany, Italy, the Netherlands, and Russia. CEEC are used as transit countries towards Western Europe. All Italian major organized criminal groups have relationships with the cartels.

The Russian-organized criminal groups have targeted, in Southern Europe, countries like France, Italy, and Israel (in addition to Austria, Northern Ireland, Finland, Germany, Switzerland, and the UK).

The Chinese Triads, after having selected the Netherlands as their first bridgehead, have expanded towards Italy and France in the area (and for the rest of Europe, they are present in Belgium, Germany, and UK).

Looking from the side of Italian criminal organizations, we can find that groups from Brazil, Egypt, Tunisia, and former Yugoslavia are in contact with Cosa Nostra, Camorra, and 'Ndrangheta. Cosa Nostra, in turn, has specialized contacts with Argentinean, Chilean, Israeli, Jordanian, Moroccan, Polish, and Syrian organizations. Camorra has links with Argentinean, Colombian, Jordanian, Somalian, and Uruguayan groups, while the 'Ndrangheta finds support from allies in Chile, Czech Republic, Dominican Republic, Israel, Poland, Rumania, Slovakia, and Turkey.[50]

The end of the Cold War worked differently on these three centers of gravity. In Italy, it helped to break old connivances and to weaken significantly older dominant groups and families. In Turkey, apparently it did not modify preexistent situations, although the increase in publicity and in pressure from allied countries might help in time to change things. In Russia and Georgia, it gave more or less free rein.

While these three centers concentrate a significant amount of criminal power, one should avoid jumping to the conclusion that the Eastern and Central Mediterranean basins are Mafia-ridden, while the rest is relatively clean. Whenever there are drug trafficking and money laundering, one can be assured that organized crime is at work and that its social and political nefarious effects are present.

A quick look to other relatively minor situations can be instructive. A first indicator are states that failed at different degrees within the past decade: Lebanon, Somalia, former Yugoslavia, and Albania. All these countries have experienced or continue to experience governments that can be corrupted, and their law enforcement is questionable at best.

Lebanon was one of the first cases where drug trafficking became a standard financial resource for several militias, while others preferred large-scale trafficking and kidnapping. This has had a corrupting influence over Syria, whose military and intelligence forces were heavily involved in the war and in the further pacification. Although drug production and trafficking have undergone significant changes, they still remain an important factor in the local and Syrian political life. Poppy cultivations have disappeared, to be replaced by cannabis and heroin refineries. Beirut retains a very marginal role, but the ports of Jieh, Damour, and Tripoli retain their role, while new ports are developing near the Israeli border (Byblos, Batroun, and Enn Naqoura). Lebanon is an important regional hub for deliveries towards Tel Aviv, Damascus (further on to Cyprus and Greece), Al Riyadh (via Amman) and Istanbul.[51]

Somalia, after the failure of the Western coalition policies governing U.N. missions, has become a major drug trafficking transit point. Allegedly most of the drug trafficking is controlled by the warlord Osman Atto, former second in command of Aideed. Moreover, after a drop of activity due to the death of the warlord Mohammed Farrah

Aideed, piracy continues to infest Somalia's waters through attacks where even mortar rounds and rocket-propelled antitank grenades are used to stop ships.

The whole war in former Yugoslavia cannot be understood if one does not consider the level of deep corruption of most regimes in place, no matter if some of them are supported by Western countries. In many cases, their most bloody militias had been recruited directly from the underworld of organized crime, often disguised as football clubs or hooligan groups. The Neretva Valley was and remains a place where cannabis is grown, and the whole region is known to law enforcement agencies as the Balkan Corridor or Route (by 1995, 80 percent of all heroin seized in West Europe had passed through that corridor). Due to the war in former Yugoslavia, the tracing of this corridor has changed, but not its importance. The general rehearsal of the projected Euro mass forgery was the widespread forgery of the Deutschmark, the reference currency in the area, in order to finance the costs of the wars of Yugoslavia's dissolution.[52]

It should be absolutely clear that the presence of the SFOR has only blocked open war and has forced some militias take a relatively lower profile, but its presence has been negligible in severing the criminal liaisons among political elites, armed militias and organized crime. Some U.N. and EU initiatives have started to tackle very prudently the problem, but they are severely hampered by the diplomatic constraints placed upon them and by a general lack of cooperation among different entities.[53]

Albania since 1997, when the Italians, leading a European coalition of "able and willing," intervened to help the local government restore law and order with the operation Alba, is the classic example of how transnational organized crime is a real security threat. First, through the bankruptcy of the "financial pyramids," it has generated the nightmare of a criminal republic just across the Adriatic Sea. Second, it has continued to exploit the despair of clandestine emigrants, using many of them in female and juvenile prostitution rings. Third, it has created and maintained in the north and in the south of the country grey zones which are respectively responsible for nourishing the war in Kosovo and for keeping up a stream of drugs, slaves, war weapons (50 percent of all Italian confiscations are in Apulia, the region facing Albania) and cigarettes across the Adriatic. The drugs, once imported, are starting to be produced locally. Mostly it is cannabis, whose quality and lower prices are beginning to replace Lebanese hashish, but, under the supervision of members of Cosa Nostra and of the Colombian cartels, experimental coca cultivations have been started on the local, rugged mountains. Moreover, there are several indications that the local groups have started operating morphine refineries. The same country, together with Montenegro, is the starting point for money laundering operations carried out by the NSCU, with ramifications towards Russia and Rumania.

A much less discussed, but no less important grey zone is the island of Corsica, infested by a sort of Mafia almost forgotten by international analysts. The story of Corsica as a base for transnational organized crime begins with the gradual transformation, through a series of secessions, of a terrorist nationalistic movement into a collection of organized criminal groups, as French President Jacques Chirac defined them.[54] He was the first French president to admit the problem openly, until then mostly considered an internal affair, mostly buried under the silences of successive governments of different political affiliations.

As it happens often with insular regions, Corsica was for decades one among the most economically depressed and socially backward regions of the centralized French state. After the end of World War II, national movements sprung up, advocating more resources for the island and the secession from France, following traditions displayed during the upheaval of the French Revolution, where many peripheral regions tried to oppose the dominance of the capital. The situation was worsened when the former

French colonists of Algeria (the so-called *pied noirs*—the black-footed ones) were relocated after the end of the war of decolonization of that country. But by the end of the 1960s, the revolutionary fervour had given way to a diffused and organized racketeering system, thinly disguising itself with the old ideals. The French political elite thought it more expedient to buy out the secessionist movement with tax cuts, privileges, contributions to its development, and by tolerating the creation of a parallel power structure. The tacit pact was that France enjoyed a more or less nominal sovereignty on the island, and that, in exchange, Corsicans supported in various ways the party in power, promoting at the same time their own lobbies.

Until the end of 1996, intimidating bomb attacks were still conducted so as to minimize casualties, but by the end of 1997 some still unidentified "nationalist groups" (local parlance for organized crime groups) assassinated the prefect Jean-Claude Erignac, evidently throwing the gauntlet to the French state.

As with every country facing forms of organized crime capable of controlling the territory, France has its own understandable difficulties restoring law and order on the island.[55] It must be clear, however, that Corsican organized crime is not something that can be considered as circumscribed to the island alone. Corsican groups have infiltrated various levels of the French law enforcement agencies, they have connections with the local and transnational organized crime groups present in Southern France, and, as other groups in other countries, they are responsible for serious frauds against European Community structural aid and agricultural support funds.

Spain is also another interesting and not so often mentioned base for transnational organized crime. Its local organizations, although lacking the strong image of others, are very active in drug trafficking, systematic cigarette smuggling, liaisons with trasnational prostitution rings, and software piracy. Part of the problem comes from the grey zones that straddle the Spanish-French border and that were created by the terrorist and racketeering activities of ETA. Their liaisons include Brazilian, Bulgarian, French, Italian, Moroccan, Polish, Portuguese, and Russian organizations.[56]

Drug production in the Mediterranean region occurs, according to the type of drug, among the following geographic areas:[57]

- **Cannabis:** Morocco and Russia (major producers), Lebanon and former Yugoslavia (minor).

- **ATS**: Western Europe (group of the ecstasy drugs) and CIS (methamphethamine and ephedrone).

Drug trafficking, instead, reveals the following patterns:

- **Heroin**: Afghanistan[58] has replaced the Golden Triangle as major producer, 40 percent of global heroin seizures were made in Europe (Western and Eastern alike). The drug followed three possible routes: 1. Central Asia, Russia; 2. Central Asia, Caucasus, Turkey Balkan Corridor; and 3. Iran, Turkey (much less used due to harsh Iranian anti-drug policies). Some 10-20 percent could come via Pakistan, Somalia, Nigeria, Netherlands, or Spain. Russia helped significantly to make the global connection between two producing areas that were before much more separated: Golden Crescent and Golden Triangle.[59]

- **Cocaine**, largely produced by Colombia (Bolivia and Peru have a lesser role), and Europe (Eastern and Western) is a market with an upwards trend (actually 10 percent of all world seizures happen here). While the Netherlands and Spain are the main European entry points, the air and sea trafficking routes connect the producing countries either directly or via the Brazil-West Africa or Southern Africa route. Another possible route, according to Interpol, would be directly to Russia in order to reach European markets.

- **Cannabis,** produced by the mentioned countries, plus Pakistan, Kazakhstan, and Kyrgyzstan (Colombia, Cambodia, and Thailand are minor but increasing in importance). Congo, Ghana, Kenya, Malawi, Nigeria, South Africa, and Tanzania (taken together) are important transit points and producing countries for European markets.

Summarizing at the end of this paragraph, we can say that the organized criminal and drug trafficking geography of the Mediterranean Region is marked by:

- three centers of gravity, concerning major transnational criminal organizations, namely Italy, Russia, and Turkey;

- 21 regional gravitating support areas: Albania, Croatia, Bulgaria, Djibouti, Egypt, Eritrea, France, FRY, FYROM, Georgia, Greece, Israel, Jordan, Lebanon, Morocco, Rumania, Slovenia, Somalia, Spain, Syria, and Tunisia;

- two states risking to become failed (Algeria and Russia), 10 having experienced at various degrees such a failure (Albania, Bosnia-Herzegovina, Croatia, Eritrea, FRY, FYROM, Georgia, Lebanon, Slovenia, and Somalia);

- four islands which have relevant grey zones and different degrees of organized crime control/connection (Corsica, Cyprus, Sardinia, and Sicily);

- two major (Morocco and Russia) and two minor drug producers (Lebanon and former Yugoslavia);

- three major drug trafficking routes: Atlantic Route, Balkan Corridor, Russia;

- three major drug trafficking entry points: Russia, Spain and Turkey;

- three major people-smuggling sea-routes (Morocco-Spain, Tunisia/Albania-Italy), and four land-routes (Sarajevo-Croatia-Slovenia-Italy/Austria, Istanbul-Ukraine-Poland-Germany or Istanbul-Romania-Hungary-Slovakia-Czech Republic, Istanbul-Greece-FYROM-Italy/Austria, Russia-Finland);[60]

- three regional financial offshore centers: Cyprus, Malta, Monaco;

- the presence of Chinese, Colombian, and Japanese organized criminal groups and the relative absence of North American and Mexican ones;

- dominant drugs are cannabis, heroin, and ATS, with cocaine on the increase.[61]

Transforming Terrorism. The end of governmental control and manipulation of guerrilla movements during the Cold War has produced, as in other areas of politics and economy, deregulation and delocalization, only that here we see a deregulation of guerrillas and a delocalization of their logistics. The deregulation of terrorism includes its privatization, its links to criminal organizations, and, mainly at the local level, its extension as a practice of criminal organizations. The delocalization is synonymous with globalization. These three relatively new characteristics pose a direct problem to the states in terms of diffusion of power. The privatization of terrorism is easily epitomized by the figure of the millionaire Osama bin Laden.

Instead of ideologies and political struggle, war economics are increasingly a mainspring of these civil conflicts, leading to a "degeneration" of armed movements, more and more entangling them in the vicious circle of criminalizing resources. Beyond possible tactical alliances with criminal organizations, the most worrying feature is that armed movements acquire more and more "Mafia" characteristics precisely because they engage themselves in drug trafficking. The drawback for these movements is that, in the long run, their legitimacy will be increasingly eroded in the eyes of dominated populations.

The dynamics of this involvement in crime are illustrated through three levels;

- local tax on illicit cultivations,

- involvement in commercial networks, and

- development of international networks.[62]

Through the first system, it is possible to set up fairly large private militias (brigade strength). The second level follows the first, through a tax on drug trafficking. The final level has been developed by the Lebanese Christian militias during the civil war, the TTLE (since the mid 1980s), the Kosovo Albanian organizations, and the Kurdish militants of the PKK.

The case of the PKK leader Abdullah Ocalan (the Avenger, nicknamed by his followers Apo—Uncle) is a striking illustration of the transformation of terrorism. In 1978 he founded the PKK on a Marxist-Leninist ideological basis and begun eliminating competing nationalist Kurdish formations (KUK). In 1980 the coup of the Turkish generals unleashed a systematic persecution of all pro-Kurdish groups, moderate and extremist alike. Fleeing from Turkey, he started training his fighters in 1982 in the midst of the Lebanese civil war. By 1984 he started an outright guerrilla campaign in South Eastern Turkey that cost until now 31,000 dead (17,878 rebels, 4,660 civilians, 3,835 soldiers, 247 policemen, and 1,218 rural self-defense militiamen).

Sanctuaries and help were provided by regional neighbours (Iran, Iraq, Syria) interested in creating problems for Turkey, by the USSR for political and geopolitical reasons, and in many ways by Greece, until recently locked in the long running feud with Ankara. This resulted in a very structured organization, 10,000-15,000 hard core militants (among which some German RAF terrorists) capable of controlling actively non-negligible portions of the Kurdish diaspora in the world and influencing several cultural associations, one islamist branch movement, a Kurdish parliament-in-exile, some dailies, one TV chain, and one political wing (HADEP).[63]

While at the start the costs had been borne by foreign assistance, in time systematic racketeering and drug trafficking began increasingly to fill PKK's war chests. Ocalan not only resorted to all usual, bloody terrorist tactics and suppressed even political dissenters ruthlessly at home and abroad (the crime for which German judges wanted him), but, unlike Arafat, Mandela, or the IRA, he used his position on the Turkish border to promote the passage of drugs towards Western European markets.

The war waged in Southeast Turkey would not be logistically understandable if one would not take into account the drug trafficking dimension and the extensive complicities in that trade on both sides. This aspect constitutes also the hidden political dimension on which the future of hard liners in both camps is at stake. The beginning of the end, prepared by terrible counterguerrilla Turkish campaigns, started with the end of Syrian protection, an ambiguous sign of the remaining influence that state sponsoring has on terrorism.

At a political level, only the imminent trial of Ocalan will tell if there has been a backstage agreement between Apo and the Turkish generals towards some vaguely federalist political solution. Apparently one of the goals of the Kurdish terrorist leader was to continue the political overtures of 1993 in the direction of a cease-fire and the search for some political solution, yet it remains to be seen if all the commanders of the PKK will exercise restraint or if some parts of the PKK run amok.[64]

Another interesting and much discussed case is Osama bin Laden. In the past bin Laden had actively collaborated with the CIA in Afghanistan, but he changed his mind after the arrival in Saudi Arabia of American troops, felt by him as sacrilegious. His $300 million fortune has created several terrorist training camps in Afghanistan, Pakistan, Yemen, and Somalia, with a network of 3-5,000 affiliates under the name of Al Qaeda (the Base). He is suspected of being the mastermind of the killing of 18 U.S. Rangers in Mogadishu, the Dahran bomb attack (June 25-26, 1996), and of being involved in the twin attacks in Nairobi and Dar Es-Salaam (August 7, 1998).[65]

A less spectacular, but no less important aspect of the transformation of terrorism is the network of private or religious charities that are capable of supporting low-cost terrorist networks, who, in turn, may accept state support, but do not depend on it.[66] This independence from governments is real, but it should not be exaggerated. Private initiative, despite having succeeded in putting together most of the means necessary for an international terrorist campaign, appears not to be capable of effectively mounting one like in the 1960s and 1970s. One could argue that only the systematic support capability provided by states allowed such campaigns during the Cold War. Several intelligence evaluations in 1998 indicated that the French terrorist Kelkal group was induced to use rudimentary means not only to avoid investigative detection, but also because it was very difficult to get sophisticated materiel. The same appears to happen even in Algeria, where GIA groups are forced to rudimentary production instead of relying on effective logistic networks abroad. By the way, the case of the GIA also shows how endemic terrorism can "degenerate" into clanic gangs. The name itself does not stand for a rigidly organized group, it is just a label, covering a terrorist nebula, whose *kataeb* (companies) are controlling each their own territory, managing their own racketeering and trafficking and fighting as fiercely among themselves as against the government forces.

The geography of terrorism in the Mediterranean Region can be summarized as follows:

- 20 countries with internal/endemic/civil war terrorism, inspired by nationalist/ethnic motivations (Spain, Israel, Greece, FRY, FYROM, Turkey, Iran, Iraq, Russia) or by political/religious motivations (Morocco, Algeria, Tunisia, Libya, Egypt, Israel, Iran, Iraq, Djibouti; Saudi Arabia, Bahrain);

- 3 countries affected by international terrorism (France, Saudi Arabia, Yemen);

- 5 countries designated as terrorism supporting states (Libya, Sudan, Syria, Iraq, Iran);

- 9 countries seriously violating human rights at various degrees in their counterterrorist actions (Algeria, Libya, Egypt, Israel, Saudi Arabia, Iran, Iraq, Bahrain, Turkey, FRY).

Regarding international terrorism as defined above, the Mediterranean Region is characterized by the apparently contradictory presence of a vast movement of islamist extremism, of a majority of U.S.-designated terrorism supporting states, of some of the most important terrorists and yet a very low number of casualties, compared to the potential targets in the whole area and in the Western European riverine countries.

The most striking contradiction is the recurring news of a great Iraqi terrorist offensive, possibly with the help of Abu Nidal or Osama bin Laden. It should be remembered that before the Gulf War, the alarm was launched about Saddam's supposed terrorist armada, but nothing happened. Surely quiet preventive measures are having their effect, but probably other factors also are playing their role.[67]

The first is the weakening of extremist islamist currents, exploiting the Islamic religious renaissance and particularly its integralist variants. Saudi Arabia had promoted since at least 1980 its own wahabbite variant of fundamentalism, exporting it not only to Afghanistan, but also to Algeria, Tunisia, and other countries where it succeeded in exercising influence. The presence of Western infidel soldiers on the holy land of Saudi Arabia, whose monarchy is legitimized precisely from its role as protector of the holy Muslim places, weakened severely Saudis' prestige. This circumstance was in some cases coupled with a cut of funds towards extremist groups that had supported the Iraqi cause in 1991. Moreover, the conservative islamist movement failed because it did not address revolutionary needs of the societies. Land reform was, for instance, conspicuously absent from their agenda, while they believed that a Middle East "Marshall Plan" could have furthered their goals.

On the other hand, secular forces started in a number of countries to break their ambiguous relationships with integralist islamist groups. In fact, these groups had been supported in order to fight against other political opponents (in some states they were leftwing forces, in other Palestinian groups). At the same time, the impetuous rising of religious streams in the political debate had forced more secular parties on the defensive. Some analysts noticed that, at a certain moment, two Middle Eastern leaders started vigorously drawing the attention of the international community on the danger of islamist extremism, particularly the attention of the United States. Creating this new enemy, Hosni Mubarak and Izthak Rabin succeeded in getting international support or neutrality, regaining in importance *vis-à-vis* and liquidating without too much international criticism their own armed opponents (al Jamaa al Islamiyya, Muslim Brotherhood, Hamas, al Jihad).[68]

The second factor, already mentioned, is the lessened support of certain states to terrorism, compared to the days of the Cold War. The effect of this reduced support and the fear of the propagation of islamist extremism also brought several Arab states to underwrite same basic political principles of the anti-terrorism fight, which, in turn, have lead to a better cross border cooperation among Mediterranean region countries.[69]

Finally, one should not forget that terrorism is not a winning option in several significant countries in the area. Through democratic or despotic means, the battle against terrorism is being won slowly but assuredly in Spain, Egypt, and Turkey, and, in the supposedly much more fragile petromonarchies, it appears to be a somewhat limited risk.[70]

Another aspect of international terrorism is represented by the future of its evolution, particularly regarding the use of weapons of mass destruction (WMD) and of information warfare. The debate on the possibility of the use by terrorist groups of biological or chemical weapons has gained more profile through President Clinton's declarations on that risk.

Surely the chemical attack in Tokyo carried out by the Auni Shinrikyo sect has left a deep impression in the minds of decisionmakers and law enforcement agencies, and one should not be complacent about the failure of the same sect to procure biological weapons. Nuclear terrorism, especially its variant featuring crude radiological dispersion devices (RDD), remains still a distinct possibility; therefore all preventive measures aimed at reducing the risks to civil populations are something that should be considered by the European governments, too.[71]

That said, one should acknowledge that most terrorist groups do not need to face the risks and the possible severe backlash inherent to the use of WMDs because much cruder methods are enough to attain their goals. Moreover, only a limited number of groups may present a profile of global purification and isolationist mentalities, which, in turn, might resort to extreme means regardless of any political consideration.

The so-called cyberterrorism is already a reality with which open information societies must learn to live, albeit until now no spectacular incident has reached the effect of traditional killings and bomb attacks.

On a less exotic note, a much more probable risk is given by the links between terrorism and criminal groups. In itself this feature in not new, but the way these bonds are presently fostered is different, as the French case demonstrates. Since 1994 the frontier between islamist militants and criminals has become hazy, due to an increasing interpenetration of both environments. The French anti-terrorist experts point out that the new groups emerging are bound by a more "intellectual" member or a veteran from Afghan or Bosnia; already socially excluded, they tend to create a sort of internationalist counterculture using islamism as an existing ideological anti-system tool offered by certain mosques, cultural associations, and within prisons; and, finally, their social opposition connecting internal and international terrorism is expected to increase.[72]

The diffusion of terrorist methods to organized criminal groups is particularly well-known in Colombia, where the Cali and Medellin drug cartels have employed car bombs frequently in indiscriminate attacks. In Europe the phenomenon is still relatively limited: three Cosa Nostra attacks in Italy (1994) and one Russian organized crime attack in Moscow (November 11, 1996). In the case of Corsica, we have instead the gradual transformation of a terrorist nationalistic movement into a collection of organized criminal groups, as already mentioned.

An ominous sign of the lethal potential that the manipulation of organized crime and terrorist techniques can develop in spillovers of endemic terrorism comes from India. The March 12, 1993, multiple bomb attacks using explosive cars, motorcycles, and suitcases left 320 dead and more than 1,200 injured in the business district of Bombay. The perpetrators were not terrorists, but local criminals following the directives of an Indian "godfather" living in Dubai, apparently recruited by the Pakistani intelligence to retaliate for the Indian killings of Muslims in Kashmir.[73]

A possible variant of this deadly synergy is the criminal multiservice agency, making money through criminal activities organized in "mafia"-like fashion and obtaining money and political protection through customized terrorist attacks. Although rare, there is the important precedent of the Magliana gang (1983-93).[74]

Concluding the analysis of the new risks in the area, one should draw attention to the case of Aum Shinrikyo, which has also highlighted the possibility that some sects may represent a risk for democratic governments either by violent actions (including mass suicides) or, worse, by secret political and economic infiltration, leading to the destabilization of the very foundations of democracy.

The problems are not only the undemocratic ideals and the methods advocated by these groups, but also their specific crimes against the human person (brainwashing, battering, rape, and extreme physical and psychological pressure) and at the economic level (extortion, tax fraud, money laundering, and corruption). Ironically, while Southern Mediterranean countries have more problems with religious extremism, Northern Mediterranean and more affluent countries have more specific troubles with sects.[75]

Policies.

If one might believe that coordinated and coherent policies regarding these new risks are more easily found in the Justice and Home Affairs (JHA) domain than in the defence one, reality will delude him quickly. Already in the relatively homogeneous area of EU countries, this issue has taken several years to come to maturity, and it will take some more time to produce fully satisfactory operational results. The Mediterranean Region is an even more complicated environment, where few frameworks have some chances to succeed, particularly when they affect sovereignty aspects which are terribly sensitive to many governments outside the EU zone.

Institutions are surely not the panacea, but they help in better organizing common efforts. Apart from more or less universal groupings like the U.N., Interpol, the OECD, or the G-7/G-8 or from specific multilateral initiatives (Sharm El Sheikh summit, multilateral meetings among Interior ministers or intelligence chiefs), the only institution that can do something here is the EU.

Despite the sometimes dismissive remarks of some commentators on its CFSP, the EU has altogether the consensus, relative will, and the concrete means to act in this respect. This fact was authoritatively confirmed by the policy adopted by NATO itself. EU is the leading organization, while NATO can only be seen as a facilitator.

What are the comparative advantages of the EU?

- Its successful experience concerning the JHA (also denominated the third pillar), because it succeeded first in securing consensus of sovereign countries over an intrusive agreement like the Schengen treaty and then in extending this *acquis* to the rest of European partners.

- Its multiple dimensions, political, economic, and security, embodied in the Barcelona process. These will help gradually in developing that mutual understanding that is the precondition to any scenario of partnership and democratization in the area.

- The availability of the WEU as a vehicle for concrete security initiatives, including out-of-area law enforcement missions that will be carried out on the basis of an implicit or explicit EU mandate.

- Its political profile that is, rightly or wrongly, perceived as less imposing, unilaterally acting and biased than the U.S. one.

Much of what will be mentioned is already being done, but it is useful to stress it again. What can be done by the EU?

- Continue in the gradual integration of her law enforcement and judicial space. EU countries are among the most lucrative markets for transnational organized crime and a traditional target for extremist political groups. Therefore, preventing and combating effectively these phenomena will create a zone of law and order with direct and indirect positive effects on neighbouring countries.

- Prepare her enlargement through policies that enhance formally and informally the cooperation among actors interested in stability and economic development. Few people realize that a good reform of the much decried Common Agricultural Policy will help ease the tensions created by clandestine immigration and its attendant criminality through a further opening of Mediterranean agricultural imports.

- Continue support to Russia in order to contribute as much as possible in avoiding the foundering of the state and of the economy and to prevent further inroads by transnational organized crime.

- Devise appropriate policies for the assistance to law enforcement agencies in the accomplishment of objectives of common interest among the Mediterranean partners. Europol could be developed gradually into a regional focal point for assistance and information exchange with law enforcement agencies of third countries.

Beyond the established institutional and economic aid contexts, another policy could be considered at purely intergovernmental level.

Cooperation among law enforcement agencies also has made significant strides on both sides of the Atlantic, as shown by the successful working relationship between the director of the FBI, Mr. Louis Freeh, and the general prosecutor of Palermo, Mr. Giovanni Falcone. What is lacking is a better cooperation among foreign intelligence services in the new fields of transnational organized crime, money laundering, and drug trafficking.

Here again, European governments should take the lead because their intelligence agencies suffer from excessive duplication, fragmentation, and relatively low budgets. The new strategic environment already puts an enormous strain on their limited resources concerning their traditional tasks. It would be interesting to develop a common framework and understanding in order to repeat and improve the successes achieved in the fields of international terrorism and counterproliferation.

This framework, that could be called a *European intelligence policy,* means that a new informal alternative collaboration culture should be shaped among the different intelligence services, shaping in turn their collective behaviour.

Concerning the specific new risks issue, a common discussion among intelligence directors could be started on basic requirements (a first one could be to include financial and organized crime within the broader analysis of foreign governments), leading gradually to joint assessments and eventually to the joint training of analysts in this area. Another subject that could be broached in this context is the division of labour between internal security and external intelligence services at a European level.[76]

ENDNOTES - CHAPTER 2

1. That is, Portugal, Spain, France, Italy, Greece, and Turkey.

2. That is, Mauritania, Morocco, Algeria, Tunisia, Egypt, Jordan, and Israel. Libya is still out due to the freezing of diplomatic ties after the Lockerbie incident, but might in the medium term be involved again in principle. The partners of dialogue do not fully coincide between the two security organizations.

3. The *Western European subregion* includes Portugal, Spain, France, and Italy. The *Balkan/Black Sea subregion* comprises Slovenia, Croatia, FRY, Federation of Bosnia-Herzegovina, FYROM, Albania, Greece, Romania, Bulgaria, Moldova, Ukraine, Russia, Georgia, and Turkey (Hungary being a bridge towards Central Europe). The *Middle East/Red Sea subregion* includes Syria, Jordan, Iraq, Iran, Saudi Arabia, Bahrain, Qatar, United Arab Emirates, Kuwait, Oman, Yemen, Djibouti, Somalia, Eritrea, Sudan, Egypt, Israel, Palestinian Territories, and Lebanon. The *Maghreb subregion* is represented by the classic quartet of Libya, Tunisia, Algeria, and Morocco, where Mauritania has been politically added.

4. For a succinct review of the different theories and a good bibliography, see Paul B. Stares, ed., *The New Security Agenda, A Global Survey,* Tokyo-New York: JCIE, 1998. Besides the chapter on North America (Florini-Simmons), for the concerned area, see also the chapters on FSU (Medvedev), Western Europe (Politi), and Middle East (Shehadi).

5. Just to name some examples for each mentioned category of risk, the repeated civil wars in the republican and imperial Rome, the Cossack revolt (18th century), the "brigandage" in Italy (19th); Arab, Norman, Mongol, Turkish migrations throughout the Middle Age; white settlers' migrations in the Sioux and other Amerindian tribes' territories (19th); the availability of water and fertile land before modern agricultural techniques; the availability of timber for navies before the spreading of iron hulls; religious terrorism in the Mashreq (the sect of Assassins) and in India's different kingdoms (Thug sect); and piracy in different centuries.

6. Giovarnbattista Vico, *Principi della scienza nuova,* 3rd ed., 1774.

7. See *International Military and Defense Encyclopedia,* Trevor N. Dupuy, *et al.,* eds., Washington-New York: Brassey's, 1993; Edward N. Luttwak, *Strategy, The Logic of War and Peace,* Cambridge MA: Belknap Press, Harvard University Press, 1987, p. 180. For the scope of

the paper, the definitions of Henry H. Kissinger (strategy as the manner by which a society secures its future); of Basil H. Liddell Hart (grand strategy as guide and coordination of all the resources of a nation or an alliance to attain the political objectives established); of Edward Luttwak ("grand strategy is the highest level of interaction between any parties capable to use unregulated force against one another"); and of Helmuth Schmidt (grand strategy as the harmonization of national economic and security policies among Western countries, since no one individually can achieve security) are used.

8. See also Barry Buzan, "Rethinking Security After the Cold War," *Cooperation and Conflict*, Sage Publications, Vol. 32, No. 1, pp. 5-28, for an analytical point of view.

9. It is important to keep in mind that in this context the word "challenge" is synonymous with "risk" rather than with the concept of outright threat. This is also necessary in order to qualify the seriousness of different challenges.

10. This applies also to Abkhazia, Albania, Chechenya, Cyprus, Iraq, Israel, Kosovo, Ossetia, Palestinian Authority Territories, Spain, Trasnistria, Turkey, or Yemen. Lebanon and Bosnia were cases, as was Vietnam, where a quasi-conventional war, a conventional war, or an international low intensity conflict were merged with an insurrection.

11. For an overview of a sample the different definitions proposed, see W. Hagan, "Organized Crime Continuum: A Further Specification of a New Conceptual Model" in *Criminal Justice Review,* 1983, p. 8, in which he lists 13 different conditions for organized crime, defined by 15 different authors, and finds 11 elements that could be included in the concept of organized crime; Didier Bigo, "Pertinence et limites de la notion de crime organisé," in *Relations internationales et stratigiques,* 20, Hiver 1995, pp. 134-8; Peter Kopp, "Analyse Economique des Organizations Criminelles," pp. 139-43; Marcelle Padovani, "Le modele Cosa Nostra," pp. 113-15; Gianluca Fiorentini and Sam Peltzman, eds., *The Economics of Organized Crime,* Cambridge: Cambridge University Press, 1995, pp. 1-30; Pierre Tremblay et Maurice Cusson, "Marchés criminels transnationaux et analyse strategique," in Marcel Leclerc, ed., *La Criminalite Organisee,* La Documentation Frangaise, 1996, Paris, pp. 19-42; Ernesto U. Savona, "La regulation du marché criminel," pp. 263-264. In general, the paper will try to avoid the terms "mafia" or "mafiosi."

12. Ad Hoc Group on Organized Crime, *Report on the Situation of Organized Crime in EU*, 1993. This definition could gradually replace the older definition adopted by the OIPC-Interpol since 1988.

13. For a more thorough discussion on the definitions of transnational security risks, see also Alessandro Politi, *Nouveau risques et sécurité europeenne*, Cahier de Chaillot nr. 29, IES-UEO, Octobre 1997, Paris, pp. 4-11.

14. According to Dutch Justice minister Winnie Sordrager, however, 50 percent of the hashish seized in the Netherlands arrives from France and Belgium, while 80 percent of the seized heroin from Germany and Balkan countries. See Associated Press, Rotterdam, April 22, 1997.

15. For an essential survey of definitions of terrorism, see Louis Rene Beres, "The Meaning of Terrorism for the Military Commander," *Comparative Strategy*, Vol. 14, No. 3, July-September 1995, Basingstoke: Taylor & Francis, 1995, pp. 287-99; Paul Wilkinson, "Terrorist Targets and Tactics: New Risks to World Order," in Alison Jamieson, ed., *Terrorism and Drug Trafficking in the 1990s*, Aldershot: Dartmouth Publishing Co., 1994, p. 179; Alain Joxe, "Un concept fourre-tout: le terrorisme," in *Le Monde Diplomatique*, April 1996, pp. 6-7; Vittorfranco S. Pisano, "Contemporary Terrorism and the West," in *Occidente*, October 4, 1994, p. 28-29.

16. U.S. Department of State, *Patterns of Global Terrorism: 1995*, Office of the Coordinator for Counterterrorism, Washington, April 1996 (Ambassador Philip C. Wilcox, Jr., Coordinator for Counterterrorism). The definition itself is drawn from the Title 22 of the United States Code, Section 2656f(d) and has been used for statistical and analytical purposes since 1983.

17. The U.S. Department of State specifies that the term "noncombatant" is interpreted to include, in addition to civilians, military personnel who at the time of the incident are unarmed and/or not on duty. Also considered acts of terrorism are the attacks on military installations or on armed military personnel when a state of military hostilities does not exist at the site.

18. See L. R. Beres. The principle of just cause maintains that an insurgency may exercise law-enforcing measures under international law. This argument is deducible from the existence of an authoritative human rights regime in international law and from the corollary absence of a central enforcement mechanism for this regime. It is codified *inter alia* at the Report of the Ad Hoc Committee on International Terrorism, U.N. GAOR, 29th sess., supp. no. 28, at 1, U.N. Doc. A/9028 (1973); see also Article 7 of the U.N. General Assembly's 1974 Definition of Aggression. Article 7 refers to the October 24, 1970, Declaration on Principles of International Law Concerning Friendly

Relations and Cooperation Among States. The standard of just means has been brought to bear on non-state actors in world politics by Article 3, common to the four Geneva Conventions of August 12, 1949, and by the two protocols to these conventions. Protocol I applies humanitarian international law to conflicts fought for self-determination. A product of all armed conflicts that are not covered by Protocol I and that took place since the Diplomatic Conference on the Reaffirmation and Development of International Humanitarian Law Applicable in Armed Conflicts that ended on June 10, 1977, the protocol brings irregular forces within the full scope of law. Protocol II, also additional to the Geneva Conventions, concerns protection of victims of noninternational armed conflicts. This protocol thus applies within the territory of a state between its armed forces and dissident armed forces.

19. Although it remained difficult to understand in the development of the case until the end of January 1999, how some German and Italian politicians continued to ignore that the PKK leader was seriously involved in drug trafficking, and whose political/freedom fight rationale begs some questions.

20. A precursor case was the attempted investigation by the U.N. of massacres allegedly committed by the new ruler of the Democratic Republic of Congo, Laurent Desire Kabila. It would have been difficult to distinguish between his responsibilities as guerrilla chief and as president of the new republic, and in both cases he remained legally accountable.

21. That is, where indigenous attackers constantly target people within the same country—the denominations express increasing degrees of violence. Examples of endemic terrorism might be found in Northern Ireland or Spain, while civil war is ongoing as of January 1999 in Algeria.

22. Citizens of another country are attacked in an area plagued by local, usually endemic terrorism, e.g., if a European dies in a bomb attack against a bus in Tel Aviv.

23. Citizens of another country are attacked in an area adjacent to that plagued by endemic terrorism, e.g., Tunisian border guards are attacked by Algerian terrorists.

24. Support in different kinds by non-state actors—or by governments on an occasional basis—to armed/terrorist groups or to their front political organizations, acting in the theatre where endemic terrorism or civil war is ongoing, e.g., the Islamic charities' networks or the pro-IRA fund raising actions in the United States.

25. Continuous and/or decisive support by governments to armed/terrorist groups, acting in the theater where the confrontation is happening, as, for instance, the support of Syria and Iran to the Hezb'allah in Lebanon. This category includes all manipulations of armed/terrorist groups made by intelligence agencies. If a group is based in a particular country, this amounts to sponsoring by that country, not to a support role.

26. It can receive international support or state sponsorship, again including all intelligence manipulations in the preceding note. This terrorism can be perpetrated in support of an endemic terrorist confrontation (e.g., attacks by the PKK in Western Europe); in support of a wider political confrontation at political, ideological, or religious level (e.g., the bomb detonated on December 23, 1995, at the office of the Peruvian Honorary Consulate, claimed later by the Anti-Imperialist Cells—AIZ, the successor organization to the RAF); and as a proxy for indirect confrontation between governments.

27. Covert operation has here a narrower meaning, since much of the intelligence manipulations in categories 5 and 6 normally fall into this bracket. Covert operations can be the French retaliations after the bomb attack in Beirut in 1986, or the Iranian-sponsored killings of dissidents in Germany, proved in April 1997.

28. Such may allegedly be the case of several "death squadrons" in Latin America during the Cold War, of a spate of bomb attacks in Italy in the late 1960s or mid-1970s, or of the GAL (Group of Anti-terrorist Liberation) in Spain. It should be noted that even within a nondemocratic country, the creation of clandestine terrorist groups muddles the existing chains of command and political power constellations, as in Algeria for instance.

29. In the year 1991, heroin overdose casualties amounted to 4,843, only among the eight countries of the Schengen space. The medium annual increase is, allowing for statistical fluctuations, around 600-700 dead. See Marie-Christine Dupuis, *Stupifiants, prix, profits,* PUF, Paris, 1996, p. 139. Concerning the United States, in 1995, overdose casualties amounted to 8,400 people against 530,000 drug-related hospital emergencies. See *Strategic Assessment 1994,* H. Binnendijk and P. Clawson, eds., Washington: Institute for National Strategic Studies, National Defense University, 1997, pp. 202-203; see also note 59.

30 Stephen Fidler and Jimmy Bums, "Illicit Drugs Trade is put at $400bn," *Financial Times*, June 26, 1997, p. 4. According to the *World*

Bank Atlas 1994, The World Bank 1994, this estimate must be related to a yearly money laundering turnover of at least $1 trillion.

31. See Alessandro Politi, "Russian organized crime and European security," in European Commission, Reinhardt Rummel and Sabine Weyand, eds., *Illicit trade and organized crime - New threats to economic security?,* European Union External Relations (DG-1) - SWP, Luxembourg, 1998, pp. 39-46.

32. See Bertrand Gallet, "La grande criminalité organisée, facteur de déstabilisation mondiale?," in *Relations Internationales et stratégiques, Grande criminalité organisée: dessous et enjeux,* nr. 20, Hiver 1995, pp. 95-98. The rapporteur of the Loi de programmation militaire 1991-93 at the French Assemblee Nationale spoke of "zone grises" defined as *"regions devenues inaccessibles et hostiles à toute pénétration, où aucun gouvernement n'est en mesure de faire appliquer les regles minimales du droit"* (Regions that have become inaccessible and hostile to any penetration, where no government is capable to enforce the minimal rules of law). Generally these grey zones are places where a civil war is ongoing (Afghanistan, the border regions of Burma and Thailand), where political confrontation and infringements of the law are a normal means for controlling any type of trafficking (the Beqa'a Valley, the Andine Cordillera, the Chinese region of Xinjang, some parts of Northern and Southern Albania). But they can also be areas where the nation-state has disappeared (e.g., former Yugoslavia during the war, Somalia); where guerrillas, militias, and drug traffickers hold sway (e.g., jungles and other rough territory); lawless suburbs in major third world cities and in a fair number of cities in the industrialised countries. See Xavier Raufer, "The New post-Cold War Terrorist Threats," in *Democracy & Security,* Issue 7, May 1996, GIRIS/IGRIS. Although there are some ideas that the cyberspace of Internet could be considered a grey zone for some criminal undertakings, it simply cannot be considered neither inaccessible nor hostile to any penetration. A further classification sees the distinction between grey zones, chaotic territories, and concrete jungles. Chaotic territories are those at the border of different old empires and at the crossing of different cultures, left to their own devices and to their chronic instability (Central Asia, Caucasus, former-Yugoslavia). Concrete jungles are found in each megalopolis and its own slums or bidonvilles (Cairo, Istanbul, Karachi, Lagos Lima, Los Angeles, Rio de Janeiro). See VV AA, CHEAr, GRR nr. 12, *Défense et sécurité à l'horizon 2000, Nouveaux défis, nouveaux moyens,* Paris, September 1995, pp. 35-27.

33. See also VV AA, "Transnational Crime: A New Security Threat?," in *Strategic Survey 1994/95,* London: International Institute for Strategic Studies, Oxford Press, 1995, pp. 25-33.

34. James Holden-Rhodes, intervention at the seminar "New Risks and European Security," WEU-ISS, November 28-29, 1997, Paris.

35. According to recent estimates, the Camorra is made up by 132 "families," Cosa Nostra by some 130-186 *cosche,* the 'Ndrangheta by 150 *'ndrine,* the Nuova SCU by 51 families, the Russian groups should be some 12,000, 300 among which have an international dimension (including Georgian ones), while the Turkish-Kurdish clans should be 12-10. See F. Rizzi, "L'oro, ultima frontiera del crimine," *Il Messaggero,* September 24, 1998. According to other sources in Russia, more than 6,000 criminal groups and more than 150 criminal societies are active, while in Ukraine some 400 criminal groups are present. See Paul B. Stares, Sergei Medvedev, *Former Soviet Union*, p. 89.

36. See "BKA sieht mit Unbehagen der Einfiffirung des Euro entgegen," in *Frankfurter Allgemeine* (further *FAZ*), November 20, 1998; "700 Fltichtlinge kommen iiber die Adria nach Italien," *FAZ,* December 28, 1998; John Mason, "Organized Crime Licks Its Lips Over Forgeries," *Financial Times,* January 9, 1999; John Mason, "Criminals Will Profit from Euro," *Financial Times,* January 20, 1999; "Mafia Prints Millions of Counterfeit Euros," *The Telegraph,* January 31, 1999, www.telegraph.co.uk:80/et (January 31, 1999); "Mafia stava falsificando euro," RAI TV, February 26, 1999. The last news report refers to the first confiscation of a fully equipped printing shop in Palermo by the police forces, following a lead of the SISDE, the internal intelligence service.

37. See "Mafias y Estados son complices, segun el Observatorio de la Droga," *El Pais* (on AFP source), October 16, 1998. Serious organized criminal infiltrations should also be considered in the mentioned offshore centers. See IASOC, Criminal Organizations, *Organized Crime: The International Report, Cyprus,* (on Reuters source), www.acsp.uic.edu/iasoc/crim org/volIO-4/artOg.htm (23/9/1998).

38. See Alessandro Politi, pp. 45-46.

39. See Paul B. Stares; Sergei Medvedev, *Former Soviet Union*, table I., pp. 84-85; Phil Reeves, "Russian Spies Running Protection Rackets," *The Independent,* November 18, 1998; "Meurtre à Saint-Petersbourg," *Le Monde,* November 24, 1998; Massimo Calabresi, "The East Mafia," *Time,* November 30, 1998; Alain Lallemand, "Mafia russe: l'Europe du crime," *Le Point,* December 19-26, 1998; Nicolas

Bannister, "Terror Threat to Business," *The Guardian,* December 29, 1998.

40. See *Associated Press,* February 9, 1999, mentioning an unclassified CIA report on proliferation to the Congress. Interestingly enough, the other country mentioned is China, another major center for organized criminal activities.

41. See Paul B. Stares, Sergei Medvedev, *Former Soviet Union,* p. 89, reporting a testimony of former CIA director John Deutsch. The same official estimated a total of some 30 countries in 1994 and of 50 by 1996 where the presence of FSU organized criminal groups was signalled.

42. Cosa Nostra in Sicily, despite Fascist energetic repression, never did disappear; Camorra was, after World War II, a constant feature of the Neapolitan hinterland and of its Campania Region, while the 'Ndrangheta became more visible in the 1970s. On the other hand, the SCU in Apulia was practically a spawn of the Camorra in the first half of the 1980s.

43. Laundering takes place in Cyprus, Sweden, and Switzerland.

44. See Dominique Dunglas, "Italie, les negriers de l'Adriatique," *Le Point,* December 14, 1998; Alberto Berticelli & Marco Dal Flor, "Ancora sangue a Milano, altri due morti," *Il Corriere della Sera* (further *Corsera*), January 10, 1999; Rose-Marie Borngässer, "Albaner haben die Mafia längst verdrängt," *Die Welt,* January 11, 1999; Richard Owen, "Immigrants Take Blame for Crime Wave in Milan," *The Times,* January 12, 1999; Kerstin Becker, "Gangster führen einen Seekrieg in der Adria," *Die Welt,* January 12, 1999; Paul Betts, "Murder Now the Fashion in Italy's Fashion Capital," *Finantial Times,* January 12, 1999; Hans-Jürgen Schlamp, "Operation Schwarzer Mann," *Der Spiegel,* April 1999, January 25, 1999; Eva M. Kallinger, Konkurrenz für die Mafia, April 1999, *Focus*, January 25, 1999; Peter Münch, Unglücke ohne Zeugen, *Süddeutsche Zeitung,* January 15, 1999.

45. See Richard Heuze, "La derive terroriste a Naples," *Le Figaro,* October 5, 1998.

46. Mrs. Alessandra Sgarella was a Milanese entrepreneur whose captivity, ended last year, passed 200 days. It is still unclear if the ransom of more than 2 million Euro ($2,4 million) was paid.

47. As an example, local police forces are still facing, despite repeated arrests, the powerful narcomafia of Cerignola. Its power was

such that it was able forbid the peddling of drugs in the city, while allowing it in the nearby villages.

48. See Alexandra de Montbrial, "L'empire des mafias," *Le Nouvel Observateur,* November 11, 1998; Nicole Pope, "La multiplication des scandales politico-mafieux menace le premier ministre turc," *Le Monde,* November 12, 1998; Marc Semo, "Le pouvoir turc gangrené par la mafia," *Libiration,* November 19, 1998; "BC, Ministerprasident Yilmaz durch MisBtrauensvoturn gestürzt," *FAZ,* November 26, 1998; Wolfgang Koydl, "Der Mann der Zuviel wuBte," *Suddeutsche Zeitung,* December 17, 1998; Jason Bennetto, "Gangs Smuggle 4,000 Migrants in a Month to UK," *The Independent,* December 29, 1998; "MWE, Die Meisten Opfer kommen aus Polen," *FAZ,* January 8, 1999.

49. See Camera dei Deputati, *Rapporto sulla criminalità organizzata (anno 1996),* presentato dal Ministro dell'Interno (Napolitano), Atti Parlamentari XIII Legislatura, doc. XXXVIII-bis, n. 2, Stab. Tipografici Carlo Colombo, Roma, September 1, 1997, pp. 375-440.

50. One of their specializations is human trafficking of Chinese nationals towards Germany as main entry point via Moscow, Czech Republic, Slovakia, Hungary, Poland, Slovenia, Bulgaria, and Rumania.

51. See "Shrinking Crops and Multiplying Networks," *La Dépêche Internationale des Drogues,* n' 46, August 1995, (www.ogd@ogd.org, 22/2/1999).

52. Since 1988 Interpol warned about the importance of this route, stretching from South West Asia through Turkey (via Istanbul and Ankara) through Bulgaria and Yugoslavia to Italy and Austria. The new tracing is Turkey, Greece, FYROM, and Albania (ports of Dürres, Vlöres, Särände). See Alison Jamieson, "Background and Characteristics of the World Illicit Drug Traffic," Alison Jamieson, ed., *Terrorism and Drug Trafficking in the 1990s,* Aldershot: Dartmouth Publishing Co., 1994, pp. 69-109; Vladimiro Odinzov, "Droga e prostituzione nel dopoguerra bosniaco," in *La Repubblica,* January 29, 1996, p. 10; Alessandro Politi, p. 22; Nicololas Mikletic, *Trafics et crimes dans les Balkans,* PUF, Paris, 1998; Camera dei Deputati, p. 436.

53. The U.N. International Police Task Force (IPTF) has the task of assisting local police forces in fighting against crime, but it has no enforcing powers, with obvious consequences. The EU-sponsored Customs and Fiscal Assistance Office (CAFAO) has succeeded in starting a cooperation between the Republika Srpska and the

Croat-Moslem Federation in order to stop smuggling orchestrated by organized crime, exploiting the loopholes between the two Bosnian entities. It remains to be seen how long it will resist political pressures. See Kevin Done, "Former Bosnian Foes Unite to Crack Down on Customs Fraud, *Financial Times,* October 15, 1998.

54. See also Andrew Jack, "When Nationalist Struggles Give Way to Banditry," in *Weekend Financial Times*, August 10-11, 1996, pp. 1-11; and VV AA, *Les dossiers du Canard enchaine,* La Corse demasquee, nr. 60, Juillet 1995, Paris.

55. See Pascal Istorza and Dominique Versini, "La Cuncolta perd son leader," *Le Point,* October 6, 1998; Franck Johannes, "Perquisitions autour de la Cuncolta," *Libiration*, October 14, 1998; Jacques Follorou, "Le juje Bruguiere a etabli un lien entre un nationaliste corse et un ancien policier," *Le Monde,* October 29, 1998; "Santoni libere, un desaveu de la methode Bruguiere," *Libiration*, November 11, 1998; Pascal Ceaux, "La police judiciaire supconneMathieu Filidori," *Le Monde,* January 15, 1999; Jacques Folloroux, "Rivalites et conflits ont retarde l'enquete sur l'assassinat de M. Erignac," *Le Monde,* January 15, 1999; Paul Silvani, "M. Chevenement reprend sa croisade en faveur de l'instauration de l'Etat de droit en Corse," *Le Monde,* January 18, 1999; "Corse: Bruguiere tente la piste intello," *Libiration,* November 20, 1998.

56. See J. Y., "Mas de 60 detenidos en la desarticulacion de una red de narcotraficantes," *El Pais,* October 29, 1998; Jose Diaz de Tuesta, "Espana se situa come terce pais de Europa en pirateria informatica," *El Pais,* November 4, 1998; Juan Arias and Jesus Duva, "Maflas espanoles y rusas controla el trafico de prostitutas brasilenas, segun un informe," *El Pais,* November 10, 1998; "Le boom de la contrabande de cigarettes en Europe," *Liberation,* December 29, 1998.

57. See UNDCP, Information Sheet nr. 2, www.undcp.org/undcp/gass/info2.htm (September 23, 1998).

58. With the contribution of Pakistan and, on a minor level, of the neighbouring Central Asiatic countries, i.e., Turkmenistan, Uzbekistan, Kazakhstan, Kyrgyzstan, and Tadjikistan.

59. Respectively Afghanistan, Iran, Pakistan, and Burma, Laos, and Thailand.

60. See "Europe's Smuggled Masses," *The Economist,* February 22, 1999.

61. One should, however, not forget that in the areas of the Arabian Peninsula and the Red Sea, the khat drug is often used. A synthetic variant (Methcathinone), known on the street as "Cat," has started being produced. As of *1997,* khat was not an internationally controlled substance, although the DEA chose to list it among the forbidden substances, even if not always very consistently.

62. See Alain Labrousse and Michel Koutouzis, "Geopolitique et Geostrategies des Drogues," *Economica*, 1996, Paris, pp. 28-30.

63. See Felix Kurz and Georg Mascolo, "Besonders mutige Kampfer," *Der Spiegel,* November 9, 1998; "Portrait: World's Most Wanted," *The Guardian,* November 25, 1998; "Von der alten PKK is wenig übriggeblieben," *FAZ,* November 27, 1998; Marie Jego, "L'implacable ascension du Parti des travailleurs du Kurdistan," *Le Monde,* December 4, 1998; Nemo Aziz, "Ocalan ist die Antwort auf die turkische Kurdenpolitik," *FAZ,* December 29, 1998; Hans Leyendecker, "Mord auf personliche Anweisung," *Süddeutsche Zeitung,* January 18, 1999.

64. Evangelos Antonaros, "Nicht alle PKK-Kader schworen der Gewalt ab," *Die Welt,* November 10, 1998; see Marie Jego, "Abdullah Ocalan aurait recemment negocie 'une solution politique' avec les generaux turcs," December 10, 1998; Michael Evans, "Britain Fears New Terrorist Attacks," *The Times,* February 17, 1999; Caroline Emcke, Annette Grossbongart, Udo Ludwig, and Georg Mascolo, "Blutrache fur Apo," *Der Spiegel,* September 8, October 22, 1999; Ley, "Deutschland droht neuer Terror durch PKK," *Süddeutsche Zeitung,* February 22, 1999.

65. See Magdi Allam, "Il miliardario di Allah e l'esercito del terrorismo," in *La Repubblica,* June 27, 1996, p. 4; and Guido Olimpio, "L'impazienza di Sonny e la tela di ragno," *Corsera,* August 6, 1996, p. 7; James Walsh, "Osama bin Laden," *Time,* December 22, 1998. One cannot avoid comparing bin Laden with Giangiacomo Feltrinelli, an Italian presumed terrorist millionaire known in the 1960s. The latter died probably while handling an explosive charge. Bin Laden is a financial manager of terrorist activities who takes care not to have companies under U.S. legislation and not to use dollars that could be tracked by the U.S. intelligence services.

66. See Aaron Karp, "The Demise of the Middle East Arms Race," in *The Washington Quarterly,* Vol. 18, No. 4, Autumn 1995, Washington, CSIS, 1995.

67. See "Saddam + Ben Laden?," *Newsweek,* January 5, 1999; James Risen, "Master Terrorist is Believed to be in Iraq," *IHT*, January 28, 1999; Gerold Buchner, "GroB-vater des Krieges," *Süddeutsche Zeitung,* January 29, 1999; Vernon Loeb, "Has the U.S. Blunted bin Laden?," *Washington Post,* February 17, 1999; "Bin Laden was Stopped Seven Times," *USA Today,* February 24, 1999.

68. On the other hand, it should be taken into account that the U.S. bombings against Osama bin Laden created a political backfire. Bin Laden's prestige, already high due to his strong anti-corruption stance, has risen throughout the Arab and Muslim world. See Tim Weiner, "In Islamic World Bin Laden's Esteem Rises," *The New York Times,* February 8, 1999.

69. It is true that Arab countries still uphold the exception that the liberation struggle of Palestinians against Israeli occupation of their territories cannot be defined as terrorism, but one should not forget that in due time the distinction of just cause/just means can, and should, be applied to both contenders in that land.

70. According to some analysts, Hamas is today is an irrelevant force, and the brigade Izzeddin al Qassem consists of some six persons. See also Christophe Ayad, "Un an apres Louxor, le chaos islamiste," *Liberation,* November 17, 1998; Christophe Ayad, "Yemen: assaut contre le Jihad," *Liberation*, December 30, 1998; Patrick Cockburn and Gary Finn, "Yemen Seeks Extradition of Militant London Imam," *The Independent*, January 26, 1999; Mona Eltahawy, "More Than 100 in Court as Egypt Cracks Down on Militants," *The Guardian*, February 5, 1999. Concerning ETA, see Jean-Hebert Armengaud, "L'ETA tente par l'adieu aux armes?," *Liberation*, October 29, 1998; L. Gomez and L. Galan, "HB reclama en Roma y Londres una negociacion politica con ETA," *El Pais*, November 11, 1998; Luis. R. Aizpeolea, "Aznar admitio que el comunicado de ETA 'abre la esperanza de una paz definitiva,'" *El Pais*, December 23, 1998. It should be remembered that all Gulf petromonarchies were considered very vulnerable to Shi'ia subversion, but, indeed, since 1980 no significant revolution has taken place on the model of the Iranian one.

71. See Alessandro Politi, "Terrorism, Domestic and International Ramification: A European Perspective," and also Richard A. Falkenrath, "Nuclear, Biological and Chemical Terrorism: Understanding the Threat," both in James Brown, ed., *New Horizons and New Strategies in Arms Control,* Albuquerque: Sandia National Laboratories, 1999, pp. 257-258 and 193-243, respectively; James L. Ford, "Radiological Dispersal Devices," *Strategic Forum*, INSS, nr. 136, March 1998; Judith Miller and William J. Broad, "Clinton Describes

Terrorism Threat for 21st Century," *The New York Times,* January 22, 1999; AP, "Doctors may be key to bioterrorism;" *The New York Times*, February 17, 1999; C.D., "La diplomatie obscure des cyberterroristes," *Le Figaro*, January 14, 1999.

72. See Herve Gattegno and Erich Inciyan, Depuis 1994, "la frontiere entre militants islamistes et delinquants est devenue incertaine et permeable," in *Le Monde*, April 4, 1996, p. 11. The Shalabi group, dismantled in 1994, mixed intimately organized crime, drug trafficking, and extremist Islamism.

73. CHEAr, p. 36-37.

74. See Giuseppe D'Avanzo, "Nicoletti e i 'ragazzi' della Magliana," in *La Repubblica*, May 30, 1996, p. 17. It appears to have been involved more or less directly in the abduction of the premier Aldo Moro, a bomb attack to a train, the homicide of a political journalist, and in the liberation from the Red Brigades terrorists of a minor politician through contacts with the Camorra. Italian police deputy chief Gianni De Gennaro believes, instead, it was simple ordinary criminality in contact with other criminal powers.

75. See Pablo Ordaz, "Mas de 100.000 espanoles viven atrapados en las redes de 200 sectas destructivas," *El Pais*, November 11, 1998; Ross Dunn, "Millennium Suicide Sect Found in Israel," *The Times*, November 24, 1998; Ph. Br. and E. In., "L'Eglise de scientologie reste sous la menace d'un nouveau proces," and "Un service de reinseignement organise de facon quasi militaire," *Le Monde*, December 16, 1998; Nikolaus Nowak, "Spanien is beunruigt über den Vormarsch der Sekten," *Die Welt*, January 19, 1999.

76. See Alessandro Politi, ed., *Towards a European Intelligence Policy*, Chaillot Papers, nr. 34, WEU ISS, Paris, December 1998, pp. 3-18.

LIST OF ABBREVIATIONS

AFP	Agence France Presse (France, French Press Wire Service)
AP	Associated Press
ATS	Amphetamine-Type Stimulants
BKA	Bundeskriminalamt (Germany, Federal Criminal Office)
CEEC	Eastern European Countries
CFSP	Common Foreign and Security Policy
CIS	Confederation of Independent States
ETA	Euzkadi Ta Askatasuna (Spain, Basque language, Basque Land and Freedom)
FAZ	Frankfurter Allgemeine Zeitung
FT	Financial Times
FSU	Former Soviet Union
GIA	Groupe Islamique Anne (Algeria, Armed Islamic Group)
HADEP	Popular-Democratic Party (Kurdish party, political wing of PKK)
IRA	Irish Republican Army
JHA	Justice and Home Affairs
KUK	Liberators of Kurdistan
OECD	Organization for Economic Cooperation and Development
OGD	Observatoire Geopolitique des Drogues (France, Geopolitical Drugs Observatory)
PKK	Partiya Karkeren Kurdistan (Turkey, Kurdish Workers' Party)

RAF	Rote Armee Fraktion (Germany, Red Army Fraction)
RDD	Radiological Dispersion Devices
SCU	Sacra Corona Unita (Italy, Sacred United Crown)
SFOR	Stabilization Force
SISDE	Servizio Informazioni e Sicurezza Democratica (Italy, Democratic Intelligence and Security Service)
SISMI	Servizio Informazioni e Sicurezza Militare (Italy, Military Intelligence and Security Service)
U.N.	United Nations
UNDCP	U.N. Drug Control Project
USSR	Union of Soviet Socialist Republics
WMD	Weapons of Mass Destruction

CHAPTER 3

REGIONAL SECURITY CHALLENGES IN THE MEDITERRANEAN

Stephen Calleya

This paper examines the role the North Atlantic Treaty Organization (NATO) and the European Union (EU) are playing in the Mediterranean area and discusses the impact such international organizations can have on managing the security challenges of proliferation of weapons and arms control. An attempt is also made to conceptualize a security model that can assist in improving cooperative relations between Europe and the Arab world. A specific security proposal put forth is that of establishing a Euro-Mediterranean Maritime Coastguard that would be mandated to carry out stop and search exercises in a number of areas, including those of weapons proliferation. This analysis concludes with an assessment of regional relations to 2010. Unless international organizations address more effectively the political differences and economic disparities that continue to separate the countries along the northern and southern shores of the Mediterranean, the issues of managing the proliferation of weapons and arms control will remain more of an aspiration than an achievable goal.

A Security Model to Manage Proliferation and Arms Control: What Role for NATO?

The post-Cold War period is proving to be a revolutionary era due to the fact that dividing lines of the past have faded or disappeared completely. Yet no clear pattern of international relations has emerged in their place. This period of rapid flux presents NATO with an identity crisis that is exacerbated when seen through the lens of such a diverse area as the Mediterranean. But it also presents the Alliance with an opportunity to forge new links with Mediterranean nonmembers. Although the costs of developing an active alliance network across this waterway will be high, the costs of failing to establish such a system could be higher in the long-term, should instability from the Mediterranean spread northwards.

NATO's successful Cold War track record makes it one of the most prominent security institutions functioning today. One way to preserve this position is by leading cooperative efforts with other institutional associations that also have an interest in ensuring stability in areas like the Mediterranean. By forming coalitions and relationships with other international organizations in the basin, NATO could play a direct role in helping to prevent the emergence of conflictual patterns of relations between the Western European and Middle Eastern international regions. Such relations could easily evolve if political and military misperceptions and the increase in the proliferation of weapons is not checked in the short term. Containment of the erratic pattern of relations between the rival NATO members of Greece and Turkey is indicative of the confidence-building role the Atlantic Alliance can play at a subregional level across the Mediterranean. Participation in NATO activities will also assist in removing some of the negative perceptions nonmember Mediterranean countries harbour about the Alliance. For example, permitting countries in the Maghreb and the Levant to attend certain NATO sessions will assist in nurturing the fact that NATO is a common defense grouping and not an aggressive military alliance. In the longer term, it has also been suggested that those Southern Mediterranean nations which are emerging as democracies should be afforded observer status in NATO.[1] The inclusion of nonmember Mediterranean countries in NATO's consultative framework would help remove existing misperceptions on both sides of the Mediterranean basin and could help generate cooperative intergovernmental interaction in the sensitive area of military issues.

As the most active military international organization in the Mediterranean basin, NATO has the capacity to influence the patterns of relations across and around the basin. In the end, it will come down to the Alliance's ability to read the indigenous patterns of relations and act according to these trends. Like other international organizations operating in the Mediterranean, NATO is finding it difficult to implement a comprehensive and coherent security program in this area. Rather than solely blame the Alliance for this outcome, it seems more accurate to indicate that NATO's apathy in the South is more the combination of the Mediterranean's incoherent and diverse regional dynamics and NATO's inability to act.

The emergence of a more multipolar international system in the last 7 years has seen an increase in multilateral intrusive behavior around the world. Great powers are eager to at least appear to be acting multilaterally in their foreign policy endeavors. The U.S. emphasis on obtaining a U.N. mandate before it acts outside its borders as it did in the Persian Gulf War in 1990-91, Somalia in 1992-93, and Haiti in 1994 illustrates this trend.

This review of NATO's role in the Mediterranean is indicative of the impact international organizations have on regional dynamics. The end of the Cold War, the process of EU, and the winds of peace blowing from the Middle East have changed the parameters of Mediterranean regional politics. One significant shift is that Mediterranean littoral states are much more keen to develop active relations with the rest of the world. Although they are still apprehensive about the implications of an enhanced American or European role in the area, they actively seek relations with the West now that competition for foreign direct investment has increased.

A U.S. security presence in the vicinity as a balance against the revival of old or new hegemonic threats, or new terrorist threats under the guise of Islamic fundamentalism, is also still favored among the majority of countries in the basin. Appeals to establish a nuclear free weapons zone or to establish a multilateral security forum may find their place in the future, but so far both remain symbolic aspirations.[2]

Post-Cold War considerations have led outside powers and international organizations such as NATO to reevaluate their policies towards the Mediterranean. Conversely, regional leaders have had to explore new external alignments in light of the sea-change in the international system since 1989. Two recent changes in the dynamics of the Mediterranean regional politics may affect the nature of intrusive influence in the Mediterranean. First is the Arab-Israeli reconciliation process. The peace treaties signed between Israel and the PLO and Israel and Jordan may become preliminary steps towards eventually establishing a cooperative pattern of intergovernmental relations in the Levant. Rapprochement between Israel and the Arab countries has the additional benefit of removing one of the stumbling blocks that has prevented closer relations between the Levant and other Middle Eastern subregions such as the Maghreb and the Gulf. The series of Middle East international financial meetings held in Casablanca, Amman, Cairo, and Doha in 1994, 1995, 1996, and 1997, respectively, highlights the potential that peaceful relations can bring to this international region.[3] If stability persists, and this is no foregone conclusion, attracting foreign direct investment to the area may become a more feasible enterprise. Such a development would fit in with the hypothesis that extra-regional actors are most influential in international regional relations when they complement the basic pattern of regional alignment and conflict.

The second shift in Mediterranean politics is both internally and externally motivated. After years of being accused of marginalizing and isolating its southern flank, NATO has imitated actions taken by other security organizations such as the EU and the Organization for Security and Cooperation in Europe (OSCE) by proposing to establish closer relations with a selection of nonmember countries in the Mediterranean area, incorporating the Levant and the Maghreb.

At first, it might appear that NATO could attempt to establish some kind of outer zone of suzerainty in the Mediterranean. In reality, it must be stressed that NATO has yet to formulate a coherent vision of long-term goals that could justify such possibilities. In addition, NATO's enlargement agenda towards the East, and the plethora of security issues it will have to contend with *vis-à-vis* Russia, will leave very little diplomatic resources to begin tackling the multitude of security challenges which exist across the Mediterranean. At most, NATO's most recent outreach program towards a selection of nonmember Mediterranean countries can promote political interaction among states in the area. It is unlikely that NATO's exchange plans will elevate cross-cultural, environmental, or military relations.

If successful in the long term, this extra-Mediterranean led effort to enhance politico-military cooperation between Europe and the Middle East could indirectly benefit trans-Mediterranean initiatives. The evolution of a more integrated and interdependent Mediterranean security community would make it more difficult for actors in the basin to upset the balance of power due to the numerous consequences they would have to confront as a result.

The fact that Western Europe has developed a multi-level international society, in which international organizations such as the EU, the OSCE, and NATO can interact with states and subnational institutions, puts this comprehensive international region in a strong position to approach security issues in the Mediterranean in a multi-institutional and multi-functional manner. Given the lack of unity in the perceptions of the countries in the Mediterranean and those powers with an interest in the area, it is unrealistic to assume that a single international organization can contend with the security challenges across the Mediterranean. A more realistic alternative is one in which a single international organization, for example NATO, complements the actions taken by others in the area. As the international organization with a large proportion of Mediterranean member-states and the most active military actor in the Mediterranean, NATO is well positioned to complement the EU's socio-economic and political endeavors in the south. But NATO should not attempt to lead European multilateral initiatives as it is not perceived as positively as either the EU or the OSCE, for that matter, by the majority of countries located in the Mediterranean. For example, NATO's Cold War military record makes it an unattractive partner to several countries in the Middle East. An enlarged NATO presence in the Mediterranean could even increase accusations of "neo-imperialist" designs by Arabists and Islamists and thus fuel support for the already very active Islamic fundamentalist groupings operating in various subregions of the Middle East. American leadership in NATO also makes this organization appear more like a vehicle of great power interests than one concerned with advancing Mediterranean causes.

Absent the creation of a trans-Mediterranean international forum, which would certainly be perceived as much more representative of Mediterranean regional interests and not some self-referenced or great power interests, the EU currently appears the most acceptable international organization across the Mediterranean that can intensify cooperative patterns of relations throughout this area.

Post-Cold War international relations show that multilateralism has failed to address effectively the increase in domestic regional hostilities. Over the last 5 years, most regions of the world have been touched by a resurgence of such intolerance based on traits that include ethnicity, language, and religion. The Mediterranean space is no exception. The *ad hoc* and often ineffective international response to many of these crises has cast a question mark on the relevance of the multilateral mechanisms designed to contend with different types of problems, i.e., of an international nature. Civil conflict and regional tensions are not the only security issues that need to be addressed in the Mediterranean. Yet, international organizations must adapt their *modus operandi* if they are to play a pivotal role in diffusing such contentious issues as environmental degradation, economic disparities, migration, weapons proliferation, and narcotics trafficking.[4]

The United Nations remains the principal international organization for achieving such multilateral endeavors. The U.N. is, however, already suffering from overstretch and cannot be expected to focus on such an extensive list of challenges on its own. Other institutions and agencies in the area such as NATO, the EU, the Western European Union (WEU), the OSCE, the Arab League, and the Arab Maghreb Union will also have to play a supportive role to the U.N. if an effective multilateral Mediterranean mechanism is to emerge. In a world without a political, ideological, or geographical strait-jacket, each institution or agency can play on its comparative advantages to ensure maximum effectiveness.

Multilateral agencies must however be cautioned against expecting rewards from their efforts in the short-to-medium term. In an area as diverse as the Mediterranean, regional coordination and cooperation is probably the most that can be initially achieved. For example, a more active OSCE in the Mediterranean can lead to an increase in political, social, and environmental exchanges. Nonmember OSCE states in the Mediterranean have already shown a keen interest in cooperating in this forum, and there has also been a call to extend associate membership to this area.[5] Such multilateral governmental action could lay the groundwork for similar exchanges at a transnational level. If supplemented by nongovernmental organizations which are already active in the area, existing disparities between the Western European and Middle Eastern international regions can be gradually bridged.

Several countries bordering the Mediterranean have sought external support to help create a single institutional framework in which discourse and dialogue on Mediterranean issues can take place. On the other hand, states such as Libya and Syria remain reluctant to actively engage themselves in such endeavors for a number of reasons: sometimes because of animosities dating back to former colonial days, and also due to mutual rivalry among themselves for spheres of influence. The proliferation of weapons in North Africa and the Levant continues to be fuelled by systemic, regional, and internal motives. Key regional actors, including Algeria, Libya, Egypt, Syria, and Iran, are engaged in an active search for geopolitical "weight" and national prestige in the post-Cold War world.[6] The political and economic fault-lines that exist along a north-south and south-south axis also provide motives for proliferation.

The superpower track record in the Mediterranean offers two cautionary notes in this respect. First, external actors can only influence and not dictate regional dynamics.[7] International organizations such as NATO must therefore read and decode the mixed signals originating in the Mediterranean if they do not want their effort to consolidate a sphere of influence across this waterway to result in a conflict-based international region.[8] If cross-border political and military measures are introduced in consultation and agreement with the Mediterranean states, NATO's outreach scheme towards the south could act as a catalyst toward regional collaboration in other areas.

If nonregional actions are perceived as attempts to dominate intra-Mediterranean patterns of interaction, the latter could retaliate by uniting and becoming less cooperative in their dealings with external actors who have substantial political and economic interests in the area.

This would certainly be the case if such a trans-Mediterranean backlash included the key oil and gas producers.

In the post-Cold War period, domestic politics play a major role in foreign policy considerations. This trend is likely to continue as internal interest groups become more assertive. This is especially the case in countries across the Maghreb, particularly Algeria, where Islamic movements are already constraining government policies. If current Arab regimes are not pressured by external actors at both a bilateral and multilateral level to establish working relationships with other political activists within their boundaries, the aspiration of nurturing more intense cooperative patterns of trans-Mediterranean relations will surely recede.[9]

Failure to identify and complement regional patterns of relations functioning around the Mediterranean area will also ultimately result in increasing discord among NATO member-states. In recent years distinct subregional dynamics have on several occasions shed light on such chords of disunity which exist within the Alliance. Greek-Turkish rivalry almost resulted in the outbreak of hostilities in early 1996 over the contested Aegean Islands, and procurement of armaments by these two countries remains among the highest in the western world.[10] Disunity among NATO member-states, particularly the United States and France, is also apparent in the unilateral Middle East policies which they have been put forward. Transatlantic differences of opinion towards the Mediterranean surfaced again in late 1996 when France, with the support of Germany, Spain and Italy, unsuccessfully called for NATO's Southern Command headquarters in Naples to be taken over by a European admiral as part of a general effort to enhance Europe's contribution to the Alliance.[11] It could also be argued that, whereas enlargement towards central and eastern Europe has assisted in boosting NATO cohesiveness, the Mediterranean is serving as a strategic backdrop which is fueling transatlantic differences. This thesis perhaps helps to explain NATO's reluctance to attempt introducing a more comprehensive strategic framework towards the south, opting instead for a more *ad hoc*/selective engagement approach.

It is a truism that the end of the Cold War has released the superpower grip on the Mediterranean. But the indicators discussed above suggest that one type of intrusive dominant system (bipolar superpower model) has been swept aside, only to make room for a different type of intrusive dominant system (multipolar great power model). This more multipolar design is reflected in the increase of activity registered by international organizations in regional relations. The more non-Mediterranean multilateral organizations, such as NATO, come to dominate patterns of relations in the Mediterranean area, the more they are likely to stifle a resurgence of intra-Mediterranean patterns of relations. As a result, contemporary European international organization involvement in the Mediterranean is best seen as a boundary management exercise, which aims at safeguarding the regional dynamics of integration in Western Europe from those of fragmentation which are active in the Middle East.

A Euro-Mediterranean Response.

At the first Euro-Mediterranean Conference which took place in Barcelona in November 1995, the 27-partner countries established three principal areas of cooperation: a political and security partnership with the aim of establishing a common area of peace and stability; an economic and financial partnership with the aim of creating an area of shared prosperity; and a partnership in social, cultural, and human affairs in an effort to promote understanding between cultures and exchanges between civil societies.

The main task at the Euro-Mediterranean ministerial meeting in Malta in April 1997 and the informal ministerial meeting in Palermo in June 1998 was for the member-states to elaborate more specifically on implementation of the partnership program and to set up short-term action plans so that tangible cooperative ventures could commence.

At the top of the agenda was the endorsement, or at least elaboration, of a security charter that will lay the foundations for the peaceful resolution of crisis situations and conflicts throughout the Euro-Mediterranean area. Such a charter would enable the partners to identify the factors of friction and tension in the Euro-Mediterranean area and to carry out an assessment of how such destablizing focal points can be managed.

In actual fact the Malta Declaration indicated that very little headway has been registered in implementing such an aspiration:

> The Participants take note of the work of Senior Officials on a Charter for peace and stability in the Euro-Mediterranean region, and instruct them to continue the preparatory work, taking due account of the exchanged documents, in order to submit an agreed text at a future Ministerial Meeting when political circumstances allow.[12]

The vagueness of the above phrase is a clear indication of the lack of progress that has been achieved in conceptualizing a framework for setting up a pan-Euro-Mediterranean security arrangement. The partner countries failed to commit themselves to an incremental work program that would at least seek to create the necessary cooperative relations that would allow for the introduction of such a charter.

They have also avoided hammering out a specific timetable within which such a framework of analysis can be carried out. As a result, it now seems more logical if the Euro-Mediterranean process (EMP) countries start to dedicate their diplomatic resources to defining a package of confidence-building measures that would create the necessary atmosphere within which a more elaborate mechanism, such as a charter, can be fleshed out.

When it comes to the direct tangible endeavors that the EMP should seek to realize, these can primarily be classified into time-oriented categories. In the short term, the 27-partner countries must introduce a basic type of confidence-building measure network that will contribute to removing the curtain of prejudice and misperceptions that continues to divide the Mediterranean along a North-South axis.

Such a network should eventually also assist in managing and containing the large number of security challenges that risk upsetting stability across the Euro-Mediterranean area. The long list of security issues that could derail the EMP includes the proliferation of weapons of mass destruction, maritime safety, environmental pollution, narcotics trafficking, and the flow of illegal migration.

At the moment there are no elaborate mechanisms to contend with such security crises or even an incident such as an accidental collision at sea between transport tankers crossing through the Straits of Sicily, or the alarming rate of degradation which is currently taking place in the environmental sector. One must also mention the proliferation of drug consignments which are reaching ever deeper into the civil societies of the Mediterranean, and the accentuation of illegal migratory flows from south to north which risks destablizing the legal structures of the state.

A confidence-building initiative that can be introduced as part of the political and security charter of the EMP is that of establishing a flexible security framework that is already addressing security issues as those outlined earlier. It will set the stage for tackling more sensitive security challenges which include intolerant fundamentalism, demographic expansion, and outright conflict.

At this point in the partnership process, a concerted effort should be made to investigate the feasibility of setting up a Euro-Mediterranean Maritime Coastguard (EMMC). The EMMC would be mandated to carry out stop and search exercises in a number of areas: maritime safety, maritime pollution, narcotics trafficking, the transport of illegal migrants, and the proliferation of weapons. Such an early warning and crisis prevention mechanism should be introduced in accordance with the principal of consent and open to any of the Euro-Mediterranean partner-states that wish to participate in such a flexible soft security arrangement. In order to ensure that such a security model can become operational in the shortest period possible, the EMMC should consist of sectoral types of soft security cooperation.

For example, any two or more EMP members can formulate cooperative alliances in specific sectors, such as that pertaining to narcotics trafficking, without having to wait until all partners are in a position to introduce such measures. Such a plan will enable the EMMC to evolve along subregional security fault-lines in the first instance until it becomes feasible to establish a fully fledged Euro-Mediterranean Coastguard at a later date.

In addition to strengthening political and security channels of communication, the establishment of such a Euro-Mediterranean early warning and conflict prevention network will assist in cultivating more intense crisis management mechanisms in an area where these are lacking. In order to ensure that such a flexible security arrangement moves beyond the conceptual stage in the shortest time-frame possible, its primary mandate may be limited to the following codes of conduct: fact-finding and consultation missions, inspection, and monitoring delegations. Such traditional rules of engagement may also be supplemented by operations that include the facilitation of humanitarian relief, particularly in times of natural disasters. At a later stage, situation centers may be set up around the Mediterranean to monitor activities under this mandate.

Only after such a threshold has been reached, should a concerted effort be made to spell out the parameters of a security charter which will include both confidence-building and crisis prevention measures that seek to further advance regional disarmament. The introduction of a Euro-Mediterranean security charter will also assist in creating a climate where the partner countries can develop command and control mechanisms to intervene as early as possible in crisis situations. Acting only after an aggressor has acquired territory or access to natural resources is to force the unwelcome choice between a massive military response and a major strategic debacle. The later the international community and security organizations intervene, the larger the cost and the less chance to restore stability.

Prospects for the Future: A Regional Assessment to 2010.

A number of indicators extant today can be used to project the strategic environment in the Mediterranean to 2010. Unless these indicators change significantly, the environment for the first 10 years of the next century will be set by the year 2000. The speed with which the events in Europe and the Middle East are moving makes it likely that the shape this part of the world will take by 2010 will be clearly discernible by the end of this century. The United States and Europe will continue to depend on the Persian Gulf and North Africa for much of their energy supplies. They will however be joined by the likes of China and India that will need to satisfy their growing energy demands and therefore access to these areas will remain a high foreign policy priority.

In the first half of the 1990s the Mediterranean showed signs of becoming a cooperative dominant area. But in the past 2 years there has been an increase in conflictual relations throughout the Mediterranean and a resultant shift to an indifferent type of region. Fault-lines along a north-south and south-south axis have become more apparent, with no sign of a process of regional transformation taking place.

As relations stand, two scenarios are possible: the first is one in which a number of Mediterranean countries manage to integrate at both a regional and international level, while the rest collapse completely. The second is one in which the majority of countries in the Mediterranean fail to integrate and are marginalized from the international political economy.

As patterns of relations across the Euro-Mediterranean area stand, the majority of littoral countries in the Mediterranean are unlikely to integrate into the global political economy that is emerging. Transnational ventures will remain limited, with states in the area more concerned with intra-state issues than with inter-state types of cooperation.

What is thus required is an urgent concerted effort by the Mediterranean states themselves to create a transnational network upon which cross-border types of economic and financial interaction can take place. If the Mediterranean is to compete and prosper in the global village of tomorrow, it must nurture an environment where people, products, ideas, and services are allowed to flow freely. At the moment there are too many bottlenecks in the system.

In contrast to the cooperative South-East Asian and Latin American developing regions, the Mediterranean currently consists of a number of subregional constellations, i.e., Southern Europe, the Maghreb, the Mashreq, the Balkans, that are evolving along separate and distinct paths. Perhaps the label that best describes the pattern of relations in the area is "fragmegration" which denotes the integration efforts being pursued by the EU Southern European countries and the fragmentation type of relations that continue to dominate the southern and eastern shores of the basin. In fact, the lack of cohesion and unity achieved to date somewhat mirrors regional dynamics manifesting themselves across central Africa.[13]

During the first 10 years of the new millennium, the United States will shift its foreign policy concerns in the region further east, focusing on the management of relations in the Mashreq and the Persian Gulf. The rest of the Mediterranean will become a EU sphere of influence once a common foreign and security policy is introduced. In the interim, the EU will continue to contain instability that may emerge along its southern periphery through NATO.

The Mediterranean has shifted from an imperial British lake in the 19th century to a superpower sea in the 20th. On the eve of the 21st century, the Mediterranean is more akin to a fault-line between the prosperous North (the haves), and an impoverished South, (the have-nots). The key development to watch in the Mediterranean in the next decade will be whether the phase of cooperative competition that has dominated post-Cold War relations to date is eventually superseded by an era of conflictual competition. This is sure to happen if states on the lower levels of the development curve come to the conclusion that they are not going to be able to move up the ladder anytime soon. If this age of indifference scenario does take hold, disorder will dominate Mediterranean relations and, as resources are depleted, the region will become an economic wasteland.

In the post-Cold War world that has emerged, the patterns of relations in the Mediterranean have already moved away from a cooperative security dominant framework to a more competitive security based model. If trends continue as they have been, the Mediterranean is destined to become a geo-strategic cross-cultural zone of indifference. Security risks will multiply, demographic growth will exacerbate economic problems, and the developed world will adopt a selective engagement approach towards the area.

The only way this scenario can be avoided is if NATO and the EU adopt a policy of strategic optimism towards the Mediterranean. Based on the theory of realism, the doctrine of strategic optimism is one in which international organizations seek change in a positive direction by identifying those areas where such progress can be made. When drawing up security policies to contain the proliferation of weapons, European security organizations must ensure that their efforts to contain such risks do not result in them becoming part of the problem.

A more transparent and engaging NATO policy that complements a overhauled EU Euro-Med Partnership process is thus necessary if an effective collective security framework is to be established in the area. This should be supplemented by a more proactive approach by international economic institutions such as the World Bank and the IMF in their dealings with the region, an approach that assists the Mediterranean countries to adopt more of a self-help mentality. Only then will efforts to contain the proliferation of weapons have a serious chance of being effective in the Mediterranean.

ENDNOTES - CHAPTER 3

1. Rodrigo de Rato, "Cooperation and security in the Mediterranean," *North Atlantic Assembly Report*, 1994, p. 17.

2. "Proposals for an integrated security in the Mediterranean," *Palma Report*, June 1992.

3. Edmund Blair, "Winning over the world's investors," *MEED*, Vol. 39, No. 40, October 1995, pp. 4-5.

4. E. Anyaoku, "The Commonwealth and the new multilateralism," *The Round Table*, No. 331, July 1994, p. 318.

5. Maurice Abela, Maltese Ambassador to the OSCE, statement presented at the OSCE Mediterranean Seminar, Tel Aviv, June 1996.

6. I.O. Lesser and Ashley J. Tellis, *Strategic Exposure, Proliferation Around the Mediterranean*, Rand, 1996, pp. 31-34.

7. Stephen C. Calleya, *Navigating Regional Dynamics in the Post-Cold War World, Patterns of Relations in the Mediterranean*, Dartmouth, 1997, Ch. 7.

8. Stephen C. Calleya, "NATO and the EU in the Mediterranean, What Relationship?," in *NATO's Southern Flank*, House of Commons Defense Committee Report, Session 1995-96, London: HMSO, March 1996, pp. 43-54.

9. Andrew J. Pierre and William B. Quandt, *The Algerian Crisis: Policy Options for the West*, Washington DC: Carnegie, 1996.

10. Richard Owen, "Old Aegean Foes," *The Times* (London), December 18, 1996, p. 33.

11. Joseph Fitchett, "U.S. tries to fend off Paris on a NATO post," *International Herald Tribune*, December 4, 1996, p. 8; and Joseph Fitchett, "War over Naples," *The Economist*, November 30, 1996, pp. 34-35.

12. Stephen C. Calleya, "The Euro-Mediterranean Process After Malta: What Prospects?," *Mediterranean Politics*, Frank Cass Publications, Vol. 2, No. 2, 1997, pp. 1-22.

13. James N. Rosenau, Rountable on "Is International Studies an Anachronism?," International Studies Association Annual Convention, Minneapolis, MN, March 20, 1998.

CHAPTER 4

NATO IN THE MEDITERRANEAN

Mario Zucconi

After the end of the Cold War, the greatest part of NATO's energies, operational activities, financial resources, and policy disputes have been spent on, addressed to, and originated from troubles in the Mediterranean region. From the drawn-out Balkan experience, the Alliance derived the stimuli and pressures to adapt to new missions, create flexible capabilities to respond to non-Article 5 security, and offer itself as the organizing element of larger, international stabilization forces. In the Balkans—if only from 1995 on—the Alliance established the credibility of its capabilities and of its members' collective will. It solidified its authoritativeness as main instrument of international stability.

After the end of the Cold War, for a while it looked like the United States was drastically cutting down on its presence and interest in this area. However, the Bosnian crisis compelled it back to a strong conmitment toward stability there. Overall, and for some time in the future, the United States is bound to remain an essential and most influential actor with regard to the Mediterranean theater. But due to the character of many of the sources of instability here, it is most important that the main Western European countries and European institutions take more responsibility, develop mechanisms and strategies for collective action, and invest much more than they are presently doing in creating stability around the Mediterranean.

The Mediterranean: Not a Unitary Geopolitical Concept.

In recent years, Western policymakers and NATO officials have increasingly expressed concern about the Mediterranean as an area of instability. They have also referred to it as to an area of allied interest. The Mediterranean is the small lake in which the powerful U.S. Sixth Fleet is stationed. And in Naples resides a double-hatted U.S. admiral—both commander of that Sixth Fleet and Commander-in-Chief of NATO Southern Command (AFSOUTH or Allied Forces South.)

However, the Mediterranean is not a geopolitically defined area—as it could be considered with regard to the time of Rome and Carthage, or Sparta and Athens. It is not an area with distinctive and unitary political characters. And, in fact, it may encompass today a number of different major geopolitical areas, of different and most important international problems. Moreover, the view of where the main issues lie in the Mediterranean changes considerably in Washington and in the Western European capitals. Not even the limits of this area are precisely defined. The Commander of the Sixth Fleet oversees operations from Gibraltar to the Black Sea and from the Baltic to South Africa. The Mediterranean is also the main base from which power was projected in the Persian Gulf since the Kuwait crisis of 1990-91.

And the fact that the Mediterranean is not a unitary political problem is not irrelevant. The polarization of international power during the Cold War carried the possibility, by pressing and negotiating with Moscow, of dealing with issues as diverse as Syria's attempt to destabilize Jordan in September 1970, or the military uprisings in the Shaba region of Zaire, or the guerrillas' attempt to overthrow the Nicaraguan government in the 1980s, or the worrisome presence of Cuban troops and military instructors in several parts of Africa for almost two decades. And if, in fact, Moscow was unable to deliver much of what was expected of it, the important point is that the Soviet international influence helped justify intervening in a range of disparate cases. In contrast, the separate, discrete crises of the post-Cold War world—and of the Mediterranean area in particular—require difficult, individual explanation and a case-by-case rationale for intervention.

An Area of "Growing Instability"?

It has become commonplace among political analysts to relate recent sources of instability to the end of the Cold War. On the contrary, most of the issues we had to deal with in recent times in this vast area are old ones. No doubt, a crisis brewing for a long time in Yugoslavia reached the boiling point when systemic pressures on that state diminished in the early 1990s. But the root causes of that crisis are economic and political, and began to emerge and steadily grow at the beginning of the 1980s. The issues that sour Turkish-Greek relations—disputed territory in the Aegean, Cyprus, Greek alleged support for Kurdish separatism in Turkey—have been there for a long time. A half-century of Arab-Israeli dispute, political and religious issues, and oil make the whole Middle Eastern area one of great political pressures and instability.

On the shores of the Black Sea, the end of the Soviet state freed political pressures, ethnic rivalries, and competition among ruling elites that are today a source of instability (in an area again, of great interest for production and movement of oil and gas). But the civil war between the Turkish army and Kurdish guerrillas in Eastern Anatolia is an older problem, going back to the early 1960s. And that between the Iraqi Kurds and Baghdad goes back to the middle 1970s.

While their aspiration is not a unified Kurdistan for the different Kurdish communities in different states, the Kurds are at the source of a number of important political problems in the area. In October 1998 Ankara threatened to attack Syria militarily because of the hospitality that state was known to be offering leaders of the Kurdistan Workers Party (PKK). But then, if Turkey has recently established an important military cooperation with Israel, its problem with Syria (caused, first of all, by control over water resources) is beginning to grow into a larger problem of regional alignments—with Syria finding support in Greece and Iran.

West of Suez, the main source of instability—different militant brands of Islamic fundamentalism—is, once more, older than the end of the Cold War. It is a relatively recent problem in Algeria, but a much older one in Egypt. Libya, of course, is a problem of its own. And, finally, if there is a common, unifying character of the instability of the southern shore of the Mediterranean (with the exception of Israel, of course), it is the general conditions of economic and political backwardness of the area.

Strategic Importance of the Mediterranean.

Needless to say, the states and issues mentioned above are of primary importance for the well-being of the industrialized world and for overall international stability. Italy imports more than 50 percent of its gas solely from Algeria. And to Spain, Algeria makes up 70 percent of its supply. To France, Algeria means not solely gas but also a large community of foreign-born residents and still important political ties.

Washington may be less directly concerned by the Algerian civil war, but for half a century has been a most influential actor in the Middle East. Its ability to influence the flow and price of oil—related in turn to its ability to deal with Arab-Israeli issues and with other ones in the region—long has been the main reason for its lasting, hegemonic position among the industrialized countries.

Turkey may be the case the importance of which the Western allies—but especially the Western Europeans—

continue to underestimate. It is a country that, we can say, lies at the intersection of different main political and cultural areas and currents. It is the industrial state bordering the raw material-producing south of the former Soviet Union. Had Turkey, its power, and infrastructures not been available and Ankara unwilling to pay the serious costs paid for it, the conduct of the operators in the Gulf in 1990-91 would have been much more complex and costly.

In Washington, there is today growing awareness of the strategic importance of a country such as Turkey. However, doubts, ambivalence, and great reluctance continue to be present in the debate about the U.S. commitment to the stabilization of the Balkans.[1] Are the Balkans, among the different security issues in the Mediterranean, less important or marginal?

"We don't have a dog in this fight," Secretary of State James Baker said in 1991 to qualify the U.S. interest in that crisis.[2] Still, if most Western countries looked at the Yugoslav crisis at its outset with a simplistic "vital interest" approach, all came out of it in 1995 realizing that the West can ill-afford large-scale conflicts in adjacent regions, even if the countries involved are economically irrelevant. Flows of refugees and terrible abuse of human rights carried into everybody's living room by CNN-type TV broadcasting have become issues as vital politically as the unimpeded flow of oil through the Persian Gulf. And as long as the Western European allies are unable to take care of that or similar problems, the domestic and international pressures deriving from them are as important for far-away Washington as they are for closer-by Paris, Bonn, or Rome.

The importance of the Mediterranean in security terms derives not from the fact that six NATO member-countries are on its shores, as many analysts pointed out until recently, but rather from the fact that it is an area of great interest, adjacent to the European continent and an area which, unfortunately, is also characterized in the overall by great instability. Many analysts agree that if NATO is going to have to fight again in the near future, it will be in the Mediterranean region. And even more, if there is any possibility of activation of Article 5 of the North Atlantic Treaty (that is, collective territorial defense), that possibility today concerns the states bordering the Mediterranean and, first of all, Greece and Turkey.

Militarily a Profound Restructuring of the Alliance.

Not that there is lack of awareness, particularly among officials and the military in Western countries, of the relevance and complexity of Mediterranean security issues. NATO senior officers are especially aware of the conditions and pressures that are profoundly reshaping the Alliance. In Mons, Belgium, the atomic bunker built to shelter the Supreme Allied Commander, Europe (SACEUR) in case of attack will probably be visited by growing numbers of schoolchildren and their teachers in the coming years. In Naples, in contrast, both the Sixth Fleet Command and AFSOUTH compound are being rebuilt in view of the possibility of missile attacks from somewhere in the Middle Eastern region.

Moreover, even while much attention was being given to the enlargement of NATO in Central Eastern Europe, the largest part of allied planning, operations, and allocation of resources had to do with the problems the Allies encountered in the Mediterranean region—Bosnia above all, in the last 7 years. More precisely, while NATO enlargement is mostly a political-diplomatic exercise and in the end may shrink down to an operation of consensus buttressing for the Alliance (especially in the U.S. Congress), the Mediterranean is where NATO wears its camouflage and flak jackets and moves around in armored personnel carriers and tanks; where it uses its fighter-bombers and naval units. It is in the Mediterranean that NATO, as a collective body and structure, went into combat for the first time in its history. It is there that the Western countries need today to exert effectively their military power. Finally, it is the pressure produced by instability in the Mediterranean that was the motor of the profound reshaping and adaptation of the Alliance that has taken place since the early 1990s.

The Gulf war and immediately after that the conflict in the former Yugoslavia were the two most important experiences that caused the Alliance to refocus its interests and adapt to new missions. An issue always present in allied relations, that of the "out-of-area" tasks, became again a central one after the Soviet intervention in Afghanistan. However, Washington's pressures at the time managed only to have put explicitly on record the unwillingness of Western European countries to assume a role in non-Article 5 situations. In the Gulf, most Western allies intervened, but especially the French remained rigidly opposed to labeling the allied participation as a NATO operation.

That stand became impossible to maintain when the political pressures deriving from the Yugoslav conflict combined in 1991-92 with the uncertain post-Cold War legitimacy of the Alliance. Thus the first decision to participate in international missions outside the Treaty area came in June 1992 at the Oslo North Atlantic Council. That was 2 months after the outset of the Bosnian conflict, and it was the beginning of an adaptation that from 1995 on would turn NATO into the main institutional actor in maintaining stability in the Balkans.

In the same context of political necessity deriving from the Bosnian conflict, other important developments took place. After much agonizing over the issue, Germany decided in favor of participation in allied operations outside the Treaty area. And because France wanted to have a part in the decisions that now counted, it announced in 1995 its willingness to come back after almost 30 years to the military structures of the Alliance (even though later, in a context of diminished pressure, it tied that participation to other conditions). Similarly, Spain began to broaden its NATO participation with the same military structures.

The Partnership for Peace (PfP) program became a useful framework in the post-Dayton Allied intervention in Bosnia. That experience, in turn, gave substance and a better focus to the PfP program. It is, once more, in that context of real operation that the idea, first advanced in January 1994, of flexible Combined Joint Task Forces (CTTF) began to shape up.

Two final points should be made with regard to Bosnia and the Balkans as a motivator of evolution of the Alliance. The Bosnia experience—years of suffering for the main Western capitals, followed by the proved effectiveness of the U.S.-NATO commitment in September 1995—brought a great clarification with regard to power structures and institutions which can effectively deal with important sources of instability. In most Western European capitals, the post-Cold War urge to establish a European security identity (ESDI) and related structures quickly receded as NATO proved effective, especially because of its essential U.S. component. At the Berlin summit of June 1996, the French accepted the idea that any ESDI would be sought within and not outside NATO.

And, finally, because of the pressure deriving from Serbian repression in Kosovo, we may be today at a defining moment with regard to NATO non-Article 5 operations. In October 1998, Richard Holbrooke coerced President of the Federal Republic of Yugoslavia Slobodan Milosevic into accepting Western conditions under threat of a NATO attack. The protracted NATO air campaign of August-September 1995 gave credibility to the threat of the bombings. What was new this time, concerning the Gulf with respect to December 1990, to August-September 1995, and to the very policy established by the North Atlantic Council in December 1992, is that the Western military instrument was used in the negotiations with the explicit opposition of Russia, a permanent member of the Security Council. One may agree or disagree with the decision then taken to Western capitals, but the point is that it will probably remain as an important development in the life of the Alliance, and that such a development came about, once more, because of instability in the Mediterranean.

Politically Serious Disagreement Over Mandate.

The growing importance of the Mediterranean theater for the future of Western security does not immediately translate into a corresponding, broad consensus among the Allies, into well-thought-out general plans and corresponding resources. In fact, the Allies continue to fail to make adequate investments and adapt rapidly enough to the changing security environment. NATO (and Western security arrangements) seem to be pulled in two different directions: fast adapting its military structures to new problems and missions, and having its potential effectiveness limited by the political differences among the Allies about where, when, and how to intervene.

To start with, contingencies increase and resources dwindle. Awareness of the problem is kept mute, and the mandates to deal with those issues remain precarious—when not controversial. American officials point out that 80 percent of military contingencies involving the United States since the disappearance of the Soviet Union (December 1991) have occurred within the Sixth Fleet's zone of responsibility.[3] And Admiral T. Joseph Lopez, former Commander-in-Chief of AFSOUTH, in a lecture given 1 year ago, was reminding his audience how the 15 countries of concern to NATO's Southern Region in the 1980s have now become more than 40—and often, one may add, with new and individual problems.

And possibly, the main problem is not so much the dwindling budget and reduced force structure, as much as the lack of overall, articulated strategies and of clear determination to be engaged in upholding stability in this area. In fact, there is much improvisation and, in large measure, inability to come to grips with the crisis before the issue becomes an intractable one. In interviews with this author at NATO in Brussels in June 1998 about what to do and when to act with regard to Kosovo, several senior officials and military officers started by warning that the arrival of Christiane Amanpour, the CNN reporter, in Pristina meant that NATO "had to do something"—needless to say, an indication of lack of overall policies, of strategic planning and even of well-defined mandates.

Since 1993, all ministerial North Atlantic Councils (NAC) and summits have mentioned the Mediterranean. In 1994 a Mediterranean Dialogue was started with five, then six, countries in the proximity of the Southern shore (Egypt, Israel, Mauritania, Morocco, Tunisia, and Jordan.)[4] NATO officials point to the carrying out in early 1998 of a CJTF-type exercise in the Southern Region, with eight countries participating and the first one to develop concrete operational procedures. People implementing Western policies in the Mediterranean stress the importance of a visible presence of Western power as a deterrent. Admiral Lopez repeatedly spoke about "forward engagement." However, the dialogue initiative or the recent exercises are more a sign of the recognition of a need than the beginning of an adequate response to existing problems.

Of course, it is not easy to move Western security policies toward a new focus. The NATO Southern Command during the Cold War not only had to guard a smaller number of countries, but was doing that with a clear focus and a well-defined threat. Indeed, the Western alliance developed mostly around the problem posed by the presence of Soviet power in Europe. It is easy to enlarge NATO to Central Eastern European countries, for no one doubts that those countries belong today to the expanded European zone of peace. Enlargement is a no-risk initiative and with immediate political dividends. Its financial costs remain undetermined and can always be delayed to future fiscal years. A U.S. administration can always blame the Europeans for being irresponsible in that respect. The Europeans can always say Washington should pay for what at the Madrid summit came out as an American version of enlargement.

In contrast, Bosnia alone has meant the disbursement of 7 billion dollars a year since 1995. And those are financial resources that need be found, year after year, in different parts of the budget of the countries participating in it. The same applies to the Gulf war—many tens of billion of dollars in the end found through a fund-raising campaign in the United States and in other Western countries.

A Broader Approach to Western Security.

But even a better understanding among Allies on NATO's new competencies and more sufficient resources are only a small part of the remedy to adequately deal with the different sources of instability in the Mediterranean region. Except for a few issues, the response to which is solely military (such as Saddam Hussein's policies), most other issues require a complex array of instruments to be dealt with—beginning with economic power. Were the Western European countries able to unify and effectively exert their potential influence, they would be decisive in different critical issues in the Mediterranean area.

The Western European countries created mechanisms for producing a common foreign and security policy (CFSP, with the Maastricht and Amsterdam Treaties). If the European Union (then Community) failed to control the crisis in Yugoslavia in 1991, officials and analysts often explain that that was before it created the new mechanisms. One analyst found that the Yugoslav crisis "was premature," for Europe was then in the process of redefining itself.[5] But 3 more years of war, the successive stabilization period, and then the new Kosovo crisis proved the European CFSP mechanisms unable to produce policies any more unified and effective than those of the pre-Maastricht Community. In 1998, a small, manageable but also highly visible operation in Albania to stabilize politically the situation there was left to the Italians and French to carry out. They refused any European institutional support and labeling.

Decades of specialization in the international roles played, with the United States as the single power dealing with most non-European crises and sources of instability, are difficult to substitute with a culture of shared responsibility. Moreover, with the regional issues left to themselves and no longer fed by the global U.S.-Soviet rivalry and linked to the compellance of strategic weapons, those issues became tempting occasions for raising the political profile of different countries or for testing one's new influence. The result is a diminished ability to steadily act collectively for most influential Western European capitals, foreign policies more dependent on domestic politics, and, at times, even frivolous policies. In the former Yugoslavia, even more important than for the additional firepower it brought with it, the United States has been essential as the unifying element of Western will and power.

The result is a vacuum of jurisdiction among the Western countries over different issues or even different regions. (Whose responsibility was dealing with Yugoslavia? Where were the Europeans?) The collective intervention then takes place only when the situation creates too many direct, unbearable pressures—but also when an issue, largely manageable early on, has become an intractable one, as in the former Yugoslavia. And at that point, the outside intervention ends up being necessarily massive, only military, costly, risky, and requiring a long-term commitment. In the former Yugoslavia, the United States and NATO intervened after other collective instruments failed in the early phases of the crisis. However, that does not necessarily mean that NATO was the sole right instrument—the lack of a real institutional "common" European policy and the inability to intervene early in the crisis are other explanations for the failure of the Western countries to deal with an issue before it becomes totally militarized in character.

The regions around the Mediterranean are where the West will have to make the largest investment for stability and for defending its interests in the near future. Except for a few ones of military nature, most issues need be dealt with through an early commitment, a broad array of instruments and, above all, economic ones. NATO's capabilities can contribute significantly and need be present and visible—but not be the substitute for other forms of influence.

ENDNOTES - CHAPTER 4

1. Typical or even extreme positions in opposition to the U.S. commitment in the Balkans are aptly presented in the chapter on NATO of the *Cato Handbook for Congress: Policy Recommendations for the 106th Congress*, Washington, DC: Cato Institute, 1999.

2. Cited in Richard Holbrooke, *To End a War*, New York: Random House, 1998, p. 27.

3. See William Drozdiak, "Sixth Fleet is Smaller but Still on Vigil to Move Fast to Crisis Area," *WPI International Herald Tribune*, August 20, 1998.

4. For a short history of the initiative, see Jette Nordan, "The Mediterranean Dialogue: Dispelling Misconceptions and Building Confidence," *NATO Review*, July-August 1997.

5. James E. Steinberg, "The Response of International Institutions to the Yugoslavia Conflict: Implications and Lessons," in Steven Larrabee, *Europe's Volatile Powder Keg: Balkan Security after the Cold War*, Santa Monica, CA: RAND Corporation, 1994.

CHAPTER 5

EUROPEAN UNION SECURITY PERCEPTIONS AND POLICIES TOWARDS THE MEDITERRANEAN

Roberto Aliboni

This paper takes into consideration, first, the security challenges the European Union (EU) member states perceive with respect to the Mediterranean area, and, second, the policy responses of the EU states to such challenges and perceptions. Mediterranean security perceptions comprise an uneven set of military and nonmilitary challenges, with an emphasis on the latter. The paper begins by examining military challenges and moves then to nonmilitary ones. Finally, it considers the European overall Mediterranean security doctrine which links the two clusters of challenges.

This Mediterranean security doctrine explains policy as well as institutional responses actually undertaken by the EU states in the 1990s. Such responses are considered in the last section of the paper. A brief conclusion provides an assessment of the EU Mediterranean policy effectiveness.

Military Challenges: Proliferation.

No state in the Mediterranean areas of the Middle East and North Africa (MENA) would be capable of conducting a full military attack on European countries and, in fact, no such threat is minimally perceived or even taken into consideration in the Northern part of the region (maybe with the exception of Turkey with respect to Syria). Military challenges and related risk perceptions in the North concern proliferation of weapons of mass destruction (WMD) and their delivery means.

According to many analysts, WMD and related missiles proliferation is less a threat than a risk for the European countries and the West. Its effects are likely to be less of military than diplomatic and political character. This is due to a number of factors, like:

- The pulling force towards proliferation, irrespective of its actual military effectiveness, is the political necessity to earn some strategic "weight" and status from the possession of WMD and missiles. As noted by Lesser and Tellis, these states want to be "taken seriously" by the West (as well as by neighbors).[1] During the Cold War, these states could obtain strategic weight internationally by aligning or not aligning themselves in the framework of the global East-West confrontation. In a sense, WMD and missiles are a substitute for alignment in the post-Cold War world. By the same token, possessing WMD is regarded, particularly by Arab states, as a proof of their technological capacity, allegedly improving their political and strategic status.

- On the other hand, there is no doubt that many MENA states feel insecure with respect to both regional enemies and the West. In this sense, WMD must be regarded as a form of gross military and political deterrence or as an instrument of interdiction and coercive diplomacy.

- Many analysts point out that MENA countries' WMD and missiles are essentially targeted on their Southern neighbors. As a matter of fact, it is in the South-South context that MENA states face real military threats and more often than not have proven to be willing or able to resort to military instruments to solve their disputes, by diplomatic coercion as well as other forms of conflict. The North is not a primary target of Southern WMD and missiles, at least from a narrower military point of view.

- Finally, whichever their use and motives, because of MENA's poor industrial and technological background, the military effectiveness of their WMD and related projection capacities are challenged by many analysts.

Despite the importance of nonmilitary motives, their poor effectiveness, the lack of an adequate industrial background, their uneven development and their mostly South-South orientation, there is no doubt that southern proliferation of WMD and related delivery means affects regional stability in a very general sense. From a narrower military angle, it makes the European Union and its principal allies (the U.S. forces deployed in Southern Europe and Turkey) more vulnerable. Southern Europe is already encompassed by a number of delivery vehicles. Even if such exposure remained a minor military threat to the EU and EU allies' security, still it would bring about a degree of political and military interdiction. Dealing with a growing instability with less freedom of maneuver might prove very difficult and risky.

The EU states belonging to NATO have recognized the risks put forward by proliferation in the NATO Istanbul Declaration of 1994. In the November 1995 Barcelona Declaration,[2] signed by the EU states and 12 non-EU Mediterranean partners, there is a joint commitment against proliferation beside other commitments to contain or diminish the level of armaments, as well as their offensive or inhumane nature.

Nonmilitary Security Challenges: Migration, Terrorism And Criminality.

Although recognizing proliferation as a major risk, EU states' concerns are focusing on nonmilitary security challenges. First, the basic European feeling is that much of the Mediterranean armed conflict is linked to global rather than regional factors and trends. Proliferation, just to quote an example, is not precisely a regional, Mediterranean trend. Containing such military trends and solving outstanding armed conflicts in the area require an international management to which the EU can contribute but cannot tackle in isolation.

Second, the EU aims at working out the conditions for stability in the Mediterranean area, by acting principally on political, social, economic and cultural factors. In the European vision, instability in the Mediterranean stems essentially from these nonmilitary factors. Economic and social underdevelopment coupled with the rule of authoritarian regimes brings about instability domestically. Such domestic instability turns regionally into spill-over effects which intrude in Europe and affect European security. What is at stake is not national security in a conventional sense, but the security of European democratic polities and the welfare and civic order of the latter as they have developed after the end of the Second World War.

The most important spill-over effects concerning the EU are related to immigration, terrorism and internationally organized criminality. These issues are contemplated by the third chapter of the Barcelona Declaration. As a matter of fact, rightly or wrongly, they are more and more important and visible in the daily political and social life of the European members of the Union.

Immigration is not a threat to employment, although unemployment is currently raging in Western Europe. With a European demographic growth approaching zero (particularly in Southern Europe) and a very poor propensity by young Europeans to accept menial jobs and mobility, immigrants are in fact almost badly needed economically. Western Europe, however, is not prepared to accept immigration (or more immigration) for political and, most of all, cultural reasons.

As a matter of fact, situations are varying from country to country because of very different legal, historical, political and cultural legacies regarding immigration and citizenship. While in Great Britain and in some Northern European countries there is an articulated relationship between communities and the state which allows for the presence of even numerous immigrant groups and a relatively high degree of cultural-political autonomy of the latter, in Southern Europe and in Germany this same relationship is definitely less flexible. This lack of flexibility makes relations with culturally assertive communities, like Muslim ones, very difficult, for these communities either do not accept assimilation (a mainly French solution) or just feel discriminated and marginalized (like in Germany, Spain and Italy) because, as well as they may be treated (but this is not always the case), they do not get the recognition they wish.

As a result of difficulties in accommodating a growing migration from the Mediterranean and other numerous areas (among which the Balkans play a political role definitely more important than that played by Mediterranean peoples), in Europe xenophobia and racism are increasing and giving way to organized political movements. Besides exacerbating tensions stemming from migration anyway, these developments put strains on the democratic character of the European polities. This is a first important risk perceived today in Europe by concerned democratic people and leaderships. At the beginning of the 1990s, the EU Commission had explicitly warned about such risk and consequently advocated the necessity of a more articulated and important European Mediterranean policy.

A second risk comes from political links between immigrated groups, notably Muslims, and respective sending countries. European inability and unwillingness to integrate immigrated people, increasingly turning into xenophobic and racist criminal attacks on individuals and groups or mistreatment, is resented by Muslim and Arab public opinion in sending countries as an evidence of a wider and fundamental European-Christian hostility towards Islam and Arabs. In this respect it is linked to early

European hesitation to intervene in Bosnia to defend Muslims. This alleged European hostility stirs in Muslim communities a sense of danger and reinforces their spontaneous identitarian assertiveness. Islamist activism is diffuse in Europe as a form of defense and identifying assertiveness backed by substantive relations with religious-political organizations at home. In this way, migration brings the Islamist movements' anti-Western hostility inside Europe and tends to exacerbate difficulties in international relations.

To a large extent, immigration is a source of conflict and instability just because the European states are unable to agree on common policies. Joint policies to control immigration are now operated within the Schengen agreement (which provides for free movements of European citizens among a number of EU member states). Cooperation within the Schengen agreement remains weak, however, because it is not yet predicated on more articulated joint policies with respect to migrants staying and working in the EU states. This risk to European security is largely due to European inertia.

To some extent, the link between migration and Islamist anti-Western attitude we have just talked about explains also European involvement with terrorism. Immigration, in fact, brings about an environment in which terrorists are able to move with relative ease. While MENA terrorism is a new development in the United States, Europe is not new to terrorism originating from these regions. Sometimes Europe is no more than a logistic base or a battlefield, like in the "Mikonos" affair. In other cases, Europe is more or less directly involved for its past colonial links (as in the case of France with current Algerian terrorism) or because it is regarded as a more or less direct player with respect to Islamists' domestic and international interests.

Finally, immigration and terrorism link up with international criminality. Though an evil in itself, illegal immigration is more and more becoming a business managed by international criminality, functionally or operationally associated with other kinds of traffics, like drugs and armaments. Illegal traffic organized by international criminal gangs is another effect of instability. Intra-state and inter-state conflict as well as terrorism start the vicious circles of drugs and displaced persons trafficking in order to finance arms transfers. The unfinished cycle of conflict in the Balkans and in Northern Iraq-Southeastern Anatolia has shown the strict and formidable intermingling of criminality, conflicts and migrations.

Structural Causes.

These challenges are regarded by European analysts and governments as proximate causes of instability and insecurity in the Mediterranean. These proximate causes trace back to structural causes, however, i.e. the roots of instability and insecurity. In the Mediterranean area two main clusters of structural causes can be identified: (a) the weakness of Arab regimes and governments on the grounds of political legitimacy; (b) the lack of good governance and political freedom bringing about political and social disruptions and economic underdevelopment. As the latter is not a secondary source of political radicalism and systemic opposition, the two clusters intermingle.

Figure 1 is an attempt at mapping out the EU vision of the hierarchy of structural causes of instability in the Mediterranean and their linkages[3]. The figure is also a guide to EU policy responses intended to correct such causes or contain their effects. To be sure, the links established in the figure are not necessarily valid from a scientific point of view: on policy grounds, however, they are helpful as they point out the political values and expectations which direct EU action. While this section describes the networking of structural causes of instability, as interpreted by the EU, next one will provide an overview of the policies worked out by the EU to attain stability in the Mediterranean.

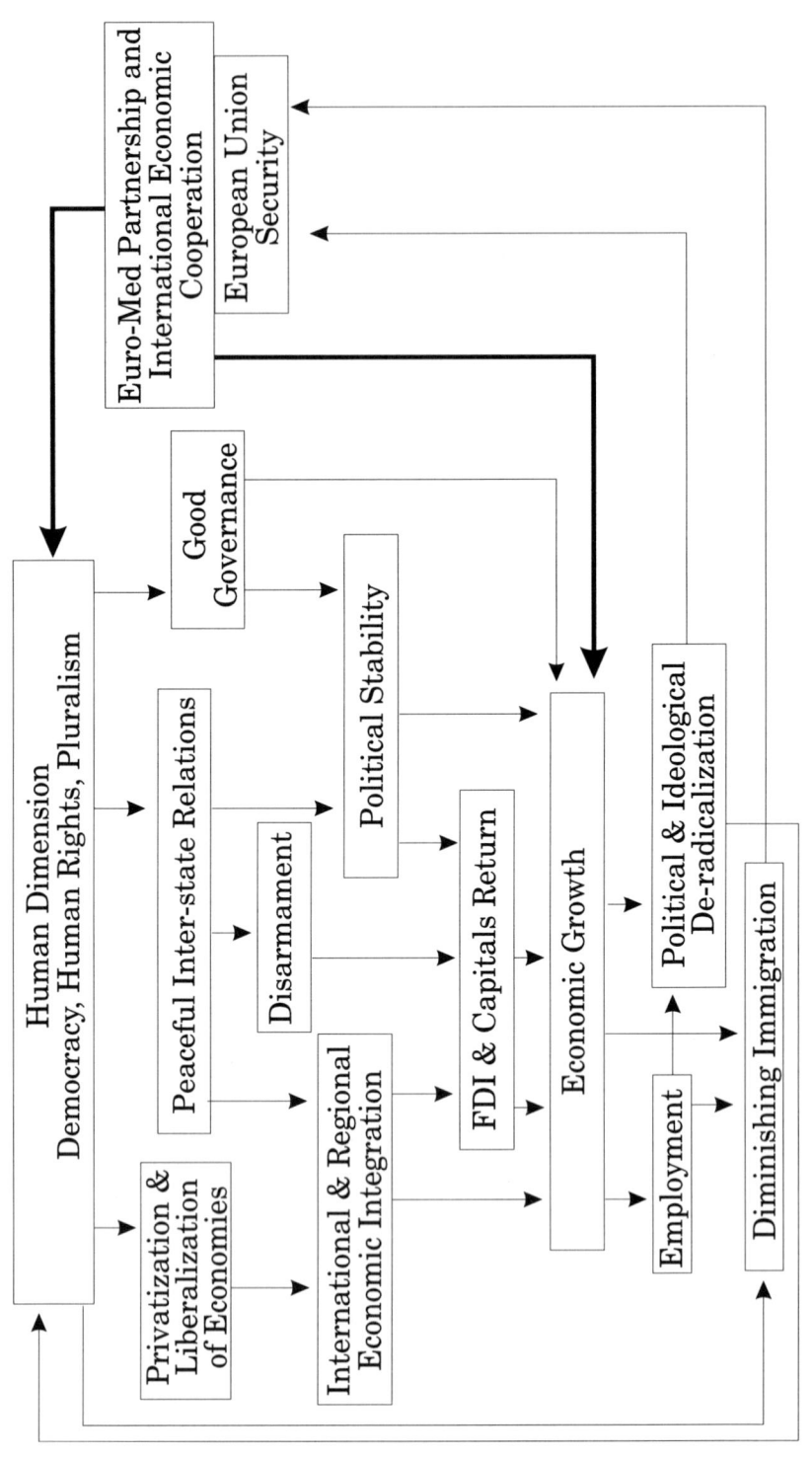

Figure 1. Systemic Relationships between Political and Economic Factors in the Euro-Med Partnership Doctrine.

The Barcelona Declaration principles and aims are largely inspired by the model of cooperation and integration of the EU itself. In a 1993 document of the EU Commission related to the "Future Relations and Co-operation between the Community and the Middle East," it was stated that:

> The Community's own experience demonstrates that war between previously hostile parties can be made unthinkable through economic integration. While this model cannot easily be transposed to the Middle East, it does suggest that the development of regional economic co-operation can be a powerful tool in reducing the level of conflict, making peace irreversible and encouraging the people of the region to learn to leave in peace.[4]

Strongly influenced by EU's experience in dealing with post-Communist Central-Eastern Europe, the Barcelona Declaration puts forward a systemic interplay among democracy, integration, and peace as the basic ingredients to affect root causes of instability.

Consequently, the agenda suggested by the Declaration starts from the necessity to use the Euro-Mediterranean Partnership (EMP) to introduce democracy and pluralism as well as strengthen political legitimacy and its underlying civil society. The emergence of such factors would allow, in turn, the achievement of inter-state relations based on peaceful resolution of disputes and the respect of the fundamental principles of international law (recalled in detail by the Declaration, in the same way as the Helsinki Declaration).

According to the model shown in Figure 1, the consolidation of peaceful relations between states would bring about stability in international as well as in intra-state relations. The existence of peaceful relations, especially in the Middle East, would open the way to a substantive disarmament and to the possibility of achieving some degree of regional economic integration.

Democratization is understood as a factor that changes and reduces the role of the state in the economy, making it possible to liberalize the latter and proceed to privatization. This development would help regional economic integration and cooperation. At the same time, the overall domestic and regional stabilization coupled with the strengthening of the market economy would allow for capital abroad to return home (an extremely significant amount in the MENA region) and for foreign capital to enter in the form of direct investments and new technologies.

Economic growth made possible by political stability attained in intra-state as well as inter-state relations would allow for reducing unemployment, particularly in relation to young generations, and lowering poverty. These would be key factors in discouraging political radicalization as well as emigration.

By indicating the introduction of democracy as the first mover of the virtuous circles described above, the EU with the Barcelona Declaration has pointed out the structural causes of instability in the Mediterranean and the character and primary sources of insecurity in the area, at least from its point of view. The Declaration is not an explicit analysis of such causes but alludes to them indirectly by setting an agenda directed at eliminating and containing such causes of instability. This is the topic of next section.

The Euro-Mediterranean Security Agenda.

In the Euro-Mediterranean security agenda, as outlined by the Barcelona Declaration, there are two policy layers: a broader one directed at shaping the structural factors which would allow for stability and, thus, security in the Mediterranean; a narrower one constituted by specific policies to be implemented jointly and cooperatively by the members of the Euro-Mediterranean Partnership.

All in all, the Barcelona process resembles the CSCE/OSCE experience. It is a cooperative security scheme, in which the players are expected to gradually attain security and escape security dilemmas by the use of cooperative instruments (instead of being guided by policies of balance of power and deterrence). The cooperative security scheme envisaged by the Barcelona Declaration is strongly predicated on a concept of comprehensive security, in which both military and nonmilitary factors are included and integrated. This is reflected (and is the outcome) of the EU analysis of Mediterranean instability on which, as argued in the above, the security scheme is predicated.

It must be added that from the point of view of the EU, the emphasis on nonmilitary factors does not come from objective analysis only, but also from the very "civilian" nature of the European Union. The Treaty of Amsterdam, having failed once again to provide an operational and well integrated Common Foreign and Security Policy (CFSP) to the Union, remains more a civilian-economic power than a politico-military one. Having said that, however, it would be wrong to think that the EU is not pursuing military or military-related cooperation in the Mediterranean. Although to a minor extent and with poor effectiveness, military cooperation is tried nonetheless.

On this backdrop, the broader and structural layer of EMP cooperative security scheme is tasked to provide a common code of conduct, which includes a set of basic principles for international cooperation and peaceful relations. The aim is similar to the Helsinki Act: the Barcelona Declaration commits its members to democratization, pluralism, the implementation of the state of law, respect for human rights and minorities, good neighborly relations, etc. as the frame which would make cooperative security work. Like the CSCE, the EMP is politically binding only. Its pivotal mechanism is the political dialogue, which is conducted in its institutions: the biennial Conference of Foreign Ministers, the Euro-Mediterranean Committee for the Barcelona Process (Euro-Med Committee), and the High Officials Committee. The political dialogue is aimed, first, to create cooperation needed to make the cooperative security scheme emerge and, secondly, to manage jointly what cooperation is actually worked out.

The narrower layer makes reference to the three chapters of the Declaration. The first and third chapters envisage a set of specific policies related to security, in practice to the military and nonmilitary factors that have been pointed out in the two previous sections: WMD and missiles proliferation coupled with other military trends, and migration, terrorism and organized international criminality. The second chapter envisages strong support to economic development and the integration of the Southern Mediterranean economies in the international setting by the creation at 2010 of a free trade area.

As for nonmilitary factors, it is important to note that the Barcelona Declaration emphasizes the necessity of promoting the cultural dialogue between the different parts of the Mediterranean as a tool working across the board, i.e., in relation to the varying social and human dimensions that are involved in the broad notion of Mediterranean security and peaceful relations. The Declaration gives special emphasis to the role of civil society in reinforcing cultural understanding and, most of all, promoting political and economic liberalization and cohesiveness in their respective societies.

Beside the aforementioned diplomatic and political instruments that can be used within the political dialogue, incentives to democratization are provided by a small fund devoted to support of nongovernmental initiatives to reinforce and spread democracy (Meda-Democracy). On the other hand, the fund designated for developmental aid is considerable (a little bit more than 4 billion ECU for concessional aid and as much from the European Investment Bank). The incentives to promote democracy, and to respect human rights and law, are supported by a strict scheme of "conditionality" that is related to the disbursement of aid.

As for the military factor, the Barcelona Declaration points out the prominent necessity to stop or contain proliferation. At the same time, it stresses other targets of arms control, arms limitation and disarmament, as well as the necessity to promote confidence-building measures and introduce conflict prevention capacities into the scheme. The relevant key passage of the Declaration points out that the Parties will:

> consider practical steps to prevent the proliferation of nuclear, chemical and biological weapons;
>
> refrain from developing military capacity beyond their legitimate defence requirements, at the same time reaffirming their resolve to achieve the same degree of security and mutual confidence with the lowest possible levels of troops and weaponry and adherence to CCW;
>
> promote conditions likely to develop good security, prosperity and regional and subregional cooperation;
>
> consider any confidence- and security-building measures that could be taken between the Parties with a view to the creation of an "area of peace and stability in the Mediterranean" including the long-term possibility of establishing a Euro-Mediterranean pact to that end.

This set of measures is named by the Declaration the "area of peace and stability." To establish the "area," Senior Officials have begun setting out two main agendas: the Action Plan and, later on, the Euro-Mediterranean Charter for Peace and Stability. While the Action Plan would be a list of measures and policies that the Partners would pick up and negotiate over time according to priorities and modes they would remain free to gradually agree upon, the Charter would be an institutional framework with a normative ambition and a stronger mechanism of political dialogue. In a sense, the Charter would be the "Euro-Mediterranean Pact" mentioned at the end of the just-quoted passage and its substance would resemble the

Stability Pact in Europe established by the EU within the CSCE/OSCE.

The Barcelona Declaration is not exhausting the military instruments available to the EU for achieving security in the Mediterranean. Beside the principles and policies the EU shares with its Mediterranean partners in the framework of the EMP, instruments available to the Union in the framework of the WEU and multinational forces set up by members of the Union, like Eurofor and Euromarfor, must also be taken into consideration (although they are not directed specifically to the Mediterranean). These instruments are part of the defense forces of the Union, its members and its allies, and tasked primarily to their national security. There is no doubt, however, that their use is intended for cooperative purposes. These purposes are listed by the 1992 Petersberg Declaration, in which the WEU members have pointed out that military forces answerable to the WEU are to be used eventually for the management of crises as well as for peacekeeping and humanitarian missions. Eurofor and Euromarfor, made answerable to the WEU (as well as NATO and other regional security organizations) by the governments of France, Italy, Portugal and Spain, are endowed with a special maritime mobility and for this reason have a natural destination to act in the Mediterranean (although not necessarily there).

Since 1993 the WEU has conducted a Mediterranean Dialogue with Mauritania, Morocco, Algeria, Tunisia, and Egypt (since 1995). In the first semester of 1998, the WEU Council decided to enlarge its dialogue to Jordan as well. The dialogue amounts to biannual meetings with representatives of these countries to exchange information. Recently, the non-WEU Mediterranean partners have been invited to visit, first, the WEU Torrejón Satellite Center (Spain) and, secondly, the WEU Planning Cell in Brussels. Principally because of the EU members reluctance to make the WEU work effectively, this organization's Mediterranean agenda (not unlike other agendas) proved weak. The Mediterranean Dialogue operates as a very broad confidence-building measure directed to enhance transparency. The establishment of Eurofor and Euromarfor, on the other hand, was not welcome by the Mediterranean partners (and countries at large) for these forces are not included in an explicit cooperative framework and would thus operate unilaterally.

Conclusions.

EU security perceptions with respect to the Mediterranean are predicated essentially on nonmilitary structural causes. Proximate causes of instability may well be of military nature, like proliferation. Still, nonmilitary proximate causes, such as migration or terrorism, are seen as most important. Accordingly, EU instruments to deal with security in the Mediterranean are less military than political, economic, and cultural in their character.

It would be a mistake, however, to believe that the EU is overlooking military and military-related instruments and issues. The cooperative security scheme envisaged by what the Barcelona Declaration defines as the "area of peace and stability" is very important not only because the EU is aware of the fact that in the middle-longer term the level and quality of armaments in the region will be decisive for its overall stability (and will be no less important than nonmilitary factors), but also because acquiring a capability to manage military and military-related relations is an important element for EU's ongoing political and defense integration. In fact, from the point of view of the EU, while Barcelona policies directed at improving economic development, containing illegal immigration, and countering terrorism as well as international criminality are of the utmost importance for European security, the implementation of the "area of peace and stability" corresponds to a no less important investment from both the point of view of security in the area and EU's political identity. In the light of these purposes, what is the balance sheet of the Mediterranean policies set out by the EU in the 1990s?

In its 3-year life, the Euro-Mediterranean Partnership has duly progressed in implementing its agenda of economic cooperation, but less so in shaping the varying aspects of security cooperation envisaged by the first and third chapter of the Barcelona Declaration. In fact, the balance sheet, after the second ministerial meeting in Malta (April 15-16, 1997) and the ad hoc ministerial meeting held in Palermo on June 4-5, 1998, is somehow disappointing in this respect. It must be added that it is maybe disappointing more in relation to migration, terrorism and criminality than the "area of peace and stability."

While the standstill in the Middle East peace process has been a serious stumbling block on the road to build up the "area of peace and stability," the EU and EMP inertia with respect to illegal immigration, terrorism and criminality is explained by the modest level of integration in the Union in relation to such matters, particularly immigration. In more general terms, the weakness of the CFSP is an important factor in slowing down the EU Mediterranean security agenda. It must be also noted, however, that despite some rhetoric, especially in Southern Europe, EU security concerns concentrate elsewhere than in the Mediterranean, i.e., in the Balkans and in Russia.

ENDNOTES - CHAPTER 5

1. Ian O. Lesser and Ashley J. Tellis, *Strategic Exposure-Proliferation around the Mediterranean*, Santa Monica, CA: RAND, 1996, p. 7.

2. The English text of the Declaration is published by *Mediterranean Politics*, Vol. 2, No. 1, Summer 1997, pp. 177-187.

3. This section is a version of part of an earlier study published in Italian by the author: Roberto Aliboni, "Riforme economiche nel Mediterraneo: il contesto politico" ("The political context of economic reforms in the Mediterranean"), in G. Barba Navaretti, R. Faini, eds., *Nuove prospettive per la cooperazione allo sviluppo. I processi di*

integrazione economica e politica con i paesi del Mediterraneo (New perspectives on development cooperation. Political and economic integrative processes with the Mediterranean countries), Bologna: Il Mulino, 1997, pp. 183-222.

4. Communication from the Commission of the European Communities, COM 93 (375), September 8, 1993.

CHAPTER 6

ARAB PERCEPTIONS OF THE EUROPEAN UNION'S EURO-MEDITERRANEAN PROJECTS

Mohammad El-Sayed Selim

Introduction.

In October 1994 the European Union (EU) announced a proposal to establish a Euro-Mediterranean Partnership (EMP). According to this proposal, the EMP was directed towards "support for establishing a zone of stability and security and creating conditions for lasting and sustainable rapid economic development in the Mediterranean countries." The proposal reiterated two main dimensions of the Partnership, namely, establishing a Euro-Mediterranean Zone of Political Stability and Security, and establishing a Euro-Mediterranean Economic Area. The objective was to establish a free trade area in all manufactured products between the EU and the Mediterranean countries, preferential and reciprocal access for agricultural products, and a free trade area among Mediterranean countries themselves. "The Euro-Mediterranean free trade zone would constitute the biggest free trade area in the world covering 600-800 million people in some 30-40 countries." The EU Proposal also promised financial support of Ecu 5.5bn for the period 1995-99 to help Mediterranean nonmember states to realize these objectives. It also called for a Euro-Mediterranean conference.

The projected Euro-Mediterranean ministerial conference was held on November 27-28, 1995, in Barcelona, Spain. The conference attendees witnessed heated debates between the EU and nonmember Mediterranean countries' representatives on the elements of the partnership. However, the final declaration issued by the conference, the Barcelona Declaration, reflected to a large extent the European viewpoint, as far as the nature of peace and stability and the free trade area that will be established by the year 2010.

The EU drafted a model "association agreement" with the southern Mediterranean countries as the starting point of the partnership negotiations. Negotiations have been conducted separately between the EU and would-be Mediterranean partners. So far, they have resulted in partnership agreements with Morocco, Tunisia, Jordan, and Israel. Negotiations are under way between the EU and Egypt, Syria, and Lebanon.

Each of the Mediterranean partners was handed a model draft agreement, and negotiations evolved around this draft. The final agreements were more or less modifications of the draft agreements. The draft agreements and the final agreements contained seven main items, namely:

Political Dialogue. The establishment of a regular political dialogue, between Egypt and the EU, that would cover all issues of common interest, and would be held at regular intervals and whenever necessary at ministerial and senior official levels and through all diplomatic channels.

Free Movement of Goods. The establishment of a free trade area over a transitional period lasting a maximum of 12 years starting from the date of entry into force of the agreement. Custom duties on industrial products exported by the EU to Mediterranean countries would be progressively abolished, but industrial products originating in these countries would be imported into the EU free of customs duties and charges as soon as the agreement was finalized without quantitative restrictions or measures. Agricultural and fishery exports of each party would be allowed access to the other party's markets free of customs duties within a pre-set quota and in specific seasons.

Rights of Establishment and Services. The exchange of the right of establishment of one party's firms on the territory of the other and the liberalization of the provision of services by one party's firms to consumers of service of the other.

Competition and Other Economic Provisions. The elimination of all agreements and practices that restrict or distort competition. However, certain concessions were given to Mediterranean countries for a limited time period, such as the right to continue state aid to their firms, but such aid would be limited to what was necessary in order to maintain and restore the viability of firms. Further, the parties shall provide suitable and effective protection of intellectual and commercial property rights in line with the highest international standards. The parties would promote the use by Mediterranean countries of the EU's technical rules and European standards for industrial and agricultural products and certification procedures, and would also conclude agreements for the mutual recognition of certifications. The EU would also assist in areas of activity suffering the effects of internal constraints and difficulties or affected by the process of liberalizing its economy and foreign trade.

Cooperation in the Areas of Education and Training, Science and Technology, and Environment. Special emphasis was put on industrial cooperation with a view of modernizing and restructuring the industrial sector, including the agri-food industry in Mediterranean countries. The draft agreements and final agreements also referred to the promotion and protection of investment, cooperation in standardization and conformity assessment, financial services, agriculture and fisheries, transport, telecommunications and information technology, energy, tourism and cooperation in customs matters, statistics, combating money laundering, and drug use and trafficking.

Cooperation in Social and Cultural Matters. These included reciprocal treatment of the workers of each party in the territory of the others. The EU and the Mediterranean countries will also enter a dialogue on any social matters that are of interest to them such as migration and the conditions of migrant workers, the promotion of the role of woman, family planning, the promotion of human rights, and cooperation in the area of strengthening mutual understanding.

Financial Cooperation. This would include financial support by the EU to facilitate reforms aimed at modernizing the economy, updating economic infrastructure, promoting private investment and job creation activities, and alleviating the effects on the Mediterranean economies of the progressive introduction of the free trade area.[1]

Arab countries reacted differently to the EU proposal. Within each country there were also different reactions of various political and economic groups. Such reactions will have long-term implications for the viability of the projected EMP. The objective of this essay is to review the perceptions of Arab countries to the projected EMP; and to assess the policy implications of these perceptions to projected partnership.

Perceptions of the Need to Establish the EMP.

Arab governments acknowledged the need to respond positively to the European proposal. Egypt's official response to the projected partnership was positive. This response was clearly articulated in the public debate that was initiated after the Barcelona conference and in other statements and documents of the Egyptian Foreign Ministry. A concept paper circulated by the foreign ministry endorsing the EMP argued that the European proposal must strive to create a Euro-Mediterranean economic area that would enhance the position of the partners in this area within the international economic system, achieve peace, stability, and security in the Mediterranean, and promote a dialogue among Mediterranean civilizations. It added that the EMP should be based on the consensus of the partners, thereby reflecting the diverse interests of the Mediterranean countries. It should not conflict with other commitments of the partners.

Egypt's Foreign and Industry Ministries were the most outspoken advocates of the Egyptian-European Partnership (EEP). They defended the agreement mainly on grounds of market expansion, job creation, and increased foreign investment. Egyptian manufactured products would get free access to the huge European market. This would lead to industry expansion and the generation of job opportunities. Foreign investors would also be tempted to manufacture in Egypt in order to benefit from the customs duty-free European market. According to Egypt's chief negotiator with the EU,

> the EEP conformed with the goal of Egyptian economic development. It would generate more job opportunities, and open a huge market of U.S. $800 million to Egyptian exports. Through the EEP, Egypt would be granted U.S. $2 billion and loaned another U.S. $2 billion to develop industry, education, training, and scientific research within the next 3 years. The EEP provides Egypt with privileges such as the progressive reduction of customs duties over 12 years.[2]

Ibrahim Fawzy, Minister of Industry in 1995, was almost deterministic in presenting the case of EEP to the Egyptian business community. He contended that the post-Cold War era was the era of grand economic blocs. Egypt was a small country, and, as a result, it had to join a large bloc or it would risk marginalization. Consequently, the EEP was "a compulsory option." The EU was not out to control the Egyptian Market because Egypt's import potential was limited. The EU's goal, according to Dr. Fawzy, was to "develop Egypt" and to "create an economic bloc to confront the American bloc and the East Asian bloc." Egypt would also gain access to the huge European market, and that would generate 1.4 million job opportunities annually. That the projected agreement did not include the freedom of labor movement into its provisions was not a disadvantage. This would serve to stop the "brain drain" from Egypt to Europe. The choice for Egypt, he added, was not the United States or East Asia, it was the European Union.[3]

The projected EMP was also viewed as complementing the Mediterranean Forum (MF) that Egypt had lobbied heavily to establish in 1994. The Egyptians argued that the MF, which is a purely Mediterranean framework, could serve to regulate cooperation between the Mediterranean countries that are members in the EMP. Both institutions could mutually reinforce each other.

The Tunisian government perceived the EMP as urgently needed to ensure better utilization of resources, achieving co-development in the Mediterranean, and securing the process of democratic transformation. Ben-Yehia, Tunisia's Foreign Minister, argued in his address at the Forum of the Constitutional Democratic Party in November 1995 that the EMP "provided the Mediterranean with a historic opportunity that could enable the area to formulate a comprehensive strategy for development."

Despite their serious misgivings about the EMP, the Syrians joined the EMP negotiations in 1997, arguing that it could bring about certain gains. The Libyans, too, have clearly expressed their desire to join the EMP.[4]

How do we account for the Arab endorsement of the basic idea of the EMP despite their major reservations (which will be outlined at a later section)? Arab desire to join the EMP is an outcome of Arab tremendous economic linkages with the EU. The EU is the major trade partner for all Arab Mediterranean countries. It is also a major donor of economic aid and technology. The Arabs fear that these interests will be jeopardized if they do not join. Further, the Arabs perceive the EMP as a mechanism to counterbalance American economic hegemony in the Middle East. They would like to see a more active European role in the Middle East as Europe is perceived to be less biased towards Israel than the United States is. Finally, the Arabs hope that through negotiations they will be able to persuade the EU to give them more concessions than have been already offered in the draft association agreements.

Arab Perceptions of the Scope of the EMP and Its Impact on Arab Regional Cooperation.

In 1992, European countries suspended all forms of multilateral cooperation in which Libya was involved. The rationale for the decision was that such cooperation would only be resumed after Libya hands over two Libyans suspected of being involved in the downing of an American airliner. In this context, the 5+5 formula was suspended, and Libya was not invited to participate in the negotiations to build an EMP. Although Arab countries began negotiations without Libya, most of them contended that Libya should be brought into the Euro-Med process, including the Egyptian Foreign Minister and the Moroccan Prime Minister.[5] However, they did not specify whether this should occur immediately or after the resolution of the Libyan-Western crisis. Arab interest in bringing Libya into the EMP stems from a major concern over its potential negative impact on inter-Arab regional cooperation.

There is also a concern that the EMP will establish a system of vertical cooperation between each Arab country and Europe, thereby jeopardizing horizontal Arab cooperation, especially the prospects of establishing an Arab free trade area. In response to this concern, the eight Arab governments participating in the EMP, in addition to Libya and Mauritania, launched a system of regular consultations to benefit from the experience of the EMP in promoting inter-Arab economic cooperation. The last meeting of this group was held in Cairo, Egypt, in July 1998.

Arab Perceptions of the Economic Aspects of the EMP.

Of all the dimensions of the EMP, the economic ones were the most severely and widely criticized by the Arabs. This is understandable, given the expected strong impact of the EMP on Arab economic security.

The issue of the Arab agricultural exports to the EU was the major stumbling block in the ongoing negotiations. In the case of Egypt, whereas the draft agreement exempted European industrial exports to Egypt from all Egyptian tariff and nontariff barriers, it put restrictions on Egypt's agricultural exports to the EU. The EU offered limited increases in the quotas of Egyptian agricultural exports, extensions of the importation seasons, and granted more agricultural products entry to the EU market. The Egyptians rejected this offer. They argued that the association agreement must maintain a balance between the liberalization of industrial trade and agricultural trade. Each party was entitled to benefit from the areas in which it enjoyed a relative advantage. The liberalization of Egypt's agricultural trade with the EU would not hurt European agriculture as such trade represented a small fraction of the EU's total agricultural production and importation. Further, Egypt was a net importer of European agricultural goods. The EU's agricultural exports to Egypt were almost five times Egypt's agricultural exports to the EU. According to the 1995 statistics, Egypt's agricultural exports to the EU were U.S. $154 million, and its total exports from the EU were U.S. $840 million. The association agreement had to address this trade imbalance if the philosophy of the association were to be based upon the economic development of Egypt and reciprocal commitments. The strategy of the 1977 Egyptian-European protocol that restricted Egyptian agricultural exports to the EU was no longer a viable one, not only because of the new association philosophy, but also because of Egypt's growing exportation potential and the centrality of the agricultural sector to its economy. Almost 56 percent of the Egyptians depended upon this sector. Among the southern Mediterranean economies, the Egyptian economy is the most dependent upon agriculture; that called for a different strategy than the one applied to Tunisia, Morocco, or Israel, countries which had already signed association agreements with the EU.[6]

During the negotiations, Egypt offered the EU four alternatives: (1) full liberalization of agricultural and industrial trade; (2) *de facto* liberalization of Egyptian agricultural exports by exempting more agricultural exports from customs duties and increasing the quotas and exportation seasons, so the value of Egypt's agricultural exports would reach U.S. $1.5 billion; (3) the full liberalization of the exportation of certain Egyptian agricultural exports without quotas; and, (4) any other EU alternative that would create a balance in Egypt-EU agricultural trade.[7] The Egyptians also demanded the removal of unjustified nontariff barriers such as the designation of specific ports for the entry of Egyptian agricultural products and the exaggerated sample quantities required for laboratory testing.

The term "Four Ghosts" referred to four items in the projected association agreement that had generated a public controversy within the Egyptian business community concerning their potential impact on the country's economy. These items were related to Standards and Specifications, Rules of Origin, Intellectual Property Rights, and Competition Policy. Egyptian businessmen argued that these items would act as nontariff barriers, hindering the flow of Egypt's exports to the EU. Egypt's chief negotiator for the agreement, Ambassador Gamal Bayoumi, introduced the term, "the Four Ghosts" of the agreement, to describe these items. In his judgment, business apprehensions about these items were not totally justified. According to him, these items were like ghosts. Once subjected to the light of day, they would disappear.

With regard to Standards and Specifications, the EU proposed to approximate the European rules governing them and to achieve mutual recognition of certificates within this field. Egyptian exporters would have to conform to the EU norms and specifications that were tailored to the needs and tastes of European consumers. Egyptian exports would find it difficult to adapt to these rules in 12 years. According to Farid Khamis, the head of the Egyptian Industries Union, it took Europe 200 years to reach these standards, and it was not fair to force Egypt to conform to them in 12 years.

The second item is the Rules of Origin. The EU proposed a Unified Protocol on this item to all its Mediterranean partners, to be annexed to each agreement. The critics of the proposed agreement argued that the Unified Protocol would impose a ceiling on the value of the nonoriginating materials as a percentage of the total cost of the final product. This was in contradiction with the Uruguay Round Agreements that required a minimum local added value. According to the EU proposed formula, as the total cost of the final product diminishes, the value of the nonoriginating materials should also diminish. As Egypt had a relative advantage in the area of the cost of labor, which means lower final cost, Egypt can only use a limited amount of nonoriginating materials. Khamis argued that this was a nontariff barrier imposed by the EU and would result in the destruction of Egyptian industries. However, Bayoumi pointed out the principle of multilateral and bilateral cumulation in the agreement as a major advantage to Egyptian economy. Such principle would promote regional cooperation.

In the field of Intellectual Property Rights (IPRs), the EU asked Egypt to accede to seven international treaties relating to IPRs. Egypt was already a member of three of these treaties. IPRs would be applied 3 years after the finalization of the agreement. Under the Uruguay Round agreements, Egypt enjoyed a 5-year grace period, extended to 10 years in the case of the pharmaceutical industry.

Whereas some Egyptian academics argued that IPRs would have a positive effect on the flow of foreign direct investments to Egypt, others contended they would constrain Egypt's ability to use modern technology and would negatively influence the pharmaceutical industry and the availability of medicine at reasonable prices.

The fourth "ghost" was the rules governing competition. The EU proposed that its rules of competition should be used as a reference point, arguing that the harmonization of competition legislation was vital for the smooth functioning of economic relations between both sides. This approach would require Egyptian businessmen, in the case of any future trade dispute concerning rules of competition, to resort to European and international law firms within the territories of the EU, which would entail high costs.

The EMP was subjected to severe criticisms by Arab professional and businessmen associations. Perhaps the most crucial of these criticisms were the following:

- The flawed philosophy of the EMP. The EMP evolved around the notion of trade liberalization. Historical experience testifies that such a notion did not necessarily result in economic development. The experience of the East Asian tigers pointed out that they achieved development not because they opened their markets to imported industrial products, but because they had not pursued that strategy.

- No new concessions were given. The EMP did not give Arab nations any more major concessions than those provided under the present Euro-Arab Protocols, such as the 1977 Euro-Egyptian and Euro-Syrian protocols and those under the 1994 Uruguay Round agreements.

- Erosion of Arab industries. Critics of the agreement contended that providing European industrial products with full access to the Arab market would result in the destruction of indigenous industrial production. Arab industries would not be able to compete with European ones, even after the transitional period that was viewed as insufficient to restructure Egyptian industries.[8] Nabil Al-Gaja, the representative of the Syrian private sector in the Euro-Syrian negotiations, argued that Syrian industries will be destroyed, and that the Syrian treasury will lose U.S. $220 million annually as a result of the loss of customs duties.[9]

- Social instability. The critics argued that the destruction of Arab industries resulting from the EMP would lead to the loss of job opportunities. The integration into the European economy would also result in rising social expectations without real economic development. All of this would lead to various forms of social instabilities and dislocations.

- Insufficient European aid. Although the amount of economic aid promised to the Mediterranean countries was the largest in the history of EU-Mediterranean relations, the critics contended that such aid, if compared with what has been promised to Eastern Europe, was insufficient. EU promised Eastern European countries, whose total population was 96 million, aid of U.S. $8.8 billion. But it offered the Mediterranean countries, whose total population was 203 million, only U.S. $6 billion. If one recalls that the Mediterranean countries are less developed than their Eastern European counterparts, one would comprehend the limited aid promised under the EMP.[10]

Arab Perceptions of the Politico-Security Aspects of the EMP.

Although Arab countries accepted the major principles of the political dialogue suggested by the EU, they criticized these principles as lacking a clear reference to the peace process in the Middle East. They argued that the EMP would entail a Mediterranean economic regional cooperation that would include Israel. Such cooperation was not likely to materialize without an agreement on the basic political elements of the future relationships between the Arabs and the Israelis.[11] They contended that, without the Madrid peace process, the Barcelona agreements would have never materialized. Consequently, no progress on the Barcelona formula would be possible without a corresponding progress on the Madrid formula. Barcelona was organically linked with Madrid. As it became clear that the Netanyahu Israeli government was determined to destroy the Madrid process, the Arabs expressed deep misgivings in the second ministerial meeting of the EMP, held in Malta in 1997, on the future of the EMP. The participants failed to agree on the basic principles of a politico-security charter because the Europeans were reluctant to deal with Arab concerns over the Israeli occupation of Arab territories.

Further, the Arabs resented the reluctance of the EU to discuss the issue of the presence of nuclear weapons in the Middle East. Although the Barcelona Declaration referred to the elimination of weapons of mass destruction (WMD) from the Middle East, it tended to focus on chemical and biological weapons, leaving the Israeli nuclear arsenal untouched.

In fact, there is a strong feeling among the Arabs that the EU is giving Israel preferential political and economic treatment that it is not willing to extend to the Arabs. This was clearly spelled out by Egypt's Foreign Minister Amr Moussa in his address at the Euro-Egyptian Cooperation Council in October 1996.

Finally, the establishment by four EU countries of the European Force (EUROFOR) and European Maritime Force (EUROMARFOR) added to Arab apprehensions about Europe's real objectives. The European countries did not consult the Arabs. They suspect that Europe has not ruled out the use of force if it is necessary to achieve European goals.

Conclusion.

Although Arab countries have accepted the principle of establishing an EMP, they have expressed strong misgivings about its likely impact on their economies and the structure of the peace process in the Middle East. The arguments in Egypt, Syria, Tunisia, and Morocco seem to be the same. Arab industries would be destroyed, and Europe is a reluctant partner in the Middle East peace process. As a result, as long as the EU insists on its unidirectional approach, the Arabs will be ambivalent partners in the Barcelona process. This is evident in the case of Tunisia and Morocco. Although the two countries have signed partnership agreements with the EU, they are now having second thoughts about the viability of this process. In Egypt there is a deep concern about the potential impact of the EMP on Egyptian agriculture. Further, the unilateral military actions of some EU countries in the Mediterranean will only serve to reinforce Arab suspicions.

ENDNOTES - CHAPTER 6

1. For a review of the main provisions of the association agreements by a Tunisian scholar, see al-shazly al-Ayary, "The Barcelona Declaration Under the Light of the Euro-Tunisian Association Agreement," *Arab Economic Journal*, Vol. 5, Spring 1996, pp. 5-66.

2. These views were articulated by Ambassador Gamal Bayoumi, in *Al-Ahram* (Cairo), April 28, 1995, and October 23, 1995.

3. Statements by Ibrahim Fawzy, then Minister of Industry, *Al-Ahram,* October 13, 1995.

4. Statements of the Syrian and Libyan representatives at the Arab-Euro meeting in Cairo, *Al-Ahram*, July 27, 1998.

5. Foreign Ministry, Arab Republic of Egypt, "Concept Paper: the Future of the Euro-Mediterranean Cooperation," and mimeo

statements of al-Youssefi, Prime Minister of Morocco, *Al-Hayat*, July 2, 1998.

6. Statements by Saad Nassar, member of the Egyptian delegation to the Euro-Egyptian partnership negotiations, *Al-Ahram*, October 28, 1995, December 16, 1995, April 16, 1996, April 27, 1996, and June 29, 1996.

7. Foreign Ministry of Egypt, 1996.

8. These criticisms were articulated by manufacturers of cars and home appliances. Car manufacturers pleaded for the inclusion of an item that would oblige their European counterparts to import 50-60 percent of the components of their cars from Egypt if it would be exported to Egypt. *Al-Ahram*, April 14, 1998.

9. Quoted in *al-Ra'y Al-Am* (Kuwait), February 13, 1998.

10. For a full review of these criticisms by a Libyan scholar, see A. al-Hussaini, "The European Union and the Future of Arab Foreign Trade," *Arab Economic Journal*, Spring 1998, pp. 31-65.

11. Interview with the ambassador of Egypt to the EU, *Al-Ahram*, July 25, 1996.

CHAPTER 7

THE SECURITY CHALLENGE IN KOSOVO: TOWARD A REGION-STABILIZING SOLUTION

Steven L. Burg

Introduction.

The current violence in Kosovo has already drawn the United States and its NATO partners to the brink of another military intervention in the Balkans. Intervention in Bosnia, however, has demonstrated the difficulty of resolving such conflicts by force alone, as well as the difficulty of extricating oneself from involvement once troops have been deployed. Despite the apparent irreconcilability of the three sides in the Kosovo conflict—the Milosevic leadership in Belgrade, the Albanian leadership in Kosovo clustered around Ibrahim Rugova, and the Kosovo Liberation Army waging an armed struggle against Serbia—there may yet be a way to resolve the conflict short of military intervention. To do so, however, will require the discovery of innovative political solutions to the clash between the claims of an ethnic group to national self-determination, and the claims of a state to preserve its territorial integrity. This is the conflict of competing principles that underlies many such ethno-regional conflicts, and the solution adopted in Kosovo may well determine the course of similar conflicts elsewhere in the Balkans; most immediately, of course, in neighboring Macedonia, where a large Albanian minority with close ties to Kosovo is waging its own struggle for greater recognition.[1]

There is no way to reconcile the competing and conflicting claims of the Serbs and Albanians to historical or political "ownership" of Kosovo. Any explicit effort to choose between these claims must result in failure. Instead, a solution must focus on stabilizing medium-term relations between Belgrade and Kosovo without shutting off any future options, so as to permit the negotiation of a longer-term solution. The process of resolving the conflict must first provide an interim agreement that immediately alleviates the present state of repression in Kosovo and begins restoring both Kosovo and Yugoslavia to "normal" social, political, and especially economic activity. It should contribute in the medium-term to weakening the social bases of support for violence among both Kosovar Albanians and Serbs, and open possibilities for democratic development in Kosovo and the rest of Yugoslavia, without which no longer-term solution is possible. Interim arrangements should give way quickly to transitional arrangements that create pathways to a lasting negotiated resolution of the conflict. Neither the interim agreement nor the transitional arrangements should preclude either side from pursuing its long-term goals through continuing peaceful negotiations.

The scholarly literature on ethnic conflict focuses on three main strategies for managing conflict: integration, power-sharing, and partition.[2] Four European examples of the application of one or more of these approaches to the solution of ethno-regional conflict are sometimes cited as potential "models" for the solution of the conflict in Kosovo: the power-sharing approach adopted in Belgium,[3] the cultural and territorial autonomy strategy adopted in the South Tyrol/Alto Adige region of Italy,[4] the partition strategy adopted in the Jura region of Switzerland,[5] and the autonomous communities/devolution strategy adopted in response to ethno-regionalisms in Spain.[6] These models have drawn the attention of Western scholars and some Serbian analysts.[7] Developments in Spain, in particular, are now the object of intensive scrutiny sponsored by the Belgrade regime.[8] Kosovar Albanian writers, in contrast, have focused in their public discourse almost exclusively on arguments denying Serbian claims to rule over Kosovo and advancing Kosovar claims to outright independence for the region.[9] The recent example of the settlement negotiated in Northern Ireland, which incorporates elements of power-sharing, may now also draw the attention of Westerners or Serbs interested in solving the crisis in Kosovo. But none of these conflicts was/is directly equivalent to the conditions present in Kosovo, and none of these solutions can be applied wholesale to the Kosovo conflict. Rather, selected elements of these examples of the successful management of ethno-regional conflict must be adapted to the particular, and difficult conditions in Kosovo.

Constraints.

A solution to the conflict in Kosovo must take into account certain constitutional, political, economic, and regional parameters, which are themselves in some ways contradictory. Constitutionally, Kosovo is a region within Serbia, which is itself a republic of the federation of Yugoslavia. This is the status presently recognized and supported by the international community as part of its efforts to underscore the inviolability of borders in the region. This simple fact distinguishes the conflict in Kosovo from that in Bosnia-Herzegovina and complicates its solution. It is also the status on which the Serbian leadership insists, and on which the Serbs base their opposition to international third party involvement in what they define as an "internal" matter. Yet, the refusal to recognize or accept this status is at the heart of the nationalist resistance movement among the ethnically Albanian Kosovars. The Kosovar Albanians argue that the constitutional/international legitimacy of this status ceased to exist when the former Yugoslavia ceased to exist. Kosovar leaders further argue that the persistent pattern of repression and abuse carried out by the present Serbian regime negates any claim it might have to rule over Kosovo. The apparent deadlock between Serb and Albanian positions is, in many ways, similar to the deadlock between Republican and Unionist positions in Northern Ireland prior to negotiations. Kosovar leaders, however, insist on their right to establish their own independent state rather than demanding immediate integration with the Albanian state across the border—although many Kosovars openly advocate integration of all Albanian populated territories into a "greater Albania."

No formula that retains the existing constitutional status of the province—or simply returns to the *status quo* prior to 1988—will be acceptable to the Kosovars. Indeed, no Kosovar political leadership can afford to accept such a formula in the face of the armed opposition of the Kosovo Liberation Army (UCK), which has demonstrated its readiness to assassinate individuals it deems to have betrayed its nationalist-separatist goals. Hence, any solution to the Kosovo conflict must reconcile the contradictory—indeed, seemingly irreconcilable—Serb and Albanian positions by finding some formulation that addresses both the demand for independence and the demand to uphold territorial integrity, and thereby gives both the moderate Kosovar Albanian leadership and the Serbian supporters of compromise some basis for mobilizing their respective constituencies in support of a settlement.

Politically, a compromise settlement must also take into account the fact that Serbian leaders and many Serbs—including intellectuals otherwise inclined toward "liberal" positions on the national issue—fear the consequences of Albanian participation in Serbian, or even Yugoslav politics.[10] For the local Serbs of Kosovo, the return of the Albanians to formal political participation raises the threat that the Serbs of Kosovo might be reduced to an oppressed minority—a fear magnified by the prospect that Kosovo might become independent. For Milosevic, the return of Albanian voters, and the representation and participation of a self-governing Kosovo entity in the federation raises the prospect of a weakening of his hold on power—both locally, in Kosovo, and on the level of the federation. At the same time, however, the Kosovar Albanians refuse to participate in either Serbian or Yugoslav politics, for they view such participation as acknowledging or even legitimating the constitutional status to which they object. They view participation as undermining their claim to full independence as the only acceptable expression of their right to self-determination. For the Kosovars to accept a settlement, therefore, it must hold out at least the possibility—if not the inevitability—that further negotiations would result in independence.[11] This is an inevitability that some Serbian intellectuals already accept—they are concerned not so much with preventing independence for Kosovo (or some part of it) as with preventing independence for Kosovo from becoming a precedent for the further disintegration of Serbia.[12] This perspective opens the possibility of achieving an interim solution that affirms territorial integrity, but leaves the door open to later separation, as does the Northern Ireland agreement.

Thus, while Serbian leaders refuse to recognize Kosovar claims to independence, they do not wish to see the Albanians re-enter Serbian and Yugoslav political life. The Serbian leadership (Milosevic) would be content to allow the Albanian refusal to participate in Serbian or Yugoslav institutions to go on indefinitely. Indeed, for many Serbs, the prospect that Kosovar Albanians might have influence over internal Serbian matters, as they did under the provisions of the 1974 Yugoslav and Serbian constitutions, is unacceptable. Hence, any solution to the Kosovo conflict that attempts to uphold the territorial integrity of Serbia and Yugoslavia—as may be required by the regional constraints noted below—must include some form of participation in a common state. But, it must also allow the Serb and Albanian communities each to avoid the influence, or perceived domination, of the other at either the local or federal levels. Such contradictory arrangements are characteristic of the power-sharing approach as adopted in Belgium, and of the autonomy/devolution strategy adopted in Spain.

Some Serbs assign special emotional significance to Kosovo because of the importance of the region in the historical development of the Serbian nation—an argument often couched in terms of Kosovo as the "Jerusalem" of the Serbs.[13] However, Albanian analysts sometimes make similar arguments about Kosovo, centered on the historical importance of events in Prizren for the formation of the modern Albanian nation.[14] Other Serbs outside of Kosovo focus their concerns on the fate of the many important Serb cultural institutions and monuments in Kosovo, such as the monasteries of Pec, Decani, and Gracanica, rather than on the region as a whole. Any settlement of the conflict over Kosovo will have to address at least these specific concerns in an effort to defuse the larger emotional issue among the Serbs. Yet it will have to do so in a manner that does not devalue or neglect the cultural and historical institutions of the Albanians.

Opposition to any settlement can be expected to be fierce within some constituencies in Serbia. For nationalist-extremist Serbs who win election to the Serbian/Yugoslav parliament from Kosovo, the return of Albanian voters to the Serbian and Yugoslav electorate will eliminate their *sinecures* and, perhaps, reduce their numbers in parliament. Some Serbian analysts suggest that Serbs who emigrated from Kosovo might become a base for political opposition to such a settlement and to any Serbian politician who agreed to it. It is therefore essential that any settlement be accompanied by the delivery of concrete benefits to Serbia that can be used to mobilize support among the general population. Nor can a settlement allow the continued impoverishment of the Kosovo population. Economic assistance to the province will be required to create support within the Kosovar population for a peaceful approach, and draw support away from the UCK. Extensive economic authority over the region will have to shift from Belgrade to Pristina. But the Serbs are unlikely to sign any such agreement unless it offers parallel benefits to Serbia/Yugoslavia. While assistance to Kosovo will most likely require the allocation of even more resources than are presently being committed through the U.S. Agency for

International Development (USAID) and other Western agencies, economic benefits can be delivered to Serbia most easily by matching Serbian implementation of each agreement with the lifting of economic and other sanctions, on a carefully linked basis.

Finally, a solution to the Kosovo conflict must be constructed with certain regional constraints in mind. The most immediate of these are the probable consequences of a settlement in Kosovo for Albanian-Macedonian relations in Macedonia. The large and restive ethnic Albanian population in Macedonia is territorially concentrated in provinces along the borders with Kosovo and Albania, and is closely linked to both Kosovo and Albania through personal, familial, and political ties. Although political views among the Albanians of Macedonia are diverse, there are strong popular sentiments and political support for ethno-regional autonomy, or even outright independence. The UCK has claimed responsibility for isolated bombings carried out in Macedonia, and may be active in the country. The formula adopted in Kosovo must therefore underscore the territorial integrity of Yugoslavia and, perhaps, even Serbia, if it is not to lead almost immediately to the disintegration of Macedonia. Similarly, nationalist Serbs in Bosnia (*Republika Srpska*) will scrutinize any settlement in Kosovo to find a basis for legitimating their own claims to independence on the basis of self-determination, as will some Montenegrins, Muslims in the Sandzak, and Hungarians in Vojvodina. For a solution in Kosovo to avoid escalating conflicts in these neighboring regions, it must provide clearly for the territorial integrity of the existing state (Serbia and Yugoslavia) within the limits imposed by the need to accommodate Kosovar Albanian demands. Such an approach does not, it should be made clear, constitute "rewarding Serbia." Indeed, if elements of the settlement contribute to democratization in Serbia, then it will produce additional pressure for change in the current regime.

Relevance of Other Cases.

The clash between ethno-regional demands for autonomy or independence and the claims of an existing state to sovereignty and territorial integrity, as well as the presence of an armed movement carrying out violent action against state authority, was/is common to most of the other European cases of ethno-regionalism cited above. The Basque ETA and the Irish Republic Army (IRA) provide close parallels to the Kosovar UCK. The intensity of the conflict in Kosovo has already reached levels equal to, or more deadly than the worst period of "troubles" in Northern Ireland. In South Tyrol and the Jura, in contrast, violence was more limited and, in the Jura, of more limited duration. In Belgium, and in the Catalan region of Spain, there was little or no violence associated with claims to self-rule. Yet, even in the cases of violent conflict, peaceful settlements were reached. The ethno-regional conflicts in Belgium, Spain, Switzerland, and Italy all have been resolved and institutionalized, and the conflict in Northern Ireland now appears headed toward the institutionalization of a peaceful settlement. These successes may be attributable to factors and conditions that are not—as yet—present in Kosovo. One of the challenges in forging a settlement in Kosovo, therefore, is to induce conflict-resolving behaviors in the conflicting parties in the absence of these factors.

All five European ethno-regional conflicts were resolved in the context of democratic states, although the conflicts in Spain each involved a centuries-long history of center-periphery tensions, and a decades-long history of cultural repression under the fascist authoritarian regime that preceded democracy. The autonomy/devolution strategy adopted in Spain was an essential element of the transition to democracy itself. Democratization and devolution/autonomy were mutually-reinforcing processes in Spain. Nevertheless, the negotiations of regional autonomy agreements were long and contentious processes, in which central institutions proved resistant to relinquishing power to the regions. Moreover, democratization and devolution/autonomy did not immediately end the violence in the Basque lands. Indeed, ETA violence, and especially the use of the military in a counterinsurgency role, endangered not only democracy, but devolution as well. Violence in the Basque lands ended only when the successful development of the autonomous ethno-regional community within a democratic Spain, and the deepening of a democratic political culture, undermined the popular legitimacy of ETA demands and methods. The support of the European Community for democratization, and especially the promise of membership contingent on democratization was an important factor contributing to success in the Spanish case. Both Basque and Catalan nationalists—like ethno-regional leaders in Belgium—recognized that the Spanish state provided a path, or gateway to membership in the European Community, which they highly valued and which was not otherwise available to them.

Successful resolution of the conflict in Northern Ireland has taken place in the context of two well-institutionalized democratic states—the United Kingdom and the Republic of Ireland—that exercised enormous influence over the conflicting parties. The convergence of interests between these two states in ending the violence and achieving a peaceful settlement, and their commitment to democratic principles of governance that enjoy widespread legitimacy in the population of Northern Ireland itself, pushed the conflict toward settlement. Similarly, the South Tyrol conflict was settled in large part through negotiations between democratic states—that is, between the state within whose territory the conflict was taking place (Italy), and the neighboring state with which the local minority identified, or at least shared an ethnic identity (Austria). The commitment of the external, "homeland" state (or European Community, in the case of Spain) to democratic processes, and especially its rejection of the violent alternative, eliminated an important basis of resistance to negotiated settlement on the part of the nationalist-separatist/independence movement. However, as the Basque, Tyrolian, and Northern Ireland cases demonstrate, violence in the form of terrorist acts often continues to occur even after a conflict is well on the road to solution. Security arrangements that address this problem, and which are acceptable to both sides, are therefore essential elements in a negotiated solution to such conflicts.

The democratic context, and especially the strength of a democratic political culture, was an especially important factor in Belgium, and Switzerland as well. In these cases, the inclination and institutional mechanisms to resolve conflicts through compromise were already well-established. The principle that all interests should be represented and participate in decisionmaking processes in Belgium pre-dated the rise of ethno-regionalism. Representation of ethno-regional identities and interests was thus introduced into the Belgian party system without major upheaval in the 1960s. This facilitated the process of constitutional change and the institutionalization of ethno-regionalism in the 1970s. Paradoxically, a similar process of institutionalizing such cleavages in national decisionmaking institutions and processes was unfolding in the former Yugoslavia at the same time. But in the Belgian case, power-sharing facilitated an increasingly-complete dismantling of the common state through peaceful means, and creation of distinct, ethnically-defined, territorial entities with increasingly comprehensive independent decisionmaking authority. There is now little left of the Belgian state over which the territorial entities can argue, other than the existence of the state itself. In the former Yugoslavia, in contrast, power-sharing produced deadlock, which accelerated the descent into war. Although political culture is difficult to quantify, there is little doubt that the inclination to democratic compromise in Belgium and Switzerland is a critical factor in explaining successful conflict resolution in these states, and that that inclination cannot be established in Yugoslavia in the short-run, if ever.

Two factors appear to have held Belgium together throughout the dismantling process. One was the continued presence of a shared identity that overarches the ethno-regional identities. The second, and more important factor was the presence of interests and identities that cut across the ethno-regions and provide the basis for common political action in central decisionmaking institutions. The most important of these, of course, has been class identity, and the class interests and political agendas that cut across the ethno-regions. The presence of common, cross-cutting interests and identities led to preservation of the unified market and, therefore, the requisite common monetary, financial, and other economic institutions and functions of the Belgian state. In Spain, too, the disintegrative effects of devolution and the creation of autonomous communities were counterbalanced by strong economic interests that linked Catalonia and the Basque lands to the rest of Spain. Perhaps the most important factor contributing to peacefulness in Belgium as well as Spain, however, has been the strongly democratic character of the state, and the resultant high level of legitimacy of existing decision-making processes. Democratic legitimacy created the certainty that no single actor could or would attempt unilaterally to override a decision arrived at through established decisionmaking processes. In Belgium, these factors contributed to moderating the expanding mutual veto power enjoyed by each of the ethno-linguistic/regional groups, making compromise on the dismantling of common state institutions and the devolution of state powers possible.

Power-sharing has led to a more complete dismantling of the state in Belgium than in Spain. That dismantling process is unlikely to go further because of the apparent absence of any further economic or material gains to be made by the regional leaderships from eliminating the common state entirely, the difficulty of resolving the status of certain ethno-linguistic border regions (including Brussels), and the unpredictability of the consequences of full dissolution for membership in the European Union. In the absence of such limiting factors, the features of power-sharing might very well have provided the institutional and organizational foundations for successful partition of the Belgian state.

In the Swiss case, both the principle of local self-determination and the mechanism of territorial partition were recognized long before the political movement for an independent Jura intensified its efforts and a separate group initiated violence. The path toward a peaceful settlement was initiated when Bern cantonal authorities responded to separatist intransigence by opening a reconsideration of the issue that did not exclude any outcome. Partition was carried out through a series of changes to the Bern Canton constitution and referenda at the regional (Jura), district, and local (commune) levels that allowed local communities to express and—under certain conditions—to act on their preferences, independently of the overall majority. (A referendum on the federal level to amend the Swiss constitution was the final step in the process.) As a result, the creation of the Jura canton left Bern divided into noncontiguous areas. Despite provocation by separatist extremists that included the use of violence, and the escalation of tensions that accompanied some local referenda,[15] the entire process of partition was carried out peacefully, and with due regard for the preferences of minority populations that constituted local majorities.

Thus, in all the cases cited above, the prior existence of well-established democratic political cultures or the presence of influential and democratic outside actors committed to peaceful settlement, or both, were important factors contributing to successful conflict resolution. In some cases, mechanisms for addressing demands for self-rule were already well-established, such as the power-sharing principles operating in Belgium and the principles of partition and territorial self-rule operating in Switzerland, and these were applied to the conflict at hand. In other cases, new arrangements were negotiated by actors committed to both democracy and peace, as in Spain and Northern Ireland. In all cases, however, the process of resolution—from immediate or interim settlement to eventual partition—was agreed in advance; that is, political actors on both sides defined the "road map" for resolving the conflict and then adhered to it. Willingness of Kosovar Albanian and Serbian leaders to agree on such a road map thus represents only the first step in the settlement process; they must also adhere to it even in the face of internal opposition.

The pluralism of political actors in the regions was a critical element in the ability of regimes and regional actors to negotiate settlements in Belgium, Switzerland, Spain, Italy, and Northern Ireland. In each of the ethno-regions, the nationalist-separatist or independence movement—and especially the advocates of violence—faced political competition from other parties or movements interested in compromise, or even loyal to the larger state. In some cases, the constituency of support for compromise and moderation was rooted in "immigrant" populations with strong ties to the larger state. But economic interest—the economic ties of local actors to the larger state and its market (or the larger European market accessible through that state)—played a key moderating role in Belgium and in both Catalonia and the Basque lands of Spain. Thus, democratic culture, political pluralism, and cross-cutting economic (and therefore, political) interests, as well as supportive external actors, are important factors explaining successful cases of ethno-regional conflict resolution. Most of these conditions are not as yet present in Kosovo. However, while neither the neighboring "homeland" state (Albania) nor the existing state (Yugoslavia/Serbia) is democratic or supportive of negotiating a solution, other external actors (including the United States and the European Union) may be able to provide incentives to negotiate an interim settlement, and to assist in mobilizing popular support for an interim settlement once it is concluded. In order to increase the probability of a stable, long-term solution, an interim settlement should be constructed so as to support processes of pluralization and, eventually, democratization in both Serbia and Kosovo. But one should have no illusions about the difficulties of negotiating a long-term solution in the absence of genuine democracy in either Serbia or Kosovo.

Mechanisms adopted for the management of ethno-regional conflicts in nondemocratic contexts share many of the characteristics of the settlements achieved in democratic contexts. In Russia, for example, the dispute between Moscow and Tatarstan over sovereignty was settled by the devolution of limited self-administration authority to Tatarstan, which included symbolic concessions to the statehood of the territory. Although the February 1994 treaty located most authority in the federation, it did give local government control over natural resources, housing and family law, and granted the right to alternative military service to the local population. The treaty assigned joint authority to the federation and local republic governments in the administration of transportation, social welfare (including health, culture, sport, and education and research), and police and security services. Agreement between Tatarstan and Russia was, to be sure, facilitated by two unique structural factors: first, the fact that Tatarstan is located wholly within Russia, with no other international borders; and second, the large proportion of ethnic Russians in the population and the important roles they play in the local economy. Russia faced no realistic security threat from the Tatarstan sovereignty movement.

The situation in Chechnya offers a sharp contrast to the situation in Tatarstan. In Chechnya, the conflict between Moscow and local nationalists/separatists was especially violent, and Moscow realized that it could not achieve a military solution to the conflict. It was this realization that led to agreements that de-escalated the armed conflict through a withdrawal of Russian forces, stabilized local government, and restored some degree of confidence by establishing joint Russian-Chechnyan administrative bodies. These agreements opened the door to peaceful negotiation of a political settlement by freezing the status of the region for 5 years. But they did not provide a long-lasting solution. In both Tatarstan and Chechnya, de-escalation of the conflict involved significant concessions by the center to local self-administration and, in the case of Chechnya, opened opportunities to negotiate more extensive local autonomy.

Once regional conflict in a nondemocratic context turns violent, however, there is a tendency for it to become prolonged, and to be resolved by force. The conflict in the Sudan between the Muslim government and secessionist Christian forces in the south remains unresolved even after 15 years of conflict. In Ethiopia, the Eritrean secessionist movement succeeded only after a 30-year armed struggle that ended with a military victory over the government and cost 500,000 lives. In Sri Lanka, it was the government that eventually achieved a costly military victory over Tamil separatists after 15 years of fighting. But even where one side or the other has achieved a military victory, violence has reemerged, fueled by the lack of a political resolution of the ethno-cultural and political issues at the foundation of the conflict. Thus, a political agreement between the conflicting parties that resolves these issues (or at least provides mechanisms for reducing frictions over them) seems essential to a stable settlement. Indeed, the failures of intervention by outside forces to resolve the conflicts between the Kurds and Iraq, between Armenian secessionists in Nagorno-Karabakh and the Azerbaidzhani government, and between the Sri Lankan government and secessionist Tamils, caution against becoming involved in any intervention in the absence of a prior political agreement between the warring sides—even if that agreement is imposed by outside pressures.

Potential Elements of an Interim Settlement.

External Supports. Elements of the devolutionary strategies negotiated in democratic and nondemocratic cases can be adapted to devise a settlement for Kosovo. But the clear absence of democratic political cultures on both sides of the Kosovo conflict will require outside actors to provide significant negative and positive incentives for each side to accept norms of behavior consistent with a peaceful settlement. Salient external actors must establish clear limits on the aspirations or expectations of local actors. They must promise and deliver rewards for compliance with these limits, as well as imposing costs on those who violate them. The ethnic "homeland" state—Albania—must not only support a peaceful settlement, but it must actively reject the violent alternative. While it may be unreasonable to expect any leadership of Albania publicly to oppose the UCK, that leadership can—with support from the United States and Europe—exercise more effective control over its border so as to reduce the flow of arms and other supplies to the UCK. The leadership of Albania can also provide important political support to a Kosovar leadership that undertakes the task of negotiating a settlement. Outside actors will also have to provide the negative and positive incentives necessary to persuade the "host" state—Serbia/Yugoslavia—to forego violence and repression as a solution and open the door to negotiating a solution without excluding any outcome in advance; a commitment that will have to be matched by the Kosovar Albanian leadership despite its apparent inability to control the UCK.

The Kosovar Albanian leadership is internally divided on the basis of both politics and personality. In the absence of significant progress, the Kosovar Albanian leadership may quickly fall prey to the internal violence characteristic of the Chechens—an outcome even more likely in light of the apparent absence of any linkages between political leaders around Rugova or opposed to him and the armed UCK.

The Violence/Security Issues. It will be difficult, if not impossible, for the Kosovar Albanian leadership around Rugova to enter into actual negotiations (as opposed to more tentative "talks about talks") as long as the present level of violence and repression continues. Certainly, no negotiations can succeed as long as there is no improvement in conditions. Hence, significant steps must be taken by Serbia/Yugoslavia to normalize conditions in Kosovo in order to get meaningful negotiations underway. These steps, beginning with the lifting of the state of emergency declared in 1989, would constitute confidence-building measures rather than a solution to the conflict. To take such steps would, however, raise an immediate security dilemma for Serbia/Yugoslavia: how will security be assured in the face of UCK violence?

In other cases of ethno-regional conflict that turned violent, such incidents continued to occur even after the conflict moved toward settlement (as in the Basque, Tyrolian, Northern Ireland cases) or after an apparent agreement or demilitarization had been reached (Chechnya). The deployment of NATO forces to Albania and Macedonia to assist in securing the borders of Kosovo against the infiltration of arms and guerrilla forces from these states (and against the movement of armed guerilla forces from Kosovo into Macedonia) can play an important role in preventing further escalation of the violence inside Kosovo, and thereby make it somewhat easier for the Yugoslav government to de-escalate its own use of force in the region. It can also help prevent spillover of the conflict into neighboring countries. The deployment of NATO forces inside Kosovo to prevent such violence is not practical.

NATO forces cannot be deployed under conditions that would leave them defending a situation that might easily become defense of the *status quo* rather than progress toward a settlement (the fate of the U.N. Protection Force (in Bosnia) or, even more problematic, the *defacto* dismemberment of a state through armed intervention—an act likely to arouse considerable opposition in the United

Nations and other multilateral organizations from other states vulnerable to internal ethnic conflict. Deployment of NATO forces inside Kosovo will produce a *defacto* partition along the lines of deployment. If NATO troops are deployed in an effort to end the violence in the province, they may very well face the task of suppressing UCK violence. A NATO air campaign directed against Serbia and Serb targets in Kosovo would almost certainly encourage such violence. Short of a NATO intervention in support of an independent Kosovo, the Yugoslav leadership will insist on its right to defend the security and territorial integrity of the state.

The right of a state to defend its security and integrity is one that the Yugoslavs cannot be expected to give up. But efforts to end the violence associated with other ethno-regional conflicts suggest how the exercise of that right by the Yugoslavs can be subjected to scrutiny and constraints. In the Basque lands, where a terrorist organization remained actively opposed to an emerging settlement, the security issue was addressed through creation of a joint Basque-Spanish security commission. A key element in the Khasavyurt accord ending the fighting in Chechnya was the establishment of similar joint Russian-Chechnyan commissions. In Kosovo, the creation of a joint security commission consisting of Yugoslav (federal) Serbian, Kosovar Albanian, and international actors might provide an equivalent solution.

Such an organization could provide effective verification of events, and oversee a rapid, phased reduction to "normal" levels of the military and special police units in the province—or to levels consistent with the level of violence that continues to be directed against the regime. It could also begin the process of reforming civil police organizations in the province. This commission could also exercise international monitoring of judicial and penal institutions in the province. The presence of international monitors would serve the interests of both the Yugoslav/Serbian leadership (intent on retaining the ability to defend itself against what it defines as terrorist acts, as well as against unfounded charges of repression) and the Kosovar leadership (intent on defending its people against the use of force for repression and intimidation).

However, it is important to note that even in democratic Spain, use of the military in a counterinsurgency role nearly derailed the regional autonomy approach. Cooperation between the Serbian and Kosovar Albanian leaderships is not likely to be achieved if the extensive use of force against the Kosovo population is sustained for much longer, and especially not if it escalates. But, in the almost certain event of continued attacks by the UCK after the onset of negotiations or implementation of an interim agreement, the joint security commission will be faced with the challenge of overseeing the legitimate use of force in Kosovo.

Only the accession of the UCK to a cease-fire agreement can avoid this dilemma. In Northern Ireland, the IRA participated in peace talks through its political party, *Sinn Fein*. The talks produced an agreement in principle on the necessity of decommissioning (disarmament) by all paramilitary organizations, to be overseen by an independent international commission. While disarmament has not yet taken place and is unlikely ever to take place, the agreement in principle contributed to establishing an atmosphere supportive of a cease-fire. In Kosovo, however, no existing political party appears to have such links to the UCK, and the UCK has not yet established a political party of its own. Any Kosovar Albanian leadership committed to negotiating a settlement of the conflict will therefore have to establish its influence, if not some degree of control, over the UCK if it is to make any cease-fire agreement credible. This might be possible if Kosovar Albanian leaders could deliver both a reduction in Yugoslav security/military forces in Kosovo, and international monitoring of the forces that remain. But it is unlikely to happen if Western involvement appears aimed too clearly at supporting independence for Kosovo.

The negotiations over Northern Ireland also produced a commitment by the British government to "normalization of security arrangements and practices" and "as early a return as possible to normal security arrangements in Northern Ireland, *consistent with the level of threat and a published overall strategy.*"[16] This formulation offers a possible solution to the dilemma of reconciling the Serbian/Yugoslav government's insistence on the right to combat what it views as terrorism, and the Kosovar Albanian demand that violence against the civilian population be halted.

International Monitoring. The restoration and expansion of international monitoring missions in Yugoslavia would be required in order to establish such a joint security commission. But no restoration of international monitoring missions is likely to take place until Yugoslavia's insistence on restoration of its membership in the Organization for Security and Cooperation in Europe (OSCE) is addressed. Hence, the initial steps toward negotiations over the future status of Kosovo will require a complex set of tradeoffs among Kosovar, Serbian (Yugoslav), and international actors.

Yugoslav leaders will have to accept the return of OSCE monitoring missions to their country, and a significant expansion of the authority of OSCE monitors in Kosovo to enable them to participate effectively in a joint Kosovar-Serbian-Yugoslav-OSCE security commission. It is unlikely that nongovernment organizations could supply the police/military expertise necessary to the success of such a commission. The OSCE-NATO relationship might provide the institutional means through which to furnish such expertise, but without involving NATO as an organization on the ground inside Kosovo.

Kosovar leaders will have to accept "normalization" with international monitoring instead of independence as a short-term outcome, as well as the right of the Yugoslav government to continue to carry out security operations *consistent with the level of threat,* and conducted in a manner *consistent with OSCE human and civil rights norms.* Agreement on "normalization of security arrangements and practices" should include an explicit plan for the phased reduction of the number of Yugoslav security and military forces in the region over time. Agreement on "normalization" and international monitoring should be accompanied by agreement between Serbian/Yugoslav leaders and Kosovar Albanian leaders to enter into good-faith negotiation over the longer-term status of the province. Successful implementation of the normalization/monitoring agreement and the onset of good-faith negotiations should be recognized by the international community as a sign of significant progress, and result in some improvement in the status of Yugoslavia in the international community.

"Joint Administration." Initial negotiations should therefore be focused at the outset on achieving a "normalization" of social and political conditions in Kosovo, paralleling the "normalization" of security arrangements. "Normalization" should not be understood as a solution in itself, but as a means of creating conditions under which the compromises necessary to achieve a solution might become possible. The "normalization" of social, economic, and political conditions in the province will require an immediate interim resolution of the ongoing dispute between the Albanian Kosovar and Serbian leaderships over the division of competencies between Serbian and Kosovar authorities, so as to permit public institutions such as schools and health facilities to function normally.

The deployment of NATO forces to Albania and Macedonia, a step that would strengthen the security dimensions of this package, need not and should not be part of the interim agreement itself. But deployment should be undertaken as a means of supporting the operation of the joint security commission described above, as well as strengthening NATO intervention capabilities.

Potential "Transitional" Arrangements.

The interim agreement outlined above consists very largely of confidence-building measures. They do not constitute a solution to the conflict over control of Kosovo. In order to provide a medium-term, or "transitional" solution to the constitutional issues surrounding Kosovo in a manner that does not destabilize the region, it will be necessary to grant substantial independence to the Kosovar Albanians, but not necessarily to Kosovo. This distinction between territory and ethnic community lies at the heart of the Belgian approach. It allows each ethno-linguistic group to exercise the right of "self-determination" through "self-administration" of those activities most directly related to ethno-linguistic cultural identity. Such self-administration of cultural affairs transcends, rather than replaces, territorial divisions. Thus, the Albanian and Serbian "communities" of Kosovo could be granted extensive powers of self-administration in such areas as education and occupational training; youth, sport, and cultural activities; and the media, although the precise areas of cultural self-administration would have to be left to negotiations between the parties themselves.

At the same time, self-administering territories or regions could be established within Kosovo, based primarily on the ethnic composition of the population. Elected authorities in these self-administering regions would take over the formulation and implementation of public policies with respect to such matters as local planning, public works (roads, transportation, utilities, etc.) housing, agriculture, local resources management, and other activities usually associated with local government. As in Belgium, ethnically-mixed areas might be designated as dual-culture regions (Prishtina and Pec, for example, might be treated in a manner analogous to the treatment of Brussels) and existing administrative units (*opstina*) that overlap a demographic divide might be divided between regions (as Brabant was divided between the Flemish region, the

Walloon region, and Brussels). Regional authorities would be prohibited from actions that violate the rights of citizens, including the rights of citizens to exercise self-administration over cultural affairs through their cultural "communities." Particularly significant cultural institutions or monuments of a cultural community would be subject to the administration of that cultural community rather than the region in which they are located, although the cultural community would necessarily have to negotiate with the regional authority over a whole host of practical issues. The definition of objects subject to such administration would be determined through negotiations, but could be facilitated by reference to the already existing list of significant historical/cultural monuments established during the communist era, with the participation of Kosovar Albanian communist officials. The extra-territorial dimension of cultural self-administration would address Serbian concerns outlined earlier.

The territory of Kosovo would thus encompass two self-administering cultural communities (Albanian and Serbian) and a number of self-administering regions (to be determined through negotiation, but including regions with predominantly Albanian population, predominantly Serbian population, and mixed population). Although there has been some public discussion in Yugoslavia of a recent proposal to devolve governmental authority in Serbia to geographical regions, the self-administering regions proposed here involve the creation of substantially smaller units (the regional devolution proposal foresees the division of Kosovo into two regions: "Metohija" and "Kosovo").

Because of the presently nondemocratic nature of the Yugoslav/Serbian state, the national judicial institutions of the state cannot be relied upon to provide just judgments when the actions of public authorities in Kosovo are challenged by citizens claiming the violation of their rights. An alternative path for citizen challenges to public authority can be established by incorporating the right of citizens to appeal to European transnational institutions, as is the case even in the agreement on Northern Ireland. To establish such a right, however, would require the admission of Yugoslavia into the corresponding transnational organizations—an additional reason for including this as part of the initial, confidence-building measures outlined earlier.

The need to secure justice in Kosovo extends to the victims of past repression, as well. The return of Kosovar Albanian personnel who left or were expelled from public institutions is one element of the interim agreement and must be achieved expeditiously. As part of the transitional arrangements, a judicial review process must be established for cases involving arrests, prosecutions, and convictions for activities protected by the human and civil rights norms articulated in Helsinki documents and usually not considered criminal in democratic states. Because the Helsinki process documents are not binding treaties and because these documents contain potentially contradictory elements to which the Serbian and Kosovar sides may simultaneously appeal, it may be necessary to obtain international representation in the judicial review process to secure the interpretation of these documents in a manner consistent with democratic norms. As in Belgium, and more recently Northern Ireland, the organization and decisionmaking rules of the provincial organs of government would have to incorporate power-sharing principles that assured each group the opportunity to participate in, and influence the shape of, each decision. The adoption of such principles in Kosovo must avoid the deadlock of a mutual veto, and can do so if most governmental functions are devolved to the communities and regions. Moreover, establishment of both cultural and regional communities with their own separately-elected authorities would create opportunities for the emergence of inter-ethnic cooperation among those responsible for technical, or functional issues in the regions and, perhaps, the emergence of shared values and interests among them. This might contribute to moderating tensions during the ongoing negotiations over the longer-term status of the province.

Provincial-Republic Relations. As a transitional measure, Kosovo would have to be granted "self-administering" (i.e., autonomous) status. All autonomous power of self-administration would be exercised by the elected leaderships of the self-administering cultural communities with respect to cultural affairs. The kinds of activities to be carried out by these communities was suggested above, but the precise list of legal competencies of these communities would have to be negotiated by the two sides. With respect to local or regional affairs, the autonomous power of self-administration granted to the province would be exercised by the elected governments of the self-administering regions, with the precise list of competencies to be negotiated.

Provincial-Federal Relations. Provincial-federal relations are at the heart of the conflict over Kosovo. The "transitional" arrangements for Kosovo must include the convening of further negotiations on long-term arrangements for governing the province itself and defining its relationship to the rest of Yugoslavia. This is necessary in order to make it possible for Kosovars to participate in federal institutions without fear that, by doing so, they will give up the opportunity to change them. But it must also make it possible for them to continue to boycott such participation. Some changes in the federal parliament paralleling those outlined for the republic parliament may be necessary as part of the transitional arrangements. These may include defining the size and composition of the Kosovar parliamentary delegation, as well as its role in parliamentary decisionmaking.

From a "Transitional" to a Long-Term Solution.

Power-sharing in the context of a province that is still part of Serbia and continued subordination to the federation in international and security affairs is unlikely to satisfy the demands for independence on the part of Kosovar Albanians. These relationships must become the focus of further negotiations, with no limits on their eventual outcome. Movement toward further autonomy for Kosovo in these areas is, effectively, movement toward independence. The so-called "third republic" scenario, in which Kosovo is separated from Serbia to become the third republic in the Yugoslav federation, is widely seen as little more than a step toward what the Serbs see as "secession," and the independence demanded by the Kosovar Albanians. Thus, if the issue of independence is to be dealt with, it must be dealt with directly, and the outstanding issues of concern to both sides must become the subjects of explicit negotiation.

It is important to define as early as possible the actual mechanisms, or process, by which independence might be secured. But negotiation of a separation process should not begin until at least the transitional arrangements outlined above have been implemented, and they have been allowed to operate over some agreed period of time—thereby creating an opportunity for inter-ethnic tensions in the region to subside. The process of separation/independence should be defined in the course of the further negotiations over the long-term status of the province. If it appears that a long-term agreement is within reach, it might be possible to leave the definition of a separation/independence agreement until long-term arrangements are operating, but this is highly unlikely. It is far more likely that separation/independence and the establishment of long-term arrangements will have to be developed as alternative proposals.

Independence, in turn, necessarily raises the question of partition; that is, of whether all or part of Kosovo should be subject to the Kosovar Albanians' claim to independence. Independence for Kosovo has long been linked to partition in Serbian discussions, but partition is uniformly rejected as an option by the Kosovar Albanians, who lay claim to the whole province. Yet, the Albanian claim to all of Kosovo serves only to provoke intense resistance to any independence for the Kosovar Albanians, at all. If separation/independence is to be achievable peacefully, both the question of independence and the question of which territories are to become independent must be decided together.

Certain lessons drawn by a Canadian journalist from the Swiss experience of creating a distinct Jura canton[17] may usefully be applied to addressing these questions in Kosovo. First, the process for achieving independence must be established in advance of any decision to separate. The negotiations suggested above to develop constitutional and other frameworks for defining the long-term status of Kosovo must develop as an alternative to provisions for initiating and carrying out a process for separating Kosovo—that is, for achieving independence. Second, the process for achieving separation/independence must be democratic; that is, it must allow local populations to express and fulfill their preferences. In the absence of a significant transitional period and a meaningful alternative to separation, even a democratic referendum will be little more than an ethnic census. Third, the expression of popular preferences must take place at the most local levels possible. The self-administering regions proposed as part of the transitional arrangements outlined above—which should reflect the actual composition of the population in the province—may also serve as the electoral units in this process. Fourth, the preferences of local majorities, articulated in a democratic referendum process, should take precedence over any provincial majority, as well as over any historical or other arguments concerning the ownership or future fate of any territory. Hence, statutory provisions for achieving separation/independence must incorporate provisions for allowing local majorities in the self-administering regions to choose different outcomes, limited only by considerations of geography.

Referenda and competitive democratic elections have provided important mechanisms for allowing populations to carry out processes of separation peacefully, and for legitimating negotiated solutions. The referendum just completed in Northern Ireland has underscored the legitimacy of the settlement process negotiated by elites. The demonstrated popularity of the settlement is likely to compel political parties in Northern Ireland to increase their support for it in order to secure voter support in the next round of elections. In Switzerland, the referendum mechanism was applied at three different territorial levels of the electorate to ensure that the separation of the Jura from Berrie canton had the support of a majority of the population in the region, and that the populations of localities in the new Jura canton agreed with their incorporation into it. By allowing for voting in relatively small communities, the Swiss referendum process permitted communities on the border of the proposed new canton to choose whether to be separated from Bern. It even allowed a noncontiguous district (Laufen) to remain part of Bern. The Swiss approach thus minimized—but did not eliminate entirely—the problem of local populations being separated from Bern (partitioned) against their will. In order to implement a Swiss-like strategy of separation/independence/partition by referendum in Kosovo, it will be necessary to secure prior agreement on the minimum criteria for allowing a given population to decide its own fate (i.e., size, location, composition, economy, etc.). This, as the Swiss experience demonstrates, would amount to agreement on the broad criteria for partition. In the absence of such an agreement, the use of a referendum might result in territorially-isolated "micro-autonomies."

Dilemmas of Implementation.

The current escalation in Serbian/Yugoslav use of force against the UCK, and the violent response by the UCK, are undermining the chances for any kind of negotiated settlement. If such violence, and the forced population displacement that is accompanying it, continues much longer, no Kosovar politician will be able to mobilize popular support in Kosovo for a negotiated settlement. These developments thus are more likely to lead to prolonged guerrilla warfare in the province than to a negotiated settlement of the conflict.

The interim agreement outlined above will not provide a basis for other groups to mount demands against Serbia/Yugoslavia or other states. But it will prove exceedingly difficult to prevent Muslims and Hungarians in Yugoslavia, and Albanians in Macedonia, from seeking the same "self-administering" status granted to Kosovo and the Kosovar Serbs and Albanians as part of the "transitional" arrangements proposed above. In Spain, for example, it proved impossible to limit the grant of autonomy to the "historic" regions of Galicia, Catalonia, and the Basque lands; the movement for autonomy quickly spread to all of Spain, which now contains 17 autonomous regions, with differing elements of autonomy. In Serbia, the province of Vojvodina has the same constitutional status as Kosovo and may claim the same rights of self-administration. In Vojvodina, Serbs constitute the majority and Hungarians the largest minority, but only about 17 percent of the population. Much of the Hungarian population is, however, located along the border with Hungary, raising the prospect that populations in these areas might seek the same right to separation/independence as the Kosovar Albanians. And the lack of constitutional status as an autonomous province cannot be expected to prevent the Muslims of the Sandzak region from demanding the same treatment as the Kosovar Albanians, as well.

However, by limiting the interim and transitional arrangements to the realm of statutory rather than constitutional change, and by deferring the issue of separation/independence until after transitional arrangements are operative, it may be possible to weaken the attractiveness of these changes for other groups. Moreover, by adopting the three-tiered, referendum-based approach to the question of separation/independence outlined above, Serbs in Vojvodina (more than 57 percent of the population) and in "narrow" Serbia (almost 90 percent of the population) could defeat any such proposal in a democratic referendum at the first stage; although the Hungarians of Vojvodina and Muslims of the Sandzak could demand the same right as Kosovar Serbs to pursue preferences that contradict those of the regional majority.

The potentially most destabilizing consequences of the approach outlined above may appear in Macedonia. Nationalist-separatist sentiments have been growing among the large and restive ethnic Albanian population in Western Macedonia in recent years. But the strategy of self-administration differs only in degree, not in kind, from the Macedonian strategy of granting local communities extensive, self-government rights. The main difference—and what may be the most disconcerting element from the Macedonian perspective—lies in the extra-territorial cultural rights and the joint administration of common cultural institutions such as the university called for by the approach outlined here. Control over Skopje University has been a focus of Albanian-Macedonian confrontation, and the university is, itself, a bastion of Macedonian nationalist resistance to equality between the cultures. Hence, implementation of the above changes in Kosovo might lead to renewed confrontation over Skopje University, as well as demands for the establishment of self-administering regions in the Albanian-majority areas of western Macedonia.

Paradoxically, however, movement toward ethnic Albanian self-administration in Kosovo may actually reduce separatist pressure in Macedonia. Much of the nationalist-separatist leadership among the Albanians of Macedonia consists of individuals formerly from Kosovo. To the extent that conditions in Kosovo are normalized and Kosovar Albanians gain extensive autonomy through self-administration, some Macedonian Albanians may be drawn back to Kosovo to participate in the construction of Albanian institutions there. Much of the pressure to create an Albanian university in Tetovo, for example, can be traced to the effective closure of Prishtina University to the region's Albanian population. Restoration of Prishtina University to normal operations may very well draw students and faculty away from Macedonia and thus relieve pressure to create an Albanian university in Tetovo.

The steps outlined above for an interim agreement and transitional arrangements are not likely to provoke further unrest among the Bosnian Serbs. The potential powers of the Bosnian Serbs and the *Republika Srpska* in the post-Dayton constitutional system of Bosnia-Herzegovina already exceed those proposed here for Kosovo. It is movement toward the long-term, or "final," status of Kosovo that may provoke renewed political demands by the Bosnian Serbs for independence. Steps toward granting Kosovar Albanians the opportunity to achieve independence through democratic means will likely set off similar demands not only among the Bosnian Serbs, but among the Bosnian Croats, as well as the Albanians of Macedonia. Thus, while it is essential to the preservation of regional stability that the "transitional" arrangements for Kosovo outlined above be achieved as soon as possible, it is also essential that movement beyond these arrangements—to the definition of the long-term, or "final" status of the province—be deferred for as long as possible. The Bosnian Serbs and Croats already enjoy more autonomy and greater blocking power over the Bosnian government and Bosnian Federation, respectively, than is granted to the Kosovar Albanians by the strategy outlined above—not to mention military power. Only the successful operation of transitional institutions in Kosovo offers the possibility of achieving agreement on a long-term solution that amounts to *de facto* autonomy within the framework of the Yugoslav, or even Serbian, state and the protection of other state borders—in Macedonia and Bosnia—against secessionist pressures. External support for both the integrity of existing borders and the operation of such transitional arrangements is essential to that success.

ENDNOTES - CHAPTER 7

1. I have explored the Kosovo-Macedonia connection in my contributions to *Toward Comprehensive Peace in Southeast Europe,* Barnett R. Rubin, ed., New York: Twentieth Century Fund Press, 1996.

2. See Timothy D. Sisk, *Power Sharing and International Mediation in Ethnic Conflicts,* Washington, DC: United States Institute of Peace Press, 1996; Joseph V. Montville, ed., *Conflict and Peacemaking in Multiethnic Societies,* Lexington, MA: DC Heath and Co., 1990; and Donald L. Horowitz, *Ethnic Groups in Conflict,* Berkeley: University of California Press, 1985.

3. For background, see Arend Lijphart, ed., *Conflict and Coexistence in Belgium,* Berkeley: Institute of International Studies, University of California, Berkeley, 1991. For more recent developments, see Robert Senelle, "The Reform of the Belgian State" in Joachim Jens Hesse and Vincent Wright, eds., *Federalizing Europe?,* Oxford: Oxford University Press, 1996, pp. 266-324; and Richard Lewis, "The Example of Belgium," *Global Forum Series Occasional Paper* No. 96-01.2, Durham, NC: Center for International Studies, Duke University, April 1996.

4. See F. Gunther Eyck, "South Tyrol and Multiethnic Relationships" in Montvile, ed., *Conflict and Peacemaking,* pp. 219-238; Hurst Hannum, *Autonomy, Sovereignty, and Self-Determination: The Accommodation of Conflicting Rights,* Philadelphia: University of Pennsylvania Press, 1990, pp. 432-440; and Oliver Schmidtke, "Ethnic Mobilization in South Tyrol," *Innovation,* Vol. 11, No. 1, March 1998, pp. 25-42.

5. See Kenneth D. McRae, *Conflict and Compromise in Multilingual Societies: Switzerland,* Waterloo, Ontario: Wilfrid Laurier University Press, 1983, pp. 185-213; and Scott Reid, *Canada Remapped: How the Partition of Quebec Will Reshape the Nation,* Vancouver: Pulp Press, 1992, pp. 23-36.

6. Juan Jose Solozabal, "Spain: A Federation in the Making?" in Hess and Wright, eds., *Federalizing Europe?*, pp. 204-265; and Robert P. Clark, "Spanish Democracy and Regional Autonomy: The Autonomous Community System and Self-Government for the Ethnic Homelands" in Joseph P. Rudolph, Jr. and Robert J. Thompson, eds., *Ethnoterritorial Politics, Policy and the Western World,* Boulder: Lynne Rienner Publishers, 1989, pp. 15-43.

7. See, e.g., Nina Dobrkovic, "Juzni Tirol-model za resavanje polozaja i statusa nacionalnih manjina?" (South Tyrol-Model for

resolving the position and status of national minorities?), in *Medjunarodniproblemi*, Vol. 44, Nos. 3-4, 1992, pp. 272-286; Pedrag Simic, "The Autonomy Statue of Trentino-South Tyrol—a [E]uropean model for the Kosovo crisis?" in Josef Janning and Martin Brusis, eds., *Exploring Futures for Kosovo: Kosovo Albanians and Serbs in Dialogue,* Munich: Research Group in European Affairs, August 1997, pp. 39-48; and Radmila Nakarada, "Svajcarsld model resavanja sukobw. preduslovi i granice njegove primene najugoslovenski slucaj" (The Swiss model of resolving conflicts: preconditions and limits of its application to the Yugoslav case), in Tomas Flajner and Slobodan Samardzic, eds., *Federalizam iproblem manjina u viseetnickim zajednicama* (Federalism and the problem of minorities in multethnic communities), Belgrade: Institute za Evropske Studije, 1995, pp. 115-138.

8. Reported in a confidential conversation, Belgrade, May 1998.

9. The gulf between Serbian and Kosovar Albanian views is evident in the materials from three recent meetings convened by outside actors. See Project on Ethnic Relations, *The New York Roundtable: Toward Peaceful Accommodation in Kosovo,* Princeton: Project on Ethnic Relations, 1997; Ger Duijzings, Dusan Janjic, and Shkelzen Maliqi, eds., *Kosovo-Kosova: Confrontation or Coexistence,* Nijmegan, Netherlands: Peace Research Centre, University of Nijmegan and Political Cultural Centre 042, 1997; and Janning and Brusis, eds., *Exploring Futures for Kosovo.*

10. This view was expressed during a discussion with several Serbian analysts which was organized by the Center for Policy Alternatives in Belgrade in May 1998.

11. This was a key conclusion of the Council on Foreign Relations Working Group on the South Balkans. See *Toward Comprehensive Peace in Southeast Europe,* Barnett R. Rubin, ed., New York: Twentieth Century Fund Press, 1996. See also the conclusion of the New York meeting of the Project on Ethnic Relations, cited above.

12. Discussion at Center for Policy Alternatives, May 1998.

13. See, e.g., the emotional cultural-historical arguments in Branislav Krstic, *Kosovo izmedju istorijskog i etnickogprava* (Kosovo between historical and ethnic rights), Belgrade: Kuca Vid, 1994; and in several of the contributions to Veljko B. Kadijevic, ed., *Kosovo i Metohija: izazovi I odgovori* (Kosovo and Metohija: challenges and responses), Belgrade: Institut za geopoliticke studije, 1997.

14. See, e.g., Rexhep Ismajli, *Kosova and the Albanians in Former Yugoslavia,* Prishtina [?]: Kosova Information Centre, n.d., p. 14.

15. These are generally ignored in scholarly treatments, but reported by Reid, a freelance journalist, in *Canada Remapped*, pp. 34-35.

16. Text of the agreement, sections on "decommissioning" and "security," as distributed by the British Consulate-General in Boston, Office of Press and Public Affairs.

17. Reid, *Canada Remapped*, pp. 32-36.

CHAPTER 8

THE CULTURAL SCOPE OF BALKAN SECURITY

Stefano Bianchini

SECURITY: A CHANGING NOTION

According to a common and largely shared opinion, security is a notion strictly connected to the defense of a state. As a result of concerns of policymakers, experts on international relations and strategic studies have placed a special emphasis on the military and diplomacy, as the two scopes able to guarantee security, exclusively or primarily. Short-term and long-term measures are taken into consideration in this framework, albeit a certain attention has been paid in more recent times even to the economic sphere.[1]

In many respects, this "traditional" approach to security has been founded in truth in the past decades. Different factors contributed to this, for example, the long-term attitudes to power policies and the relevance of the pattern based on the balance of powers; the peculiar relations between the camps during the Cold War ("containment" and "roll back" in the American policy, the "besieged fortress" in the Soviet policy, détente and nuclear balance in both approaches); the worldwide increasing interdependence in politics and economics. All these features mirrored a situation where the military and diplomacy played an evident crucial role in international relations.

Nevertheless, and however provocative it may sound, these approaches are inadequate to understand and face the challenges of the post-Communist international balance and particularly the Balkan events. In fact, a radical change occurred in Europe when communism collapsed. New trends, which were perceived with difficulty in the previous decades, emerged powerfully. In this context, security is depending increasingly on a wide variety of factors. Besides the military, diplomacy, and economic interdependence, other features crucially contribute to define the sense of security of a political community. A special evidence has been showed by demography (particularly the rate of birth and the immigration/emigration flows); by the domestic degree of economic and social development of different strata and regions; by the quality and the distribution of information and media systems; by the attractive power of symbols and myths in a group; by the complex and contradictory relations between history and memory. All these elements have a great impact on the perception of security of people and political communities.

Additionally, the 20th century has been a century characterized by a predominant role of ideologies. An unpredictable acceleration of the stages of social developments—through the industrial revolution, the role of machines, the improvement of medicine, the mass society, and, finally, the universal suffrage—has imposed an epochal transformation to human societies. On the one hand, a new system of production (with industries, services and, later, new communication systems) emerged, while world space was shrinking drastically, time was pressing increasingly, and the health of populations improved significantly.[2] On the other, the sources of legitimization of powers and the system of selection of the elites, which remained similar for thousands of years, radically changed when the whole adult population of a political community, regardless of sex, education, or income, had the right to vote and was included into the institutions. In the end, the system of building human societies has changed quickly and radically in few decades.

In this new system, political elites sought to preserve their predominant role by obtaining the support of the population by any means, legal or illegal, ethic or violent, according to the situations and the countries. Consistently, different values, political beliefs, foci of identification and loyalties, political knowledge and expectations, and cultural backgrounds of the populations became increasingly relevant in a political community and in the relations between rulers and ruled.

Therefore, political cultures increasingly influenced policymakers and different strata of a society since the beginning of the 20th century. Hence, it is evident that even the perception of security has to be considered in this framework. In fact, the impact of these transformations on security issues is relevant indeed.

The emphasis on these aspects, however, does not mean that the impact of the military and the diplomatic factors are to be underestimated or marginalized, both in general terms and in the specific context of the current Balkan crisis, either at local or international levels. Simply stated, referring to a deep changing context may better clarify that any approach to security issues restricted to the military and diplomatic factors only, is, today, inadequate to understand the evolution of the events and to influence their developments, particularly in the Balkan peninsula. In fact, and despite the successful intervention of NATO in Bosnia in 1995, stabilization of the area is unlikely to be reached in a short while, and even in medium terms, mainly because of the neglected (by international subjects), but extremely relevant, cultural scope of the Balkan crisis.

In other words, the origin of the Balkan crisis in the 1990s cannot be traced back merely in an attempt to establish a political and military predominant role of a state (or a group of states, or a specific leadership, or a specific political elite) over a certain territory or region. We are not facing a crisis where the aggressor can be merely identified with a state whose leadership wishes to recast the regional balance of powers by establishing its predominant role through a medium-sized power policy.[3]

Truly, the reasons why this interpretation of the events has been often supported by some Balkan leaderships is understandable, because they wished to present themselves as the "victims of the aggressor" by appealing to a traditional scheme of international conflicts. However, they offered an "easy political answer" to a problem which is, in fact, more complex.

The "power policy" interpretation, in fact, is powerless to explain why, during the Yugoslav secession war, all the parties involved violated cease-fires and agreements systematically, in spite of their being internationally mediated or even imposed. Additionally, this interpretation fails to clarify why all the parties involved carried out domestic policies aimed at sanctioning individuals and groups who wished to reestablish dialogue between the populations of the parties. Particularly in the Serbo-Croatian cultural space, all parties promoted ethnic cleansing, violence against civilians including rapes, regardless of the, albeit evident, different responsibilities of leaderships in provoking the war.

The more the separation from those events is chronologically growing, the more this picture is becoming evident, in spite of the fact that sources of information are still fragmented. As a result, not only is the "power policy" interpretation showing a lack of effectiveness, but also the categories of aggressors and victims strictly applied to State attitudes are becoming powerless to explain what happened and what should be needed, in order to find a lasting solution to the crisis.

Crucially, aggressors and victims did exist and are still existing (for example, in the Kosovo case). This is not disputed. What is disputable is to what extent and to which subjects these categories have been ascribed. In fact, the effectiveness in applying these categories with the goal of understanding the events depends on the peculiarities of the conflict. In the Balkan case, the conflict was provoked only to a certain extent by wishes or aspirations of power policy.

On the contrary, instability in the Balkans has been mainly provoked by a political culture, namely nationalism, which has been used by local political elites in order to redefine the territory of the state and its membership.

Truly, nationalism as a political culture played a crucial and progressive role for a certain period, particularly during the 19th century when emancipation and modernization were the main goals to be achieved with the overcoming of the backward institutions of the great empires. In this context, Giuseppe Mazzini has played an indisputable influential role.[4]

Since then, however, the world changed deeply, and political ideologies changed as well. At the end of the 20th century, any attempt at identifying the political thought and action of Giuseppe Mazzini with those of Radovan Karadzic sounds extremely difficult. Still, each relies on nationalism and claimed (or claims) to be a nationalist. Nevertheless, and albeit any comparison between these two personalities is an hazard, the enormous distance between Mazzini and Karadzic makes evident the transformation of nationalism: in fact, this political culture has been gradually transformed in a peculiar state/party ideology.

As a result of this transformation, a realistic approach is currently unavoidable by both scholars and policymakers. It means that both have nothing to do but recognize the nature of this change. This change implies that, especially in the Balkans, nationalist ideology and nationalist political culture have gradually become effective tools used by political elites for recasting the territory of a state and its membership. In this context, members of a newly established political community have difficulty being considered as "citizens," but are something else that has still to be defined. Additionally, it has to be emphasized that nationalist transformation of the society and state is considered by nationalists as a crucial prerequisite for (a) the achievement of political modernization, (b) economic development and (c)—extremely important—the security of the state and its members.

All these factors roughly lead to the conclusion that the idea of state is the main focus of post-Communist transition in the Balkans, in Eastern Europe, and to a certain extent even in East-Central Europe.[5] In fact, after the Communist collapse, the meaning, the scope, and the perspectives of any change have implied the recasting of the state as *the* powerful structure able to guarantee the conditions for development and wealth. This belief was not only a legacy of Communism (in spite of the fact that the state did play a central role under Communist rule). It was also a legacy of the pre-Communist period, when backward countries in Eastern Europe faced the challenge of development in very difficult conditions, because they lacked capital, and technologies were increasingly expensive. Without a rooted and reliable financial system, these societies were doomed to rely on the fiscal system of the state, in order to collect resources for development. This crucial role played by the state was studied effectively by Alexander Gerschenkron and other prominent scholars of economic history in the 1950s and 1960s.[6] We do not need to insist further on these aspects. Additionally, we can emphasize that such a process, encouraging the state to become *the* lever for development, has strengthened its magnet role for bureaucracy and policymakers who tried to use it as a tool for establishing their predominant control over society.

After the collapse of three political systems in 80 years (namely, the empire, the interwar authoritarian state, and the Communist state)[7]—when, simultaneously, a mass society was created—the implications of these factors have proved to be extremely broad: changes of the state structure, in fact, have implied changes of territories, of people, of history, of language, of monuments and symbols, because the legitimization of the newly created realities needed both a confirmation from an asserted continuity of the past and the charging of previous failures to "outer subjects." Consistently, the establishment of new forms of control over the society and a management of power, both in terms of development and corruption, according to the quality and the choices of the ruling class, appeared a great opportunity to many groups and individuals.[8]

Since the goals of corruption, self-social promotion, and self-enrichment were not openly claimed for evident reasons, new political parties turned their attention to state-building and development issues, by emphasizing that the economic crisis of the 1980s had been provoked by neighboring peoples or countries. By blaming "otherness" and claiming development simultaneously, nationalists in particular were able to collect significant support from an exhausted population and, at the same time, to emphasize the achievement of the development of the community as the main goal of their political action.[9]

In this sense, a radical change occurred to the idea of State, because this was considered the prerequisite for strengthening political modernization, economic development and (ethnic) security. As a result, nationalism— better, its ethno-nationalist interpretation— has been promoted by the new ruling class as a state or state/party ideology with the aim of encouraging and spreading simultaneously into the population a peculiar set of political beliefs, expectations, foci of identifications, symbols, and perceptions of self. Thanks to this, the cultural identification of rulers and ruled has become the main source of both the legitimization of power and security of the newly established political communities.

Crucially, nationalist political culture has proved to have a great impact in the society in terms of (a) legitimacy of the rulers; (b) loyalties of the ruled; and, (c) state-building processes. In this context, which has been even strengthened by uncertainties of post-Communist transition, the nationalist approach is aggressive in order to recast territory and membership of the states. While competing with each other for territories, they follow similar mechanisms in domestic policies because they share a common idea of security and stability through cultural homogenization. This explains why ethnic homogeneity has been pursued by all nationalisms in former Yugoslavia. As cynical it may appear, differences in their aggressive policy and praxis depended primarily on the quantity of weapons nationalist movements had when they sought to carry out their project.

Milosevic first made nationalism a tool for political actions and popular support in Serbia; the dismemberment of Yugoslavia and the war were provoked by him. The brutality against the population, the systematic massacres, and the humanitarian disasters which occurred from Slovenia to Kosovo since the beginning of the 1990s are definitely to be considered the outcome of his policy.[10] However, he was not the sole culprit of those events or of those that followed. Besides the political responsibility of the Slovenian leadership, which is unquestionable, although often neglected, a largely-shared nationalist political culture made possible the war of HVO against Bosnia, the ethnic cleansing of Krajina by the Croatian Army, the Kazanj massacre against the Serbs of Sarajevo, and the killing of no-nationalist Albanians in Kosovo by the UCK.

In all the above-mentioned cases, nationalism has been the political culture which created turmoil and insecurity. By way of confirmation, it was not by chance that the way of conducting the war in the Yugoslav region in the 1990s differed from previous European experiences radically. Instead of battles between opposing armies, the Yugoslav secession war was characterized by an aggression primarily against civilians. Traditional battles played a secondary role, because the question of borders, however important, was less relevant than the goal of achieving (a) ethnic homogeneity, (b) forced assimilation and/or at least (c) the subjugation of the "other" within a certain State.[11]

In contrast, brutality of attitudes characterized military operations of both regular and irregular corps when they faced ethnically mixed areas (as, for example, in the case of Vukovar), anti-nationalist individuals, and those who declared themselves as "Yugoslavs." The fate of the latter is particularly interesting. With the Yugoslav collapse, Yugoslavs lost their country and their foci of cultural identification, because Milosevic embezzled the name of "Yugoslavia" in order to establish his control over the property of the federation. Additionally, no one significant political organization or country in the international arena claimed the protection of the right of self-determination for "Yugoslavs."[12]

As a result, the categories of "aggressors" and "victims" are to be recast, not with reference to the ethnic membership, but by taking into consideration the political culture to which they belong. In other words, "aggressors" are not whole people, but nationalists of all peoples; "victims" are not people in a generic way, but those who share an intercultural or multiple identity.

In sum, because the traditional intercultural web of the Balkans is put under discussion by nationalists, the current Balkan dilemmas on state building and security—which emerged since the Dayton Agreement was signed in 1995—confirm how the nationalist idea of state and the persistence of destabilization are strictly connected.

THE BALKANS UNDER NATIONALISM: A COMPARATIVE PICTURE OF THE SITUATION

Let us observe what is going on in the area recently. A short comparison among the situations of Kosovo and rump Yugoslavia, Bosnia, Croatia, Macedonia, Albania, Slovenia, and Moldavia offers a good picture of the role played by political cultures in a security/insecurity context.

Kosovo and FRY.

In Kosovo, both the parties in conflict do not seem interested in reaching a compromise. A perspective of autonomy in the Serb context is rejected by Albanian leaders with good reason; they fear that autonomy can be threatened by Serb leadership at any time to come, as it has occurred in the past. In contrast, Serb leaders are reluctant to accept autonomy, and they have good reason, too. The international recognition of Slovenia and Croatia in 1992 has proven that administrative borders may be recognized as international borders in the event of a claim for independence led by the majority of a local population.

Independence of Kosovo is firmly rejected by Serbian leaders, who claim their right to protect state borders in a context which has been *de facto* legitimized by the International Community through the mechanism of recognition adopted for successor states of the Soviet Union, Czechoslovakia, and Yugoslavia. In contrast, any change of this principle may lead to a threat of stability in Bosnia, Macedonia, and Cyprus. Indeed, the perspective of a partition of Kosovo is questioned, too, and can lead to a war. In fact, both Serb and Albanian parties claim their sovereignty over territories with rich natural resources. In the end, the large autonomy of Kosovo in a federation of three equal subjects is rejected by Montenegro. The solution has been seen as an attempt at diminishing the current overestimated role of Montenegro in the federation, particularly in a period when Milosevic aims at doing it. In the end, Milosevic is aware that the participation of the Albanians in Serb polls and/or the full membership of Kosovo in the federation may affect seriously his predominant position in the country and even provoke his political defeat. In other words, the three subjects involved in the issue (Albanian, Serb, and Montenegrin political elites) are unwilling to find a political solution at least in medium-to-short terms. They lack a mutual confidence as an outcome of 10 years of tensions and Serb repression of Albanians claims. This situation has led both the parties in Kosovo to violate the agreements imposed by the diplomacy of the contact group, and the agreement reached by Milosevic and Holbrook in October 1998 in order to stop (or postpone) NATO intervention has been rejected repeatedly by Fehmi Agani (and not only by UCK, FARK, and Adem Demaqi).

Meanwhile, the autonomy of the University of Belgrade has been suppressed without any international reaction, and state control over the media systematically imposed. As a result, an international military operation in Kosovo is doomed to radicalize the situation and particularly make impossible the persistence of Kosovo within Serbia. This means that changes in state borders will be forced by an international intervention. The unavoidable outcome of this is that the ethnic state is a welcome solution. In such a case, the risks of a destabilization of Bosnia, Macedonia, and Albania are likely to be strengthened. In conclusion, the Kosovo question reveals an evident geopolitical scope, which is strictly connected with a broad problem of state-building.

Bosnia.

At the end of 1998, the picture in the Serb camp is not so dark as it may appear. In fact, recent elections have proved that a political differentiation is increasing, in spite of the fact that the radical Nikola Poplasen has been elected president of the entity. In contrast, both the assembly of the entity and the Serb representative in the Bosnian presidency are characterized by more moderate approaches than those of the president of the entity. Additionally, members of the Serbian elite are increasingly attracted by the idea of being the first Serbs to be included in a process of European integration in the event that the support of European Union (EU) to Bosnian integration is going further. This perspective is really serious and may open new differentiation processes between Serbia and the Republika Srpska.

The new European common currency which has been instituted in 1999 is another factor that can have a great impact as a magnet on Bosnia, and particularly on the attitudes of local policymakers. The most popular currency for the everyday needs of the population, the German mark, presumably will be replaced by the Euro soon. As a result, Bosnia possibly may be included in the EU, although any specific process of enlargement to this country has not been started yet.

It will be extremely interesting to see how the future of Bosnia will evolve in the years to come in connection with the European integration processes. On the contrary, it seems that threats to the Bosnian integrity can emerge in the Croatian camp. Although in Herzegovina political differentiation is increasing, and the hard-liner Ante Jelavic has been elected to the Bosnian Presidency with only 52 percent of the votes (in the past elections, the Croat candidate, Kresimir Zubak, got 88.7 percent of the poll), it is a fact that the most extremist member of this government is Jelavic. Tensions between Croats and Muslims are emerging on many occasions, while domestic events with neighboring Croatia are not encouraging. In this context, a negative repercussion is likely to be the outcome because of the efforts made by U.S. representatives who forced the reluctant Muslim leaders to sign a special treaty with Croatia in November 1998, in order to accomplish Dayton Agreements. This was, in fact, the most ambiguous part of the treaty because its nationalist interpretation (from both the Croatian and Serb sides) is in evident contrast with the goal of preserving the integrity of Bosnia, also included in the Dayton Agreements. As a result, a similar treaty between the Republika Srpska and the rump Yugoslavia presumably will be signed, despite opposition efforts by Biljana Plavsic and Milorad Dodik in 1997.

In such a way, the process of differentiation in the Serb camp can have a negative impact on attempts at relaxing tensions in the area. Hard-liners and the Radical party will be encouraged to achieve their goal of erasing borders between Serbia and Republika Srpska. Additionally, this perspective will be strengthened whether Serb borders in rump Yugoslavia are going to be changed in Kosovo as a result of a war. In the end, the future of the Bosnian State is still truly disputed. Integration and disintegration are still to be considered open options, for domestic and international reasons.

Croatia.

In Croatia, Tudjman's succession has commenced. A great economic crisis is threatening the country because of the high value of the currency and the lack of production. The Dubrovnik bank scandal and the death of Gojko Susak have strengthened a settlement of the accounts within HDZ. Despite the information launched by the press, it is not true that only soft-liners resigned recently. Even a hard-liner but dogmatic figure such as Andrija Hebrang was forced to resign when he started to make order in the ministry of defense where the Herzegovinian lobby, and particularly the young and ambitious Ivic Pasalic, were absolute bosses. A quite intricate connection is emerging between the economic/financial interests of a powerful group within the state and the role played by this group in defining the Croatian interest in Bosnia. In other words, the effort of HDZ hard-liners to establish their own strong control over the ruling Croatian party is likely to affect Bosnian stabilization by encouraging Herzegovinian extremists to carry out the goal of Croatian unification. By contrast, HDZ is clearly loosing its appeal in the ballots. Local elections in Osijek and Dubrovnik in Fall 1998 confirmed a coalition of opposition parties was able to get a solid majority, successfully defeating HDZ. This perspective, however, can encourage both a split in HDZ between soft- and hard-liners and the attempt of hard-liners to get a stronger control over the levers of power before their central power system in Zagreb is seriously threatened. In conclusion, the political future in Croatia is dominated by an uncertainty which may have effects, not only within Croatian borders but also in neighboring countries—particularly Bosnia. Also, a repercussion in relations with Slovenia and Serbia, with which a series of contested issues need to be resolved, is not excluded.

Macedonia.

In Macedonia, the key issue for the future of the country is the complexity of the ethnic question. How the relations between Slav Macedonians and Albanians may evolve plays a predominant role. The elections of November 1998 provoked a great change in the government of the country when a new contradictory coalition of nationalist and civic parties defeated the former communists, and a new balance emerged in the country. The reasons for this change are based mainly on social dissatisfaction rather than on ethnic tensions, and this is why a coalition between Macedonian nationalists of VMRO and the newly created civic party led by Vasil Tupurkovski (the Democratic Alliance) became possible. Furthermore, Tupurkovski is the strongest candidate for the 1999 presidential elections when current President Kiro Gligorov will be unable to run again. In other words, Macedonia is facing a drastic turnover. However, stability is still unpredictable. Macedonian-Albanian ethnic polarization is far from overcome, although the most extremist of the Albanian parties, the PDPA led by Arben Xhaferri, has been included in the government with VMRO and DA. Paradoxically enough, the moderate Albanians of PDP (which supported former Communists in the past government) were not. In this framework, it is unclear whether the coalition can survive when old unsolved issues (such as that of the Tetovë University) are coming back again to the agenda. Truly, both VMRO and DA pointed out that economic recovery is their first and main commitment; however, they do not share similar ethno-political strategies. VMRO is still a Macedonian nationalist party, while DA is a civic movement which includes in its own ranks members of Serb, Roma, and Albanian minorities. It can be expected that a contrast between these two parties will emerge after the presidential elections as Tupurkovski needs the VMRO support to win. However, he may not need the support of VMRO after the elections if ethno-national relations worsen. In this context, the role of the Albanian parties will be crucial, taking into consideration the impact of the Kosovo events.

Strong links were established between Albanians of Kosovo and of Macedonia during Titoist Yugoslavia, as well as after the dismemberment of the country when Serb repression policies increased dramatically in Kosovo. As a result, migration flows from Kosovo to Macedonia intensified, threatening ethnic balance in Macedonia and making more interdependent the events in Serbia and Macedonia. In this context, appeals to moderation can lose any effectiveness, and Albanian politicians will be encouraged to claim independence or the establishment of an autonomous region, at least while Macedonian parties oppose both these goals. In the end, many unpredictable factors are still affecting regional stability. In other words, as in Albania, the further existence of the Macedonian State remains under discussion, and the possibility of a collapse has not been avoided yet.

Albania.

Turmoil in Albania is far from being contained. The collapse of the state is still a possible outcome as a consequence of several factors.

After the election of a new, young premier, Pandeli Majko, untainted by a communist past and committed to overcoming Berisha-Nano animosity, the country approved in a referendum on November 22, 1998, a new Constitution, still strongly contested by the Democratic Party. Previously, this party boycotted the Parliament and the commission where the draft of the Constitution was prepared in order to reject any compromise. The attempt was that of convincing the population that the current government has no legitimization. A further step of this policy was that of claiming new elections with the hope of revenge over the socialists. In fact, the real victim of such an approach was the reliability of the political institutions of the country, which was affected by the double collapse of the state in 1991 and in 1997.

To make the picture even darker, these developments are occurring simultaneously with the worsening of the Kosovo issue. Politically, the Kosovo leadership established good relations with Berisha and the Democratic Party since the early 1990s, while serious contrasts emerged with Fatos Nano when he met Milosevic in Crete in Fall 1997. Meanwhile, the Albanian governments of Nano and Majko proved unable to reestablish their control over the northern borders of the country, where Kosovo's war was becoming an economic lifeline. In this framework, the relations between the two military forces operating in the Yugoslav region (FARK and UCK) deteriorated and endangered the territorial integrity of Albania, because of the flows of weapons, armed irregulars and refugees across the borders.

Since 1997, the situation has become increasingly complicated. In fact, the attempts of Berisha at taking advantage of the crisis in Kosovo are likely to increase negative reactions of the Albanian population in the south of the country. Truly, Berisha does not seem to have a great support in the country, but his relations with the Kosovar political elite are still close, and it cannot be excluded that Berisha may have a new opportunity to take over the power in the event that Kosovo is included in Albania. However, it remains to be seen whether this perspective will be accepted in the south or lead to a new collapse of the Albanian State by encouraging a North-South or Gheg/Tosk confrontation. In other words, because of the weakness of Albanian political institutions in a unstable regional context, the risk of a new collapse of the state is still possible and may be provoked by an interaction of factors, most of them unpredictable.

Slovenia and Moldavia.

Albeit geopolitically marginal in respect to the Balkans, both Slovenia and Moldavia are to be considered countries open to possible threats in terms of regional security. Two-thirds of both land and maritime borders between Slovenia and Croatia are contested. Despite repeated attempts at mediating, bilateral relations are sometimes exacerbated. In these cases, tensions increase suddenly with unpredictable outlets which can lead Ljubljana to a nationalist confrontation with Zagreb—under the pressure of extremist movements which are at the moment contained into the opposition ranks, but which have sometimes proved to have a significant impact on the population.

As for Moldavia, the country is located in a delicate geopolitical crossroad between two big destabilized areas, the Balkans and the Commonwealth of Independent States (CIS). By way of confirmation, a document recently signed in Chisinau by the leaders of Moldavia, Ukraine, and Romania urged Russia to withdraw its troops from Transdniester region, a reminder of a careless international public opinion that another recent ethno-national conflict was not over. In fact, the Russian Duma has not yet ratified the treaty that ended the 5-month war in 1992. Furthermore, domestic tensions in Russia, combined with the uncertainties of the economic and political (presidential) situation, may intertwine with the international developments in Kosovo in the event of a NATO intervention without a supporting vote of the Security Council. As a result of worsening East-West relations, Duma is likely to postpone indefinitely the withdrawal of the troops still arrayed in the CIS by affecting simultaneous relations in the area. In this context, because Russian policymakers are still uncertain whether to build a civic state, an ethno-nation state or—again, when possible—an empire, it is evident that local tensions and a possible subsequent international intervention are doomed to have a great impact on the process of state-building in a broad area, where, additionally, the form of state-building may eventually have destabilizing effects.

FINAL CONSIDERATIONS AND PROPOSALS

This rapid overview makes evident the following conclusions:

- The different crises in the Balkans are strictly intertwined. They require an overall solution, which cannot be found when a situation is exacerbated and the International Community appeals to military or diplomatic tools only, in order to restore a truce.

- The main factor which connects these crises is nationalism, namely its idea of state which is embodied in the attempt at establishing an ethno-national legitimization of powers. However pursued, such a legitimization affects security in neighboring countries, because it is based on both mistrust towards the "others" and disputed historical/territorial/cultural claims. With these premises, the future of a political community is increasingly built against (and not along with) neighbors. As a result, defense reasons encourage a country which perceives itself as threatened to react in similar ways. In the end, the criteria of geopolitical arrangement that will be carried out by local and international subjects in a specific area are going to influence radically the future of the whole Balkans, in terms of rules and patterns to be applied in the name of the "equality" of nations.

- The effectiveness of the military and political tools of the International Community in order to create (even force) conditions for stability at the beginning, and later for peace, run serious risks of being influenced by the political culture of local political elites. In this context, a great disaster in terms of regional and

European security may be achieved if the appealing to military and diplomatic intervention is interpreted by the local parties as a support offered by the International Community to a nationalist approach against the other.

This can be particularly the case of Kosovo, which differs radically from those of Bosnia and Albania in the 1990s. Previously, in fact, NATO intervention in Bosnia was authorized by the United Nations (U.N.) and became possible because the Bosnian war had been considered an international war provoked by domestic uprising, with direct support coming from Serbia and Croatia. (Truly, this interpretation of the facts has been denied by a contested decision of the Hague tribunal which pointed out the civil character of the Bosnian war and dropped a long series of charges in the Tadic case. In contrast, this approach has been later overthrown by a different court, which emphasized the international scope of the war and the Croatian military involvement in its decision on the Celebici case.)[13]

As for Albania in 1997, the "ALBA" operation was formally requested by the local government.[14] In this context, the Kosovo situation is peculiar indeed. On the one hand, a military intervention of NATO is likely to be opposed by the veto of Russia and China in the Security Council; on the other, it has no chance to be requested by the Serb government. Albeit for different reasons, these attitudes are originated by a common principle—the absolute sovereignty of the state. In the former case, because Russia and China are concerned for possible domestic consequences in delicate issues such those of Chechnya and Tibet; in the latter, because Serbia wants to protect its borders.

As a result, without an undisputed U.N. legitimization, the military intervention of NATO is going to be "simply" considered an action of a military alliance, rather then an action of the International Community (however this concept may have a sense). Whether security has to be guaranteed by worldwide recognized supranational institutions (as the U.N.) or by the most powerful military subject is a topic for a specific study on security and international relations, which exceeds the approach of the present analyses. Rather, let the attention of the reader turn to the impact that both these forms of interventions (with or without U.N. support) are going to have on the perception of the state in the specific context of Kosovo and the Balkans. In fact, it is evident that the political culture, which suggests and supports such a military action, is based on the conception that the absolute sovereignty of the State has to be contained.[15]

This is neither an accident nor an unpredictable outcome of the post-Cold War politics. Truly, since the end of World War II, an increasing series of events has confirmed that state sovereignty as a principle is coming to an end. After the Communist collapse and the end of the Cold-War confrontation, this trend has been even more strengthened. Both globalization and regionalization are threatening the predominant role of the nation-state, the Westphalian system of international relations and the principle of absolute sovereignty of the state. This change is a great challenge for the existing political communities and one of the main repercussions of the post-Communist transition.[16]

Consistent with this general framework, the threat of a military intervention in Kosovo has been justified in 1998 in order (1) to stop Serb repression, (2) to stop a humanitarian disaster, and (3) to reestablish the autonomy of the region. In other words, the goals to be achieved by a possible military intervention in Kosovo are doomed to affect the sovereignty of Serbia/Rump Yugoslavia in a very peculiar way, because its main reason—as it was stated in the NATO camp—is the desire to change the domestic policy of this state, not its borders.

By contrast, the current predominant political culture of the local political and military elites suggests exactly the opposite interpretation. Namely, both Albanian and Serb leaderships consider that a NATO intervention has to be encouraged, or blamed, because it aims at diminishing the territorial sovereignty of Ramp Yugoslavia, while the impact of the action on domestic policy is largely neglected. This interpretation is largely shared by the current leaderships of the other Balkan States.

In a sense, an approach emphasizing territory rather than domestic policy is understandable in a nationalist context. Actually, the intimate nature of nationalism does not allow accepting the idea of a both "inner and outer contained sovereignty of the state." However, this general approach is softened, as for the outer sovereignty, because, at least temporarily, a state may suffer a loss of territory because of a war. Additionally, a state may submit to strong international pressures as an outcome of an adverse balance in the system of international alliances, which can be reversed when a new opportunity emerges. In contrast, any threat to inner sovereignty is not even taken into consideration, for the simple reason that it is unthinkable.

As a result, a great cultural misunderstanding threatens the effectiveness of any action promoted by international bodies in the Balkans. In other words, the goals of military interventions and other engagements of international bodies in the Balkans need an evident anti-nationalist cultural support if they want to be effective.

In fact, nationalism as a state ideology is a threat to international security because it aims at strengthening the sovereignty of the state against neighbors, while the International Community—through the role of the U.N., the creation of an International Penal Tribunal, the protection of human rights, and the process of European integration, just to mention a few—is increasingly supporting interdependence, multilateral cooperation, a new supranational legal system, and, finally, a containment of sovereignty extended to domestic policies. The events at the end of 1998, with the arrests of General Pinochet in

Great Britain and of Kurd leader Ocalan in Italy, are a confirmation of a general trend of interdependence and containment of the state, which is not any more the sole institution able to persecute a crime committed within its borders.[17]

It is exactly this interdependence that is clashing with nationalism as an ethno-cultural ideology and a form of protection of the absolute sovereignty of the state. Because nationalism is a mutant with multifaceted statements, it may express forms emphasizing either sovereignty or a mix of ethnicity and sovereignty. This quite complex picture makes unclear—for the concrete political world—the boundaries between "civic" and "ethnic" nationalism, albeit they are well-defined in the more sophisticated academic world.[18]

Additionally, the persistence of a "national" legitimization of state powers is contributing to stress the ambiguous nature of the nation-state, weakening the effectiveness of international actions. In fact, it is evident that any, open or surreptitious, support to a nationalist goal against another nationalist one is doomed to affect the international effort to find a peaceful solution to tension. Furthermore, in this case, a sense of dissatisfaction and revenge may arise among local elites, encouraging the search for an outer, more powerful "protection," which can be used, once it has been found, for further destabilization.

These mechanisms are well-known. However, it is the persistence of a "national" legitimization of state powers that makes evident why the European Community has been powerless in facing the Yugoslav crisis in 1991. Moreover, the difficulties which arose during the negotiations for the Maastricht Treaty, the political and cultural limitations which suffered from the final version of the treaty, and the attempts at containing the European integration process within the economic sphere for a longer period of time, have a common origin and can be explained mainly in a context of resistance to interdependence coming from an obsolescent leadership seized with the idea of nation.[19]

In the end, this framework permits an understanding of why the Balkan challenges on the threshold of the new millennium are embodied in a modern (or maybe post-modern) process of change in international relations, rather than originated by medieval attitudes and traditions. The focus is on the state-building process through a new articulation of the roles of state and nation. New patterns are emerging from the current Balkan tensions and showing a potentially attractive ability, which is a serious threat to peace.

As a result, stabilization and security in the Balkans can be achieved only in a new, anti-nationalist framework, which has yet to be built. This means that the national legitimization of state powers has to be overcome and new patterns offered in terms of:

- secularization;
- citizenship;
- softening borders;
- free flows of labor and capital;
- democratic management of differences; and,
- recognition of existing multiple identities within individuals and within communities, with an evident impact on state symbols, use of languages, administration (devolution), education systems in terms of flexibility, and permeability of cultures.

The main assumption is as follows. The more neighboring societies are articulated and mutual knowledge is rooted, the more security is strengthened. By contrast, the more neighboring societies are closed, homogeneous and without communication, the more their insecurity is going to affect peace in the area.

In this context, the actions of the international community may be effective and prepare a lasting security framework for Europe if they are supported by a clear strategy of encouraging permeability and communication among neighboring countries in the Balkans. Definitely, the implementation of such a strategy may provoke the opposition of local political elites, as in the case of current nationalist leaderships in the Balkans. However, because the sovereignty of states is under discussion even in domestic policies, this opposition cannot stop an international engagement in order to encourage alternative education systems, strengthening democratization (through the free flow of ideas and their free representation), and freedom of the media.

Since the Helsinki agreement was signed in 1975, the policy of human rights played a crucial role in preparing the collapse of communism.[20] A similar approach has to be developed towards nationalism. In this sense, strengthening alternative political cultures[21]—which are emerging all over the Balkans, while needing strong supports in order to break isolation in the country—is to be considered a prerequisite for stabilization.

Furthermore, as mentioned above, the threat of an international intervention in Kosovo has confirmed that the principle of the sovereignty of a state can be affected when an ethnic group is persecuted and collective rights are denied. However, in the Balkan context, the effectiveness of an international engagement depends mainly on its ability to encourage regional permeability and flexibility. This can be done through a series of tools able to guarantee, for example:

- the autonomy of the universities in Serbia, Bosnia, and Croatia;

- the freedom of media;

- the education in history and political science (which means civic education) of the population; and,

- the education of specific categories of workers, such as teachers, policemen, judges, and all those who play a relevant role in spreading a sense of belonging to democratic institutions as the institutions of the whole society.

It is quite evident that the lack of democracy in Serbia is worsening the Kosovo issue and, vice versa, the worsening of Kosovo issue is affecting the existence of a civil society and the role of anti-nationalist opposition in the country. Therefore, no political solution of the Kosovo issue will cause dramatic repercussions in Macedonia, Albania, Bosnia, and Cyprus, at least.

Crucial questions include: Are military interventions and diplomatic or other international engagements justified when an ethnic community is threatened only? Is the ethnic issue the unique one that may affect regional security? Or, vice versa, is the lack of democracy in a country the main factor that is affecting security? If the answer is the lack of democracy, as the author of this chapter does believe, this means that nationalism and democracy are incompatible, as well as are nationalism and security. As a result, without a radical change in political culture, namely a change able to distinguish democracy from nationalism and to offer security to individuals and groups as well as the respect of ethnic identities without nationalism, it is impossible to have an effectiveness in military and political actions in the current Balkan and Eastern European crisis.

ENDNOTES - CHAPTER 8

1. Compare, for example, Dale C. Copeland, "Economic Interdependence and War: A Theory of Trade Expectations," *International Security*, Vol. V, No. 20, 1996; Peter Paret, ed., *Makers of Modern Strategy: From Machiavelli to the Nuclear Age*, Oxford: Clarendon Press, 1986; James E. Dougherty and Robert L. Pfaltzgraff, Jr., *Contending Theories of International Relations*, New York: Harper

& Row, 1981; Kenneth N. Waltz, *Theory of International Politics*, New York: Random House, 1979; Klaus Knorr and Frank N. Trager, eds., *Economic Issues and National Security*, Lawrence: Regents Press of Kansas, 1977.

2. David Harvey, *The Condition of Postmodernity*, London: Blackwell, 1990.

3. See Stefano Bianchini and Robert Craig Nation, eds., *The Yugoslav Conflict and Its Implications for International Relations*, Ravenna: Longo Editore, 1998; Susan L. Woodward, *Balkan Tragedy*, Washington DC: The Brookings Institutions, 1995; Stefano Bianchini and Paul Shoup, eds., *The Yugoslav War, Europe and the Balkans: How to Achieve Security?*, Ravenna: Longo Editore, 1995; Leonard J. Cohen, *Broken Bonds. Yugoslavia's Disintegration and Balkan Politics in Transition*, Boulder: Westview Press, 1993.

4. Compare Maurizio Viroli, *For Love of Country*, Oxford: Oxford University Press, 1995; Federico Chabod, *L'idea di nazione*, 4th ed., Bari: Laterza, 1979; Giuseppe Mazzini, *Scritti politici*, Torino: utet, 1972; Giuseppe Mazzini, *Scritti editi e inediti di Giuseppe Mazzini*, Imola: Galeati, 1976.

5. Stefano Bianchini and George Schopflin, eds., *State Building in the Balkans*, Ravenna: Longo Editore, 1998.

6. See Alexander Gerschenkron, *Economic Backwardness in Historical Perspective*, Cambridge, MA: The Belknap Press, 1962. Compare with the following studies: Francesco Privitera, *La transizione continua*, Ravenna: Longo Editore, 1996; Daniel Chirot, *The Origins of Backwardness in Eastern Europe*, Berkeley: University Of California Press, 1989; John Lampe and Marvin Jackson, *Balkan Economic History*, Bloomington: Indiana University Press, 1982; Iván T. Berend and György Ránki, *Economic Development in East Central Europe in the 19th and 20th Century*, New York: Columbia University Press, 1974.

7. Stephano Bianchini, *Atlante geopolitico dell'Europa centro-orientale*, in "Limes," n. 1, 1996, pp. 95-123.

8. Fadil Ademovic, *Beznadje zla*, Sarajevo: Medjunarodni Centar za mir, 1997; Nebojsa Popov, ed., *Srpska strana rata*, Beograd: Republika, 1996; Rada Ivekovic and Dunja Blazevic, *Hommage à Sarajevo. Destruction de l'image/Image de la destruction*, Paris: L'Harmattan, 1996; Adil Zulfikarpasic, Vlado Gotovac, Miko Tripalo, Ivo Banac, *Okovana Bosna. Razgovor*, Zürich: Bosnjacki Institut, 1995; Mark

Thompson, *Forging War*, London: Article 19, International Centre Against Censorship, 1994.

9. See Ivan Siber, "Psychological approaches to Ethnic Conflict in the Territories of Former Yugoslavia," in Dusan Janjic, ed., *Ethnic Conflict Management. The Case of Yugoslavia*, Ravenna: Longo Editore, 1997; Stefano Bianchini, *Sarajevo. Le radici dell'odio*, 2d ed., Roma: Edizioni associate, 1996; Sabrina Petra Ramet, *Balkan Babel*, Boulder: Westview Press, 1996.

10. Srebrenica 1995, Sarajevo: Institut za istrazivanje zlocinaprotiv covjecnosti i medjunarodnog prava, 1998 with documents; Smail Cekic, *The aggression on Bosnia and Genocide against Bosniacs 1991-1993*, Sarajevo: Institut za istrazivanje zlocinaprotiv covjecnosti i medjunarodnog prava, 1995 with documents.

11. See Sefer Halilovic, *Lukava strategija*, Sarajevo: Marsal, 1997; Kasim Begovic, *Bosna i Hercegovina od Vanceove misije do Daytonskog sporazuma*, Sarajevo: Bosanska Knjiga, 1997; Xavier Bougarel, *Bosnie. Anatomie d'un conflict*, Paris: La Découverte, 1996; Heni Herceg, *Ispodvijesti*, Split: Feral Tibune, 1995; Stefano Bianchini, "Yugosklavism and Nationalism: the Rebirth of National Serb Interest," *South East European Monitor*, Vol. 2, No. 1, 1995, pp. 50-66; Slaven Letica, *Divlje misli*, Zagreb: AGM, 1993; Zoran Obenovic, *Srbija i novi poredak*, Nis: Gradina, 1992; Dobrila Gajic-Glisic, *Srpska vojska*, Cacak: M. T. Spasojevic, 1992.

12. See Melita Richter Malabotta, *L'altra Serbia: gli intellettuali e la guerra*, Milano: Selene Edizioni, 1996; *Federacija Bosna i Hercegovina: drzava i civilno drustvo*; Zagreb: Novi Liber, 1995; Rada Ivekovic, ed., *La Croatie depuis l'effrondrement de la Yougoslavie. L'opposition non-nationaliste*, Paris: l'Harmattan, 1994.

13. Compare M. Cherif Bassiouni, *Indagine sui crimini di guerra nell'ex Jugoslavia*, Milano: Giuffrè, 1997; International Criminal Tribunal for the Former Yugoslavia, *Indictment: Delalic, Mucic, Delic, Landzo (Celebici)*, The Hague: Press and Information Office, 1996; International Criminal Tribunal for the Former Yugoslavia, *Indictment: Tadic and the Others*, The Hague: Press and Information Office, 1995.

14. See Pino Agnetti, *Operazione Alba*, Stato Maggiore della Difesa Novara: De Agostini, 1997; and *Albania, strategia e linee d'azione della diplomazia italiana gennaio-ottobre 1997*, Roma: Ministero degli Affari Esteri, 1997.

15. Luigi Ferrajoli, *La sovranità nel mondo moderno*, Bari: Laterza, 1997.

16. Michael Heffernan, *The Meaning of Europe*, London: Arnold, 1998; Gerard Delanty, *Inventing Europe. Idea, Identity, Reality*, New York: St. Martin's Press, 1995; Altiero Spinelli, *La crisi degli Stati nazionali. Germania, Italia, Francia*, Bologna: Il Mulino, 1991.

17. See Andrew Linklater, *The Transformation of Political Community*, Cambridge: Polity Press, 1998; Karl Cordell, ed., *Ethnicity and Democratisation in the New Europe*, London: Routledge, 1998.

18. Compare Anna Krasteva, ed., *Communities and Identities*, Petekston, Sofija, 1998; Will Kymlicka, *Multicultural Citizenship*, Oxford: Clarendon Press, 1995; Tiziano Bonazzi and Michael Dunne, eds., *Cittadinanza e diritti nelle società multiculturali*, Bologna: Il Mulino, 1994; Raymon Breton, "From Ethnic to Civic Nationalism," *Ethnic and Racial Studies*, Vol. 2, No. 1, 1988, pp. 86-102.

19. Zekerijah Smajic, *Evropska unija i zemlje bivse Jugoslavije*, Sarajevo: Oko, 1997; Paolo Facchi, Melita Richter Malabotta, Claudio Venza, eds., *Conflittualità balcanica. Integrazione europea*, Trieste: Eitre, 1993.

20. Francois Fejtö, *La fin des démocraties populaires*, Paris: Séuil, 1992; E.Fanara, ed., *I diritti dell'uomo da Helsinki a Belgrado: risultati e prospettive*, Milano: Giuffrè, 1981.

21. Stefano Bianchini, "Political Culture and Democratisation in the Balkans," in Geoffrey Pridham and Tom Gallaghan, eds., *Democratisation in the Balkans*, London: Routledge (forthcoming); Marilyn Rueschemeyer, ed., *Women in the Politics of Postcommunist Eastern Europe*, New York: Sharpe, 1998; Stasa Zajovic, ed., *Zene za mir*, Beograd: Zene u crnom, 1997; Mary Kaldor and Ivan Vejvoda, "Democratization in East and Central European Countries, *International Affairs*, Vol. 73, No. 1, January 1997, pp. 59-82; Esad Zgodic, *Gradjanska Bosna*, Tuzla: Ritam, 1996.

CHAPTER 9

SOUTH-EASTERN EUROPE AT THE BRINK OF THE NEW CENTURY: THE SECURITY ASPECT

Valeri Ratchev

Introduction.

The sole mentioning of the Balkans (or southeastern Europe, as all the countries of the region prefer it to be called) is often sufficient to spoil the mood of and to introduce skepticism among the participants at any conference on international security issues. That immediately reminds them of the scenes of violence on the TV screens since the end of the 1980s, starting with Timisoara in Romania, passing through Bihac and Srebrenitsa in Bosnia and Herzegovina, and ending in practically any village in Kosovo.

It would be wrong to say that people were not used to seeing violence on TV before 1989. The terrorist acts in Northern Ireland and Spain, for example, were not pleasant to watch, either. The difference, however, is not so much in the essence of the problems, but rather in their political interpretation, in their print and televised media coverage. *The Balkans in Fire: Nightmare in Yugoslavia, Balkan Ghosts: A Journey through History, Fifty Years of War and Diplomacy in the Balkans, Balkan Tragedy: Chaos and Dissolution After the Cold War*, and *Summer in the Balkans: Laughter and Tears After Communism* are only samples of the titles and headlines of books and publications by such prestigious international figures as James Hill, Yves Delay, Robert Kaplan, Carol Sforza, Susan Woodward, and Randal Baker. The apotheosis of this rhetoric is in the words (and the way of thinking) of a senior European diplomat, "Whether we like or not, NATO has become the sheriff in

Europe's 'Wild Southeast'."[1] In Bulgarian parlance: a word spoken is past recalling.

The Situation in the Balkans.

Rightly or not, the Balkans will enter the 21st century as a by-word for instability and conflicts. Researchers from all over the world are seeking the roots of this unhappy situation in the conflicting nature of the Balkan peoples, in the heritage of the Ottoman Empire and the Cold War, in the contradictory policy of the great powers for centuries and, even now, aiming at redistribution of the space of the region, and in new geopolitical and economic interests.

The truth probably includes elements of all these reasons. However, what is strategically important for all the nations of the region is that ongoing and potential conflicts isolate it from the rapid integration processes in Europe, divert huge resources from development programs, increase the technological backwardness of the countries and of the regional infrastructure as a whole, and immensely reduce the standard and quality of life of all peoples.

As a result of these circumstances, the Balkan Peninsula became a specific space from the perspective of European security:

- the largest military operation in Europe for half a century was carried out in this region;

- this is the region, where, contrary to all other parts of Europe, the level of heavy armaments continues to be maintained at the highest possible level, and in many cases is being increased;

- the level of political contacts between the Balkan countries continues to carry signs of geometrical configurations (the well-known axes and triangles) from the beginning of this century, instead of applying the necessary contemporary approach;

- the regional infrastructure, the economic exchanges, and the regional distribution of labor are still at a very low level compared to the other parts of Europe; and,

- the standard and quality of life of the Balkan peoples lag considerably behind that of the rest of Europe, and this makes the region unattractive, even for its inhabitants.

Risks and Threats to Security.

The main threat to security in Southeastern Europe is the economic, social, and ethno-religious instability emerging against the background of still powerful nationalism, of aspirations for national and ethnic self-determination, and of related territorial disputes. The collapse of the totalitarian form of government activated a number of latent contradictions, hidden forcefully by the old regimes. These contradictions create new risks and challenges to security.

The dismantling of the biggest Balkan state began with the collapse of the bi-polar system. The bloody Yugoslav quake sent tectonic waves all over the region that caused threats of different degrees to the neighboring countries. The 5 years of war in former Yugoslavia, the 2 1/2 years of efforts to implement the Dayton Peace Agreements, the new orientation of the former communist states, the Albanian and the Cyprus crises—all these circumstances profoundly altered the geo-political picture of the region. From a political prospective, the Balkans are so radically different now that the use of the term, *Balkans*, is already unreasonable.

The level of stability, the security policy orientation, the relations with the other European states, the European Union (EU), the United States, NATO, and Russia, for the countries of the Northern Balkans (Slovene, Croat, Bosnia, and Herzegovina) are completely different from those of the southern sub-region (Bulgaria, Romania, Greece, and Turkey) and the central sub-region (Albania, Macedonia, and the Federal Republic of Yugoslavia). It is precisely in the Central Balkans where the ongoing and potential conflict sources are concentrated. On the background of this approach to the configuration of the Balkans, the crisis of the last decade is the epicenter of the tensions that sends its tectonic waves to the southeast.

In the northern sub-region, the tensions, accumulated in the period after World War II, resulted in the rupture of the Yugoslav Federation by force of arms. After a long "starting period," however, the commitment of the West was of a high intensity and eventually lead to a large scale peacekeeping operation, to the Dayton formula for creation of a new state, and to a program for economic recovering of the region.

The shift of the conflict to the central Balkan sub-region could be expected because of the almost identical character of the contradictions and their nonsettlement in the framework of the Dayton process in Bosnia and Herzegovina. Although similar in roots, the cases of Kosovo, Macedonia, and Albania are very different from the ones in the north, and very little of the accumulated experience can be mechanically applied. Precisely these circumstances opened the way for some Bulgarian initiatives on Kosovo that were supported by its neighbors.

The contradictions in the Southern Balkans are of another nature and do not stem from the crisis that began in Yugoslavia a decade ago. Their dimensions are at a higher strategic level because they affect the interests of the United States, Russia, and the states of the EU in the Eastern Mediterranean and the Middle East. Nevertheless, there is a threat of a chain reaction of the conflict spreading from the central sub-region to the Southern Balkans.

Flash Points.

Three crisis areas with different degrees of intensity dominate in Southeastern Europe:

- the "hot crisis" in Kosovo and the issue of Albanians in Macedonia;

- the "fading (for the time being) crisis" in Bosnia and Herzegovina; and,

- the "cold crisis" in the Aegean Sea and Cyprus.

There was nothing unusual in the development of the Kosovo crisis. In Chechnya and Kurdistan and in Africa and Central America, the regular armies deal with the rebels and the separatists in the same way—through cleansing of the ethnic groups and the social groupings that support them. The Serbs applied the same tactics in the beginning of the war against the dismantling of the Yugoslav Federation. The Croats and the Bosnians did the same towards the end of the war.

Throughout the Kosovo crisis, the West could not find the right tune. It declared some Serb operations as legitimate defense against the separatists and others as requiring immediate NATO interventions, while the cleansing operations in Central Kosovo in July 1998 were passed with silence. The western countries looked on as actors in a drama in which they play the roles that they have chosen *themselves*, depending on *their* culture and using their *own* languages.

For the time being, NATO succeeded in halting the violence without military intervention, but much time was wasted. Because of this, the main motive for such an intervention became the refugee problem. There is no doubt that this problem is important, but its possible solution will not eliminate the roots of the conflict in the province. The Albanians will probably accept some parts of the agreements, but giving up the demands for independence will not be among them. The Serbs will also make concessions on obvious issues, but giving up the *de facto* control over Kosovo and the border with Albania will not be among them.

The problem is that none of the parties involved in the conflict—the Serbs, the Albanians, or the part of the international community that has authorized it to make decisions—has a strategy for its real solution. The lack of strategy creates the possibility for offensiveness of the claims, opens the door for expansionism, and leads to permanent escalation of pretensions of an Israel-Palestinian type.

The way in which the conflict was prevented at this stage is characterized by some important elements that will leave a lasting imprint on the future situation in the region.

- It was admitted that the conflict is stained with blood to a stage when "the victims cannot be forgotten." Whatever the political development in the future is, these victims will hang as a "sword of Damocles" over the ethnic peace in the province.

- Although the western leaders and media see the roots of evil in the person of Yugoslav President Slobodan Milosevic, the United States again decided to negotiate with him for the solution of a crisis created by his government. The end of the Milosevic era is postponed for the indefinite future. The questions are for whom is that "good," and for whom is that "evil."

- The countries of the region were once more isolated from the decisionmaking on issues that concern their vital interests, although the West admitted that the mistake to isolate the neighbors around the Dayton Agreements should not be repeated. There are continuous statements that partnership and associated membership status make states participants in the crisis management, the last ones with which the United States and NATO coordinated their intentions and acts were the countries of this region. And this is an overstatement, in fact these countries were not consulted at all. There was no Euro-Atlantic Partnership Council (EAPC) mechanism, there was no "strategic partnership." There was just a note requesting air space corridors that could be dispatched with the same wording to Sweden as well.

- Despite the obvious potential "domino effect," the approach to the management of this crisis was again dominated by military threats. The efforts to force the Albanians to work out a common position in a few weeks that they have not succeeded in doing in 20 years is an example of pseudo-diplomacy. The only result of the diplomatic pressure on Serbia was the consolidation of the nation around Milosevic's political camarilla. The pick was reached when Milosevic was called to Moscow to accept the demands of the Contact Group, while at the same time in Brussels, Rugova was instructed to avoid negotiations.

- The solution of the crisis even at this stage put an end to Russia's geo-political presence in the Central Balkans. Bulgaria and Romania were lost for the Russian cause forever. For the first time, Serbia felt Russia's weakness on its back and will probably no longer count on its support. The area of the Northern and Central Balkans will remain under NATO's hat, with all evolving consequences.

The other regional conflict, one that could be qualified as a "fading" or "cooling" crisis, is the one in Bosnia and Herzegovina, in other words, the zone of action of the Dayton Peace Agreements. This crisis became a strategic challenge of a new type for the democratic community. It is precisely in Bosnia and Herzegovina where the NATO horizons started to expand, and the idea that peacekeeping operations outside the Alliance's zone of responsibility could, if not be dominant, be at least equally important for the collective defense.

Second, it is very important to note that in Bosnia and Herzegovina, NATO demonstrated abilities to overcome contradictions with nonmember countries and other international organizations, such as the Western European Union (WEU) and the Organization for Security and Cooperation in Europe (OSCE). Russia's participation in the peacekeeping operations is a historic precedent of cooperation with NATO and facilitated the signature of the Founding Act in May 1997.

Third, the NATO peacekeeping Implementation Force (IFOR)/Stabilization Force (SFOR) operation demonstrated that, in a period of general reduction of the armed forces, the activities in coalition and cooperation between armed forces of different states is the approach that will lead to the creation of a base for a collective instrument for maintenance of international peace and stability.

What is new in the development of the situation in Bosnia and Herzegovina is the change of the general situation.

- The Milorad Dodic government was the first in the Bosnian Serb Republic that was pro-Dayton, and this facilitated the implementation of the agreement. A nationalistic-oriented government took over after the last elections in 1998, and it remains to be seen how this will influence the future developments. The Muslim-Croat Federation improves slowly as a state formation, but the national and religious disunion at the community level is still very strong. It remains evident, however, that further implementation of the Dayton Peace Agreement is impossible without external pressure, including military presence.

- The SFOR contingent is the only dominant military force in the region, and, as a result, no threat exists that the Bosnian Serb army will confront the international forces in the implementation of their future missions. The Bosnian Federation Army is being slowly formed, and its main problem is the lack of well-trained commanders. The Serb army is losing its superiority in heavy armaments, but it is still much better manned with qualified personnel.

- The probability of resuming the combat activities is practically nonexistent for the time being. The threats to security come mainly from the unsolved issue of the return of refugees and the related possible clashes at a local level. The existence of scores of armed criminal groupings and persons that pillage the population and the refugees in the less controlled regions is also a serious problem.

The disputes between Greece and Turkey on Cyprus and the Aegean Sea are a sort of Cold War with an unpredictable prospective. Two elements continue to further complicate the situation.

- The first is last year's official statement of the EU and the leading member-states that they are not ready to consider the application of Turkey for full membership (at least for the time being). Despite some softening of the EU position, Turkey again was not invited to participate in the Vienna Summit in December 1998 as a potential member of the Union. The scalding of the more than two decades-long ambitions of Turkey introduces new elements in its European and Balkan policy. They can hardly be expected to be entirely positive to Europe, although Ankara is likely to initiate steps for improving the bilateral relations with the Balkan countries, Greece excluded. Last year, certain differences of the U.S. and Turkish positions concerning the regional military cooperation could be registered. The fading of the European integration goal will inevitably feed the pro-fundamentalist moods and actions in the country.

It should not be forgotten, however, that Turkey is a very important factor with regard to the Balkans, and it is of common interest that its political stability is preserved.

- The second element was the deal between Russia and the Republic of Cyprus for delivery of ground-to-air missiles C-300 to the Greek Cypriots, i.e., their deployment in the integrated Greek-Cypriot defense space. This led to the freezing of initial *detente* between Greece and Turkey. The decision to deploy the missiles on Crete Island and the possible purchase of other types Russian ground-to-air missiles by Nicosia will hardly ease the tensions between Greece and Turkey. The present situation leads to the following conclusions that may change under the influence of new developments: (1) in the Cyprus issue there is another "player"—Russia; (2) a chain of contrameasures and possible answers to them will probably follow; (3) it will give another argument for delaying the beginning of possible political negotiations; and, (4) the policy of all external factors to the region will have to become more cautious.

It is evident that, whatever the international mediation efforts might be, the solution of the open issues between Greece and Turkey continues to be in the hands of the two countries.

Transnational Risk Factors.

The organized crime in Southeastern Europe is growing, due to the transition processes in some of the countries and the existence of sources of tension and military conflicts in the Balkans as well as in the adjoining geo-strategic regions. One of the main "traditional" (the so-called Balkan) roads for narcotics traffic to Western Europe passes through Southeastern Europe from the "Golden Crescent" (Pakistan, Afghanistan, and Iran) as well as from Syria, Lebanon, Iraq, and Turkey. (It is estimated that 75-80 percent of the heroin in Western Europe passes through this route.) "The Balkan Road" is also used in the opposite direction—for the transportation to the Near and the Middle East of chemicals produced in Western Europe needed for drug production. In the last years, growing efforts are being observed for the creation of new channels for drug traffic.

There is a tendency for increasing the illegal traffic of arms, ammunition, and explosives. Several channels pass through the Balkans—from Western Europe to Turkey and the Middle East, from Russia to former Yugoslavia (through Romania, Bulgaria, and Greece), to Turkey and the Middle East, from Serbia to the neighboring countries, and, recently, from Albania to Kosovo and Macedonia. The increase of the quantities of arms, ammunition, and explosives in the illegal markets in the Balkans is an objective factor for the expansion of political and criminal terrorism.

The traffic of strategic goods and raw materials is a relatively new phenomenon in the region. Besides the usual criminal results, this traffic creates a real danger of nuclear, chemical, and bacteriological terrorism on a regional, European, and world-wide scale.

Due to its geographic situation, Southeastern Europe is one of the migration "highways" from Asia and Africa to the developed countries of Western Europe and the United States. One of the touch-lines between the Christian and the Muslim worlds passes precisely here, and there is a constant danger of infiltration of Islamic fundamentalist groups and activists. The balance of security of the Southeastern European countries is particularly sensitive to these processes. In fact, in defending their national interests, the countries of the region, including Bulgaria, are buffers on the way of the migration waves.

The region is very vulnerable to money laundering. The liberalization of the internal and external economic relations and the great increase of the number of financial and credit institutions in the new democracies of the region, that are not being sufficiently controlled, create favorable conditions for money laundering.

The acts of terrorism in southeastern Europe show that the degree of terrorist threat is very different in the different countries of the region. The terrorist activities have mainly internal characters. At the same time, the different terrorist pressures on the states lead to differences in their reactions. The varying degrees of preparedness of the defense systems of the individual countries create a field of maneuver for terrorist organizations and conditions for the "transfer" of terrorism. This converts internal terrorism into a regional threat.

The Caspian Energy Resources: Impact on Southeastern Europe.

The picture of southeastern Europe will not be complete if the situation in the adjoining region—the Black Sea, the Caucasus, and the Caspian Sea—is not kept in mind.

The shallow waters of the northeastern Caspian Sea have become an obsession for the world's biggest industry and some of the world's most powerful countries. Geological studies have suggested that the salt dome there sits atop a potentially gigantic oil field, called Kashagan, and that, together with the large Tengiz field nearby and thousands of other smaller wells in the region, could be worth billions to the companies that control it—and to Kazakhstan itself. In recent months a near hysteria has enveloped Kashagan for perhaps the richest prize of this decade's high-stakes competition for Caspian oil and natural gas.

The U.S. Government has made the energy-rich region a strategic priority. The official statements in the winter of 1998 suggested that the goal of the United States is to have the investment and revenues generated by the Caspian and Caucasus region's energy resources play a crucial role in furthering its economic and political development. Even then the United States strongly opposed the construction of pipelines through Iran that would be of interest to neither the western countries nor to Russia.

The United States declared that it supports the construction of multiple pipelines in order to ensure unimpeded oil and gas supplies in the future. "We strongly support the development of transport routes for Caspian energy through Russia, which we believe is in the interest of all the regional states," Jan Kalicki, the U.S. Commerce Department envoy to the region, said on February 25, 1998. He particularly supported the completion of the Caspian Pipeline Consortium (CPC) project from Kazakhstan to Novorosiisk.

This considerably diverges from the recent U.S. stand. Washington wants to deprive the neighborhood toughs, Russia and Iran, control over more than a token share of the oil from Kashagan.[2] To do that, the United States has proposed the construction of a massive 1,087-mile (1750 km) east-west pipeline, which would start from Kazakhstan and Turkmenistan, then run west under the sea to Baku, the capital of Azerbaijan—and the center of the Caspian oil business. From there, it would cross Georgia and terminate in Ceihan, a Turkish port city on the Mediterranean. The key is that no oil would pass through Russia or Iran.

What is odd about the rush on the pipeline issue is that nobody yet knows whether Kashagan is flush with oil or only a major dud. The results of the definitive drilling tests by a consortium of major oil companies that should have started in December 1999 will not be available until next summer, at the earliest. Still no one has forgotten the early seismic studies showing that Kashagan could be two-and-half times as large as Kazakhstan's Tengiz, the Caspian's largest proven field. Tengiz has 6 billion to 9 billion barrels of producible reserves—a remarkable field by world standards. The governments backing Baku-Ceyhan worry that, unless the pipeline is started soon, a major geo-strategic opportunity will be missed.

But the uncertainty, plus generally soft prices for oil world-wide, has set off a tense squabble between the oil companies, which would have to foot most of the estimated $4 billion pipeline bill, and the U.S. Government which is determined to press ahead with the project.

In the end of October 1998, the oil companies—among them Shell, Mobil, and British Petroleum—held a top-level meeting with U.S. officials to discuss the matter. The outcome of the talks was as muddy as some recent disappointing dry holes in the Caspian. "We all agreed that Baku-Ceyhan makes sense. What we need to do is find ways to make it commercially viable in the shortest possible time." said an American official. "Baku-Ceyhan is going to happen. The main reason is that the governments want it, and politics do matter," Jan Kalicki, the U.S. Commerce Department envoy to the region, said.

In the meantime, it was announced that the Western oil consortium would be prepared to build a shorter pipeline, which would terminate at Georgia's Black Sea port of Supsa. It would be roughly half the length of the Baku-Ceyhan plan—and cost roughly half as much.

U.S. Government officials considered the Supsa idea a temporary solution. Before their meeting with oil executives at the end of October 1998, they were at pains to dismiss any notion that the original pipeline idea was untenable. Deputy U.S. Secretary of State Stroub Talbott called reports of its imminent demise "wrong and inaccurate." Washington's Caspian allies also spoke out. Turkish president Suleyman Demiril said: "Azerbaijan is determined [to go ahead with the Baku-Ceyhan plan], Georgia and Turkey are determined, and the United States is backing the project."

In Ankara, Turkey, on November 3, 1998, the presidents of Turkey, Azerbaijan, Kazakhstan, Georgia, and Uzbekistan signed a joint statement, supporting the Turkish Baku-Ceyhan project. The statement, that has a "symbolic character," was signed also by U.S. Energy

Secretary William Richardson. The surprise was the last-moment withdrawal of the President of Turkmenistan without further explanations.

Just before signing the statement, Turkish Foreign Minister Ismail Jem threatened that his country might address itself to other energy sources and producers to cover its needs if the "mistake" were made not to finalize the Baku-Ceyhan project. He repeated Turkey's position that it would not allow the Bosporus and the Dardanelles (the Straits) to become a "pipeline."

Commissary of the European Commission Christos Papautsis emphasized, however, that "from a political and strategic point of view, it is better that more than one route exists" for the transportation of the Caspian oil, adding that Russia should not be excluded. The diversification of the energy supplies is one of our principle goals in guaranteeing these supplies, he added.

The unsolved status of the Caspian Sea is an obstacle to the development of the Caspian energy projects. More important, however, is that many of them are competing and may cause serious conflict situations in the region.

It can be expected that, at this stage, the ambitious plans of many companies for exploitation and transportation of Caspian gas and oil will not be implemented. Actual investments are considerably lower than previously announced, and the conclusion may be made that the goal is the conservation of the Caspian fields rather than their real and complete exploitation. This is due both to the international conjuncture (energy overproduction and considerable decrease of their international prices) and to the interests of the main geo-political and economic actors.

In the regions that are main energy transport knots, a serious increase in the political, social, and ethnic tensions may be expected, even to the creation of more large-scale conflicts. That is particularly valid for the Caspian states, Turkey, and the Balkans.

What conclusions could be made from the available information?

- The U.S. Government is considering the issue as a strategic and political one; its main goal is to isolate Iran and Russia (it is to be discussed which of the two should occupy the first place in this negative rating). In fact, the United States is trying to isolate the whole Eurasian region (the oil field countries and Turkey excluded) from the supply route to the world markets.

- As it is still not absolutely sure that the Caspian oil and gas are worth the huge investments that are planned, the interests of the U.S. Government and those of the major oil companies do not entirely coincide. Another reason for such possible differences is that the Caspian oil and gas may undermine the world energy prices that are at a low even without the appearance of the new supplies.

- Although five countries (Turkey, Azerbaijan, Kazakhstan, Georgia, and Uzbekistan) plus the United States already supported the Baku-Ceyhan project, this should not be regarded as anything more than a political declaration. The implementation of the project will inevitably lead to economic contradictions that will be not easy to solve. Turkmenistan's last-moment withdrawal is an indication of this.

- Russia evidently will be against the southern route as the only solution. Moscow will insist on the western route (using the already existing pipeline to the Black Sea port, Novorossiisk) and probably much more on the future north-western pipeline (through Russia, Ukraine, and Poland to Western Europe). It is almost sure that Russia will be supported by Ukraine and Poland (mainly for economic reasons), but very probably will be also supported by several EU countries, particularly Germany and France. Guaranteeing the diversification of the energy supplies will be among the main arguments for such support.

The main conclusion for us is that the Balkans (Bulgaria and Romania, and, to a certain extent, Greece) will again remain outside of the energy highways to Western Europe. Nobody seems to be very keen to invest in a pipeline under the Black Sea from Novorossiisk or Supsa (Georgia) to Romania and Bulgaria (at least for the time being). In the best case, some oil will be delivered by tankers to the Black Sea ports of the two countries, but the quantities will be marginal. The situation with the gas might be slightly better because of the existing infrastructure. The project for construction of a gas pipeline from the Bulgarian Black Sea port of Burgas to the Greek Aegean Sea port of Alexandroupolis will still remain under question. (Russia has already declared that it will not support the project because it is economically unprofitable.) The political, strategic, and economic importance of Turkey will increase enormously, compared to her Balkan neighbors.

Conflicts and Integration.

Security is the key word for any region, and, of course, for the Balkans, too. Investing in the security of this region as a whole will certainly have a direct positive impact on the zones of conflict as well. In such a case, the conflict will not only be "capsulated" and the risk of its expansion beyond its zone will sharply diminish, but a sort of political "magnet" will be created, attracting the sides of the conflict to a certain type of behavior encouraged by external factors. Such a powerful "magnet" or stimulation should be membership in the EU, and—as far as security is concerned—in NATO, of countries with proven political stability and democratic development.

In fact southeastern Europe has its strategic advantages. The region is a linking point between East and

West, between North and South. It is a strategic, political, economic, and information linch pin of the EU to the Commonwealth of Independent States (CIS) and Central Asia. The region shapes the NATO Southern Flank, it increases the Alliance's strategic depth without significantly extending its outer borders.

The countries of southeastern Europe may have an important contribution to make to conflict prevention and the struggle against the new threats to international security. If integrated, they will be a reliable ally in preventing the proliferation of weapons of mass destruction, and in cutting the channels for illegal traffic of narcotics and arms. These are threats against the security of Europe and the United States, but not all the allies are ready to fight them unconditionally.

The crises in Former Yugoslavia and Albania and the problems in Cyprus and the Aegean Sea have a painful influence on the image of the whole region. Several countries that were not involved in any conflict, and even contributed substantially to the success of international efforts for their solution, are *de facto* partially isolated geographically, economically, and politically from the processes in the part of Europe west of the conflict zone. They are in the shadow of the conflicts that determine the ways of political thinking and behavior. The general characteristic of the countries of the region is their insufficient decisiveness in carrying out the obviously needed radical reforms in the economic, internal, and foreign policy fields. The rating of the Balkan countries from an economic and financial point of view is low, and to a great extent continues to be determined by the conflicts' intensity.

As a result, a conceptual vacuum is created concerning the states of the region. Western Europe and the United States define their main accents and strategy using the conflicts as a point of departure (starting point). Their actions are directed mainly by "point decisions" (often unfortunate), aimed at settling already existing military-political crises. The economic and social aspects of the conflict solution are not sufficiently considered (if at all), and no strategy for the political and economic investment in the region is worked out. The military and political-military measures have priority in the attempts to master the situation.

In its policy towards southeastern Europe, Russia, as a power with traditional interests and influence in the region, also has as a main priority the settlement of the crises in Bosnia and Herzegovina and in Albania and Kosovo. Russia also tries to maintain friendly relations with the governments there, to preserve the inherited military-strategic balance in the region through which to encourage the countries to adopt a policy of neutrality, and, above all, to ensure favorable conditions for functioning of the Russian infrastructure energy systems passing through or feeding the countries of the region. These energy systems became a part of the political instrument for achieving Russia's goals in the region. (Boris Yeltsin stated, "What is good for GASPROM is good for Russia.")

It should be emphasized that in this context the Balkan states are not offered the possibility to actively defend "their case." In a much lesser degree, they are regarded as serious (and reliable as far as investments are concerned) allies in the efforts to build up a homogeneous security zone. Despite their ambitions, they are forced to feel rather as a part of the problem than a part of the solution.

The countries of the region are particularly sensitive to some aspects of the implementation of the Western integration concepts. NATO has always been considered here as a political test for the attitude of Western Europe and the United States to the Balkans. Excluding countries such as Slovenia and particularly Romania from the first enlargement wave dispatched to the region a clear signal of the prematurity of the expectations. The ground was created for spreading doubts concerning the place of the region in the geo-strategy of the 16 capitals. Concerns were revived of the establishment of new separation lines between the countries of Central and Eastern Europe that share the same political heritage and do not dramatically differ in their post-communist development. The "Yalta/Malta" syndrome became actual again in several countries. The governing reformist majorities in countries such as Bulgaria and Romania were forced to render an account of why countries, distant from areas that are neuralgic for the Euro-Atlantic security, were preferred to join the first group invited to adhere to the Alliance.

In Expectation of Washington 1999.

With the approaching of NATO's 50th Anniversary and the Washington Summit, the public debate on the Alliance's enlargement is inflaming again in the candidate countries. The reactions of the "strong" candidates—Romania and Slovenia—to the Madrid Summit decisions were that of deception, and even offense, because of placing them among the "second rate states." The NATO member-states that supported their candidacy were declared "friends forever," even some heads of state became honorary citizens of the unfortunate candidates. Those who were against almost became enemies of the nation.

In Bulgaria the decisions of the Madrid Summit were accepted with understanding from both supporters and opponents—it was clear to everyone to what extent the Bulgarian candidacy was desperately late and to what extent the country was unprepared for the task when the decision was taken.

Despite everything else, all Balkan countries have the bitter impression that they still are the "bad boys," and there are still numerous and important considerations for their isolation from the real integration that have nothing to do with strategy or even politics.

It is still not entirely clear whether new states will be invited in Washington or if the issue will be left for the future. If we judge the words of Secretary of Defense William Cohen in Portugal, no new invitations are foreseen in April 1999. If we judge the statements of some European leaders, they will insist on a second group. However, this is an internal NATO debate and will obviously remain that way. It is understandable that the Alliance needs time to absorb the three new members and to make the needed conclusions on the basis of accumulated experience.

The improvisations on the thesis—will there be another wave of NATO enlargement in April 1999—are unfruitful and even senseless. While we were dealing with such improvisations in 1994-1997, we missed the time to carry out the necessary reforms that were successfully done by Poland, Hungary, and the Czech Republic. We should not be upset that the opinion not to invite any country in 1999 is prevailing. Our main task is to achieve the criteria for membership with the clear understanding that, due to the NATO open-door policy, our turn will inevitably come in due time. A different long-term development would be unfortunate not only for the candidate-countries, but the Alliance and the European security as well.

The countries of southeastern Europe, however, continue to make enormous efforts in order to attract attention. Some extremes can also be watched: effective promotions are being carried out, avalanches of PfP actions are being proposed, and multinational military formations are shooting up like mushrooms and are expecting a crisis anywhere so that they may demonstrate their high "NATO-like" abilities. All this is understandable and even right because the stakes are very high. At the same time, however, this strains the questions that naturally emerge, the main one being, "If the enlargement is postponed indefinitely (we should not forget that the enlargement costs were calculated for a period of 10-12 years), what will the European security system look like?"

It seems obvious that the promised all-European security system will be replaced by a *collective* security system for the NATO and EU member-states, and *cooperative* system for the others. On the border between them, a very important division line will emerge. From a purely military point of view, this is not all that essential, but it becomes extremely important because of the restrictive measures for crossing the borders, of trade protectionism, of information and cultural domination, etc.

If NATO does not expand, the military aspect of the security of the countries that remain outside the Alliance will not change considerably; it can hardly be expected that bilateral or multinational regional military alliances will be formed, even under the threat of new crises. What will change, however, is the assessment of the general security level, the state of the so-called *enhanced national security*.

It is a question of principle for us whether the NATO member-states are in a position to change their enlargement philosophy from "adherence of stability" to "adherence for stability." This is unthinkable today, but precisely this attitude opens possibilities to those who have "other" geo-strategic and geo-economic interests to draw the conclusion. If the conflicts stop the integration, then the best way to keep enormous areas fluid is to maintain the conflict situations through arms sales, supporting ones and confronting others, economic and customs restrictions, splitting friendly and friendly to our enemies states and governments, etc.

So we come to the question, "Will NATO continue to emphasize and develop the collective defense as a dominant function, i.e., if Article 5 of the Washington Treaty is stressed, how will the difference between membership and partnership be gradually eliminated (what was promised in a lot of statements after Madrid)?" Defense, even if they try to modify the notion, is dealing with precise concepts, such as war theaters, adversaries, military potentials, strategic and operational areas, etc. In Southeastern Europe we are trying to adopt the liberal way of thinking, but it is very hard to understand how our Partnership for Peace (PfP) will compensate for the advantages of the membership.

These questions may be easy to answer from an academic point of view, but they are very difficult to answer from a political point of view. Our governments need success in order to carry out political and economic reforms, success that should have a small but steady development. And when practically everything in our countries is invested in integration, and this integration is practically non-existent, one day somebody may ask unpleasant questions about the wasted resources, about the wasted political confidence, and about the lost opportunities. We hope that in NATO, nobody fools himself that in their present shape EAPC and PfP may exhaust the integration issue. It is fully possible that the NATO and EU states close themselves in their own problems (they have enough of them and have full right to do so because their governments must also render accounts of the spent resources), and to marginalize their strategic responsibility of the countries which are still in "the gray zone." This will not be the end of life in the Balkans, and all the people will not emigrate to the West. But the picture in southeastern Europe will be complicated and its development—unpredictable:

- For a long period, the *borders* between the Balkan countries will remain *frontiers*. These frontiers will have to be protected and defended. The issue of the military balance will continue to occupy the militaries' minds when they propose or make decisions on defense issues. The defense of a classical type will be a main trend of the military buildup and the basic task of the military policy. The regional military cooperation will consist rather in compensating the imbalances than in an expression of a high mutual confidence.

- The threat of the "domino effect" will paralyze the relations between the countries of the region for a long time. Kosovo, the Serb Republic in Bosnia and

Herzegovina, Montenegro, Macedonia, Albania, the Turks in Bulgaria and Greece, the Kurds, Cyprus—all these are elements of one and the same domino. The problem of the Balkans, however, is not in the ethnic diversity, the problem is in the poverty. A poverty that is not very different than the one in the beginning of this century when the Balkans became known as the "powder keg" of Europe. Today, however, the poverty is placed in a new political and information environment. This environment complicates the solution of the problems "at peace-work," it unifies causes that are at a distance of many hundreds of kilometers.

- The policy of Western Europe towards the eastern part of the continent will be dominated by the big states. The weak relations of the Balkan countries with the EU combined with the further restrictions due to the future adherence of the Czech Republic, Poland, Hungary, and Slovene in EU will lead to shrinking of the markets, the communications, the political contacts, and the cultural exchanges. If to all this is added the possible limitation of the U.S. presence and the practically complete disengagement of Russia from European affairs, their policy will have no alternative and no corrective. For the countries that fall in the zone of direct interests of some Western European countries, this could be the source of a progressive development. For all the others, however, the solution will be to return to the Russian and Ukrainian markets where the crisis will lead to a demand for goods that are not of the quality of the western or Japanese, but are of much lower prices. The increased trade exchanges with Russia and Ukraine will not be based on direct payments but on barter. And our 10-years' experience shows that barter is the most powerful source of illegal income and organized crime.

- The liberal and pro-western intellectuals will be the first to perceive the lack of perspective in their own countries and will seek ways to realize themselves abroad. This will have as a consequence the diminishing of the reserve of democratic politicians. At all elections the political elite will be gradually replaced by figureheads of the economic groupings. Every crisis will revitalize the nationalistic moods, just because no other ideology will get support. The civil society institutions, whose creation required such enormous efforts in the last years, will gradually politicize.

- Evidently, we have to admit that in the Balkans *there are problems which are impossible to solve*. The impossibility to solve them is, above all, a consequence of the lack of resources. The problem solution of all sorts is becoming more and more expensive, and the lack of operative resources is becoming a critical factor in crises management and conflict prevention. The lack of resources results in lack of alternatives. The lack of alternatives makes the armed forces the only real argument. That is why Turkey adopted a $125 billion rearmament program, Greece declared the purchase of modern weapons, Romania is negotiating a deal to buy combat helicopters, and Macedonia is planning to deploy a 30,000-man army.

We understand that the enlargement of a military-political alliance like NATO by accepting new members, and going through difficult political, economic, and social reforms in a radically changed international environment, is a very complicated and long process. We do not underestimate the complexity of the tasks which NATO and the member countries have to solve in this context. But at the same time, we expect from NATO a reciprocal act of solidarity, giving Bulgaria concrete perspectives. We are convinced that we have the right to expect that in the final documents of the Washington Summit, Bulgaria at least will be especially mentioned as a serious applicant for membership, and South Eastern Europe will be defined as the natural direction of the next phase of the enlargement process.

Going Ahead: Alone? Together?

When discussing the security issues in southeastern Europe, it is difficult to say what is pessimistic and what is realistic. It is even more difficult to make concrete and specific suggestions to Balkan governments to do this in Bosnia, or that in Kosovo, or something else in Cyprus. The approach of the countries of the region—reserved or positive—is very important.

- We may criticize the hasty, short-sighted decisions in the first stages of the Yugoslav crisis which certainly exacerbated an already tense situation.

- We may shake our heads critically at the optimism with which the United States thought that a crazy-quilt pattern, as concocted in Bosnia, might work effectively.

- We may reproach the EU, the United States, and the United Nations that they have known for years that Kosovo would sooner or later explode, yet they did nothing to prevent it.

- We may regret that, in particular, the EU has not been able to go beyond talks, visits, and high-flying words and take any positive steps.

- We may be also critical of unrealistic schemes, such as bringing the war criminals to justice, which have not gone beyond a few paltry cases.

What the countries of southeastern Europe can do is to:

- Inform and advise both the international organizations and the major power governments on situations which we, because of our proximity and of our greater knowledge of the area, are better equipped to know and to assess;

- Keep in touch with each other in a spirit not just of cooperation, but rather in the awareness of a common problem in our own backyard;

- Talk in a friendly and firm way to all parties involved, official or unofficial, trying to show them that any gain they may secure by the force of arms is bound to cost them much dearer in terms of losing touch with the realities of this beginning 21st century; and, finally,

- Show by our own example of creative cooperation that the path we have chosen for our countries, as members or candidates in the European construction, is more promising for our future.

An extraordinary example of a positive approach to the regional cooperation is the establishment of the Multi-National Peace Forces-Southeastern Europe (MNPFSEE) by seven countries—Albania, Bulgaria, Greece, Italy, Macedonia, Romania, and Turkey. This may be considered as an extremely positive achievement, because MNPFSEE unites three NATO member-states, they unite two of which do not maintain the best possible relations, two countries that have no diplomatic relations and the name of the one is disputed by the other; they consist of countries with very different status in the European and Euro-Atlantic institutions.

The establishment of these forces is a practical expression of the political will for military cooperation with the goal of building confidence among neighboring states. MNPFSEE is a concrete element of the military reform and the preparation for accession to NATO, and a way to materialize the new policy of participation in solving the security issues in cooperation with the democratic international community.

And last but not least, the establishment of MNPFSEE demonstrates that, when the spirit of cooperation prevails over the differences, our region has a future.

ENDNOTES- CHAPTER 9

1. William Drozdiak, *International Herald Tribune*, October 14, 1998.

2. Steve LeVine, *Newsweek*, November 2, 1998.

CHAPTER 10

TURKISH CHALLENGE AND EUROPEAN OPPORTUNITY: GREEK FOREIGN POLICY PRIORITIES IN A POST-COLD WAR SETTING

Theodore A. Couloumbis

Greek Foreign Policy Priorities in a Post-Cold War Setting.

The post-Cold War period (let us better call it the 1990s) seems to have falsified the prophesies of both the universal order and the universal disorder schools of thought.[1] At present, the world appears to be moving toward a new variant of *bipolarity* defined primarily in economic rather than military/political/ideological terms. One pole groups advanced, industrial, and democratic states; while the second pole comprises regions of the Third World and the former Soviet bloc that are characterized by economic scarcity and underdevelopment, as well as by political systems that vacillate between traditional authoritarianism, unstable democracy and praetorian managerialism.

The first pole, a world island of economic interdependence, democracy, and political stability, is made up of North America, the European Union (EU), Japan, and the remaining economically advanced countries of the Organization for Economic Cooperation and Development (OECD). Greece has managed to consolidate its presence in this zone of stable interdependence by virtue of entering the European Community on January 1, 1981.

In the second pole, the so-called "poor south" of the planet, one finds countries with developing economies and conflict-prone polities that are unable as of yet to sustain consolidated systems of democracy founded on pluralist and self-balancing civil societies. Recent and well-publicized examples of flash points in this region include humanitarian nightmares in Rwanda, Burundi, Congo (Kinshasa), Algeria, Zaire, Bosnia, Chechnya, Afghanistan, Kashmir, Cambodia and North Korea, just to name a few.

Hovering somewhere between the two poles are some of the former communist countries of central, eastern, and southeastern Europe. These states are in the middle of a very sensitive transition process that will either guide them safely into the ranks of the pole of stability and peace, or to the second pole of instability, civil strife, and war. Unlike former Yugoslavia and certain regions of the former Soviet Union, countries such as Poland, the Czech Republic, Slovakia, Hungary, Romania, Bulgaria, Slovenia, and the Former Yugoslav Republic of Macedonia (FYROM) seem, despite occasional difficulties, to be moving well on the road to a market economy and consolidated democracy.

Greece belongs institutionally to the pole of stability but, unlike its remaining EU partners, it borders on a region of fluidity and real or potential conflict north and east of its frontiers. Therefore, the gamut (nearly) of Greece's political parties as well as an overwhelming majority of public opinion have supported, increasingly since the mid-1980s, the process of Greece's multidimensional integration into the mechanisms and institutions of the Western family of nations. The dominant paradigm premised on multilateralism and reflecting Greece's foreign policy priorities could be summarized as follows.

The first priority of foreign policy since 1974 has been the consolidation of democracy and the adoption of an economic convergence strategy (with the more advanced EU partners) designed to safeguard Greece's historic European option. In their efforts to secure full integration into the "hard core" of post-Maastricht Europe, Greek policymakers, whether drawn from the ranks of New Democracy (in government between 1990 and 1993) or of PASOK (in government since October 1993), have avoided the so-called dilemma between a Europeanist and an Atlanticist profile. They have opted instead for a Euro-Atlanticist stance (akin to the British, Portuguese and Italian models) recognizing that there is adequate complementarity in a strategy that pursues political and economic integration through the EU and, simultaneously, relies chiefly on NATO for the provision of the collective defense and collective security values.

The second (first from a defense and security standpoint) priority in Greek foreign policy is the maintenance of a sufficient regime of military balance in the Greek-Turkish nexus of relations. Since 1974 (following the Turkish invasion and continuing occupation of northern Cyprus), all of Greece's political parties have been perceiving Turkey as posing a major threat to Greece's territorial integrity in the Aegean and in Western Thrace. In this connection, Greek bipartisan policy calls for the maintenance of an adequate balance of forces (especially in the air and sea) while avoiding highly destabilizing and economically costly arms races. NATO has been repeatedly urged by Greece's foreign minister, Theodoros Pangalos, to seriously consider the development of an intra-NATO dispute settlement mechanism which would help resolve differences peacefully as well as strengthen the appeal of the Atlantic Alliance as a collective security as well as collective defense providing institution.

Under the Constantinos Simitis government (but also under New Democracy rule in 1990-93), the Greek stance vis-à-vis Turkey's oft-declared European option has been to move away gradually from a strategy of *conditional sanctions* and toward one of *conditional rewards*. In other words, Greece now openly declares its willingness to lift its objections (given its veto power in the EU) to the building of a close relationship between the EU and Turkey, provided the latter abandons its threats of going to war over the Aegean question and contributes substantively toward a functional and mutually acceptable solution to the Cyprus problem, permitting the reunification of Cyprus as a federal, bizonal, and bicommunal state that is also a member of the EU and NATO. Cyprus could thus become one of the first candidates for NATO expansion in the Eastern Mediterranean setting.

The remaining priorities of Greek foreign policy involve relations with post-Communist Balkan neighbors and with the non-EU and non-NATO states of the Mediterranean region. In the case of the Balkans, after a painful interlude (1992-94) of near involvement in a regional imbroglio, Greece has opted for a multilateralist foreign policy (together with its EU, WEU, OSCE and NATO partners) designed to contribute to successful transition policies toward democracy and market economy in each of the states north of its borders. After smoothing its troubled relations with Albania and FYROM and while continuing to cultivate good relations with Bulgaria and Romania, Greece has also proceeded to adopt a purely equidistant stance (vis-à-vis Serbia, Croatia, and Albania) in the questions of Bosnia and Kosovo, respectively. The Greek policy toward the Balkans could be summarized today as "not becoming a part of the problem but joining, instead, the coalitions of the willing that act collectively as part of the solution." In this respect, Greece has joined Western peacekeeping and peace enforcement initiatives in Albania, Bosnia, and elsewhere in former Yugoslavia, including its mid-May 1997 participation in PfP military exercises on the territory of FYROM and mid-summer 1998 NATO exercises in Albania, together with troops from the United States, Italy, and Turkey, among others.

The process of EU and NATO enlargements fits well with Greece's strategic objective of encouraging stability and peace in the Balkan region, thus distancing the unpleasant contingency of having to face a second diplomatic/military front in addition to what has been widely perceived as a clear and present danger emanating from Turkey. Further, Greece's substantive support and involvement in EU regional, developmental programs fit the strategy of a multilateral and stabilizing presence in the Balkans.

With respect to Greece's role in the Mediterranean, the multilateralist formula applied to the Balkans is the orienting principle for Greek foreign policy in this region as well. Here the opportunities for NATO and EU initiatives are more than apparent. The EuroAtlantic community has every incentive to extend the values of security and cooperation into this structurally unbalanced region (where the EU North is rich and demographically stable while the non-EU South is economically disadvantaged and demographically explosive). For the time being, the EU/MEDA fund, which amounts to a very substantive sum of 4.7 billion Ecus for the 1995-99 period, is a concrete and much needed first step in a gradual convergence strategy designed to facilitate economic and political development in the disadvantaged littoral states of the non-EU Mediterranean south.

Greek policymakers also find that NATO offers excellent opportunities for military cooperation (beyond confidence-building measures) between the alliance and critically important eastern Mediterranean states such as Egypt, Jordan, Israel and Cyprus. The opportunities for substantive cooperation between NATO and these states will increase geometrically if the nexus of Greek-Turkish difficulties (which we will address later in this chapter) is adequately addressed, and Cyprus is permitted to join the ranks of NATO and the EU (given the overwhelming benefits that such a prospect ensures for both communities on the embattled island).

Finally, in Greece's list of priorities, the relationship with the United States occupies a critical position. There has been a dramatic improvement in the U.S.-Greek relationship during the 1990s. One could argue that the profile of this relationship from 1947 (the Truman Doctrine) to 1974 (the collapse of the Athens dictatorship) had been of the classical patron-client variety. The United States, a dominant superpower, and Greece, a strategically located but internally divided small state, could not have avoided the center-periphery dependence relationship. It was, indeed decisive American intervention in the 1947-49 period which prevented a Communist take-over in the Greek Civil War. The victors, the majority in Greece, were indeed grateful, and Harry Truman's statue was erected overlooking a central and busy Greek boulevard. However, the vanquished, a sizable minority, viewed the United States as an "evil Empire" that had been responsible for their final defeat in 1949.

In the 1950s, 1960s, and early 1970s, Greek-American relations were adversely affected by a constantly escalating Greek-Turkish conflict over the fate of the island of Cyprus. Perceptions in Athens were that the United States was systematically tilting in favor of Turkey (whose strategic value was heavily exaggerated by American strategic thinkers). Anti-Americanism assumed even greater proportions by what the Greek people considered an American stance of benign neglect (if not outright support of the dictators) during the 1967-74 period, when Greece was placed under the oppressive regime of the Athens Colonels. The Greek military regime not only violated basic human rights but also triggered a criminal coup against President Makarios of Cyprus (July 15, 1974) which—in turn—led to the Turkish invasion and the subsequent occupation of 37 percent of Cypriot territory.

In the years following the restoration of democracy in Greece (1974), despite the anti-American rhetoric of Andreas Papandreou and his left-of-center political party (PASOK), the image of the United States began improving again. The gradual consolidation of democracy, the incorporation of the vanquished of the Civil War into the political process, continuing economic development, entry into the EU (January 1981), the alternation of Left-and-Right-of-Center parties in power, and the establishment of strict civilian control over the Armed Forces, have permitted Greece to move in the direction of becoming a "civil society." Pluralistic discourse and the rise of independent and antagonistic media (radio and television that had been previously state controlled) have also permitted the kind of complex public exchange that reduces dogmatism and challenges Manichean (light vs. darkness) oversimplifications.

A Path toward Greek-Turkish Reconciliation.

The points of friction between Greece and Turkey are multiple, and much ink has been spilled in description, analysis, and interpretation of these problems as well as in the presentation of a variety of Greek-oriented, Turkish-oriented, and third-party perspectives.[2]

Regardless of the merits and demerits of the case of each of the disputants, the central question that needs to be asked is whether Greece and Turkey, which have been involved in an undisguised Cold War since the mid- to late-1950s, will be better off in a condition of protracted conflict, as compared to entering into a new phase of mutual and active engagement and even cooperation. Unequivocally, the answer is that both countries would be much better off if they were to reach a final reconciliation, a new historic compromise, reminiscent *of* the Lausanne settlement of 1923, and the Venizelos-Ataturk treaty of friendship of 1930.

The Imia islets and Cyprus crises of 1996, however, underscore the ease with which a state of protracted tension between the two countries may degenerate into organized violence and warfare. Hopefully, the leaderships in Greece and Turkey will have realized by now that Greek-Turkish war is unthinkable because, to begin with, it will isolate both belligerants from their Western institutional affiliations. Further, even if Greece or Turkey were to secure some marginal territorial gains after some initial battles, a chain of revanchist conflicts will surely follow, classifying both countries as high risk zones with a devastating impact on their economies and societies.

The ingredients of a lasting settlement, given the current international setting, can only be based on the assumption that Turkey will cement its West European profile. Greece, since 1974, has developed durable and tested democratic institutions and has become a member *of* the EU. Turkey is currently at the crossroads of the great choice between a European and a non-European orientation. Like post-World War II France and Germany, Turkey and Greece can bury the geopolitical divisions of the past, accept and respect the territorial status quo that emerged after World War II, and resolve to proscribe the use of the force in their bilateral relations.

A comprehensive Greek-Turkish settlement will most likely not be achieved without a just and mutually acceptable solution to the prickly problem of Cyprus. Cyprus has long been at the center of Greek-Turkish issues and still remains so. As long as the present situation in Cyprus continues, whereby the armed forces of Turkey occupy 37 percent of the island's territory, Greek-Turkish relations will remain tense, and a solution to Cyprus question will most likely not be forthcoming.

A genuine settlement of the Cyprus problem, which is today "ripe" for a solution,[3] would exclude *enosis (union* of Cyprus with Greece) and *taksim (partition* of the island). The historic compromise, therefore, calls for independence of a federal, bizonal, and bicommunal state, along the lines of the Makarios-Denktash (1977) and Kyprianou-Denktash (1979) agreements. Furthermore, Greece and Turkey cannot, and must not, attempt to impose a settlement on Cyprus. Reconciliation and peace in Cyprus are matters for the two Cypriot communities to agree upon.[4]

The new state of Cyprus that will emerge, following a putative agreement between the representatives of the Greek and Turkish Cypriot communities, will be given an excellent chance to survive and prosper if, at the time of its second birth, the "Federal Republic of Cyprus" were to become *simultaneously* a member state of the EU and, if deemed desirable, NATO. EU membership, together with genuine collective guarantees, demilitarization (except for the British sovereign base areas), and a United Nations (U.N.) or preferably a NATO-commanded multinational implementation force (until mutual confidence is established), will allow the troubled Cypriots to forge gradually a long-lived unity based on all the rights, duties, and freedoms that democracy provides.

A genuine settlement of Cyprus, while presupposing political equality of the two communities, cannot rest on a premise equating (in terms of shares of territory, gross national product, and federal parliamentary and executive powers) the 80 percent of the Greek-Cypriot community with the 18 percent of the Turkish-Cypriot community. In fact, all states and governments in the ethnically volatile Balkan and eastern Mediterranean regions must begin to abide by a simple and logical rule of behavior; otherwise, the chance of having peace in the region will be very slim. This rule could be articulated as follows: "Treat minority communities and other dual identity groups residing in your own country as well as you would expect third countries to treat minorities and other dual-identity groups that are ethnically related to you." For example, Greece should treat its Moslem (i.e., Turkic, Pomak, and Roma minority in western Thrace as well as it would like Albania to treat the Greek minority in southern Albania. Similarly, Turkey should treat (i.e., offer similar rights and guarantees) its Kurdish community in eastern Turkey as well as it would prefer Turkish minority communities to be treated outside of Turkey, whether in Cyprus, Greece, Bulgaria, or elsewhere. Albania, to give one more example, should treat the Greek minority in southern Albania as well as it would like Albanian minorities living in neighboring states to be treated. One could proceed offering examples involving a variety of states with ethnically heterogeneous populations in the eastern Mediterranean and Balkans, as well as in other parts in the world.

Turning to the Aegean dispute, a much needed historic compromise between Greece and Turkey must rest on two general and two operational principles of foreign policy behavior. The first general principle involves the mutual denunciation of the use of force by Greece and Turkey (e.g., by both countries signing and ratifying a non-aggression pact). The second general principle, which follows from the first, is that the Greek-Turkish dispute(s) in the Aegean will follow the road of peaceful settlement involving time-tested methods such as bilateral negotiations and, in case of deadlocks, arbitration and adjudication.

The two operational principles apply to Turkey and Greece respectively. For the benefit of Turkey and other sea faring countries traversing the Aegean, it must be made clear that the sea will not be transformed into a "Greek lake." For the benefit of Greece, it also must be made clear that the Aegean cannot be partitioned or subdivided in any fashion that encloses (enclaves) Greek territories such as the Dodecanese and eastern Aegean islands into a zone (or zones) of Turkish functional jurisdiction. The two principles together add up to the mutual acceptance of the status quo and the mutual commitment to exclude force as an instrument of policy in the relations of the two countries.

Concluding Remarks.

Looking from a Greek perspective at the record of Greek-Turkish relations since the July 1997 Madrid summit, the optimist would say the glass is half full, the pessimist would retort it was half empty, and the pragmatist might say to both "get a smaller glass." The arguments that the optimists tend to employ include the following: Greece's domestic conditions (political and economic) have improved considerably since the days of the Papandreou succession saga (November 1995-July 1996); Greece has a prime-minister with a pragmatic and Eurocentric orientation who has managed to establish control over his party, while enjoying a comfortable majority in parliament and projecting a credible image abroad. The party of the loyal opposition, under youthful and modernizing leadership, has lowered the tones of criticism on vital foreign policy questions abandoning a "tradition" in Greek politics of automatic dissent on all issues in order to score points with the permanently frustrated Greek public. In Madrid (1997) the Turkish President (with the implicit blessing of his armed forces) committed his country to the non-use of force and to the employment of peaceful process for the settlement of disputes. The obdurate behavior of leaders such as Rauf Denktash and Bulent Ecevit has met with mildly to highly critical responses in the international community, and Turkey (and the Turkish Cypriots) is singled out as primarily responsible for the lack of progress in the tortuous Cypriot peace process. All this is happening while the inflation of Greece is falling toward the 2.5 percent mark, and the remaining Maastricht (EMU qualification) criteria are within plausible striking distance before the end of 1999.

The pessimist, wearing dark glasses, shakes his/her head and dismisses the above as reflecting a mixture of utopian thinking and mirage-making. For the pessimist, the Maastricht regime is being pursued at the expense of the poor and disadvantaged in Greece. Turkey is continuing, despite Madrid, to escalate its revisionist demands in the Aegean and in Cyprus, and the "good boy" approach adopted by the current Greek government is being perceived in Ankara as a sign of weakness. Exhibiting a longing for the now gone "strong, proud, and charismatic" leadership, the pessimists are sounding the alarm for the declining Greek population that is "turning decadent, consumerist, selfish, and, at best, indifferent." Greece, for the pessimist, still has a chance to survive if it arms well, abandons wishful thinking, trusts less on the so-called solidarity of its European partners, and embarks on an international crusade condemning Turkey for its miserable human rights record and for its reliance on force so as to attain its foreign policy objectives.

ENDNOTES - CHAPTER 10

1. The literature on post-Cold War systemic changes is vast and growing. On the side of those predicting a new world order founded on a concert of great powers that projects the values of pluralism, democracy, and market economy, see Francis Fukuyama, *The End of History and the Last Man*, New York: Free Press, 1992; and Charles A. Kupchan and Clifford A. Kupchan, "The Promise of Collective Security," *International Security*, Vol. 20, No. 1, Summer 1995, pp. 52-61. On the other side, predicting the return of history in a world of great conflict, see Samual P. Huntington, *The Clash of Civilizations and the Remaking of World Order*, New York: Simon and Schuster, 1996; and Zbigniew Brzezinski, *Out of Control: Global Turmoil on the Eve of the 21st Century*, New York: Scribner, 1993.

2. For a detailed and detached review of the positions taken by Greece and Turkey on their bilateral dispute(s), see Andrew Wilson, *The Aegean Dispute*, Adelphi Paper No. 15., London: International Institute for Strategic Studies, 1979-80; see also Theodore A. Couloumbis, *The United States, Greece and Turkey: The Troubled Triangle,* New York: Praeger, 1983; Thanos Veremis, "Greece," in Douglas T. Stuart, ed., *Politics and Security in the Southern Region of the Atlantic Alliance,* Baltimore, MD: Johns Hopkins University, 1988, pp. 137-156; Ali L. Karaosmanglou, "Turkey's Security Policy: Continuity and Change," in Douglas T. Stuart, ed., *Politics and Security in the Southern Region of the Atlantic Alliance,* pp. 157-180; Tozun Bahcheli, *Greek-Turkish Relations Since 1955,* Boulder, CO: Westview, 1990; and Monteagle Stearns, *Entangled Allies: U.S. Policy Toward Greece, Turkey and Cyprus,* New York: Council on Foreign Relations, 1992.

3. In the view of the author, the end of the Cold War offers powerful incentives to the parties in the dispute (Greek and Turkish Cypriot communities) to proceed with a settlement which would add to all Cypriot citizens' welfare and security by facilitating the entry of Cyprus into the EU and its defense umbrella, NATO.

4. It should be noted, however, that any settlement that does not enjoy the concurrence of Greece and Turkey will be less likely to take hold and succeed, given both Cypriot communities' close affinities with Greece and Turkey respectively.

CHAPTER 11

TURKISH SECURITY CHALLENGES IN THE 1990s

Duygu Bazoglu Sezer

Introduction.

This study will use the term "security" to refer primarily to its external dimension rather than internal, and to the political-military aspect of security rather than its purely political, diplomatic, and social aspects.

It is nobody's secret that Turkey is faced with a domestic challenge to its territorial integrity in the form of Kurdish separatism led by the the Kurdish Workers' Party (PKK) since 1984. It is also widely known that the Kurdish question has negatively penetrated several areas of Turkish foreign policy, souring Turkey's diplomatic and military relations with many of its traditional friends and allies. Two developments in September 1998 have caused a deep sense of disillusionment in Turkey: the re-sponsorship by Washington of preparations for Kurdish autonomy in Northern Iraq, and the meeting of the so-called "Kurdish deputies" at the Italian parliament with several Italian parliamentarians on September 29.

This paper will limit the discussion of the role of the PKK for Turkish security to those cases where its manipulation of the external environment to enhance its ability to weaken the Turkish resolve to resist has been narrowing the threshold of human and material damage acceptable by Turkey. The sanctuary and direct assistance provided to the leadership of the PKK by Syria is the most glaring example of such cases. For years Turkey has maintained that the freedom enjoyed by the PKK in Syria and the Bekaa Valley in Lebanon allows it to consolidate its power base so as to inflict increasingly greater, and therefore unacceptable, damage to Turkey. In early October 1998, Turkish and Syrian troops stood face-to-face across the border following the Turkish warning of October 1 to Damascus that it either cease to nurture the PKK or else face the consequences.

This paper will first survey the main features of the new security environment for Turkey, then follow with a discussion of the specific challenges as seen by it.

The New Security Environment.

Turkey has been in the forefront of those countries whose security situation has dramatically shifted in the 1990s. This shift has entailed two contradictory directions, one positive, the other negative.

On the positive side, the end of the Cold War has removed the threat of war between the United States and the former Soviet Union which, according to conventional strategic wisdom, would have escalated to the nuclear level at some point.

Turkey, situated directly on the former Soviet Union's southwestern borders and hence forming the most southeastern flank of NATO, most plausibly would have been physically drawn into such potentially cataclysmic war. The end of the Cold War appears to have greatly diminished the plausibility of such war. This has been an enormous relief for Turkey, the target of outright nuclear intimidation and attempted blackmail by Soviet leaders several times during the height of the Cold War.

However, the anticipation of near-perfect security and the concomitant peace dividend that the phasing out of the Cold War and the disintegration of the former Soviet Union heralded in the early 1990s for the world, in general, and for Transatlantic nations, in particular, has proven to be largely illusory for Turkey. Granted, the threat of general war seems to have been greatly reduced, and Russia, the sole nuclear weapons successor state to the former Soviet Union, is much, much weakened. Yet, the regional environment around Turkey breeds both old and new types of political and military risks and threats that challenge, at times intrinsically and at others extrinsically, the core prerequisite of Turkish security. I define that core prerequisite as "the preservation of Turkey's will and ability to maintain its domestic unity and socio-economic viability as a democratically-governed, independent political entity while at the same time keeping intact the country's territorial integrity."

The Crescent of Instability.

A crescent of instability encircles Turkey almost full circle: from the Balkans in the north, down to the Aegean in the west and the eastern Mediterranean in the southwest, through the northern Gulf in the south, and, finally, to the Caucasus in the northeast. No other part of the world—not even Northeast Asia— parallels this multi-regional crescent of instability in terms of its vast space, the number of inter-state and intra-state conflicts, the number of fragile cease-fires, the coercive involvement of the world's most powerful military alliance, namely NATO, for peacemaking, etc. Turkey is the only land bridge that physically connects the three sub-regions of instability situated in two continents, Asia and Europe.

This exposure to several regions of instability might have direct and indirect bearing on Turkish interests. For example, Turkish interests would be adversely affected if some of the regional conflicts resulted in the violation of the security interests of those states in the region that are friendly towards Turkey, like Bosnia-Herzegovina, Albania, Macedonia, Georgia, and Azerbaijan. Second, developments that would usher in a radical shift in the regional configuration of power through irredentist policies and/or coalition-building would threaten Turkish interests by undermining its relative standing in the region. During the 4-year war in Bosnia-Herzegovina, the idea of a possible Greater Serbia and a Greek-Serbian-Russian (Orthodox) Alliance were feared, both for their impact generally on the Balkan balance of power and specifically on what they would imply for Turkey's place in that balance. Turkey would be outnumbered and outmaneuvered.

The crescent of instability around Turkey presents it with direct challenges as well. For example, the intention of Iran, Syria and Iraq to obtain weapons of mass destruction (WMD) capability of one sort or another purportedly to counter Israeli capabilities presents a direct challenge to Turkish security. Or, the presence of Russian military bases and troops in the southern Caucasus (not only for peacekeeping in Abkhasia but also to man the military bases in Georgia and Armenia, and to stand guard at the Armenian-Turkish and Georgian-Turkish borders) certainly is not a source of security for Turkey. Such specific challenges to Turkish security will be discussed in more detail in the following pages.

Transformation of the Western Alliance.

The seriousness of the instabilities and vulnerabilities in the 1990s emanating from the regions around Turkey acquires added significance against the background of the transformation that the Western alliance has undergone since 1990, in response to the elimination of the Soviet threat and the emergence of regional conflicts such as the wars in the former Yugoslavia. Thus, NATO is no longer the NATO of the Cold War years. More specifically, the relevance of Article 5 is very much in doubt under today's circumstances. This implies that Turkey, or any other ally on the flanks, should have less confidence than it might have had during the Cold War that the principle of collective defense would be invoked in case of aggression against it. Moreover, Turkey is only an Associate Member of the West European Union (WEU), by virtue of the fact that it is not, nor is it likely to be, a member of the European Union (EU).

Other institutions of the post-Cold War security architecture in Europe have not been designed to offer hard protection or assurances, anyway. As a result, NATO ally Turkey can no longer count on its protection, presumably still in force.

Security Challenges in the 1990s: Old and New.

While for the sake of convenience one can categorize today's security challenges as "new," and "old," one would need to note the interconnections and linkages among them. Through a process of cross-mutation, new and old challenges get tied to each other at various junctures of time and space, thus acquiring complex and novel new dimensions. For example, the security challenge from Greece is old, but it has acquired altogether new dimensions in the 1990s when Athens is pursuing a strategy of the encirclement of Turkey by promoting an anti-Turkish coalition among Greece, Syria and Armenia, three neighboring countries not reputed for their friendship for Turkey.

The Threat from Greece and Cyprus.

The perception of Greece as the single most important security threat is at its zenith today in Turkey. This is ironic compared to the nearly half a century of the Cold War when this perception was not so all-pervasive, but when the two countries even went to the brink of war several times.

There is a qualitative difference in the nature of the Greek threat in the post-Cold War era. Previously, Greece posed a threat to Turkish interests in the Aegean and Cyprus. In the 1980s, immediately upon winning entry into the European Union (European Community then), it concentrated its diplomatic energies on barring Turkey's admission into the processes of European integration. Thus, the primary Greek objectives with regard to Turkey were to gain exclusive control over the Aegean, and indirectly over Cyprus; and, to secure Turkey's exclusion from Europe.

In the changed circumstances of the 1990s, Greek strategic objectives with regard to Turkey have been broadened to include the following: 1) to entertain, in Greek strategic planning, the possibility that Turkey might be headed for dismemberment by Kurdish separatism spearheaded by the PKK; and, 2) to promote the formation of an anti-Turkey regional coalition in Turkey's immediate neighborhood in the south and east by exploiting the strains in Turkey's relations with Syria and Armenia. The following pages will discuss Turkish views of the two new elements in the Greek strategy towards Turkey in the 1990s. The traditional conflict over the Aegean and Cyprus and the struggle to bar Turkey from Europe will not be addressed here.

The logic behind the two new elements incorporated into Greek strategic thinking with regard to Turkey was simple. A Turkey that might be embroiled in a country-wide civil war against Kurdish separatism; a Turkey that might be isolated by and subjected to the pressures of a coalition of unfriendly forces on its borders in the south and the east; thus a Turkey that would find itself much beleaguered domestically and externally would give Greece the freedom to pursue the realization of its objectives on the Aegean, and possibly also those on the western coasts of Turkey.

Turkey has repeatedly charged that Greece, encouraged into such thinking by the PKK's terrorist successes, has viewed the latter as a natural ally in its struggle against Turkey, extending it political and material support in order to facilitate the division of Turkey at no cost to itself.

Clearly Kurdish separatism and its terrorist arm, the PKK, have played into the hands of Turkey's antagonists in the immediate region. Any country with grievances against Turkey theoretically could, and in many cases actually have used the issue to pressure Turkey into "correct behavior." This has been true most critically for Syria, and to a lesser degree for Iraq, Iran, Armenia, and Russia. While most European countries and Washington have tried to deal with the challenge posed to Turkish territorial integrity by Kurdish separatism by applying a human rights perspective and an anti-terrorism posture, Turkey's neighbors in the east have been bound by no such constraints that inherently showed deference to the systemic features and norms of the international order which honor the territorial integrity of states. Generally speaking, Turkey's immediate neighbors have viewed the issue of Kurdish separatism more like a zero-sum game whose successful exploitation was anticipated to serve their respective self-interest. In the event that Turkey ultimately lost to the separatists and was divided, in the zero-sum thinking Turkey's loss would automatically result in gains for them, above all for Greece and Syria.

It is in this frame of mind that Turkey has been watching with concern the progression of national and regional initiatives towards the creation of what appears to be an anti-Turkey grouping in its immediate vicinity, spearheaded by Greece and Syria. The first formal manifestation of this process was the signing of a defense cooperation agreement between Greece and Syria in June 1995. In response to expressions of concern by Turkey, Syria apparently immediately assured Ankara that the agreement did not give Greece a right to use Syrian air bases.

Between 1995-98, the diplomatic horizon of Greece vastly expanded as it concerned Greece's anti-Turkish strategy. Greece simultaneously engaged in a bilateral and multilateral diplomatic campaign, first, to establish good working relations with Damascus, Teheran and Erevan on a one-on-one basis, and, second, to promote the idea of a regional grouping between Greece, a Balkan country, and three physically and culturally distant countries among whom no tradition of institutionalized multilateral cooperation had ever existed before. All of a sudden in 1995, Greece decided to launch a diplomatic initiative and to present itself as a leading external force willing and capable of making a contribution to regional peace and stability to the east of Turkey.

Since 1995, a pattern of annual consultations called Trilateral Meetings have taken shape among Greece, Iran, and Armenia with the participation of their respective foreign ministers. The first meeting took place in Athens in 1995, the second in Teheran in 1996, and the third in Athens in 1997. The fourth, and final, Trilateral Meeting was held in Teheran on September 9, 1998. In the meantime, numerous high-level bilateral visits have been exchanged among the three capitals during which a series of trade, communications, energy, and military cooperation agreements were concluded.

What is important at this point is the perception that an anti-Turkey impulse appears to have energized the momentum for cooperation among Greece, Syria, Teheran, and Armenia since 1995. The fact that these contacts have not yet assumed a militarily significant phase capable of posing a coordinated military challenge to Turkey fades in significance from a long term perspective. What one is witnessing in the Athens-Syria-Teheran-Erevan interaction is a process that has the potential to be dangerous to Turkey's long-term interests. No country would feel safe in the long term if and when it is encircled by a potential coalition of three hostile states, namely Greece, Syria, and Armenia. The Iranian motive in joining this explicitly antagonistic grouping is more ambivalent, more complex.

In summary, Turkey at this point can only determine the presence of the Greek intention to leapfrog to Turkey's east in order make life difficult for Turkey in its own vicinity. The arguments and statements of officials like Defense Minister Yerasimos Arsenis, who have declared that Greece should conclude military alliances with Iran, Iraq, Syria, Armenia, Russia, and Bulgaria to establish an anti-Turkish bloc, verify the Greek thinking behind these developments.

The military cooperation agreement between Turkey and Israel reached in February 1996 should be seen against the background, first and foremost, of growing Greek-Syrian ties in 1995. While the Arab world has reacted to Turkish-Israeli military cooperation angrily, they have failed to take into account the impact of Greek-Syrian defense cooperation on Turkish perceptions of threat.

Cyprus.

Two developments in the 1990s concerning Cyprus pose serious challenges to Turkish security—the decision by the EU to admit Cyprus as a full member at the end of accession negotiations, and the purchase by Nicosia of reportedly 30 S-300 surface-to-air missiles from Russia for deployment in southern Cyprus in Fall 1998.

Turkey is opposed to the accession of Cyprus to the EU above all else on the argument that the Guarantee Agreements of 1960 rule out the accession of Cyprus before that of Turkey. In other words, the proposed accession of Cyprus to the EU would be in violation of the international agreements that created the republic in the first place—until after Turkey has joined.

Obviously neither the arguments of Ankara nor the Turkish-Cypriot government's opposition to being excluded from the accession negotiations (except on the EU's own terms) have carried weight before Brussels. The Turkish Republic of Northern Cyprus (TRNC) and Ankara have been forced to seek their own solution to coping with the approaching new order on the island: the Greek part of the island becoming EU-territory, and the Turkish part of the island being left to struggle for survival in the shadow of a hostile neighbor protected now by the EU hat. The answer has been agreement for eventual integration between the two. Clearly, this is not the best of solutions for the long-term interests of either the Turkish-Cypriots or of Turkey. On the other hand, Brussel's decision to admit Cyprus in the first round of EU enlargement has set in motion this dynamic that has inherently invited a new, perhaps irreversible stage in over 20 years of transitional *de facto* division of the island.

Developments in the military field are not promising either. The upgrading of military relations between Athens and Nicosia with the signing of a military cooperation agreement and the adoption of a joint defense doctrine in 1993-94, and the planned deployment of Russian-made S-300 air-defense missiles at the recently opened air base at Paphos are all very serious challenges to Turkish security. Turkey has warned that it would not tolerate their deployment. Greece, for its part, has declared that it would view Turkish military strikes against Greek-Cyprus a *casus belli*.

In summary, the triangular relations between Greece, Turkey, and Cyprus have reached an unprecedented level of complexity and tension since mid-1990s. In addition, with the planned deployment of the S-300 SAMs on Cyprus, Russia will have gained, for the first time in history, a direct military/technical presence on the island. Moscow and some circles in the West argue that the sale of these weapons systems to Cyprus is a commercial rather than a strategic deal. However, simple strategic logic defies this argument; that logic dictates that a power like Russia not overlook the enormous strategic advantages such a deal would accrue to its power position in the eastern Mediterranean especially at a time when NATO's eastward expansion, the Partnership for Peace (PfP) activities in Central Asia, and the West's intense engagement in the Caspian Sea region have been taken very hard by the Russian political class.

On The Brink of War with Syria.

On October 1, 1998, Turkey issued the strongest warning to Syria to date to immediately stop supporting PKK-terrorism or face Turkish retaliation. In the days since, diplomatic channels and mediation attempts by Egypt and Iran have somewhat defused the anticipation of a

Turkish-Syrian war. This does not rule out, however, the possible use of force at some point in the near future for, as the leaderships of all major political parties have agreed, Syria's role in PKK terrorism has reached intolerable proportions, and Turkey is using its right of self-defense when threatening the use of force. The Turkish action thus comes at a moment when there is a national consensus that the country will not tolerate more damage from PKK terrorism that is sheltered and materially aided by Turkey's neighbors, most dangerously by Syria.

Is there a reasonable motive for Syria to harbor ill-feelings for Turkey? The answer lies in the following: Syria is a country which refuses to recognize Turkey's international boundaries, claiming for itself the province of Hatay, which acceded to Turkey in 1939 following a 20-year French protection since the end of World War I, which saw the dismemberment of the Ottoman Empire's Arab and Balkan lands. Damascus and Baghdad also resent Turkey's grandiose dam projects on the Euphrates River, which it has been developing on an accelerated pace only over the last 20 years. No other major upstream country has waited this long to exploit the water resources it derives from such major transboundary river systems, willfully allowing the downstream countries to get unlimited benefits from unlimited flow of water. On the basis of a Turkish-Syrian agreement worked out during the tenure of Prime Minister Turgut Ozal, Turkey is obligated to release 500 cubic meters of water per second at the Turkish-Syrian border, an obligation which it has been faithfully honoring.

Northern Iraq.

Northern Iraq is another sancutary from where the PKK has conducted its operations against Turkey with impunity. The transformation of Northern Iraq virtually into a no man's land following the Gulf War, with Kurdish warlords roaming the area, has allowed the PKK the freedom to engage in a campaign of inflicting unacceptable damage to Turkey in human and material terms.

Clearly, the unsettled question of the future status of Iraq in the regional order nourishes a most destabilizing neighborhood for Turkey. Control over Northern Iraq by Baghdad would most probably have curtailed the most destructive aspects of PKK activity. President Saddam Hussein is frustrated with Turkey primarily because of the latter's support of the Gulf War and the United Nations (U.N.) resolutions, and therefore takes anti-Turkey positions at times. Bilateral relations would be normalized, however, if Iraq resumed a normal place in the region—which would, in the first instance, require it to honor its disarmament obligations to the U.N.

The PKK is only one dimension, the armed dimension, of the question of Northern Iraq. As mentioned in the Introduction, the political and diplomatic dimension of the future of Northern Iraq is of utmost importance to Turkish security. Turks feels that any federated Kurdish state in Northern Iraq would affect Turkish security extremely negatively—hence the deep concern over Washington's revival of Kurdish autonomy in Northern Iraq.

Weapons of Mass Destruction.

Three countries in the Middle East which are known by the international community either to have had some type of WMD capability or to entertain the intention eventually to develop it are Iraq, Syria, and Iran. All three are also noted for their ballistic missile capability. These very countries are Turkey's immediate neighbors. Turkey, for its part, possesses neither the capability in any of these weapons nor the intention to develop them.

Of the three, the potential threat from Iraq's WMD and missile capabilities have been eliminated to an important extent as a result of UNSCOM's operations on the ground in Iraq—until they were halted by Baghdad last summer.

There is no assurance, however, that Baghdad will desist from a concerted effort to reacquire WMD capability in the event that Saddam Hussein somehow succeeds in ridding Iraq of UNSCOM's thorough and intrusive inspections in the future.

Until recently, Turkey tended to rationalize the growing WMD missile capability to its south in the context of the Arab-Israeli conflict, believing that Israel was the potential target. However, the current confrontation with Syria has sharpened the sense of danger to Turkey from Syrian missiles and chemical weapons, just as the Gulf War in 1991 had done concerning Iraqi missiles and chemical weapons. We did not know then that Iraq had virtually mastered nuclear weapons capability. Iran's nuclear and missile programs are serious potential security challenges not just to Turkey, but to the region as a whole. Iran insists that its nuclear program is for peaceful purposes, and that it has passed the IAEA inspections that verified Iran's compliance with the NPT. American and Israeli intelligence communities believe otherwise, pressuring Russia, Iran's major source of supply of nuclear technology, not to sell sensitive technologies to Iran. Under pressure from U.S. President William Clinton shortly before the U.S.-Russia summit in Moscow in 1995, Russian President Boris Yeltsin agreed not to sell Iran gas-centrifuge uranium-enrichment technology, which could be used to make bomb-grade uranium, and not to train Iranian nuclear physicists.

This incident was illuminating also from another perspective: that such a critical deal could be made without authorization by the Kremlin or the Russian Foreign Ministry, as neither the Kremlin nor the Foreign Ministry purportedly had prior knowledge of the intention of then Russian Minister of Atomic Energy Viktor Mikhailov to sell this technology to Iran.

Amid the controversy about Iran's real intentions concerning nuclear weapons, Turkey and other non-nuclear weapon states in the region will have to keep in mind that

Iraq advanced towards a nuclear weapons capability clandestinely, while at the same time seeming to adhere to the NPT.

In July 1998, Iran successfully tested the Shahab-3 medium-range missile. Iranian officials described the test-firing as a defensive move aimed at creating a balance in the region, meaning specifically a balance that would neutralize the American presence in the Gulf. The demonstration of Iran's medium-range missile capability is certainly not a welcome development from the perspective of Turkey, especially in view of the fact that Iran is strongly suspected—despite strong denials—of pursuing nuclear weapons capability. It is interesting that, following the firing, Iran took pains to send a message virtually to the whole world that none of its neighbors seemed troubled by the successful testing of the missile.

Russia.

Turkey and Russia do not contest each other over any hard sovereignty questions. The closest sovereignty-related controversy between the two is the Turkish decision since Summer 1994 to regulate the traffic going through the Turkish Straits in order to improve the safety and security of the city of Istanbul and its environs against the potential risks and hazards of projected increasing volumes of tanker traffic to be carrying Caspian Sea oil as it is shipped to world markets. Russia argues that the Turkish move is in violation of the Montreaux Treaty of 1936 that establishes the legal regime of these straits. It charges that Turkey is motivated by a desire to eliminate Russian territory and the port of Novorossisk as the most attractive route for the export of Caspian Sea oil to world markets.

The absence of hard sovereignty disagreements has not meant the absence of political tensions, however. Rivalry for influence first and foremost in the Southern Caucasus and secondarily in Central Asia has been the fundamental cause of the uneasiness in Turkish-Russian relations in the 1990s.

The competition over the main pipeline that would transport Caspian Sea oil to world markets is a manifestation of this rivalry in the economic/commercial realm with significant long-term political implications.

Chechen separatism in Russia and Kurdish separatism in Turkey have adversely affected the two countries' mutual security perceptions, each accusing the other of instigating separatism in order to undermine the other's territorial integrity. On the other hand, while no Turkish parliamentarian has been cited for his activities in support of Chechen separatism, Russia's Duma members have been.

Russia's regional diplomacy in general and its arms exports to Iran and the Greek-Cypriot government in particular are among the most serious challenges to Turkish security interests—even if Moscow seems to stand only in the background. Like Greece, Moscow seems to see utility in the idea of an anti-Turkey coalition among Greece, Iran, and Armenia, as suggested by ample evidence in official and unofficial statements to this effect. As mentioned before, the Turkish-Israeli military cooperation agreement of February 1996 emerged against this background of unfriendly regional diplomacy.

Notwithstanding these tensions, Russia is not likely to confront Turkey with a conventional threat in the near-to-medium term for two main reasons: political and economic stability that underwrites a country's military muscle does not seem likely to dawn on the Russian state and society in the near future, and political and economic independence in the Southern Caucasus—except in Armenia—where Russian and Turkish long-term strategic interests compete with each other most intensely seems to be getting firmer roots. The nature of Russian-Armenian relations obviously defies this generalization.

On the other hand, one cannot rule out circumstances that might lead to another type of Russia, an aggressive Russia: the coming to power of Russian ultra-nationalists in Moscow, and a new round of fighting between Armenia and

Azerbaijan in which one side might seem to be headed for defeat. A contingency of this nature might ultimately drive Turkey and Russia into the imbroglio, the former to defend Azerbaijan and the latter to defend Armenia. Russian military bases and Russian troops in their various roles scattered around Georgia and Armenia—and directly at the borders with Turkey—and upgraded forces of the North Caucasus Military District legitimized in the CFE's adaptation in 1997 will undoubtedly be activated in order to repulse any Turkish action against Armenia. If things do not go right in such a contingency, Russia might be tempted to resort either to nuclear blackmail, or failing to get Turkey to retreat, might use limited nuclear strikes. The official military doctrine and Russian elite's thinking about the utility of tactical nuclear weapons in regional conflicts have already set in place the conceptual and political framework to make resort to tactical nuclear weapons in such contingencies politically acceptable and legitimate.

Conclusion.

As the discussion in the previous pages suggest, Turkish security perceptions are dominated primarily by concerns over long-term Greek intentions to gain control over the Aegean and the Eastern Mediterranean, and over the multi-faceted regional strategy of encirclement that it has been pursuing since mid-1990s to realize those aims.

Syrian claims on the Turkish province of Hatay and implicit claims by a newly independent Armenia on parts of eastern Turkey have turned them into potential allies of Greece. It appears that in the new scheme of things in Greek strategic thinking, a weakened and possibly divided Turkey would cease to be an obstacle to the realization of Greek aspirations in the Aegean and the Eastern Mediterranean.

The challenge of Kurdish separatism to Turkish security, a challenge with powerful domestic roots, has nevertheless been magnified in its scope only in conjunction with the nurturing it has been receiving from the external environment. Turks believe that Syria, and to a lesser extent Iraq and Iran, have been extending material support to the PKK, recognized as a terrorist organization by several leading governments in Europe and by Washington. This belief has been documented by Turkish authorities—hence the recent confrontation with Syria. PKK terrorism and the support it receives from Turkey's neighbors not only threaten Turkish territorial integrity, but they forestall the consolidation of Turkish democracy.

The consequences of attempts by Turkey's revisionist neighbors to tamper with the territorial integrity of Turkey would, if eventually successful, naturally be extremely destabilizing for a very broad region stretching from the Balkans to the Persian Gulf and to Central Asia, threatening the geopolitical *status quo* for nearly two dozen countries inhabiting this vast space.

CHAPTER 12

GREEK-TURKISH RIVALRY AND THE MEDITERRANEAN SECURITY DILEMMA

R. Craig Nation

Introduction.

In the best of all possible worlds, Greece and Turkey would be pillars of stability amidst the turbulence of southeastern Europe and the eastern Mediterranean. With their privileged access to European institutions, substantial economic prospects, and powerful state traditions, they have multiple assets that could be brought to bear to help promote development and security. In reality, however, existing Greek-Turkish relations present a depressingly diverse aspect. Athens and Ankara are arch rivals, whose mutual enmity often approaches the level of preoccupation. Rather than contributing to a resolution of the Mediterranean security dilemma, Greece and Turkey are among its biggest progenitors.

Greek-Turkish rivalry is unusual in that the protagonists are very unevenly matched. Greece is a small Balkan state with a population of 10.5 million, but also a North Atlantic Treaty Organization (NATO) and European Union (EU) member with an international agenda dominated by its relationship with institutionalized Europe. Turkey has a large and rapidly growing population of almost 65 million. It has European aspirations but also a significant Asian frontier, and it confronts an international situation that is extremely threatening and complex, "at the centre of a crescent-shaped wedge of territory stretching from Kazakhstan to the Gulf and Suez and finally to the North African coast, containing the most volatile collection of states in the world."[1]

Like Greece, Turkey has been a NATO member since 1952, but its relationship with the EU is contentious. It has assumed significant commitments in the war-torn Caucasus and Central Asian regions since the break-up of the Union of Soviet Socialist Republic (USSR), its relations with Syria and Iraq are potentially explosive, and it confronts an open-ended domestic insurrection in Kurdestan with important international ramifications.[2] Greece and Turkey are highly militarized—Turkey devotes 3.8 percent of its Gross Domestic Product to defense spending and Greece 4.7 percent (against a NATO average of 2.2 percent), and both have launched ambitious military build-ups. There is, however, little doubt that the Turkish side has the wherewithal to prevail in an armed confrontation. Turkish Gross Domestic Product is approximately 1.5 times that of Greece, and in purely military terms, Turkey enjoys something like a 4-1 ratio of superiority, with 594,000 men at arms (477,000 in land armies, 63,000 in the air force, and 54,000 in marine forces) compared to a Greek force of 168,700 (116,000 on land, 33,000 in the air, and 19,700 at sea).

Despite its physical superiority, the unresolved conflict impacts negatively upon Turkey's foreign policy agenda as well. Ankara's long-standing goal of accession to the EU has been sacrificed on the alter of Greek-Turkish rivalry, and in view of the many and substantial challenges that it confronts on other fronts, eternal bickering with Greece might well be portrayed as a luxury, if not an extravagance. The rivalry is nonetheless alive and well, irrespective of the constant ministrations of NATO, the good will of innumerable mediators and profferers of good offices, and the real best interests of almost all those involved.

There are at least two reasons why this is so. First, though sometimes concerned as much with symbol as with substance, Greek-Turkish rivalry is deeply rooted and complex, with multiple dimensions that have tended over time to become mutually reinforcing. The underlying issues are neither trivial nor straightforward, and they will continue to defy facile solutions. Second, the rivalry is set in a larger spacial and temporal context, and has been sensitive to patterns of change in the geostrategic and historical environment. Greek-Turkish relations are often discussed on the basis of "ancient hatreds" assumptions that emphasize their timeless and unchanging character—what Henry Kissinger has called the "atavistic bitterness" and "primeval hatred of Greeks and Turks."[3] But the relationship is also a dynamic one, and at present is very much conditioned by circumstances specific to the post-Cold War period.

Historical and Cultural Foundations.

Greek nationalism has three foundations; the legacy of the great classical civilization of the age of antiquity, the Byzantine and Orthodox Christian heritage of the Middle Ages, and the national revival of the modern period. The classical legacy is timeless and in a sense universal, though its fundamental importance as a source of specifically Greek identity is revealed by the furor unleashed by the 19th century Austrian historian J. P. Fallmerayer's attempt to deny an organic link between the modern Greek peoples and their classical ancestors.[4] The conquest of the Orthodox Christian civilizations of the Balkan peninsula and Aegean island groups by the expanding Ottoman dynasty in the 14th and 15th centuries, culminating with the fall of Constantinople in 1453, is almost universally regarded as a tragedy of epic proportions and the prelude to a dark age of cultural effacement, the *Turkokratia* or period of unadulterated Turkish domination.

Modern Greek national identity is a direct product of the 19th century national revival, waged as a bitter struggle against Ottoman overlordship beginning with the first Greek uprising in 1821. The Greek national state, created in 1830 at the behest of the European great powers, included only about a third of the Greek peoples of the Balkan region. Thereafter, the Greek state was built up piece by piece, as the consequence of a long sequence of wars, diplomatic maneuvers, and uprisings on behalf of the goal of *enosis* or union, inspired by the *Megali Idea* (Great Idea) of uniting all the Greek peoples of the Aegean and Anatolia within a single national entity. In Turkish national memory, this process is conterminous with the long decline of Ottoman civilization, and therefore linked with the Turkish peoples loss of great power status and cultural preeminence.

The tragic culmination of the *Megali Idea* came at the end of World War I, with the defeat of the Greek expeditionary force in Asia Minor at the hands of Mustafa Kemal's new Turkish national movement, the fall of Smyrna in September 1922 and the ensuing massacre of the city's Greek and Armenian populations, and the treaty of Lausanne in 1923. The treaty regularized a Greek-Turkish border at the expense of the nearly one and a half million Greek and Turkish refugees forced to participate in an officially sponsored population transfer. For the Turks, this is remembered as the "war of independence" whose outcome ensured the survival of a Turkish national state. For the Greeks it is "the catastrophe," a cataclysmic defeat which brought a violent end to the millennial Hellenic civilization of Asia Minor. Like other peoples whose national idea rests upon a cult of martyrdom derived from a long and only partially realized struggle for independence, the Greeks' national identity has been culturally constructed as a myth of resistance to a barbaric, alien, and permanently menacing other. In the case of Turkey, national identity has been defined against the foil of rivalry with an eternal Greek enemy, always ready to take advantage of Turkish weakness, that is simultaneously resented and scorned.[5]

Outside the context of this mythic structure, of course, Greek-Turkish relations have been considerably more nuanced. The peace of Lausanne was followed by a period of rapprochement under the direction of Mustafa Kemal (Ataturk) and Elefterios Venezelos, architects of war in 1919 but by the late 1920s determined to prioritize the goal of domestic restructuring and reform. The policy survived its architects, and Greek-Turkish feuding was not a significant factor in international relations during the period 1930-55.[6] It was only with the rise of anti-British national agitation in Cyprus that the Greek-Turkish rivalry made a comeback. In the postwar decades, both Greece and Turkey were modernizing societies undergoing a process of traumatic social change, including rapid urbanization, progress toward universal literacy, and the rise of mass democratic cultures where the evocation of an "invented" national tradition against the foil of a despised rival played well in public forums. On both sides, political elites manipulated national sentiments to further their quest for power, in the process conjuring up and exacerbating a strategic rivalry that would quickly take on a life of its own.

Aegean Issues.

The essence of Greek-Turkish strategic rivalry is the struggle for physical control of the Aegean and eastern Mediterranean. This is by any measure a vital interest for both sides. For Greece, the Aegean represents an essential part of the national whole, linking the Greek mainland with major islands and island groups. For Turkey, the Aegean covers the north-south maritime artery attaching the Dardanelles to the Mediterranean coast including the port of Izmir, and the air corridors providing access for civil aviation toward the west. The Aegean and eastern Mediterranean also possess geostrategic significance as the western pole of a commercial axis stretching east and southward toward the Caspian Sea and Persian Gulf. Marcia Christoff Kurop notes that "the eastern Mediterranean and the Persian Gulf form a single entity with Turkey and Egypt providing a continental and maritime bridge between Europe and the Middle East."[7] For Margarita Mathiopoulos, the Aegean is "a geopolitical region of vital interest" as "NATO's corridor of stability between Europe, the Middle East, and the former Soviet Asian territories."[8]

In the recent past, stability has been in short supply. By imposing population transfers and clearly delineated spheres of influence, the treaty of Lausanne was broadly successful in creating a kind of equilibrium between Greece and Turkey in the region, but that equilibrium began to unravel with the emergence of the Cyprus question in the 1950s. By the 1970s, a long list of points of discord had emerged which continue to defy resolution.

Sovereignty and the Militarization of Strategic Islands.

There are some 3,000 Greek islands in the Aegean Sea, of which only about 130 are inhabited. At Lausanne in 1923 and in the 1947 treaty of Paris, which effected the transfer of the Dodecanese island group from Italy to Greece, Athens agreed to keep only lightly armed security forces on western Aegean islands and to refrain from the construction of fortifications. The militarization of selected islands was nonetheless begun in 1964, and by the 1970s, over 25,000 Greek soldiers were stationed in the Dodecanese island group adjacent to Turkey's Mediterranean coastline, on Lemnos, Samothrace, and smaller islands near the entrance to the Dardanelles, and on certain central Aegean islands.

Greece has argued according to the *clausala rebus sic stantibus* that the Montreux Straits Convention of 1936 lifts the demilitarized status of islands adjacent to the Dardanelles; that Turkey is not a signatory to the 1947 treaty of Paris and that therefore the Dodecanese can be armed; and that, especially in the wake of the Cyprus occupation of 1974 and the creation of a 4th Aegean army unattached to NATO on the eastern coast of the Turkish mainland with its headquarters in Izmir in 1975, Greece perceives a Turkish threat to which it may legitimately react on the basis of the principle of self-defense under article 51 of the United Nations (U.N.) Charter. Turkey has responded that the demilitarization of eastern Aegean islands is a legal condition of Greek sovereignty; that no essential changes in circumstances have occurred; that the Paris treaty of 1947 also applies to nonsignatories; that the Montreux convention does not change the status of Lemnos and adjacent islands; and that there was no prior Turkish threat motivating Greek actions—Ankara has only taken countermeasures in the face of severe Greek provocations. These issues remain unresolved, and the militarized islands are points of constant friction.

The problem of militarization is complemented by disputes over sovereignty. The maritime frontier between the Dodecanese group and the Turkish coast was precisely delineated in a 1932 agreement between Italy and Turkey, but since April 1996 Ankara has posed new concerns about "grey zones" of uncertain sovereignty further to the north, where the terms of the 1923 Lausanne treaty are less clear, as well as in the sea of Crete. The Turkish demand for adjudication of the issue has been portrayed as a means to obtain leverage in a future comprehensive resolution of Aegean issues, but it also has a strategic dimension.[9] The sensitivities evoked by the issue were demonstrated when a January 1996 naval incident posing the issue of sovereignty over the tiny rock of Imia (Kardak in Turkish), in the Dodecanese group adjacent to the Bodrun peninsula and the island of Kos, brought the two Aegean antagonists to the brink of war. Strong U.S. diplomatic pressure was required to reverse the course of events, in a scenario that could be replayed in any number of other settings at almost any moment.

Delimitation of the Continental Shelf.

The issue of control over the Aegean sea bed became a contentious one following the discovery of oil deposits off the island of Thasos in 1974. Bilateral negotiations begun in 1981 were broken off at Greek initiative in 1987. Turkey responded by initiating seismic activities and drilling in disputed areas, giving rise to a sharp crisis in the spring of that year. In the years since 1987, the issue has lost some of its sharpness, due in part to the steady decline in the price of hydrocarbons on world markets and to the modest extent of the resources in question, but it is far from having been resolved. Athens argues that (a) the islands facing the Turkish mainland are a part of Greece, and that Greek lands must be considered as an integral whole; (b) the Geneva convention of 1958 on the continental shelf specifies that islands possess continental shelves; and, (c) the continental shelf border between Turkey and the adjacent Greek islands must be based on the equidistance principle measured from the nearest Turkish coast. If applied in practice, these premises would give Greece effective control over nearly all the Aegean Sea, leaving only a narrow coastal strip for Turkey.

In response, Ankara has argued that (a) islands located on the natural prolongation of a continental land mass do not have continental shelves of their own; (b) the 1982 Law of the Sea Convention disallows consolidation of Aegean islands with continental Greece by forbidding an "archipelago regime" or "national integrity" principle; (c) there is no rule of law or logic that dictates an "equidistance principle" between small islands and a large adjacent land mass; and, (d) the treaty of Lausanne requires a Greek-Turkish balance that allows each side to utilize the Aegean on an equitable basis. A broad range of factors specific to the nature of the Aegean, including its semi-closed character, the Greek archipelago regime, the distribution of natural resources, mutual security interests, and accessible transportation routes must thus be considered in measuring access. Turkey's ideal solution would impose a line of division allowing it to exploit a significant part of the eastern half of the seabed. Ankara has, however, consistently refused Greek requests to bring the issue before the International Court of Justice, preferring the route of bilateral negotiations, perhaps less due to the merits of the case in question than because of the potential implications of a definitive court ruling for other unresolved disputes, notably its differences with Syria and Iraq over control of the waters of the Euphrates.[10]

Territorial Waters.

At Lausanne, territorial waters in the Aegean extended for only three miles. In 1936, Greece unilaterally expanded its own territorial waters to six miles, and following World War II, Turkey reciprocated. At present, with a six-mile limit as standard, Greece possesses 48.86 percent of the Aegean and Turkey 7.47 percent, leaving 48.85 percent as international waters. The Law of the Sea Treaty of 1985, which the Turkish regime has refused to sign, allows a 12-mile extension of territorial waters, the extension that Turkey itself applies to its Mediterranean and Black Sea coastlines. In 1995, after the entry into vigor of this treaty, the Greek parliament stated its right to enforce a 12-mile limit in the Aegean, a gesture whose realization Ankara promptly stated would become a *casus belli*. Though the Turkish response was aggressive, the Greek claim was clearly provocatory. The imposition of a 12-mile limit would bring together Greek territorial waters between the Cyclades and Dodecanese archipelagos, giving Athens hypothetical control over Turkey's vital north-south maritime route, as well as over maritime access to the Black Sea.

The issue is arguably more symbolic than real. The extent of effective control that an extension to the 12-mile limit would bring is not necessarily great. International law does not permit interdiction of peaceful commercial traffic, nor even of the passage of warships, except in cases of strong tension or open conflict. A 12-mile extension is moreover opposed by almost every other power with maritime interests in the Aegean, and not least the major NATO powers. If the issue persists, it is in some measure because of its implications for the related problem of control over airspace.

Airspace Control.

International law and the Chicago convention of 1944 require that the extent of national airspace correspond to the extent of territorial waters. Since 1931 Greece has asserted a national airspace limit of ten miles, valid for both continental Greece and the Greek archipelago, despite its formal adherence to six-mile territorial waters. From 1974 onward, Turkey has formally protested against this incongruity, and reinforced its position by systematically conducting overflights in the four-mile grey zone. These interventions are regularly challenged by Greek aviation, leading to numerous instances of mock combat and occasional crashes. Disputes over airspace have given rise to other sources of tension, including differences over the Istanbul-Athens flight region, international flight routing, terminal areas, and military flight issues such as early-warning borders, command and control areas, and the extent of air maneuvers. The argument directly affects flight borders for two NATO commands, the south-central NATO headquarters in Izmir (Izmir also hosts Turkey's 6th Allied Tactical Air Force) and the 7th Tactical Air Force in Larisa, Greece.

Treatment of Minorities.

Greece and Turkey have been chronically at odds over the treatment accorded their respective minorities. Despite the mass population transfers carried out under the terms of the Lausanne treaty, a sizable Turkish minority remained in western Thrace (in 1923 the Muslim population of western Thrace was estimated at 130,000, out of a total regional population of 190,000) together with a large Greek population in Istanbul (somewhat over 100,000) as well as smaller minorities on the Turkish islands of Bozcaada (Tenedos) and Gokceada (Imbros) (7,000 and 1,200, respectively). Lausanne made specific reference to these "Muslim and non-Muslim" minorities and guaranteed them the right to maintain autonomous religious, cultural, and educational institutions.

The Greek side is fond of pointing out that the Greek population of Istanbul has been reduced today to well under 10,000, and that only 250 Greeks remain on Gokceada and 100 on Bozcaada, while the Muslim population of western Thrace has remained fairly stable at around 120,000. Ankara retorts that a natural rate of increase would have more than doubled the minority population of western Thrace were it not for mass migration provoked by a Greek policy of denial of identity and systematic repression. The numbers are disputed, but the larger climate of hostility that infects Greek-Turkish relations probably lends some degree of truth to both positions.[11]

Athens has reacted to international criticism of its policy in western Thrace by offering a number of concessions including educational incentives and limited self-government, but it refuses to designate the minority in Thrace as Turkish, clinging instead to the "Muslim" designation used in the text of the Lausanne treaty. According to Greek sources, about 50 percent of this minority are of Turkish descent, 35 percent are Bulgarian-speaking Pomaks (Muslim Slavs), and 15 percent are Muslim Roma (Gypsies). The concerned populations have a long list of grievances that include the expropriation of land by the Greek state, denial of citizenship to members of the Turkish minority returning from trips abroad, educational discrimination, refusal of the right of election of local religious leaders or Muftis (in 1990 Greece suspended the election of local Muftis in favor of appointment by the state), and electoral gerrymandering aimed at denying the Turkish minority fair representation.[12] The status of the Greek minority and Orthodox patriarchate in Istanbul remain sore points with Greek public opinion, and, as an ethnically Turkish region with a long list of grievances that is territorially contiguous with Turkey proper, western Thrace is militarily exposed and a point of potential leverage in a larger pattern of strategic competition.

The Cyprus Question.

The beautiful island of Cyprus, mythical birthplace of Aphrodite, has a vital location some 80 kilometers off Turkey's southern Mediterranean coast and a complex political history accurately reflecting its strategic importance. Culturally and socially, it has been subjected to waves of Byzantine, Venetian, Hellenic, Turkic, and British influences. From 1571-1878 it was part of the Ottoman empire, but at the Congress of Berlin in the summer of that year, which presided over a peace settlement after the Ottoman defeat in the Russo-Turkish War of 1877-78, it was leased to Britain for use as a naval basing area. Cyprus was annexed in 1918 and declared a crown colony in 1925.

The population of Cyprus today is around 780,000, divided between a Greek majority representing about 80 percent of the total and a Turkish minority representing 18 percent. These communities traditionally lived interspersed throughout the island, including within numerous mixed villages. The anticolonial movement launched in the 1950s, however, was simultaneously a Greek nationalist movement that sought to link the call for independence to the goal of *enosis*, or attachment to Greece. The Turkish Cypriot community responded with a call for *taksim*, or partition.

In 1955 the United Kingdom, whose government had originally resisted the idea of granting Cypriot self-determination, sought to resolve the problem by convening a London conference, in the course of which a bomb exploded at the Turkish consulate at Salonika (in the immediate vicinity of the house in which Ataturk was born). This act of terrorism was eventually discovered to have been a Turkish provocation, responsibility for which became one of the items in the indictment brought against then prime minister Adnan Menderes that would lead to his execution by hanging in September 1961. The immediate result was a series of anti-Greek pogroms in Izmir and Istanbul, where over 2,000 Greeks were killed and many more driven from the cities as refugees.

Between 1956-60 Cypriot politics were dominated by the terrorist anti-British agitation of the National Organization of Cypriot Fighters (EOKA) led by Georgios Grivas, a retired army colonel with extreme right-wing political affiliations. After a British expeditionary force of over 30,000 soldiers proved incapable of controlling the violence, a Zurich agreement in 1960 defined terms for independence. Greece, Turkey, and the United Kingdom were designated as guaranteeing powers. Britain was granted two military base areas (which it still maintains), and Greece and Turkey were permitted to garrison 950 and 650 soldiers, respectively, on the island. The constitution specifically forbids attachment to another state, uniting Cyprus with Austria as the only other state in the world whose sovereignty is similarly circumscribed. The text also defined a power-sharing arrangement according to which the president would be a Greek Cypriot and the vice president a Turkish Cypriot, with four Greek and three Turkish ministers. Thirty percent of the seats in the House of Representatives were reserved for the Turkish Cypriot minority, 40 percent of commissions in the National Guard, and 30 percent of positions in the police force and civil service—percentages that granted disproportionate representation to the Turkish Cypriot community. In August 1960 Greek Archbishop Makarios III became the first president, and the Turkish Cypriot Fazil Kucuk the first vice-president, of an independent but badly divided Republic of Cyprus.

The Cypriot constitution was badly flawed and quickly proved to be unworkable. Makarios provoked the crisis that undermined the fragile equilibrium which it sought to define on November 30, 1963, by proposing 13 amendments designed to curtail the special advantages of the Turkish minority and create a unitary state. Within a matter of weeks, communal strife exploded, driven forward by the systematic harassment of Turkish Cypriots, including attempts to "ethnically cleanse" whole districts by expelling them from their homes. In 1964 a U.N. multilateral peacekeeping force (the U.N. force in Cyprus-UNFICYP) arrived on the island to police a 180-kilometer long "Green Line" of separation between the warring communities, where it has remained to this day at a cumulative expense of over $3 billion.

These events were decisive. The atrocities committed by Greek irregulars terrorized Turkish Cypriots, driving many as refugees into protected areas and shattering the island's delicate ethnic balances. Reliance upon U.N. peacekeepers was both an admission that the island's problems were unresolvable in their own terms and a panacea that made division provoked by violence appear tolerable. The Makarios government was discredited, and outside powers were quick to move into the void of power—the Turkish military contingent assuming strategic positions in the north of the island and occupying the Nicosia-Kyrenia highway, Greek forces building up to over 10,000 by 1967, and the United States taking up the role of the United Kingdom as great power sponsor and crisis manager. In both 1964 and 1967 Turkey threatened to invade the island to restore order and protect the Turkish Cypriot minority, and was only dissuaded by vigorous warnings from Washington.

In 1968 inter-communal talks began, mediated by U.S. envoy Cyrus Vance, with Rauf Denktash representing the Turkish Cypriot community and Glavkos Clerides the Greek Cypriots, both lawyers, associates since their school days, and seemingly permanent pieces of the Cypriot puzzle. But events had already spun out of the hands of local actors. The increasing intensity of East-West competition in the eastern Mediterranean, U.S. distrust for the nonaligned orientation and left-wing supporters of the Makarios regime, the increasingly desperate search of the colonels' regime in Athens for some kind of dramatic success to bolster its failing domestic support, and the quest of the Turkish armed forces, after overthrowing the government for the second time in a decade in 1971, for new sources of domestic legitimacy, created a volatile intermingling of interests which would soon set the Cyprus tinderbox afire.

In November 1973 a student uprising against the colonels' junta culminated with a massacre in the heart of Athens. Under growing pressure, the new Greek strongman Dimitrios Ioannides turned to Grivas and his right-wing nationalist allies in Cyprus, apparently hoping to restore his position by attaching the island to Greece with a sudden *coup de main*. On July 15, 1974, National Guard and Greek national contingents seized power in Cyprus, but failed in their attempt to capture and murder Makarios, who managed to escape to London with British assistance. The Cypriot presidency now fell temporarily into the hands of the former EOKA gunman Nikos Sampson, while inter-communal violence flared up in all directions. On July 19, a Turkish expeditionary force set sail from Mercin, securing control of a narrow coastal strip but failing to seize Nicosia airport. On July 22 a U.N.-imposed cease-fire took hold, and on July 24, after the Greek armed forces refused to follow Ioannides' desperate call for an all-out attack on Turkey, the Greek junta fell in Athens, with power placed into the hands of a civilian coalition led by Konstantinos Karamanlis.

The military fiasco was followed by a diplomatic fiasco in Geneva. Here, in a hastily organized diplomatic forum, Ankara presented demands for a federated Cyprus with equal status for the Turkish Cypriot minority and Turkish administration for numerous scattered ethnic cantons. The disorganized Greek government was not in a position to react to these claims, and a distracted United States (in the midst of its domestic Watergate crisis) did not choose to oppose them. After articulating its demands, and winning time to regroup its forces, on August 14 the Turkish "peace force" in Cyprus fanned out to the east and west, eventually seizing about 40 percent of the island's territory and culminating a process of ethnic cleansing that would drive about 200,000 people from their homes (180,000 of them Greek Cypriots), grouping the Turkish Cypriot population under Ankara's protection in the north and forcing the Greek Cypriot population across a military demarcation line into the south. On February 11, 1975, the process was completed by the creation of a "Turkish Federated State of Cyprus" with Denktash as president, formalized in 1983 as the Turkish Republic of Northern Cyprus (TRNC), but to date accorded diplomatic recognition only by the Turkish Republic itself.

Christopher Hitchens has argued that the essence of the Cyprus tragedy from 1960 onward was "the exploitation by outside powers of internal differences that were genuine in themselves" with the purpose "to suborn the independence of the island."[13] His thesis is controversial, but there is little doubt that, in the Cold War context within which events unfolded, specifically Cypriot issues were interpreted in the context of an overriding western interest in managing Greek-Turkish rivalry and frustrating the emergence of an independent-minded and nonaligned Cypriot regime.

Though the second Turkish invasion clearly went beyond reasonable bounds in asserting physical control over more than a third of the island, the final result was in some ways comparable to the U.S. agenda for a combination of *enosis* and *taksim* outlined prior to the invasion in the so-called Acheson plan—an imposed partition, an independent, Greek-oriented Republic of Cyprus, and a permanent Turkish presence in a northern Cypriot dependency. This was an acceptable, if less than ideal, solution, and it has proven to be enduring. For Athens the outcome was a defeat and a humiliation, but it remained in a position to cultivate special relations with the Republic of Cyprus. Ankara warded off the worst-case of a successful Greek coup, reinforced its military position, and ensured that the Turkish Cypriot community would remain dependent upon Turkish sponsorship. The United States avoided a direct Greek-Turkish clash with the potential to weaken NATO and removed the Cyprus imbroglio from its strategic agenda. Or so it thought. In fact, the Cyprus question was left as an open wound that has subsequently poisoned all attempts to effect an enduring Greek-Turkish rapprochement.

Greek-Turkish Rivalry after the Cold War.

The Cyprus problem has changed remarkably little in its overall contours in the quarter century that has passed since the Turkish invasion. The TRNC, with 37 percent of the island's territory and 18 percent of its population almost uniquely of Turkish and Turkish Cypriot extraction, is permanently occupied by approximately 35,000 soldiers of the Turkish 3rd Army. Turkey also maintains a dominant position within the TRNC's police force, militia, and secret services. The mini-state is isolated internationally and is to all intents and purposes a Turkish protectorate. To the south, across the Green Line patrolled by 1,200 soldiers of the UNFICYP, lies the predominantly Greek Cypriot Republic of Cyprus, internationally recognized as the legitimate government of the island but without any authority over the Turkish zone. The record of initiatives aimed at overcoming the impasse, pursued over decades by U.N. secretary generals, U.S. presidents, and multilateral negotiating forums, reads like an encyclopedia of diplomacy, but nothing of substance has been achieved. The Cyprus problem, like the poor, seems destined to always be with us.

The perception of stasis is, however, misleading, both in the case of Cyprus and as pertains to the Greek-Turkish rivalry as a whole. During the Cold War decades, Greek-Turkish competition was constrained by a number of domestic and international factors. Both sides were aware that they shared an overriding interest in helping to contain Soviet power. Both were significantly dependent upon their links to the North Atlantic Alliance for security assistance. Not least, because the driving force of the rivalry was not in essence strategic competition, but rather nationalistic self-other images, neither had any real reason to allow an escalation of tension to sweep out of hand. Greek-Turkish rivalry was played out in the shadow of the arsenals of the superpowers, and, like many other Cold War conflicts with direct implications for the East-West balance, constrained by the exigencies of competitive bipolarity.

The end of the Cold War has removed many of these constraints, and transformed what was a chronic but contained rivalry into a potentially more volatile and dangerous one. The new configuration of power in the "arc of crisis" along Russia's southern flank has enhanced Turkey's strategic weight, lent impetus to the emergence of a more assertive foreign policy agenda, encouraged familiar Greek fears of a bigger and more powerful neighbor, and stimulated renewed cultural friction. In the new geopolitics of the post-Cold War, the eastern Mediterranean has become a seismic point for "a multi-regional strategic calculus incorporating southeastern Europe, the Middle East, and the Caucasus."[14] As a result, the fragile Greek-Turkish relationship is being subjected to new kinds of strains and tensions that it is ill-prepared to bear.

Neither Greece nor Turkey succeeded in utilizing the window of opportunity opened by the end of the Cold War to forward a policy of reconciliation. The Greek administration of prime minister Kostas Simitis began its tenure in 1996 with proposals for the creation of a joint committee under EU auspices to ameliorate Greek-Turkish relations, but Simitis has confronted strong opposition from the national populist wing of his own ruling party.[15] On the Turkish side, disappointing economic performance, political instability (Turkey has experienced five governments since the general elections of December 1995), and a crisis of confidence in ruling institutions provoked by corruption scandals have encouraged a tendency towards nationalistic posturing and self-preoccupation. Each side, because of internal weaknesses, has opted to play the nationalism card repeatedly.

Greek-Turkish relations have also been degraded by the new tensions that have emerged in Turkey's relations with Europe. Ankara concluded an EU association agreement in 1963, and in 1987 it applied in due form for full membership, but in 1989 its candidacy was pushed to the back of the line of new post-communist democracies. In its July 1997 blueprint for enlargement entitled *Agenda 2000*, the EU eliminated Turkey from its list of candidates altogether. This gesture was partly motivated by a pragmatic awareness of developmental and demographic imbalances, and partly by a sincere concern for Ankara's less than adequate human rights record. But it also seemed to draw a line between a European "Christian club" and the lands of the East, perceived in Orientalist fashion as the domain of backwardness and cultural exoticism.[16]

Turkey's clash with the EU has coincided with an intensifying search for alternative patterns of cultural identification and diplomatic alignment, provoked by a weakening of the Kemalist consensus domestically.[17] Kemal's original vision included the rejection of the Ottoman imperial tradition on behalf of a unitary Turkish national state, centralized political control under the aegis of the progressive officer corps, strictly enforced secularism, a statist and Listian philosophy of economic development, and a pro-Western strategic orientation. The disappearance of the Soviet Union, and with it a centuries-old common border with Russia to the north, weakened one pillar of the edifice of Kemalism by calling the necessity of a pro-western alignment into question. Turgut Ozal's opening of the Turkish economy during the 1980s removed another. The electoral victory of Necmettin Erbakan's Islamic Welfare party in December 1995 and Erbakan's appointment as prime minister in January 1996 seemed to threaten a third.

These trends have been accompanied by a new interest in Turkey's Ottoman past, regarded not as a model to emulate but rather as a neglected source of cultural orientation.[18] For centuries Turkey considered itself to be the center of an autonomous geopolitical space and an independent great power, not a peripheral extension of greater Europe. The Kemalist assertion of a European destiny contradicts this tradition, but it may yet prove to be incapable of replacing it. The dynamics of the Balkan conflict, where the Bosnian Muslims and Kosovar Albanians have been widely viewed as victims of campaigns of genocide at least passively abetted by the Western powers, the outcome of the Gulf War, where Turkey is perceived to have made important sacrifices on behalf of the allied coalition and to have been rewarded by Western championship of Kurdish nationalism in northern Iraq, and the EU's apparent indifference to Turkey's professed European vocation, have all contributed to the crystallization of a sharper and less dependent Turkish national idea. The "soft coup," which led to Erbakan's resignation under military pressure in June 1997 and the subsequent outlawing of the Welfare party by the Turkish Constitutional Court, has represented a Kemalist reassertion of sorts, but at the expense of an ever-more intrusive political role for the Turkish military hierarchy, traditionally committed to the pursuit of a hard line against Athens.

Intensified political tension and cultural friction have been accompanied by aggravated strategic competition. The area's Cold War status as the "southern flank" of the extended front of East-West confrontation has become irrelevant with the demise of the Soviet Union. The strategic stakes at issue are, however, at least as great if not greater than in the past. In the post-bipolar context, Greece and Turkey may once again be perceived as part of a "Levant" that opens to the economic promise of the extended Middle East and southwestern Asia. They represent the westernmost pole of a new strategic axis stretching through the Black Sea and Caucasus to the untapped natural gas and oil reserves of the Caspian basin. Many issues concerning the construction of a main export pipeline to bring Caspian oil into world markets, including the short-term economic viability of the entire endeavor, remain to be resolved, but there is no doubt that Caspian resources represent a long-term strategic asset of some importance, and that the issue of access has upped the ante of strategic competition in the eastern Mediterranean theater as a whole.[19]

From a Western perspective, the importance of the Greek-Turkish relationship has been enhanced by NATO's extensive engagement in Balkan conflict management. There is no realistic "exit strategy" for the 30,000 NATO troops deployed since 1995 in war-ravaged Bosnia-Herzegovina. The Bosnia elections of the summer of 1998, which reinforced intolerant nationalist leadership in all three of Bosnia-Herzegovina's mutually hostile ethnic communities, made clear that NATO's peacekeeping responsibilities will be indispensable for the foreseeable future. NATO plays an important role in propping up the fragile institutions of governance in Albania and the Republic of Macedonia, and it has recently been drawn into responsibilities for monitoring the Kosovo conflict. "Whether we like it or not," argues an anonymous senior European diplomat, "NATO has become the sheriff in Europe's wild southeast. We need to expand our perception from the microcosm of Bosnia to an overall strategy for the Balkans, because NATO has become the central organizing force for the entire region."[20]

Unfortunately, Balkan turmoil has also sharpened the competitive edge of the Greek-Turkish relationship. Greek concern with Turkey's superior military potential, reinforced by the perception of an ambitious Turkish Balkan policy inspired by the imperial premises of neo-Ottomanism, has been reflected in a combative search for unilateral advantage.[21] Simultaneously, Turkey's exposure on multiple fronts makes it highly sensitive to real and imagined Greek provocations. The Aegean feud has thus become entangled with international engagement in the Bosnian conflict, the complicated relationship between Turkey and the EU, the emerging Turkish-Israel strategic partnership, the role of Turkey as an arm of the West in the politics of the Caucasus and Central Asia, the politics of NATO enlargement, and a host of other issues.[22]

Many of these dynamics have crystallized around the Cyprus problem. In 1992, then U.N. Secretary General Boutros Boutros Ghali launched a major diplomatic initiative designated as the "Set of Ideas," intended to provide a comprehensive formula for overcoming the post-1974 stalemate. These proposals, in the tradition of the U.S.-sponsored Nimetz Plan of the 1970s and U.N. General Secretary Javier Perez de Cuellar's Proximity Talks of the 1980s, recommended the creation of a Cypriot republic with a single international personality and citizenship presiding over broadly autonomous federal units in the north and south.

The Set of Ideas suggested reducing the northern zone to 28 percent of the island's territory by returning to Greek Cypriot control the Varosha district of Famagusta, the northern citrus growing area of Morphou, and 34 other villages. The federal units were to receive equal powers, with safeguards to prevent impingement upon their authority by the central government, whose responsibilities would be limited to foreign affairs, defense, federal juridical and police matters, central banking, customs and immigration, posts and telecommunications, patents and trade marks, and health and environmental issues. Politically, the hope was to resurrect the principle of proportional representation, with a Greek Cypriot president and Turkish Cypriot vice president and a bicameral legislature with 50/50 percent representation in the upper house and 70/30 percent in the lower house.

The framework was accompanied by a series of confidence-building measures (the transfer of Varosha to U.N. control and its gradual opening to commerce involving both communities, the reopening of Nicosia airport under the auspices of the U.N. and the International Civil Aviation Authority with freedom of access for both sides, and the relaxation of the Greek Cypriot embargo on the north) designed as incentives to cooperation. Greek Cypriot president Georgios Vassilou accepted the Set of Ideas as a basis for discussion, but in the end, the project broke down around the core issue of sovereignty, with Denktash demanding prior recognition of the TRNC as a condition for negotiations and formal equality between federal units including a rotating presidency, separate communal elections, strict equality in representation in governmental institutions, and a rule of consensus for Council of Minister decisions.

In the wake of this failure, the United States picked up the torch, presiding over the signing of a brief document at NATO's Madrid summit in July 1997 in which Greece and Turkey declared that they would respect each others "vital interests" in the Aegean and pledged to resolve disputes peacefully, and kick-starting U.N.-sponsored negotiations on Cyprus in the summer of 1997 at Troutbeck, New York, and Montreux, Switzerland.[23] These initiatives, like so many before them, were quickly side-tracked, this time by Turkish reactions to the EU's Agenda 2000. The failure of the Set of Ideas and subsequent U.S. proposals left many with the conviction that in Cyprus diplomacy had arrived at the end of the road.

Already in 1990 Vassiliou had opened a door leading in another direction by filing a formal application to enter the EU. Accession was a legitimate goal in view of the Republic of Cyprus' economic achievements, but it was widely considered impossible prior to a negotiated agreement between north and south. Vassiliou's real hope was probably to win negotiating leverage and to encourage the EU to become more active in facilitating a diplomatic outcome. In 1995, however, in part as a result of Greek pressure, in part as a consequence of annoyance with Turkish Cypriot diplomatic intransigence, and in part due to a desire to discipline Ankara for its continued refusal to move forward on European concerns with humans rights abuses and respect for democratic norms, the request was accepted by the EU Council of Ministers. In April 1998 negotiations on accession were formally opened. The reaction of Denktash was an uncompromising refusal to participate in any accession negotiation, accompanied by a threat to encourage the annexation of the north to Turkey in the event that EU membership should become a reality. This was not an empty threat. In the course of 1998, Turkey and the TRNC proceeded to establish a joint economic area and put into place the institutional foundations for full annexation.

The friction provoked by the EU accession agenda has been paralleled by rising military tensions. In 1993 Greece and the Republic of Cyprus announced a strategy of common defense intended to bring Cyprus inside of the Greek national defensive umbrella. Under the terms of the agreement, Greece and Cyprus have conducted joint military exercises and opened a naval and air station, appropriately named "Andreas Papandreou," on the southwest coast near the tourist resort area of Paphos. When fully operational, this facility will extend the range of Greek air-power to include a militarily vital stretch of Turkey's Mediterranean coast. As such, it has been bitterly resisted by Ankara. When, on June 16, 1998, in the midst of a European summit in Cardiff, Wales, United Kingdom, with the Cyprus problem on the agenda, four Greek F-16 warplanes and two C-130 transports visited the base as part of a military exercise, another sharp crisis in bilateral relations ensured.[24]

In 1996, the Republic of Cyprus announced the purchase of four systems of Russian-made S-300 (SA-10 in the NATO designation) surface-to-air missiles, each equipped with 12 missiles with a range of 160 kilometers.[25] The purchase, if brought to fruition, would have served several distinct functions. The missile systems are capable of contributing to a more credible defensive capacity for the Republic of Cyprus, which, at present, lacks an air force altogether. They could also also serve to protect the Andreas Papandreou facility. Less tangibly, but of considerable importance, deployment would to some extent salve the deep frustration at the lack of diplomatic progress felt by most Greek Cypriots. "The missile crisis," writes Niels Kadritzke, "is rooted in the fears of men and women who feel themselves to have been abandoned by the entire world."[26]

The announcement of an intention to deploy the missiles encouraged a good deal of belligerent rhetoric. Turkey unambiguously condemned the move as an aggressive gesture which "poses a direct threat to Turkish security," and announced its intention to attack the sites, should deployment commence.[27] Taken aback by the potentially dramatic consequences of its actions, the Clerides government offered to suspend the purchase in exchange for an acceptance of a 1979 agreement, never honored, defining the terms of a demilitarization of the island. Not surprisingly, the offer was abruptly refused.

The Turkish ultimatum made deployment an extremely high-risk undertaking, but the Clerides government confronted considerable domestic pressure to make good on its commitments. In the midst of the controversy, the Greek Cypriot minister of defense Iannakis Omirou demonstrably described the deployments as critical to Cypriot security, and threatened to resign should they be canceled or delayed. Twenty percent of the Greek Cypriot electorate presently backs a "Front of Refusal" which is committed to reunifying the island under Greek hegemony and strongly supports the missile purchase, and many Greeks are convinced that the demilitarization of Cyprus would amount to an acknowledgment of forced partition as a legitimate *status quo*. Despite these pressures, in December 1998 Clerides backed away from a commitment to deploy, suggesting the island of Crete as an alternative venue—a suggestion which Ankara promptly labeled as equally unacceptable. In the end it is likely that Turkish intransigence will be sufficient to block deployments on Cyprus. The larger climate of strategic rivalry out of which the controversy has grown will, however, remain intact.

The entire Cyprus imbroglio rests upon an extremely unstable foundation. Western policy has been built upon the minimalist foundation of sustaining the post-1974 *status quo*. Simultaneous efforts to encourage a negotiated settlement have never been accompanied by the kinds of pressure that would be necessary to provoke decisive concessions. The currently preferred diplomatic initiative is the direct heir of Boutros Ghali's Set of Ideas, calling for the creation of a "bi-communal and bi-zonal federation" that would create a facade of unity while providing the TRNC with nearly full sovereignty in all but name. But trends are at work that will soon make the *status quo* unsustainable, and the ideal of the bi-zonal federation unobtainable.[28] Diplomatic alternatives to *de facto* partition rest upon resurrecting a common Cypriot identity as a foundation for reconciliation, but on both sides of the island that identity is at risk.[29] Economic success and Greece's status as an EU member have inevitably oriented the Republic of Cyprus towards western Europe. The foundation for its high-risk strategy of accession, described by Denktash as "*enosis* through the EU,*"* is a deeply-rooted frustration with an eternal stalemate on the diplomatic front that only works to the advantage of the Turkish side.[30] Should the Republic of Cyprus come into the EU without the north, however, a gauntlet will have been thrown down that will inexorably lead toward the TRNC's annexation by Ankara.

Within the TRNC, the emigration of the indigenous Turkish Cypriot population combined with a steady influx of Turkish immigrants from Anatolia provides an ever more substantial foundation for a long-term strategy aimed at reducing the north to the status of a Turkish province. According to Alpay Durduran, head of the Turkish Cypriot opposition party *Yeni Kibris* (New Cyprus), over 40,000 Turkish Cypriots have left the island since 1974, the majority taking up permanent residence in Great Britain. The 80,000 indigenous Turkish Cypriots who remain make up almost exactly half of the TRNC's total population of 160,000 as recorded in the 1997 census.[31] The autochthonous population provides the political base of opposition to Denktash. That opposition strongly supports the agenda for a bi-communal and bi-zonal federation. But it soon risks becoming a minority within its own land.

Alternatives for the West.

The Greek-Turkish rivalry has brought low so many carefully considered programs for conflict resolution that it seems superfluous to attempt to develop yet another integrated set of proposals. In lieu of an ideal solution, it may be more useful to consider points of orientation that could be helpful in addressing or understanding the problem in new and positive ways.

1. Although it is usually treated as a unique case, the Greek-Turkish rivalry displays much in common with many other contemporary inter-state and regional conflicts. On one level it is a civilizational conflict waged across linguistic, cultural, and confessional fault lines. On both sides it rests upon a culturally constructed and assiduously cultivated image of the enemy with a strong mythic component. It is part of a larger crisis of regional order affecting all of southeastern Europe, pitting politically fragile polities one against the other in a series of contests over sovereignty and status. It is a quarrel between modernizing societies subject to all sorts of strains, where nationalism and national enmity are prone to manipulation by ambitious political elites in search of a rallying cry. It is a strategic rivalry between insecure neighbors with mutually exclusive claims to strategic terrain, maritime choke points, and air corridors, fed by an international military order that prioritizes competitive bidding for arms markets. And, at least in regard to Cyprus, it has engaged and bogged down the international community as peacekeeper and would-be conflict resolver. One part of a long-term solution to the Greek-Turkish rivalry will have to address the world order concerns—cultural, developmental, strategic—from which these kind of dilemmas derive.

2. Greek-Turkish relations are not frozen in place or immobile. From 1930-1955, bilateral relations were reasonably stable, and it was only with the emergence of the Cyprus problem that the current phase of more intense rivalry ensued. During the Cold War decades, rivalry was imbedded within the Western Alliance and constrained by the presence of a common external threat. In the post-Cold War strategic environment, these constraints have become less relevant, and the potential for an open clash has in some ways actually increased. Bilateral relations between Athens and Ankara have become an integral part of a larger pattern of geopolitical rivalry stretching from the Balkan peninsula and Aegean Sea, through the Black and Caspian Seas, into post-Soviet Central Asia. Policymakers committed to encouraging rapprochement need to be sensitive to the dynamic character of the relationship and the altered strategic context that has intensified, rather than reduced, its volatility.

3. There is also a positive side to the picture. All is not amiss in Greek-Turkish relations, and there are some grounds to hope that a self-generated process of rapprochement could eventually take hold. Building bridges between neighboring cultures, that in the end have a great deal in common through institutionalized dialogue and cultural exchange, has long been a goal of progressive minded artists, intellectuals, and well-meaning citizens. Both sides have agreed to terms of participation in a brigade-sized Balkan peacekeeping force, and are engaged in efforts to generate an ongoing regional dialogue on the foreign ministers level.[32] Neither has any interest in allowing their rivalry to slip beyond the edge of open confrontation; angling for leverage is one thing, but an out and out fight, which would inevitably be vastly destructive, is quite another. And none of the issues that have divided the two sides in the past are unresolvable in their own terms.

The International Court of Justice is a perfectly adequate venue for the resolution of differences over access to the Aegean. By applying the premise of equity, Turkey could be granted an economic zone encompassing about a third of the sea's nonsovereign area, proportional to its share of the Aegean coastline and comprising two or three broad passages stretching past the Greek islands of Chios and Lesbos.[33] Such an outcome would represent a true compromise that would deny Greece the vain hope of transforming the Aegean into a *mare nostrum*, and simultaneously recognize the Greek islands lying off the Turkish coast as integral parts of the Greek whole, rather than enclaves in the "Turkish half" of the sea.[34] The status of respective minorities could be resolved on the basis of OSCE norms, if need be, with the help of international monitoring. Even the Cyprus imbroglio is amenable to reasonable compromise. The bi-zonal, bi-communal federation agenda is far from ideal, but it takes into account the minimal demands of the respective communities and is probably the best compromise that circumstances permit.

4. None of these benign outcomes can be achieved without progress in addressing core security concerns—the Turkish military threat to Greek sovereignty and frustrated Turkish desire for fuller access to European institutions. The keys to resolving these concerns lie in the hands of the United States and the EU.

U.S. policymakers have defined Turkey as a critical strategic ally whose allegiance is to be cultivated at all costs—"I think it is very important that we do everything reasonable to anchor Turkey to the West," in the words of U.S. President William Clinton.[35] This has encouraged a great deal of tolerance for assertive Turkish policies and for the dominant political role of the Turkish armed forces, a reliable ally of the West in many ways but also the champion of a geostrategic agenda with destabilizing implications.[36] Washington has looked on impassively as Ankara has maintained an illegal occupation of northern Cyprus over several generations, pursued the chimera of a military resolution to the Kurdish question by focusing its efforts on the destruction of the Kurdestan Workers' party, repeatedly threatened its Greek neighbor and NATO partner with military reprisals, reinforced a strategic partnership with Israel that threatens to alienate much of the Arab world, launched military incursions into northern Iraq, mobilized its forces against Syria, presided over three armed coups, and most recently engineered the resignation of the democratically elected government of Erbakan's Welfare party.[37] The United States has considerable influence over its Turkish ally, and should perhaps contemplate using it in a more positive manner—to restrain the Turkish military leadership, encourage political pluralism, and deter the kind of aggressive posturing that Greece cannot help but perceive as an existential threat.[38]

The EU, on the other hand, by turning its back on Turkey's European aspirations and opening the door to accession for the Republic of Cyprus, has all but publicly lined up with Athens against Ankara. In so doing, it has viscerally threatened what can fairly be defined as Turkish vital interests. While this situation prevails, Ankara can be expected to continue to place pressure upon Greece as a source of military and diplomatic leverage. Only a more open and flexible European process can supply the positive incentives necessary to move Turkey toward a policy of rapprochement and concession. The problem of Greek-Turkish rivalry cannot be resolved so long as Ankara perceives the door that leads to Europe to be locked and barred.

5. Western policy has focused on "managing" the problem of Greek-Turkish rivalry and in so doing has contributed to perpetuating it. The more ambitious goal of transcending the rivalry by focusing on the two antagonists' core security concerns may prove to be more productive in the long term. Neither Greece nor Turkey can be coerced to accept arrangements that they do not feel contribute to their national interests, but they can be encouraged to buy into mutually beneficial trade-offs designed to integrate and reconcile. These kind of trade-offs can only be arranged within the larger European and Euro-Atlantic context.

They might include a Greek agreement to surrender claims to disproportionate rights in the Aegean in exchange for Turkish recognition of Greek sovereignty over disputed islands; a negotiated nonaggression pact guaranteed by the United States, including demilitarization agreements affecting militarized Greek islands as well as Turkish forces on the mainland in Izmir or adjacent to Rhodes; or the acceptance of a bi-zonal arrangement in Cyprus monitored by NATO with significant Turkish military participation as a prerequisite for the island's accession to the EU—the prelude to a revived relationship between Brussels and Turkey itself. However they are defined, such trade-offs should involve mutual concessions, shared advantage, and consistent Western monitoring.

All of these initiatives involve considerable risk, but there is even greater risk in not pursuing them. Greek-Turkish relations are subject to severe new pressures, the *status quo* cannot be maintained indefinitely, and, in the worst case of an open rift, U.S. and Western interests in the Mediterranean basin would suffer severely.[39] Greek-Turkish rivalry is a fundamental barrier blocking the way to an effective Mediterranean security regime and a critical risk for NATO. It is also a challenge that balanced, coordinated, patient, and persistent Western policies can still hope to confront successfully.

ENDNOTES - CHAPTER 12

1. John Redmond and Roderick Pace, "European Security in the 1990s and Beyond: The Implications of the Accession of Cyprus and Malta to the European Union," *Contemporary Security Policy,* Vol. 17, No. 3, December 1996, p. 438.

2. See Nimet Beriker-Atiyas, "The Kurdish Conflict in Turkey: Issues, Parties and Prospects," *Security Dialogue,* Vol. 28, No. 4, 1997, pp. 439-452; Henri J. Barkey and Graham E. Fuller, *Turkey's Kurdish Question*, Oxford: Rowman & Littlefield Publishers, Inc., 1998; and Michael M. Gunter, *The Kurds and the Future of Turkey,* New York: St. Martin's Press, 1997.

3. Henry Kissinger, *Years of Upheaval*, Boston: Little, Brown, 1982, pp. 147-151.

4. Richard Clogg, *A Concise History of Greece*, Cambridge: Cambridge University Press, 1992, p. 2.

5. The argument is presented from a Turkish perspective in Vamik D. Volkan and Norman Itzkowitz, *Turks and Greeks: Neighbors in Conflict*, Huntingdon: The Eothen Press, 1994.

6. Tozun Bahcheli, *Greek-Turkish Relations Since 1955*, Boulder: Westview Press, 1990, pp. 5-18.

7. Marcia Christoff Kurop, "Greece and Turkey: Can They Mend Fences?," *Foreign Affairs*, Vol. 77, No. 1, January-February 1998, p. 12.

8. Margarita Mathiopoulos, "Toward an Aegean Treaty: 2-4 for Turkey and Greece," *Mediterranean Quarterly*, Vol. 8, No. 3, Summer 1997, p. 116.

9. Niels Kadritzke, "Athenes et Ankara se disputent la mer Egee," *Le Monde diplomatique*, October 1996, pp. 14-15.

10. Frank Brenchley, "Aegean Conflict and the Law of the Sea," in Frank Brenchley and Edward Fursdon, *The Aegean and Cyprus, Conflict Studies No. 232*, London, Research Institute for the Study of Conflict and Terrorism, June 1990, pp. 1-8.

11. For a balanced evaluation, see Hugh Poulton, *The Balkans: Minorities and States in Conflict*, London: Minority Rights Publications, 1997, pp. 173-192.

12. *Turkish Minority in Western Thrace: Briefing of the Commission on Security and Cooperation in Europe*, Washington, DC: Commission on Security and Cooperation in Europe, April 1996.

13. Christopher Hitchens, *Cyprus*, London: Quartet Books, 1984, p. 51.

14. Elizabeth H. Prodromou, "Reintegrating Cyprus: The Need for a New Approach," *Survival*, Vol. 40, No. 3, Autumn 1998, p. 5.

15. Wes Jonassen, "Greece and Turkey: Still on the Rocks," *Middle East International*, June 27, 1997, p. 20.

16. Salahi R. Sonyel, "The European Union and the Cyprus Imbroglio," *Perceptions*, Vol. 3, No. 2, June-August 1998, pp. 73-83.

17. Resat Kasaba, "Kemalist Certainties and Modern Ambiguities," in Sibel Bozdogan and Resat Kasaba, eds., *Rethinking Modernity and National Identity in Turkey*, Seattle: University of Washington Press, 1997, pp. 15-36.

18. Kemal H. Karpat, "The Ottoman Role in Europe From the Perspective of 1994," in Vojtech Mastny and R. Craig Nation, eds., *Turkey Between East and West: New Challenges for a Rising Regional Power*, Boulder: Westview Press, 1996, pp. 1-44.

19. Ian Bremmer, "Oil Politics: America and the Riches of the Caspian Basin," *World Policy Journal*, Vol. XV, No. 1, Spring 1998, pp. 27-35; Rosemarie Forsythe, *The Politics of Oil in the Caucasus and Central Asia: Prospects for Oil Exploitation and Export in the Caspian Basin*, Oxford: Oxford University Press, 1996.

20. Cited in William Drozdiak, "NATO Role Grows as Threat of Force Calms Kosovo Crisis," *The Philadelphia Inquirer*, October 18, 1998, p. E4.

21. Elaborated in Peter Varraroussis, "Die griechische Diplomatie auf dem Balkan—Ruckkehr in die Geschichte?," *Sudosteuropa*, Nos. 6-7, 1995, pp. 373-384. See also Ekavi Athanassopoulou, "Turkey and the Balkans: The View from Athens," *The International Spectator*, Vol. XXIX, No. 4, October-December 1994, pp. 55-64.

22. The Ankara-Tel Aviv strategic axis has recently become the subject of particular concern, typically described in the Syrian press as

> a destabilizing element which will provoke conflicts and bring back the climate of the 1950s in the Middle East, when the politics of alliances sparked conflicts and animated hostility towards the West in general and the United States in particular.

Cited in Mouna Naim, "Vives critiques contre des manoeuvres isaelo-turcs-americaines en Mediterranee," *Le Monde*, June 7, 1998, p. 3.

23. Evan Liaris, "A European Solution" Opportunity for Rapprochement in Cyprus," *Harvard International Review*, Vol. XX, No. 1, Winter 1997-98, pp. 38-41.

24. "Greek Fighters Land in Cyprus," *The Washington Times*, June 17, 1998, p. 17; and "Turkish F-16s Sent to Cyprus," *The Washington Post*, June 19, 1998, p. 33.

25. Michael R. Gordon, "Greek Cypriots to Get Missiles From Russians," *The New York Times*, April 29, 1998, pp. A1 and A3.

26. Niels Kadritzke, "Chypre, otage de l'affrontement entre Athenes et Ankara," *Le Monde diplomatique*, September 1998, p. 7.

27. Nuzhet Kandemir, "Turkey: Secure Bridge Over Troubled Waters," *Mediterranean Quarterly*, Vol. 8, No. 4, Fall 1997, p. 10.

28. Prodromou, p. 8, argues that current circumstances "reveal the status quo option as unsustainable and irrelevant to any effort towards meaningful peace-building in Cyprus."

29. Thomas F. Farr, "Overcoming the Cyprus Tragedy: Let Cypriots Be Cypriots," *Mediterranean Quarterly*, Vol. 8, No. 4, Fall 1997, pp. 32-62.

30. Denktash's observation is cited in Redmond and Page, p. 434.

31. Niels Kadritzke, "Rêve d'Europe dans le nord de l'île," *Le Monde diplomatique*, September 1998, p. 7.

32. Ünal Cevikoz, "European Integration and Regional Co-Operation in Southeast Europe," *Perceptions*, Vol. II, No. 4, December-February 1997-1998, p. 153.

33. Kadritzke, "Athenes et Ankara se disputent la mer Egee," and Andrew Wilson, *The Aegean Question, Adelphi Paper no. 155*, London: International Institute for Strategic Studies, 1979.

34. Theodore Couloumbis and Piodromos Yonnes, "Alternative Futures in the Post-Cold War International System and Their Implications for Greece," in Heinz-Jürgen Axl, ed., *Beiträge zur Mobilisierung Südosteuropas aus deutscher und griechischer Sicht*, Munich: Südosteuropa Aktuell, 1995, p. 58.

35. Cited from remarks to reporters in Kelly Couturier, "Turkish Premier Expected to Press Clinton on Pipeline," *The Washington Post*, December 19, 1997, p. 46.

36. Andrew Borowiec, "Army Runs Turkey Behind the Scenes," *Washington Times*, July 18, 1998, p. 16; and for background, William Hale, *Turkish Politics and the Military*, London: Routledge, 1994.

37. Michael M. Gunter, "The Silent Coup: The Secularist-Islamist Struggle in Turkey," *Journal of South Asian and Middle Eastern Studies*, Vol. 21, No. 3, Spring 1998, pp. 1-12; and Ben Lombardi,

"Turkey—The Return of the Reluctant Generals?," *Political Science Quarterly*, Vol. 112, No. 2, 1997, pp. 191-215.

38. Jim Hoaglund, "Before Turkey Joins Europe," *The Washington Post*, November 2, 1997, p. C7.

39. Heinz Kramer, "The Cyprus Problem and European Security," *Survival*, Vol. 39, No. 3, Autumn 1997, pp. 16-32.

CHAPTER 13

THE STALLED PEACE PROCESS: ISRAELI-SYRIAN TRACK

Sami G. Hajjar

> Shimon Peres is a great diplomat who wants peace, Ehud Baraq is on the road to peace; but Netanyahu. is a strange man whose declarations are strange.
>
> Hafiz Al-Asad[1]

Introduction.

In this chapter, the author examines the stalled Middle East peace process and focuses especially on the Israeli-Syrian track. He argues that, for ideological and strategic security considerations, the Likud government of Prime Minister Benjamin Netenyahu is unwilling to abide by the "land for peace" formula established in the 1991 Madrid Peace Conference. Also, Mr. Netenyahu and his foreign policy advisors hold certain assumptions about Syria, whereby the return of the Golan Heights is a lesser national priority for President Asad. Syria, on the other hand, will not agree to any territorial compromises on the Golan Heights and refuses to endorse any separate deal between Israel and Lebanon. The future prospects for a lasting peace in the Middle East is in doubt. The author believes that a vigorous U.S. involvement, along with a meaningful European role, hold the best chance for reviving the peace process leading to a settlement of the Israeli-Syrian (and Lebanese) track.

On October 23, 1998, at a White House ceremony witnessed by U.S. President William Clinton and King Hussein of Jordan, Prime Minister Netenyahu and Chairman Yasir Arafat signed the Wye River Memorandum. The "Wye Agreement," as it is commonly referred to in the press, represented a considerable investment in time and effort on the part of President Clinton and his senior foreign policy advisors to revive the Palestinian-Israeli peace track and gave hope that the Middle East peace process could be resuscitated after almost 2 1/2 years of hiatus.[2] However, the agreement suffered a series of quick setbacks, including the decision of the Israeli cabinet to require added conditions for implementing the pact, and the decision of the Knesset to hold general elections in the spring or early summer of 1999 has placed the implementation of the Wye Agreement on hold at least until after Israel elects a new prime minister and a new Knesset.[3]

The peace process is again frozen. How did it get frozen in the first place? A brief background focusing on Prime Minister's Netenyahu's first 2 years in office may help to understand why and how the process was placed on hold.

Background.

The election of hard-line Likud leader Benjamin Netanyahu as prime minister of Israel on May 29, 1996, profoundly changed the tempo and direction of the Middle East peace process. Netanyahu's disdain of the Oslo agreement reached between the previous Labor government and the Palestinian Authority, his attempt to separate the Lebanese-Israeli peace track from the Israeli-Syrian track, and his insistence that the Israeli-Syrian negotiations be resumed with no preconditions and irrespective of progress made between the Syrians and the Labor government negotiators have effectively frozen the peace process between Israel and its two neighbors to the north. The current deadlock based on deeply-held ideological beliefs, sovereignty claims, and national security consideration is not likely to loosen without the continued direct personal involvement of the President of the United States along, perhaps, with a role for the European community.[4] Vital U.S. interests in the

Middle East are in jeopardy if a comprehensive peace process, begun in Madrid in 1991, is not successfully concluded.[5]

The process had its roots in United Nations (U.N.) Resolution 242 that, following the 1967 Arab-Israeli war, recognized the "inadmissibility of the acquisition of territory by war," and the need for the "establishment of a just and lasting peace in the Middle East." These aspects of U.N. 242 became popularly known as the "land for peace" formula that led to the Israeli-Egyptian peace based on the Camp David Accords of 1979. It was also the basis on which the Madrid Conference of 1991 was convened that resulted in an Israeli-Palestinian Agreement in 1993 and an Israeli-Jordanian full peace treaty in 1995. Furthermore, the "land for peace" formula generated a strong momentum toward regional peace as relations between Israel and several Arab states began to normalize.

Prime Minister Netanyahu made it clear during the election campaign and after his victory that he rejects the "land for peace" formula and will seek instead "peace with security." He vowed never to return the Golan Heights to Syria, accept Palestinian statehood, or compromise the sovereignty of Jerusalem.[6] Having made clear what he will not do, he called on the Arabs to negotiate peace with no preconditions.

A 2-day Arab summit in Cairo in late June 1996 produced a communique in which Arab leaders representing 21 nations "called on Israel to withdraw from all occupied Arab lands and to permit the Palestinians to establish an independent state with East Jerusalem as its capital." They warned that, if Israel is to delay or proceed differently, this would "compel all the Arab states to reconsider steps taken in the context of the peace process."[7] In a written statement issued by his office, Mr. Netanyahu responded, "One-sided demands that harm security are not reconcilable with peace talks. In order for the process to continue successfully and fruitfully, such demands must stop."[8]

With the hardening of positions on both sides, former U.S. Secretary of State Warren Christopher traveled to Israel for meetings with the new Prime Minister to explore ways in which the peace process could continue. Press reports following their meeting on June 25 suggested that Mr. Netanyahu,

> refused to yield on his hard-line stands that have raised fears of a slowdown in Arab-Israeli peacemaking . . . and [d]espite Christopher's lawyerly effort to skirt points of contention, Netanyahu stood firm on several points that, if maintained in negotiations, would differ markedly from what the United States has been promoting in the Middle East for the last several years . . .[9]

Still, many analysts advised then that Mr. Netanyahu needs to be given a chance to develop his foreign policy priorities. The logic of the advice was that election campaign rhetoric will eventually give way to the responsibilities of governing. As one Israeli investment manager who experienced the economic benefits of peace with the Arabs has stated, "People are a little afraid of what he [Netanyahu] says. But between what he says and what he does there is a difference—at least I hope so."[10]

During the next 2 months after the Arab summit in Cairo, a flurry of high-level meetings and diplomatic activities took place. These included the well-publicized Netanyahu visit to Washington on July 9-10 where he met President Clinton and addressed a joint session of Congress and his visit to Cairo July 18. Press and analysts' reports were mixed, but most suggested that no substantive progress toward resumption of the peace process was made because of these meetings. In fact, when in Washington and,

> Despite royal treatment, Netanyahu made no concessions to U.S. peace policies . . . Specifically, [he] did not embrace the U.S.' land for peace formula or agree to curb settlements to lift the

closure of the Palestinian territories, to withdraw troops from Hebron or the Golan Heights, to meet Yasir Arafat or to recognize Palestinian statehood. Instead he emphatically asserted that Jerusalem would forever be Israel's capital. His unabashedly hard line must have come as a surprise to many Americans, who have been assured by much of the U.S. media that he is simply 'pragmatic politician, whose views will be tempered by high office.'[11]

On the other hand, the respected Jordanian weekly *Shihan*, quoting special sources in Washington, reported that Netanyahu offered to the U.S. Administration,

> to revive the secret forum between Israel and Syria as an irreversible Israeli condition if Syria wants to join real talks that could culminate in its recovery of the Golan Heights and secure Israel against any future Syrian military threat.[12]

The report went on to detail the elements of the Netanyahu proposal including the decoupling of the Lebanese and Syrian tracks, Israeli complete withdrawal from the Golan Heights in return for guarantees for its security along certain lines including the stationing of 10,000 American troops in the Syrian Heights to monitor a demilitarized zone between the two countries, and a fair distribution of common water sources. The substance of this Israeli offer, according to the source, should have been acceptable to Syria, however, the stall in the talks had to do with mechanics, rather than details.

> The Syrian leadership sensed that the Americans and Israelis would be setting a trap for them if they proceed with the secret talks, without bringing in another world power, like Russia, that would strengthen Syria's hand in the negotiations and hold the Israelis and Americans to the provisions of the treaty.[13]

If Prime Minister Netanyahu made such an offer to the U.S. administration, this would explain why U.S. peace process coordinator Dennis Ross was dispatched to the region in late July 1996 to revive the peace talks. One would assume that if Netanyahu's secret offer to the Syrians was as inflexible on the Golan Heights as his public statements, then Mr. Ross could have had little basis on which to rekindle the stalled talks. In short, there were mixed signals on the future of the peace process and specifically the Israeli-Syrian track.[14]

Between the time of Netenyahu's election and the meeting at Wye River Plantation, there were many attempts to move the peace process forward. However, and despite many meetings between regional leaders, trips by several U.S. and European envoys, and the floating of new and fresh proposals, the peace process was no further along than where it was when Netenyahu took office in May 1996.[15] For in this time period, Netanyahu's hard-line stances were designed to change the basis on which the peace process was predicated. On the Palestinian track, he objected to the Oslo agreement entered into by the previous government as endangering Israeli security, and gave the green light for the building of a new settlement on Har Homa in East Jerusalem. The decision to build this settlement was the primary reason for the freezing of the peace process.[16]

On the Israeli-Syrian track, Netanyahu declared that negotiations must begin anew and not proceed, as the Syrians demanded, from where they left off with the previous government. Netanyahu also proposed the "Lebanon First" option—a non-starter proposal for the Lebanese and Syrians who considered it a trick designed to split the Lebanese-Syrian tracks, and therefore weaken the negotiating position of each side.[17]

Finally, it was Britain's Prime Minister Tony Blair who invited Mr. Netanyahu and Mr. Arafat to meet in London in May 1998, in an effort to restart the process, at least initially on the Israeli-Palestinian track. The London meeting succeeded only in revealing a rift between the United States and Israel over the American proposal of an Israeli withdrawal from an additional 13.1 percent of the West Bank. Before the London meeting, Arafat had accepted this proposal, but Netanyahu offered to withdraw from 9 percent only.[18] American diplomacy did eventually reach a deal with Mr. Netanyahu on the size of the withdrawal that was also acceptable to the Palestinians. That deal was, of course, the Wye Plantation Memorandum. This agreement, however, while an important step forward, is hardly the key to "unlock the door to the long-elusive regional peace between Israel and its Arab neighbors," as Vice President Gore hoped.[19] The key to regional peace remains a comprehensive "land for peace" formula.

This remainder of this chapter will focus on the Israeli-Syrian peace track. It contends that little difference exists between what Mr. Netanyahu says and what he does. The same should be true of any Likud successor to Netenyahu. The reason, besides traditional Likud ideological arguments in favor of retaining captured lands, is that Netanyahu (Likud) and his foreign policy advisors hold certain assumptions about Syria whereby the return of the Golan Heights is a lesser national priority for President Asad. In addition, Netanyahu seeks to benefit from the policy of *istifrad*—a rich Levantine-Arabic term meaning isolation, separation, seclusion, and loneliness—that could weaken Syria and leave it with virtually no bargaining options *vis-à-vis* an Israeli government that values security above peace. Finally, Israel's hand is further strengthened through its 1996 military agreement and alliance with Turkey which has created a new regional geopolitical reality in which Syria has become encircled by hostile states.[20]

The United States faces solemn challenges in trying to move the peace process forward in the current circumstances. It is difficult to assess how President Clinton's domestic political problems will impact his ability to be fully and personally engaged in the peace process. Equally uncertain are the results of the Israeli 1999 elections and the choice of prime minister. Still, even if U.S. diplomacy, during the remaining time of the Clinton administration, with all its attendant arsenals of economic and military aid is to succeed in convincing the Israeli government to return to the "land for peace" formula, the size of the aid package and the domestic political pressure the administration will have to endure may be too great a price to pay. The chapter will conclude by postulating some general policy recommendations.

The Golan Heights and Israeli-Syrian Relations.

The Golan Heights as an area of friction and contention between Israel and Syria dates back to 1949 when the two countries signed a U.N.-brokered armistice agreement to end the state of hostilities following the 1949 Arab-Israeli war. Relations between the two countries over the Golan issue could be divided into two periods. The first is the period before 1967 when the Heights were under Syrian control. The second period beginning 1967 to date is characterized by Israeli occupation of about 1,250 square kilometers of the 1,750 square kilometers that comprise the Heights, and Syria's attempt to regain sovereignty over them.

During the first period, Israeli-Syrian relations involved border incidents often culminating in major military clashes. According to Muhammad Muslih,

> At issue was the DMZ [demilitarized zone], an area of less than 100 square miles stretching from above Lake Huleh to south of the Sea of Galilee (Lake Tiberia). The zone was composed of three separate sectors of land along the Israel-Syria border. The northern sector was formed by Syrian, Palestinian and Israeli villages, while the central and southern sectors were more important from a strategic point of view because they were heavily populated and straddled the Jordan River between the Sea of Galilee and Lake Huleh.[21]

From the beginning, Israel sought to have exclusive control over the Sea of Galilee for settlement and economic purposes. Israel, acting under the counsel of its legal advisors as to the legal status of the DMZ, began:

to implement a carefully planned policy whose quintessence was the imposition of Israeli sovereignty over the DMZ. The objective was to drain the Lake Huleh marshes, win exclusive control of the Sea of Galilee, and complete Israel's Natural Water Carrier, a project whose aim was to divert water from the Jordan River to the northern part of the Negev desert in the south.[22]

Syria, therefore, was determined to check Israeli encroachment that involved such measures as the planting of mines and minefields, erection of fortifications, extension of Israeli cultivation and the restriction of the movement of U.N. military observers—all viewed by Syria as creeping annexation of the DMZ which, from a Syrian legal viewpoint, was neither under Syrian nor Israeli sovereignty. The point here is that both sides have come to regard the region as important economically and militarily for their national interests. Numerous incidents took place during the period before the Six-Day War of 1967 that demonstrated the value of the area to each side.

The second period in Israeli-Syrian relations began in June 1967 after Israel captured the Golan Heights and the high point on Mount Hermon (2,224 meters) from Syria. Acquisition of the Golan has given Israel tremendous strategic advantage with its army stationed only 35 kilometers from the Syrian capital of Damascus, allowing it to install highly sophisticated eavesdropping devices on Mount Hermon, giving it control of water sources including the Banias River—a major tributary of the Jordan River feeding it with 14,000 cubic meters of water every hour—and providing opportunities to create new Jewish settlements in the area.[23]

From a Syrian perspective, the loss of the Golan Heights makes it extremely vulnerable to an Israeli land attack, as the Heights formed a critical natural defense against Israel. Their return is a vital geo-strategic objective. Furthermore, the Israeli occupation of the Golan has had other costs. Control of the water sources was an obvious cost, given the significance of water issues in a situation of increasing shortages.[24] Israeli occupation has also meant that Syrian citizens on the Golan are left unprotected and abused. Because of Israeli policies, only 16,000 people in five Arab villages remain, compared to 130,000 people in 139 villages in 1967. Additionally, Syria regards the 15,000 Israeli settlers in some 35 Jewish settlements to be intruders on Syrian sovereignty.[25]

Compared to the first period, the 1967-to-present period in Israeli-Syrian relations has been largely characterized by the relative quiet and lack of border incidents between the two countries on the Golan with one major exception. Instead, Syria has used the surrogate Hizballah in south Lebanon as its main military weapon against Israel. The exception was the October 1973 Arab-Israeli War during which Syria attempted a surprise attack to recover its occupied territories. That war ended with the return of a small strip of territory in 1974 and the establishment of a U.N.-patrolled buffer zone between the two armies as a result of Henry Kissinger's mediation efforts.[26]

For the Israelis, the occupation of the Golan poses a serious dilemma which is reflected in the division among the Israeli public over this issue. To some, the Golan offers the opportunity to trade captured territories for real peace with Syria (and by extension with Lebanon), thus ending the 50-year old Arab-Israeli dispute. Apparently, the previous Labor government was moving in this direction, having concluded that President Asad had indeed made a strategic decision to enter into a lasting peace with Israel. Consequently, the Rabin-Peres governments were prepared to trade land for peace. To other Israelis, however, the Golan should never be given up to the Syrians, for its possession affords Israel the best security guarantee against any future Syrian attack. Finally, there are those who take a somewhat middle position, arguing for partial withdrawal as the price to be paid for peace with Syria.[27]

The late-1997 news regarding a Mossad agent who fabricated reports on Syria is likely to add an intricate dimension to Israeli-Syrian relations. Spy master Yehuda Gil, responsible for watching Syria, apparently provided false information for several years that influenced key Israeli decisions on Syria which nearly caused two wars. It was Gil's information portraying the Syrian leadership, and especially President Asad, as opposed to making peace that played a role in Rabin's decision to emphasize the Israeli-Palestinian track vice the Israeli-Syrian track.[28]

The Israeli Position.

The position of the current Likud Israeli government on the Golan Heights is largely shaped by Israel's U.N. Ambassador Dr. Dore Gold—formerly Netanyahu's principal national security advisor, and director of the U.S. foreign and defense policy project at the Jaffee Center for Strategic Studies of Tel Aviv University.

Gold's writings are largely centered on operational and tactical considerations as the principal factors to be met according to Israeli security requirements. In turn, these requirements constitute the only bases for the peace process. In addition, the U.S.-born and educated Gold argues in favor of settlement arrangements with the Syrians that would preclude the stationing of American troops as peacekeepers on the Golan. Of course, this is a very popular stance in the United States, especially among members of Congress who are loath to place American troops in what might be harm's way. Consequently, Israel must retain significant portions of the Golan to guarantee its security. Similarly, operational and tactical factors require that Israel does not withdraw completely from the West Bank, and the Oslo Agreement, that the previous Labor government concluded with the Palestinian Authority, is viewed with extreme suspicion by Gold and the Likud government.

Gold's starting premise is the existence of two types of structural asymmetries between Israel and its Arab adversaries that seriously imperil Israeli security. The first asymmetry is the wide disparity between Israel's Jewish population and the populations of its Arab neighbors that allows the Arabs to maintain relatively large military establishments. The numbers imbalance becomes more significant, considering that the bulk of Israeli formations is reserve units compared to Arab divisions that are standing active service units.

The other asymmetry pertains to coalition formation potential. Within the region, and despite inter-Arab rivalries, the Arab military have managed to form multi-state coalitions against Israel in every Arab-Israeli war. By contrast, Israel has no regional alliances save for cooperative ties with "periphery states" such as Iran under the Shah, and recently Turkey.

The net effect, as Gold sees it, is that "these asymmetries mean that the central strategic challenge for Israel is countering the potential conventional military superiority of its Arab state adversaries individually, and especially in coalition."[29]

To overcome the strategic challenge posed by the conventional military power asymmetries, Gold argues for Israeli military control of the Golan Heights and the West Bank as these occupied territories afford Israel with three important security advantages. The first is *denial*, whereby Syrian forces can no longer threaten the Sea of Galilee from the Golan and are denied the ability to control the sources of the Jordan River. Control of the West Bank denies the Arabs (Palestinians and/or Jordanians) the ability to threaten Israel's coastal plain where 70 percent of its population dwell and that is the principal site of Israeli industrial plants. It also increases the distance between the Mediterranean and the pre-1967 border that was only 10 miles and made Israel vulnerable to Arab attack at its narrow waist.[30]

The second advantage is *warning*, whereby control of the territories gives Israel early warning capabilities. In the case of Syria, Israel can detect Syrian military activities as far as the Syrian capital. The loss of the Golan has by definition denied Syria comparable coverage of the Galilee region. In the West Bank, Israeli deployment of air defense units reduces the threat of air attacks by Arab forces originating from the direction of Jordan or Iraq. Control of West Bank airspace "is vital for the defense of the skies of Israel against Arab war coalition aircraft."[31]

The last advantage is *defense*, and Gold makes it clear that this is because of Israeli control of topographically favorable terrain. The Golan Heights and the West Bank provide Israel with an excellent shield against conventional military attack. They also improve Israeli counter-offensive capability that traditionally has emphasized mobile warfare with the objective of taking the war to the enemy's heartland.[32]

Gold concluded his essay by positing the dilemma facing Israel: ". . . to hold on to all the 1967 territories and make Israel more defensible or give up these territorial barriers and reduce the enmity of its neighbors?" Put differently, the difficult security choice is between military strategic considerations and diplomatic political arrangements. The answer depends on the nature of the Middle East at any given time and "peace between Israel and the Arab states could not be superior to the relations between Arab states themselves."[33] Therefore, and with respect to Syria, Syrian intentions and capabilities are critical elements for a peace arrangement with Israel. They are, however, difficult to measure. Consequently, Israel will require agreed-upon limits on Syrian offensive capabilities in exchange for Israeli withdrawal from Golan territories. Syria may not, however, agree to any force structure reduction since it can claim threats to its security from other quarters. An alternate consideration might be a demilitarized Golan Heights. This, according to Gold, is unacceptable, for unlike the Sinai, the Golan does not provide a deep enough buffer against Syrian forces who will remain within close striking distance to Israel.

On the other hand, Gold believes that, although the Palestinians are not a military power, nevertheless Israel must have access to the West Bank as defense against potential Arab enemy attack from the east. His conclusion:

> . . . Israel will have to take a conservative approach to outstanding territorial differences with its neighbors. Premature Israeli withdrawal, while the basic elements of Middle East instability persists, [ethno-religious conflicts, frontier disputes, serious economic differences] would destabilize the region and could increase the chances of war more than continuation of the status quo.[34]

It is the desire to perpetuate the status quo that is the key to Netanyahu's attitude and policy toward the peace process. The military strategic considerations are buttressed by Likud's ideological inclination to claim the occupied territories as part of the historical land of Israel that belongs to the Jews.[35]

Since coming to power, Netanyahu's government has purposefully pursued a policy of not accommodating the "land for peace" formula that is at the heart of the U.S.-sponsored peace process. The alleged assumption is that such a formula does not guarantee Israeli security. But what about the use of U.S. forces on the Golan Heights in a post "land for peace" settlement as a buffer between Syrian and Israeli forces? Gold provides the arguments about why such a proposal is unworkable or at least undesirable.

In a Jaffee Center memorandum, Gold argued that U.S. forces on the Golan, for reasons already stated, would likely have to perform peacekeeping and peace-enforcing activities. The former involves monitoring activities similar to the Multinational Forces and Observers (MFO) in Sinai. Peace-enforcing would involve early warning and possibly to act as a deterrence force in case of Syrian hostile intent, and as a defense force in case of a Syrian attack. Gold carefully weighs each of these peace enforcing functions and notes that their performance by U.S. forces, beside negating long-standing Israeli national security doctrine by making

Israel dependent on the United States, they are likely to lead to friction between the two countries that could alter their strategic relationship. The conclusion he reached was that

> ... the presence of a large American force on the Golan Heights would, in the final analysis, be disadvantageous for Israel's security. Beyond the risks associated explicitly with the deployment of a substantial American presence on the Golan, there are a number of domestic American political factors that in any case reduce the chances that such a presence would be acceptable to the U.S.[36]

It should be evident that Gold's arguments are at the heart of the Netanyahu policies regarding the peace process. Israeli security is very important and could only be achieved by direct Israeli military strategic advantage. Peace agreements that diminish Israeli military strategic advantage or the presence of surrogate forces such as the United States as guarantors of peace are unacceptable alternatives. Given the general conditions of the region, it would be unrealistic to expect Israeli-Arab relations to be superior to existing Arab-Arab relations. Consequently, the status quo with its attendant Israeli military superiority is, for the time being, an acceptable option.

The security arguments of Dore Gold are not Likud's only supporting arguments. There are the contentions of Daniel Pipes who at one point argued that Asad was primarily interested in absorbing Lebanon. The implication is that he is willing to reach a deal by which the Golan Heights are "traded" for Lebanon.[37] Later, Pipes argued that Asad was not truly interested in achieving a settlement on the Golan; his goal, for reasons of regime survival, "is not peace but a peace process."[38] There were, furthermore, the arguments of Professor Beres and Ambassador Shoval (Israeli Ambassador to the United States) that, beyond the immediate security concerns, withdrawal from the Golan Heights would "uproot 32 Golan Jewish communities and threaten a third of Israel's water supply."[39] These arguments simply fuel the propensity of Likud to hold on to the Golan. *The Times* (London) recently reported that the number of Jewish settlers on the Golan is increasing and continues to rise. The central thesis of this report was that,

> Israel is consolidating its presence on the occupied Golan Heights to the extent that leaders of the Jewish settlers here no longer fear the land being handed back to Syria as they did before the 1996 election.[40]

To all the above discussion could be added the observation that in the post-Soviet world, the perpetuation of the status quo on the Israeli-Syrian front clearly favors the Israelis. Syria's lacking a superpower patron, and Israel's success in forging a military alliance with Turkey, mean that the gap between Israeli and Syrian military strength is widening in Israel's favor. The longer the status quo continues, presumably the less is Syria's ability to negotiate a favorable peace settlement. This is the realization that both Israel and Syria must have arrived at which explains Israeli government stalling tactics and Syrian eagerness for the resumption of the negotiations on the basis of the "land for peace" formula.

The Syrian Position.

The geo-strategic environment of the region in the aftermath of the Gulf war provided the United States the opportunity to cooperate with the Soviet Union and convene the 1991 Madrid Peace Conference based on the "land for peace" principle. Syria, which until then had depended on the Soviet Union for political and military support, concluded that relations between the two superpowers were changing rapidly, and blanket Soviet support was no longer assured. Madrid was a viable option to achieve peace. After all, Syria and several Arab states had participated in the U.S.-led coalition against Iraq and could now hope to count on a vigorous and even-handed peace role by the United States.

Syria's approach to the Madrid Peace Conference was based on two conditions: all lands occupied by Israel in 1967 were to be returned as a precondition for any peace agreement, and the peace agreement should be comprehensive. This meant that Israel must agree to withdraw from all the lands occupied in 1967. Indeed Israel's participation in the Madrid Conference meant acceptance of the "land for peace' formula as the basis for future negotiations. Syria also preferred that a comprehensive peace agreement be reached simultaneously settling all outstanding issues between Israel and those of the Palestinians, Jordanians, Lebanese, and Syrians. Such an approach would strengthen the Arab negotiating position in addition to salvaging what has remained of Arab solidarity after the Gulf war.

Syria's approach to the peace process and a detailed accounting of its negotiations with Israel was recently revealed by Walid Al-Moulalem, Ambassador to the U.S. and head of the Syrian delegation to the peace talks.[41] Ambassador Al-Moualem made it clear that Syria would never negotiate with Israel if it was not understood that Israel was willing to withdraw from the entire Golan to the June 4, 1967, international boundary.[42] In other words, the purpose of the negotiations was for Syria to regain sovereignty over all of its territory in exchange for peace and normalization of relations with Israel. He claimed that Prime Minister Rabin understood this point and committed Israel to withdrawal. The Syrian Ambassador stated:

> From Madrid onward, the only issue we would even consent to discuss was full withdrawal. Under Likud, of course, it was a dialogue of the deaf—I think Ben Aharon, the head of the Israeli delegation, was following to the letter [former Prime Minister Yitzhak] Shamir's instructions to continue talking for ten years without result. After Rabin became prime minister in June 1992, we still insisted on discussing withdrawal only. When Rabin finally realized that the Syrians would not move a step ahead in discussing any of the other elements of a peace settlement before being convinced of Israel's intention on full withdrawal, he made the opening.[43]

After Rabin was assassinated, Peres made the same commitment, and the reason an agreement was not reached then was because Peres decided to call for elections. Al-Moualem made it clear that, precisely because the Israelis accepted the principle of "land for peace," i.e., withdrawal, that negotiations were progressing on the other elements of a peace agreement including normalization, security arrangements, and the timetable of fulfillment. Al-Moualem also noted the negotiating strategy of Rabin that sought to separate each of the peace tracks that Israel was engaged in. Consequently, when progress was being made on the Israeli-Palestinian track in 1993, "he [Rabin] informed us through the Americans that he could not proceed on the Syrian track because the Israeli public needed time to digest the Oslo Accord. So he suspended our talks." Peres, by contrast, wanted to "enter the elections with a Syrian-Israeli agreement in his hand. He wanted to 'fly high and fast' . . ."[44] The Syrians, however, were not prepared to move that quickly since the issues to be settled with respect to the other elements of a peace agreement were complicated, and time was needed to sell the agreement to the Syrian public. Still, Peres called for elections less than 3 months after taking office and the talks were suspended in 1996.[45]

Syria has made its position very clear to Netanyahu's government. First, Syria has opted for peace as a strategic choice. Second, negotiations must be resumed from the point they were left off. All understandings reached between the parties concerning withdrawal of Israeli forces from the Golan and agreements about security arrangements must be considered valid. Third, the Syrian and Lebanese tracks are inseparable.

The Syrian option for peace was stated clearly by President Asad during a joint news conference in Geneva in January 1994, following meetings with President Clinton. He said,

> Syria seeks a just and comprehensive peace with Israel as a strategic choice that secures Arab rights, ends the Israeli occupation, and enables all peoples in the region to live in peace, security, and dignity, and in honor we shall make peace.[46]

This statement, made for the benefit of the Israelis and international mediators, especially the United States, was meant to convey the sincerity of the Syrians in reaching a final settlement with the Israelis if the Golan Heights are returned to Syrian sovereignty.[47] Pragmatically, Asad's "strategic choice" was the only one left for him under the circumstances. As a realist, "driven not by ideological considerations but by *raison d'etat* . . . Asad is very aware of his strategic predicament vis-à-vis Israel."[48] Lacking a superpower patron, his predicament is Syria's inability to effectively balance Israel's power or else contain it. Consequently, the peace option as a "strategic choice" exposes his weakness and, therefore, vulnerability.[49]

A major difference separates the Syrian and Israeli positions with respect to possible resumption of negotiations between them. Netanyahu believes that negotiations should be resumed without any preconditions so that "both sides would be free to raise any negotiating demand they wish . . ."[50] He justified his position on the strength of the argument that,

> there is no contractual mechanism between the two states with regard to a peace arrangement. He [Netanyahu] asserted that the United States understands it and agrees that issues discussed in talks conducted by the previous government are not binding on Israel.[51]

Put differently, Netanyahu would honor signed agreements entered into by the previous government, but is not obligated to accept his predecessor's bargaining positions. In yet another statement attributed to him, the Israeli Prime Minister suggested that he was in no hurry to conclude a peace treaty with Syria:

> We are not on the verge of war with Syria and the road to peace with it has not ended. There are obstacles on the way, but we will achieve peace. We will work for it during the current phase (phase ending in the year 2000), otherwise in the next (year 2004).[52]

Syria, on the other hand, insists that agreements reached in negotiations with the previous government, including Rabin's willingness to withdraw to the June 4, 1967, line, should be the starting point for the resumption of talks. Syrian negotiator Al-Moualem claims that the Israeli offer to withdraw from all of the Golan was in writing. This was also confirmed by Defense Minister General Mustafa Tlass.[53] To go back to point zero as Netanyahu demands, means, in the words of the Syrian Vice President Khaddam, that "the negotiations could last another century . . . since every time there is a new Israeli government we have to return to point zero."[54] Accepting Netanyahu's position would also mean accepting his harder line, and give the false impression that Syria might be willing to make territorial concessions.

Syria's hegemony over Lebanon has become its surest weapon against the policy of *istifrad*. If Israel could be denied the option of a separate peace with Lebanon, then Israel will have to continue its involvement in the increasingly unpopular "security zone" on its northern border. It also means that the goal of achieving peace between Israel and all of its neighboring states will be only half fulfilled. Not surprisingly, therefore, the relatively recent Israeli proposal to implement U.N. Security Council Resolution 425 (calling on Israel to withdraw from Lebanon) met with strong Syrian condemnation. This is because the Israeli withdrawal plan would take away an important Syrian weapon—using Hizballah against Israel.

The Israeli proposal offered to comply with Resolution 425 if Lebanon takes steps to insure security along the border. In Netanyahu's words,

> There is no policy of unilateral withdrawal, because in our assessment that would increase Hezbollah attacks into the Galilee . . . If the government of Lebanon will join us in establishing the proper security arrangements in southern Lebanon, we will be happy to get out of Lebanon in the framework of implementing U.N. Resolution 425.[55]

For Syria (and Lebanon), Israeli withdrawal must be unconditional as called for by Resolution 425. The Syrian message is clear, security on the border and peace in Galilee is obtainable once Israel agrees to withdraw simultaneously from south Lebanon and the Golan Heights.[56]

Finally, and with respect to the broader issue of alliances and "encirclement," it is not surprising that Syria's response has been an attempt to balance Israel's alliance with the United States and the more recent Turkish-Israeli alliance. Since the United States is viewed by Syria as biased toward Israel, Syria has vigorously advocated for a European role in the peace process, especially after Netenyahu came to power. President Asad believes that, given the stalemated peace process, the European Union, and particularly France, should have a role to play in the peace process, "not to replace the Americans, but to have a role along with the Americans in pushing the peace process forward."[57] It remains to be seen what role Europe can play, given "Israeli animosity toward French and European diplomatic intervention in the Arab-Israeli conflict."[58] The Turkish-Israeli military alliance has sufficiently worried Syria so that President Asad traveled to Iran in July 1997 to bolster Syria's relations with that country. Syria has also taken steps to establish contacts with Iraq, its neighbor and Ba'th Party ideological enemy. "Together with them, the Syrians could face Turkey and signal the Americans that they still have partners in spite of attempts to isolate them."[59] The Turkish-Israeli military agreement concerns not only Syria, but also most nations in the region leading to the emergence of "a front led by Egypt, Saudi Arabia and Syria."[60] It remains to be seen, however, if the new realignments taking place in the region will endure and effectively balance one another.

The above discussion discloses why the Israeli-Syrian peace track is deadlocked. The problem is the inverse relationship between the defining elements of the stalemate: Syrian demand for sovereignty and Israeli quest for security. If American diplomacy is to succeed in moving the Israeli-Syrian peace track forward, it must do so based on proposals that can accommodate these conflicting claims.

Observations and Policy Recommendations.

On May 6, 1998, Hillary Rodham Clinton, speaking to a group of Arab and Israeli teenagers, said that creating a Palestinian state is "very important for the broader goal of peace in the Middle East."[61] Not surprisingly, this statement touched off criticisms of the First Lady in many pro-Israeli quarters in and outside of the United States. However, it is precisely this realistic future assessment of the region that is required of the United States if it is to secure its long-term vital interests. One such interest is a lasting and comprehensive Middle East peace. On the Israeli-Syrian peace track, a comparable realistic assessment is the fact that Syria will not make territorial concessions in the Golan Heights, and will not waver in its demand for full sovereignty over its occupied lands. Additionally, there is absolutely no reason to believe that any post-Asad government will accept anything less.

In this author's view, the long-standing U.S. commitment, by word and deed, to the security and well-being of the State of Israel was a major factor in bringing the Arabs to the realization that Israel is in the region to stay. Today, no responsible Arab leader or citizen harbors any false hopes that Israel could be eliminated from the political landscape of the Middle East. Arab willingness to recognize and negotiate with Israel since the Madrid Peace Conference attests to this fact. Similarly, the United States must now dispel any false hopes entertained by the current and any future Likud government, and by some Israeli citizens (and their U.S. supporters), that they could permanently annex all or some of the Golan territory; just as the First Lady's statement helped dispel the notion that somehow Palestinian national aspirations could be negotiated or withered away. A realistic assessment of future regional conditions by the principals involved in the peace process is the prerequisite step to breaking the deadlock. As major mediator between the parties in the peace process, but also as the sole superpower with vital interests in the Middle East, the United States must publicly endorse the reasonable and legitimate demands of the parties—Syrian sovereignty over its occupied territories, and Israeli demands for security concerns in the Galilee and northern Israel.

With the dawning of a new international era following the collapse of the Soviet Union, a new reality has emerged in the Middle East. It is the linkage and the interconnectivity that exist between the various subregions of the Middle East. Saddam Hussein proved vividly that connection when he fired Scud missiles on downtown Tel Aviv. Also true is the interconnectivity between the various tracks of the peace process. The failed Doha economic conference of 1997 showed how failure on one track (Israeli-Palestinian standoff over the proposed settlements on Har Homa) can affect another. As the former Assistant Secretary of State for Near Eastern Affairs warned, "The United States is making a dangerous mistake by focusing its efforts in the Middle East peace process solely on Israel and the Palestinians, without also involving Syria and Lebanon."[62] The impression that the Israeli-Syrian track is deliberately being put on hold reinforces the Syrian belief that the United States is less than an "honest broker" assisting in the Israeli tactic of *'istifrad'ing'* and 'encircling' Syria.

In the Arab street, the image of the United States as responsible "honest broker" is less than positive and continues to deteriorate. Anyone who follows the Arab press and is in touch with Arab elites is constantly reminded of this fact. The most common charge is that of "double standards" by which the United States is willing to look the other way when Israel stands in violation of U.N. Security Council resolutions, but insists on the strictest adherence by Iraq to U.N. sanction resolutions.[63]

The popular negative image of the United States forces Arab governments, including friendly ones, to distance themselves from U.S. policies. In years past, Arab governments were in a far better position to influence and shape public opinion in their countries through their control of the media. But since the "migration" of the leading Arab print media (e.g., the influential dailies *Al-Hayat* and *Ashorq al-Awsat*, and magazines as *Al-Watan al-Arabi* and *Al-Wasat*) to Paris and London, and the establishment of the influential Middle East Broadcasting (MBC) television in London—regarded as the CNN of the Arab world— (because of increasing local censorship, and the Lebanese civil war that forced many free Arab press out of Beirut), local governments find it extremely difficult to continue molding public opinion in their countries. This "immigrant" and popular Arab press addresses itself to a wider Arab audience and focuses on broad regional issues. Hence, for example, the reader in a Gulf state is likely to be as informed and concerned about the intricacies of the peace process as the average reader anywhere else in the Arab world. The rapid spread of the Internet and the satellite dishes enhances this phenomenon and the interconnectivity of the region as a whole. In short, the traditional local press with its focus on the alleged accomplishments of the state, and the antics of the rulers and their progeny is rapidly becoming irrelevant.

The prevailing trend toward regional linkages and interconnectivity of issues can potentially destabilize regimes in the area friendly to the United States. Arab governments are made aware of this trend by the increasing public pressure to adopt policies more in line with popular sentiments. Ironically, these developments are unfolding while the United States is scaling down its public diplomacy efforts. The U.S. Information Agency, whose primary mission is to foster an understanding and appreciation of U.S. foreign policy among overseas nationals, is being eliminated as part of a plan to restructure the foreign service establishment.

The success of U.S. foreign policy objectives in the Middle East hinge on the outcome of a peace process that is currently stalled and frozen. Although President Clinton is understandably reluctant to undermine his high approval rating at home by pursuing a Middle East policy contrary to the wishes of the powerful pro-Israeli lobby, he is in the unique position of not having to face re-election and so can move the process forward. The President, who is likely to survive a Senate impeachment trial, must personally become once again engaged in the process, and to offer a role for the European Union in the search of a final settlement to the Arab-Israeli conflict. A European role as a mediating partner with the United States, at a time when Europe is emerging as potentially the world's strongest economic power, will send clear signals that the Western alliance with whom Arabs and Israelis have extensive economic and political relations is serious about a final just settlement.

On the Israeli-Syrian track, this means pressuring the Israeli government to accept concessions made by the previous Labor government in its negotiations with the Syrians. To argue that such a recommendation ignores the results of the 1996 Israeli elections (or the 1999 elections if Netenyahu is returned to power), and that only the Israeli government can decide the parameters of its security requirements, is to argue in favor of abandoning the peace process and U.S. interests in the region. In this regard, it is time that congressional leaders realize the anomaly of allowing their institution to be used by a foreign leader to pressure the U.S. President against his better judgement of America's long-term interests.

In return for Israeli concessions, the United States should offer Israel additional security commitments, including the possibility of stationing U.S. troops on the Golan Heights for a period of time. Similarly, the United States and Europe should see to it that every phased Israeli withdrawal from the Golan is reciprocated on the Syrian side by confidence-building measures and concrete steps toward normalization of relations between the two countries.

Finally, Dore Gold's arguments notwithstanding, it is only with peace based on the "land for peace" formula that Israel could be transformed from a nation in the Middle East to a nation of the Middle East. By pressuring for a final settlement, the United States, as the world's only superpower, transforms itself from a hapless mediator to a responsible actor. A successful peace process will also ensure the long-term interests of the United States in all of the Middle East.

ENDNOTES - CHAPTER 13

1. Quoted in *Ma'ariv*, Tel Aviv, Internet Edition, August 13, 1997.

2. For a complete text of the Wye Memorandum, see *New York Times* (Internet Edition), October 24, 1998. President Clinton's involvement included his personal participation for many long hours in the negotiations at the Wye River Plantation and his subsequent historic visit to Israel and Gaza to give impetus for the implementation of the Wye Agreement. See Deborah Sontag, "Clinton, Despite Hurdles, Sets Up Crucial Salvage Mission," *New York Times*, (Internet Edition), December 14, 1998. Also in mid-December 1998 U.S. Senator Arlan Specter (Chairman of the Senate Committee on Intelligence) who traveled with President Clinton to Israel, went to Damascus and delivered a message to President Asad from Prime Minister Netenyahu indicating Israeli interest in resuming peace talks with Syria, and also a message from President Clinton urging Syria to reach agreement with Tel Aviv on resumption of peace talks. See London *Al Hayat* (in Arabic), December 18, 1998, p. 7.

3. See Lee Hockstader, "Israel Puts Pact in Doubt," *The Washington Post*, November 1998, pp. Al, A27.

4. At the time of this writing, the situation has been made much more complicated by the impeachment of the President and his pending trial in the Senate. Give the high approval ratings that the President has in the polls, and despite his likely censure by the Senate, President Clinton can exert tremendous leverage on any post-1999 Israeli election government to move the peace process forward.

5. See The White House, *A National Security Strategy for a New Century*, October 1998, p. 52.

6. See George Joffe, "Israel After the Elections: What You See is What You Get," *Jane's Intelligence Review*, Vol. 8, No. 8, August 1996, p. 365.

7. *New York Times*, June 24, 1996, p. 1.

8. *Ibid.*, p. A8.

9. *The Washington Post*, June 26, 1996, p. A23.

10. *The Washington Post*, June 25, 1996, p. A11.

11. Donald Neff, "Netanyahu Gets the Royal Treatment in Washington," *Middle East International*, July 19, 1996, p. 4. In Cairo, President Mubarak and Prime Minister Netanyahu held a joint press conference following their meeting in which they indicated their desire to pursue the peace process, widen the circle of peace, and fulfill commitments already made. For a full text of the press conference, see *Foreign Broadcast Information Service* (hereafter *FBIS*)-96-140, July 19, 1996, pp. 13-17.

12. *Shihan* (Amman, in Arabic), July 20-26, 1996, p. 13. See *FBIS-NES*-96-141, July 22, 1996, p. 12.

13. *Ibid.*, p. 14.

14. Mixed signals have continued during and after Mr. Netanyahu's visit to Amman in early August. It may be recalled that King Hussein had, a few days earlier, visited Damascus for talks with President Asad. Press reports indicated that the King was "very optimistic and very reassured" that negotiations will continue until there is comprehensive peace. Netanyahu stated that the deadlock on how to proceed with the peace talks with Syria could be broken at once if there is goodwill on the side of Syria. The following day, however, Syria rejected resumption of talks with Israel arguing that the Israelis wanted to discuss south Lebanon without making any commitment to trade for peace on the Golan. The editor of Syria's state-run daily *Tishrin* stated the next day

that Netanyahu rejects realistic terms for peace—trading land for peace. See *The Washington Post*, August 6, 1996, p. 1/11, and August 7, 1996, p. A24. Also, President Asad stated that "The Israeli government wants 'to resume the peace process without any foundation or ground for action,' . . . I don't think that this will lead to any results." *The Washington Post*, August 8, 1996, p. A26.

15. For example, see David Makovsky, "Israel-U.S. Face-Off Looms, As Ross Goes Home Empty-handed," *Ha'aretz* (Internet Edition), March 31, 1998.

16. See "Israel's Bad Decision on Har Homa," *Chicago Tribune*, February 28, 1997, p. 22; Joel Greenberg, "Ending Silence, Palestinians Battle Israeli Units," *New York Times*, March 21, 1997, p. A11; Rebecca Trounson, "Netenyahu Shrugs Off East Jerusalem Furor," *Los Angeles Times*, November 13, 1998, p. 14; and Aliza Marcus, "Israel Asks Bids for Building Site in E. Jerusalem, Har Homa Plan Angers Palestinians," *Boston Globe*, November 13, 1998, p. A2.

17. See Hene R. Prusher, "Israel's Tough New Peace Plan Forces Syria Into Hard Choice," *The Christian Science Monitor*, August 8, 1996, p. 6.

18. See Barton Gellman, "A Gamble On Forcing Israel's Hand," *The Washington Post*, May 7, 1998, p. Al; and Lee Hockstader, "U.S. Effort Is Rebuffed By Israeli," *The Washington Post*, May 11, 1998, p. Al, 14.

19. *The Washington Post*, May 4, 1998, p. A1.

20. For a detailed discussion of this point, see the excellent article by Alain Gresh, "Turkish-Israeli-Syrian Relations And Their Impact On The Middle East," *Middle East Journal*, Vol. 52, No. 2, Spring 1998, pp. 188-203.

21. Muhammad Muslish, "The Golan: Israel, Syria, and Strategic Calculations," *Middle East Journal*, Vol. 47, No. 4, Autumn 1993, p. 613. 1 shall rely almost exclusively on this source to highlight the two periods involved in Israeli-Syrian relations on the Golan.

22. *Ibid.*, p. 615.

23. See Robert I. Friedman, "Ceding the High Ground," *Harper's Magazine*, April 1995, pp. 66-67.

24. According to one estimate, Israel uses 500 million cubic meters of Golan water per year or approximately one fourth of its annual water needs. See Ali Said Badwan, "The Golan Heights: Its Strategic-

geographic-riparian Importance," London *Amarq Al-Awsat* (in Arabic), January 29, 1997, p. 15.

25. For a full discussion of the Syrian position and Israeli actions on the Golan see Muslih, pp. 625ff; and Tayseer Mara'i and Usama R. Halabi, "Life Under Occupation in the Golan Heights," *Journal of Palestine Studies*, Vol. XXII, No. 1, Autumn 1992, pp. 78-93.

26. For a full exposition of these positions, see Muslish, pp. 622-625. Also, for a discussion on the modalities of peace between Israel and Syria, see Alon Ben-Meir, "Israel and Syria: The Search For A 'Risk-Free' Peace," *Middle East Policy*, Vol., 4, Nos. 1 and 2, September 1995, pp. 140-155.

27. Muslish, *Ibid*.

28. See *New York Times*, (Internet Edition), December 7, 1997, and *Ha'aretz*, (Israel), Internet English Edition, December 7, 1997.

29. Dore Gold, "Fundamental Factors in a Stabilized Middle East: Security, Territory, and Peace," Gottesman Lecture Series, Washington, DC: Jewish Institute for National Security Affairs, 1993, p. 6.

30. See *Ibid.*, p. 9.

31. *Ibid.*, p. 10.

32. *Ibid.*, pp. 8-12.

33. *Ibid.*, p. 13.

34. *Ibid,*. p. 17.

35. This view is also held by Moshe Arens, former Israeli defense and foreign minister and Netenyahu's political godfather, who believes that Israel must retain the Golan Heights essentially for security reasons. "We would risk paying dearly for giving it up. During the October 1973 war, the Golan was almost entirely reconquered by Syrian troops who could have gone on advancing right up to Haifa." Quoted in Alain Gresh, p. 189.

36. Dore Gold, *US Forces on the Golan Heights and Israeli-Syrian Security Arrangements*, Memorandum No. 44, Tel Aviv University: Jaffee Center for Strategic Studies, August 1994, p. 48.

37. See Daniel Pipes, "Damascus and the Claim to Lebanon," *Orbis*, Vol. 30, No. 4, Winter 1987, pp. 663-682. Dore Gold is also of the opinion that President Asad is interested in controlling Lebanon and that he might be "willing to forgo most of the Golan in favor of Lebanon. . . ." See Ilene R. Prusher, "Israel's Tough New Peace Plan Forces Syria Into Hard Choice," *Christian Science Monitor*, August 8, 1996, p. 6.

38. Daniel Pipes, "Syria's Peace Bluff: Just Kidding," *The New Republic*, January 8 and 15, 1996, pp. 18-19.

39. Louis Rene Beres and Zalman Shoval, "Why Golan Demilitarization Would Not Work," *TVI Report*, Vol, 11, No. 4, 1996, p. 12.

40. Christopher Walker, "Golan Boom Quells Settlers' Fears of Pullout," *The Times* (London), Internet Edition, March 9, 1998.

41. See interview with Ambassador Walid Al-Moualem, "Fresh Light on the Syrian-Israeli Peace Negotiations," *Journal of Palestine Studies*, Vol. XXVI, No. 2, Winter 1997, pp. 81-94. This was a rare interview by a Syrian diplomat which received wide attention in the international press, including *The Jerusalem Post*, January 31, 1997, pp. 7,19; *Al-Safir*, (Beirut, in Arabic), Internet Edition, February 2, 1997; and *The Washington Post*, January 29, 1997, p. 6. *The Jerusalem Post* wrote, ". . . the interview, exceptional in its depth, scope and candor could be the opening diplomatic salvo from Damascus in an offensive that is intended to lead to military conflict."

42. Even if Israel is to agree to return the Golan to Syria in exchange for peace, it is likely to demand adjustments in the international boundary in order to avoid the cross-border tensions and to insure control of Lake Tiberias and other water resources. See Brian S. Mandell, "Getting to Peacekeeping in Principal Rivalries: Anticipating An Israeli-Syrian Peace Treaty," *Journal of Conflict Resolution*, Vol. 40, No. 2, June 1996, p. 243.

43. *Ibid.*, p. 84.

44. *Ibid.*, p. 85.

45. For a detailed survey of the Israeli-Syrian interaction between 1991 (Madrid Peace Conference) and the suspension of the talks in 1996, see Helena Cobban, *Syria and the Peace: A Good Chance Missed*, Carlisle Barracks, PA: U.S. Army War College, Strategic Studies Institute, July 7, 1997.

46. "The President's News Conference With President Hafiz al-Asad of Syria in Geneva," *Weekly Compilation of Presidential Documents*, Vol. 30, Issue 3, January 24, 1994, p. 92.

47. A few months later, Syrian Minister of Defense General Mustafa Tlass amplified on this position, indicating Syria's willingness to cooperate with the U.S. initiative and to adhere to "the resolution of international legitimacy." See General Mustafa Tlass, "Syria and the Future of the Peace Process," *Jane's Intelligence Review*, Vol. 6, No. 9, September 1996, pp. 412-13.

48. Hisham Melhen, "Syria Between Two Transitions," *Middle East Report*, Spring 1997, p. 4.

49. Syria's vulnerability was clearly demonstrated in October 1998 when Turkey threatened military action against Syria if Syria did not end its support of Kurdistan Workers Party rebels operating against Turkey from Syrian territories. The initial Syrian reaction was to call Turkey's threat a plot with Israel to undermine Syria. However, Syria quickly sought Arab and Islamic mediation of the crisis, resulting in an agreement between the two sides whereby Syria presumably acceded to Turkey's security concerns. See "Turkey Warns Syria Again Not To Support Rebel Kurds," *International Herald Tribune*, October 6, 1998; "Syria Calls Turkish Threat a Plot," *The Washington Post* (Internet Edition), October 2, 1998; Stephen Kinzer, "Syria Agrees to Stop Supporting Kurds, Defusing Crisis With Turkey," *New York Times*, October 22, 1998; and "Turkish-Syrian Discussions," Abu Dhabi *Al-Ittihad*, (Internet Edition in Arabic), October 30, 1998.

50. Ze'ev Schiff, "Netanyahu Proposes New Syrian Formula, *Ha'aretz*, (Israel), Internet Edition, September 21, 1997.

51. See *Jerusalem Qol Yisra'el* (in Hebrew), August 28, 1997, in *FBIS-NES*-97-24, August 29, 1997.

52. See *Asharq Al-Awsat* (London, in Arabic), April 5, 1997, p. 3.

53. See Thomas Lippman, "Election Cited for Derailing Mideast Peace Move," *The Washington Post*, January 29, 1997, p. 6, and *Al-Ittihad* (Abu Dhabi in Arabic), Internet Edition, April 12, 1998, which quoted Tlass as saying "President Asad has a written document signed by President Clinton indicating the willingness of the previous Israeli Labor Government to withdraw from the Golan Heights to the June 4, 1967, line."

54. Quoted in *Al-Ittihad* (Abu Dhabi in Arabic), Internet Edition, February 17, 1997.

55. Joel Greenberg, "Israel Seeks Deal to Quit Buffer Zone in Lebanon," *The New York Times*, Internet Edition, March 2, 1998.

56. Lebanon's newly elected President, former Army Commander Emile Lahhoud, has endorsed the Syrian position on Lebanon emphasizing among other things the demand that Israel accepts U.N. resolution 425 unconditionally, that Israeli withdrawal should occur simultaneously from south Lebanon and the Golan Heights, and that the Lebanese Army will not make its mission that of preserving the security of northern Israel. See Rafiq Nasrallah, "Lahhoud Establishes The Policy Of His Country Toward Israel," Abu Dhabi *Al-Ittihad* (Internet Edition in Arabic), December 12, 1998.

57. See "Interview of President Asad With French Television," Abu Dhabi *Al-Ittihad* (Internet Edition in Arabic), July 16, 1998. France has been actively seeking a role in the Middle East, especially in Lebanon and Syria, its former "colonies" under the old League of Nations mandate system, a role which apparently Syria and Lebanon welcome. See Pia Christina Wood, "Chirac's 'New Arab Policy' And Middle East, Challenges: The Arab Israeli Conflict, Iraq And Iran," *Middle East Journal*, Vol. 52, No. 4, Autumn 1998, pp. 563-580.

58. Wood, p. 565.

59. "Syria Said To See Iran as Ally Against Israel-Turkey Front," *Ha'aretz* (in English), August 1, 1997, in *FBIS-NES*-97-213, August 4, pp. 19-97.

60. Gresh, p. 188.

61. "International Section," *New York Times*, (Internet Edition), May 8, 1998. Several months later, the Clinton administration "informally asked Israel to consider accepting the principle of an eventual Palestinian state as part of a final Wye Plantation summit document . . ." See David Makovsky, "U.S. asks: 'consider' Palestinian state," Israel *Ha'aretz* (Internet Edition in English), October 14, 1998.

62. Edware P. Djerejian, "No Talks, No Peace," *New York Times*, August 21, 1997, p. 32.

63. Gresh, p. 188.

CHAPTER 14

ISRAELI SECURITY IN A CHANGING ENVIRONMENT: CHALLENGES AND RESPONSES

Gerald M. Steinberg

THE NEW THREAT ENVIRONMENT

The threat environment in the Middle East is changing rapidly, reflecting the combined impacts of the uncertain peace process, the end of the Cold War, the unresolved Iraqi threat, concern over developing Iranian capabilities, and, most importantly, the proliferation of ballistic missiles and weapons of mass destruction (WMD) in the region. These factors have created new challenges for Israeli military planners and decisionmakers in the Mediterranean and for Israel, in particular.

As the dangers of a large-scale combined conventional attack that threatened national survival from 1948 through 1973 and beyond seem to recede (although they remain formidable), the WMD threats posed by neighboring and more distant states are growing. In 1991, Iraq possessed a large arsenal of chemical and apparently also biological warheads, as well as ballistic missiles to attack targets in Israel, as well as other states in the region. Despite over 7 years of United Nations (U.N.) inspections and sanctions, Saddam Hussein's regime has developed and implemented a vast program of concealment to hold onto considerable capabilities. Once the inspections and threat of military action are lifted, Iraq will be able to reconstitute its stockpiles in a very short period of time. As a result, Iraq remains a formidable threat to Israel and to the region.

In addition, Syria, Egypt, Libya, and Iran all possess significant chemical weapons capabilities (Egypt has had chemical weapons since the early 1960s, and used them in its campaigns in Yemen, but not against Israel). There is also increasing evidence that many of these states are developing biological weapons.

In the past, the domination of the Israeli Air Force has protected population centers from Arab air attacks, but the proliferation of ballistic missiles has increased the vulnerability of Israeli cities and other civil targets. Syria has Russian SS-21 and North Korean Scud-C missiles, Egypt is obtaining missiles and technology from North Korea, and in July 1998, Iran tested the Shihab 3, with a range of 1300 kilometers (based on North Korean and Russian technology).

These missiles are of strategic importance when combined with WMD warheads, and with nuclear weapons in particular. According to most estimates, the Iraqi nuclear weapons development program had progressed to within a year of producing a weapon before the 1991 war. Former United Nations Special Commission (UNSCOM) inspector Scott Ritter has noted that Iraq maintains the completed casings for three nuclear weapons, which will become weapons with the addition of fissile material[1]

There is also considerable evidence that Iran is pursuing nuclear weapons, using technology and facilities acquired from Russia, and Syria is acquiring a large research reactor from Russia in order to develop a nuclear infrastructure. These programs are in the first stages, and the development of a nuclear threat to Israel is still likely to be at least 5 and perhaps 10 years away, (assuming that the inspections and other limitations on Iraq continue), but the developments will be monitored carefully, and Israel must begin developing its strategic responses to these developments.

The nuclear tests conducted by India and Pakistan in 1998 may have accelerated the rate of nuclear proliferation in the Middle East. These tests shattered the relatively static global nuclear framework, and it is very difficult to predict the long-term impact of these developments.

Although the talk of an "Islamic bomb" and fears of technology transfer from Pakistan to Iran or Iraq may be exaggerated, the sudden weakening of the international nuclear non-proliferation regime could serve to increase the incentives for Iran, Iraq, and other Middle Eastern states to develop such weapons. If the responses and sanctions imposed by the United States and the international community appear to be weak in the views of the major decisionmakers in these countries, the implications will be drawn, and additional states will be willing to pursue such weapons without fear of censure or stigma. Thus, in the Middle East, the emergence of a multipolar nuclear environment in the next decade seems to be very likely.

ISRAELI STRATEGIC OPTIONS

As a result of these developments, Israeli decisionmakers and analysts have recognized the need for accompanying changes in security doctrine, budgeting, procurement, and training. For many years, Israel relied on the combination of preemption (against conventional threats, as in 1967), preventive attack, conventional deterrence, and qualitative superiority to offset the Arab quantitative advantage. In addition, since the 1960s, the perceived nuclear option provided a weapon-of-last-resort to deter threats to national survival. This policy succeeded in avoiding a direct clash with the U.S. Government, with its emphasis on non-proliferation.

For many years, American-led export-control policies may have slowed the rate of WMD and missile proliferation in the region. However, in the past decade, these limitations have become increasingly ineffective, in large part due to Russian, Chinese, and North Korean technology transfers. In addition, since the 1981 attack on the Iraqi nuclear facilities, preventive attacks (under the Begin Doctrine) have become far more difficult to implement. The WMD and missile development programs of Iraq, Iran and Syria are often placed underground and are well-defended, and the installations are dispersed over a wide geographic area. Although the combination of tightened export controls and military operations (not necessarily conducted by Israel) might, under optimum circumstances, slow the rate of proliferation, it is unlikely to be stopped. As a result, Israel will have to adapt its military doctrine to this emerging reality and threats to stability and security.

In a broad sense, three general approaches can be identified:[2] strengthened deterrence; defense; and regional alliances. (Regional arms limitation is also a theoretical option, but the experience to date in the multilateral Arms Control and Regional Security talks has not been encouraging, and it is clear that any agreements will take many years.) Each provides advantages and limitations, and the optimum security doctrine should combine aspects of all three in order to maximize the benefits and minimize the disadvantages.

Stable Mutual Deterrence.

As noted, both conventional and nuclear deterrence have been prominent aspects of Israel security doctrine for many years. In a Hobbesian world or region, in which there are no rules of conduct or recognition of common interests, and in which hatreds are very deep, the development of a credible threat to inflict unacceptable punishment is seen as the best means of enhancing stability and dissuading potential aggressors.

Since defeating the Arab armies that invaded in 1948, Israel has consistently emphasized deterrence policies in preventing attacks. At that time, the narrow borders, small population, and image of weakness and vulnerability were seen as inviting attack, and in response, Israeli leaders such as Ben Gurion and Dayan emphasized the creation of a strong army able not only to defend the state, but also to deter threats by carrying the war to the territory of the aggressors and bringing it quickly to a conclusion.

Deterrence became more important in both Israel and Arab strategies following the wars between 1967 and 1973, and for the past 20 years, the absence of major wars (with the possible exception of Lebanon in 1982) might be attributed, in part, to the success of deterrence.

Similarly, over the past 30 years, the "ambiguous" nuclear deterrent policy has been viewed as very successful. The perceived nuclear retaliatory capability is credited with preventing Egypt from going beyond a limited attack in the 1973 war, and Egyptian military sources have acknowledged this factor. In addition, the evidence indicates that the fear of massive Israeli retaliation deterred Saddam Hussein from using chemical or biological weapons against Israel before or during the 1991 Gulf War.[3] (It is now clear that the Iraqis possessed Scud warheads with chemical and biological agents at the time, and while Saddam sought to bring Israel into the war, he was not willing to accept the consequences of massive Israeli retaliation.) During the war, U.S. Secretary of Defense Cheney also invoked the prospect of Israeli nuclear retaliation to deter the Iraqi leader from attacking Israel with chemical weapons. Shimon Peres and other Israeli leaders attribute the growing Arab willingness to accept the existence and legitimacy of Israel, and to negotiate peace agreements, to the recognition that Israel's nuclear deterrent capability prevents the Arabs from achieving a decisive military victory that would put an end to the Jewish state.[4]

The Israeli monopoly has been steadily reduced as other states in the region seek to gain nuclear, chemical, or biological weapons. In response, Israeli leaders have increased the emphasis on and credibility of the threats of massive retaliation and deterrence. In January 1995, during a Knesset debate on the Iranian nuclear threat, Deputy Defense Minister Gur warned Islamic nations that if one of them uses nonconventional weapons against Israel, no one will escape the consequences of that war.

We have made this clear many times. In this issue, we will not allow ourselves to be behind and we will not expose ourselves [to this danger].... The radical Islamic world knows the nature of war. The Iran-Iraq war reached its end after 200 Iraqi missiles were fired against Teheran. This means that even the Khomenist leadership understands what happens when its people are injured. Don't think that a leader of a people with 60-65 million people could suddenly arise and go to war with grave danger without taking into consideration the terrible suffering that he would cause to his people.... Israel must take this option into consideration; Israel decided that she will exist despite the existence of nuclear weapons in the world. We have to be ready across different fronts and time frames, and in this area, we must not take any chances."[5]

Similarly, after the Iranian missile test of July 1998, Prime Minister Netanyahu remarked that "I think it should be remembered that Israel is the strongest country in the region. It has answers, and I think that every country in the region knows Israel's power."[6]

In the context of an eroding monopoly, the viability of an invisible deterrent that is entirely separate from the Israeli war fighting doctrine and order of battle is questionable. At some point, this will be insufficient and a more visible and robust deterrence capability will become necessary, capable of a credible response to different levels of threat and potential attack scenarios. There are increasing signs that the Israeli leadership is considering the requirements for these changes in its deterrent posture. Major General Yitzhak Ben-Yisrael, head of the Armaments Research and Development Administration at the Defense Ministry, indicated that the policy is being reevaluated, and noted the limitations of the invisible deterrent. "If Israel's defense doctrine is deterrence, you can't deter anyone except by showing him your capability."[7]

As long as Israel's vulnerability to a strategic first strike is very limited, survivable second strike capabilities, including the appropriate command and control systems (C3-I) are not a high priority. However, this situation is changing with the proliferation of ballistic missiles and WMD systems. If another state in the region makes progress towards a nuclear weapons capability, Israel is likely to abandon the ambiguous nuclear posture and adopt an overt nuclear deterrent. (Israel is a signatory to the Comprehensive Test Ban Treaty, and although it has not yet ratified the agreement, policy makers are normatively bound by the terms, unless the security situation changes very radically.)

In developing a strategic response, Israel has begun by investing in strategic intelligence and early warning. The Ofeq 3 satellite, which was developed and launched by Israel after the U.S. rejected Israeli requests for access to American satellite data, is reportedly capable of returning high-resolution images, and additional satellites are planned.[8] (The launch of Ofeq 4 ended in failure, but a replacement is reportedly being prepared for launch.)

With respect to delivery systems, Israel has recently acquired long-range F-15 I aircraft from the United States, with the well-publicized capability of striking targets in Iran without the need for refueling. Given Israeli air-superiority and the ability to defeat or evade air defense systems that are deployed or likely to be deployed in the region, this represents an important and flexible deterrent capability. In order to assure the maintenance of a survivable second strike, a number of these aircraft can be maintained on airborne alert during periods of crisis, as was done with other initial approach fix (IAF) systems during the 1991 Gulf War.

Israel also possesses a long-range ballistic missile capability with ranges of at least 2,000 kilometers. Although there is no official confirmation regarding the existence of the Jericho missile,[9] the evidence is clear. (The Israeli *Shavit* launcher, which is apparently based on similar technology, has placed three small satellites into orbit, and any launcher can also serve as a ballistic missile. The range will vary with the size of the payload.) With moderate hardening and underground or mobile deployment, these systems are secure against all threats with the exception of nuclear weapons. (The author of an article in *Jane's Intelligence Review* claimed that 50 nuclear warheads on *Jericho-II* intermediate-range missiles are deployed for this purpose.)

There are also unconfirmed reports that Israel is developing a cruise missile (known as the *Popeye Turbo*) with a range of 350 kilometers, to be operational in 2002.[10] The recent delivery of three new *Dolphin*-class submarines built for Israel in Germany sparked speculation regarding the possible development of a sea-based second strike deterrent. Press reports suggested that these submarines could be converted to carry "nuclear-tipped cruise missiles."[11] However, given the absence of reliable evidence and the plethora of unsubstantiated rumors dealing with Israeli strategic capabilities, these reports must be treated with a great deal of caution.

With respect to deterrence against attacks involving chemical and biological weapons, the requirements are subject to intense debate. Despite some claims that chemical weapons are the strategic equivalents of nuclear weapons, the damage caused by chemical weapons (CW) attacks, particularly from a small number of missiles with small payloads, is quite limited. As a result, the threat to use nuclear weapons in retaliation is not credible, despite the speculation that Israel might use such weapons in response to Iraqi threats to "incinerate half of Tel Aviv with nuclear weapons." Although a response in kind can be considered to provide an effective deterrent, there is no public information regarding Israeli chemical weapons capabilities, if any. (There has been a great deal of speculation on this issue, but no reliable evidence exists, one way or the other.) This issue has come to be a central aspect of the debate regarding ratification of the Chemical Weapons Convention, with opponents arguing that by ratifying this treaty, Israel would be weakening the perceived deterrent capabilities and options with respect to a chemical attack.

Deterring biological weapons (BW) attacks raises additional problems, particularly given the high degree of uncertainty with respect to the nature of the threat. If BW are, as some analysts contend, far more lethal than CW, then the threat to use nuclear weapons in response to a BW attack is credible. However, if the scale is closer to the threat posed by CW, the deterrence issues are also similar.

The Limitations Of Mutual Deterrence in the Middle East. Any decision to adopt a strategy based on mutual deterrence must face the basic requirements for stability, particularly in a multipolar environment. While the deterrence system developed during the Cold War may be deemed to have prevented war (although critics argue that the mutual deterrence strategy was flawed, and nuclear conflict was avoided despite these flaws), there are many different factors in the Middle East. In this region, the conflicts are ethno-national and not ideological, the major actors share common borders and have fought a number of conventional wars, and there are questions regarding the rationality of the leaders and their readiness to take major risks. Instead of a bipolar deterrence system, as was the case in the Cold War, Middle Eastern deterrence would be multipolar, adding additional complexities and sources of instability. The level and quality of communication is often poor (Israel and Iran do not have direct links and misperceptions are common.) The long history of violent terrorism demonstrates the willingness of some individuals and groups to kill large numbers of people in the name of a particular cause. In this environment, the creation and maintenance of a stable system of deterrence will be difficult.

At the same time, the options available to Israeli decisionmakers are limited, and, as noted above, the historical record demonstrates that deterrence based on massive retaliation and threats directed at the leadership and regime have been successful. (In the 1991 Gulf War, Saddam Hussein first indicated a willingness to withdraw from Kuwait after an American precision guided weapon penetrated a command bunker that also housed members of the Iraqi elite. When the Iraqi leader realized the extent of his vulnerability, he acted according to a rational calculus.)[12] In the absence of a preferred alternative, strengthened mutual deterrence is likely to continue to be the basis for Israel's military doctrine in the face of proliferation of WMD and long-range ballistic missiles.

Defensive Strategies and Approaches.

Until the past few years, Israeli military planners did not invest significant resources in defensive systems. The very small size of the country and the need to bring wars to a rapid conclusion in order to allow the reserve forces to return to civilian life have led to adoption of an offensive approach, in which battles are fought in enemy territory, before the Israeli population is placed at risk. In addition, the air superiority established by the IAF is also credited with protecting the country.

However, the acquisition of missiles and CW in a number of Arab countries has forced Israel to develop a defensive strategy, both active and passive. The passive approach to defense consists of the distribution of gas masks to the entire population, and the creation of "sealed rooms" in houses and other buildings as barriers to the penetration of chemical and biological agents. This population defense was applied during the 1991 Gulf War, and has been maintained since, particularly in the face of renewed concerns regarding the potential for an Iraqi attack.

At the same time, active missile defense programs have been pursued, primarily in the form of the *Homa (Wall)* ballistic missile defense (BMD) project, which includes the *Arrow* missile system, the *Green Pines* fire-control radar system, a command and control system and other sub-systems. Research and development of the *Arrow* is expected to cost over $2 billion (largely provided by the U.S. Government), and most of the technology, including the radar system, is being developed in Israel.

The operational *Arrow 2* is designed to provide terminal defense against incoming missiles, by destroying them at an altitude of between 10 and 40 kilometers. A number of development tests of the *Arrow* have demonstrated the potential for this system, particularly given the difficulties and much higher costs associated with the American BMD programs (theater high-altitude area defense [THAAD] and the Navy's Theater-Wide systems).

In May 1998, Defense Minister Yitzhak Mordechai approved a multi-year project to build and deploy the *Homa* BMD system. The U.S. Government has agreed to provide some of the funding for three *Arrow* batteries (at an estimated cost of $80 million per battery), with the first operational capability expected towards the end of 1999. In September 1998, a successful test of the integrated system, which tracked and "destroyed" a simulated target, marked a major milestone in the development process.

However, there are a number of obstacles to wider deployment of the *Arrow*. These include an unfavorable cost-exchange ratio (each *Arrow* defensive missile is expected to cost from $1 to $2 million, and an average of two *Arrow*s must be allocated to each incoming warhead, while surface-to-surface [*SCUD*]-type offensive missiles can be added at a fraction of this cost), and the ability of more advanced weapons to defeat the *Arrow*.

As an alternative, or primary layer, Israeli military planners are giving greater consideration to the development of boost-phase intercept (BPI) BMD systems. BPI has the advantage of being able to destroy offensive missiles in the first stages of their flight, while they are moving slowly, present large targets, and threaten to release their payloads over the countries that are attempting to launch these systems, rather than close to their targets, as is the case with terminal defense systems such as the *Arrow*.

A number of approaches to BPI have been considered. The United States is planning to develop and test an Airborne Laser (ABL) system carried in a modified Boeing 747 aircraft. Israeli R&D funds have been directed towards the development of a lower cost system, based on small kinetic energy "kill vehicles" (Missile Optimized Anti-Ballistic weapons or MOAB, also known as IBIS[13]) fired from hovering drones or unmanned aerial vehicles (UAVs). This approach is strongly supported by Major General (Res.) David Ivri, and some money has been allocated for conceptual studies. Critics view Ivri's role as a combination of technological enthusiasm and an effort to provide contracts for the Israeli defense industries, and BPI's future is highly uncertain.

In order to be effective, the BPI carriers must be on station near the launch sites at the time of attack, and must be able to survive attacks by air defense systems. This may be achievable for relatively short periods, particularly during times of crisis, and for longer periods with respect to neighboring countries. For example, UAV-based BPI may possibly counter the Syrian missile threat (although the farther the launch sites are from the Israeli border, the more difficult this will become), but it is much more difficult to achieve with respect to Iraq and Iran. Although the laser-based ABL has a theoretical range of 200 kilometers (or more, depending on the laser), there are many technical uncertainties, and such a large object, even if maintained far away from the launch site, would be vulnerable to preemptive attack. In addition, there are various inexpensive countermeasures, such as coating missiles with reflective paint, which could neutralize the laser.

More fundamentally, as Yisrael Tal has noted, unless the defensive system provides 100 percent protection, which no system can, it is not sufficient to protect a small country like Israel against a nuclear threat. Tal noted that

> One of the things that worries me is that among policymakers there is a certain belief that defense is stronger than offense. That is, that we can best the enemy from defense positions. This is very dangerous. The Arabs can afford to remain in a defensive posture. We cannot afford this.[14]

BMD, whether terminal, as in the case of the *Arrow*, or BPI, or a combination, may be part of a new Israeli strategy, but it will not remove the need for or primary emphasis on deterrence and assured second strike capabilities.[15]

Regional Security Alliances.

While the strategic debate continues, the development of regional security relationships, and the growth of an extensive system of security cooperation between Israel and Turkey mark a very important change. In the past 5 years, this relationship has grown to encompass use of each other's airspace for training flights and exercises, Israeli military exports and upgrade packages, consultations and exchanges at the highest levels, and a highly publicized naval search and rescue exercise involving the United States, and with Jordanian observers.

This strategic relationship and proto-alliance with Turkey has ended decades of Israeli regional isolation, and provided a balance to the Arab alliances that have linked military forces against Israel in the past. The links between Ankara and Jerusalem also serve to offset the Iranian-Syrian alliance which has been seen in Israel as an additional concern and source of regional instability. Turkey and Israel share concerns regarding Syrian threats, including missile and WMD, and also about Iranian-supported Islamic fundamentalism in the region.

Beyond the defense cooperation with Israel, Turkey is also developing a bilateral relationship with Jordan. Israel also has good, although generally unpublicized cooperative security links with Jordan, based on shared perceptions regarding Palestinian and Iraqi threats. These shared interests are likely to increase if a Palestinian state is created, and if Saddam Hussein is able to escape the international sanctions regime and resume his efforts to achieve regional dominance.

Thus it is possible that in the next decade, and depending on political developments in all three countries and the region, Turkey, Jordan, and Israel could form the nucleus of a defensive regional security structure. Political changes and reevaluations of Egyptian interests might possibly create a situation in which Cairo would join this framework, and then other states might follow.

There are, however, a number of uncertainties in these relationships, and the future may not be as cooperative as the Israeli optimists hope. If the Islamic forces gain strength, and these groups oppose security links to Israel on ideological grounds, the alliance could be frozen or rolled back. In addition, the limits of the alliance need to be defined. Turkey is likely to distance itself in the event of confrontation between Israel and the Palestinians, and Israel will avoid becoming involved in the conflicts with the Kurds and any Turkish military involvement in Cyprus.

THE CENTRALITY OF THE RELATIONSHIP WITH THE UNITED STATES

Since the mid-1960s, the strategic ties between Washington and Jerusalem have been a central and growing factor in Israeli assessments, decisionmaking, and policy. Israel receives most of its weapons platforms and much of its technology from the United States, and American military assistance helps to pay for strategic systems such as the F-15 and *Arrow*.

In addition, Israel is aware that only the United States has the potential power and global sense of responsibility to attempt to slow the process of WMD and missile proliferation in the Middle East. With Russia continuing to provide technology and assistance, particularly to Iran, and leaders in Moscow, such as Yevgeny Primakov, see such assistance as a means of increasing Russian power in response to NATO expansion and other factors, American counterpressure on Russia on these issues is extremely important for Middle East stability. In this sense, the Cold War may be returning to the region.

At the same time, there is a growing sense that both the capability and the resolve of the United States to intervene in the region is diminishing steadily. This is most apparent in the case of Iraq, but is also visible with respect to the proliferation of weapons of mass destruction (WMD) and missiles in Iran, Syria, and other states that pose a danger to the region, in general, and to Israel, in particular.

From the 1970s and through the 1980s, many U.S. intelligence and high-level policymakers consistently missed or underestimated Saddam Hussein's programs. In 1981, the U.S. Government was surprised when Israel decided it needed to destroy the Iraqi reactor, and again in 1990 when the almost completed Iraqi nuclear weapons capability was suddenly uncovered. The combination of the tilt to Iraq during the war with Iran, the pro-Iraqi lobbying of Arab states (primarily Egypt and Saudi Arabia), and the fact that the vast majority of intelligence assets were directed toward monitoring the disintegrating Soviet Union, all contributed to this complacency and the asymmetry in assessments between Washington and Jerusalem.

Following the 1990 Iraqi invasion of Kuwait, the United States responded with a major military campaign, but this war ended before Saddam Hussein had been removed from office, and without the destruction of Iraq's missiles and nuclear, chemical, and biological technology and infrastructure. Since then, Saddam Hussein has succeeded in evading the UNSCOM regime, and in maintaining, and perhaps even adding to his WMD arsenal. From an Israeli perspective, the Americans have failed to fully redeem pledges to destroy these capabilities during the 1991 Gulf war, when the Bush Administration pressed Israel to act with restraint in the face of missile attacks. Although there are many factors that have complicated the destruction of the Iraqi capability, American credibility has eroded. For the millions of Israelis who spent 6 weeks in sealed rooms with gas masks and face this prospect again, the lapses and frequent departures from a strong, consistent U.S. leadership role have a strong impact.

Although the Clinton Administration has focused on Middle East issues, the Arab-Israeli peace process has claimed most of the time and resources of those responsible for formulating and implementing U.S. regional policy in the Middle East. The accelerating proliferation of WMD in the region is often relegated to secondary status except during periods of crisis and sudden and intense activity. (In Washington, some policy makers have claimed that the freeze in the peace process has weakened the American ability to influence Arab states to support military action against Iraq. However, the evidence suggests that the causality is reversed. It is U.S. actions, or lack of action, with respect to WMD proliferation that affects the U.S. ability to influence the peace process.)

Criticisms of U.S. policy with respect to Iraqi weapons capabilities have been highlighted both in Washington and Israel. A 1998 report of the Senate Subcommittee on International Security, Proliferation and Federal Services concludes, "By speaking loudly but carrying a small stick the Clinton Administration risks its nonproliferation credibility and America's security."[16] In early 1998, following the Iraqi suspension of UNSCOM inspections, the dispatch of U.N. Secretary General Kofi Anan to negotiate an agreement over further inspections, and the subsequent agreement, was widely criticized. Claims by U.N. inspector Scott Ritter and evidence that the U.S. Government had asked the UNSCOM team to avoid searching too hard for Iraqi weapons and facilities, in order to prevent a confrontation with Iraq, were seen in Israel and throughout the Middle East as signs of American weakness and lack of resolve.[17] This evaluation increased significantly in the Fall of 1998, when the United States was engrossed in the Lewinsky Affair, and Iraq again suspended UNSCOM inspections.

Similarly, the slow American response to Russian exports of missile and nuclear technology and expertise to Iran was seen as a sign of weakness. Although Israeli intelligence information showed a steady flow of technology from Russia to Iran beginning in early 1997, the U.S. Government did not act for many months. After the U.S. Congress passed mandatory sanctions legislation in mid-1998, (and with a wide majority that insured the ability to override Clinton's veto), the Russian government announced the opening of an investigation regarding some of the firms involved in this technology transfer. At this stage, the U.S. Government imposed sanctions of these firms. However, in July 1998, the Iranians tested the Shihab 3 missile, with a reported range of 1300 kilometers (placing Israel within range), and even if all Russian assistance were stopped, it appeared that the Iranians would be able to complete the development independently.

More recently, the emergence of internal splits in Iran, and the election of Khatami has led to a "softer" U.S. approach and relaxation of sanctions, while the Iranian nuclear and missile programs, as well as support for terror and threats directed at Israel have not changed. This process has not increased Israeli confidence in the American ability to slow the flow of WMD technology to the region, or to protect Israel's vital security interests.

Perceptions of American Weakness.

In a broader sense, Israel's threat perceptions and strategic concepts very much depend on the degree to which the United States acts as the world's only superpower, and accepts the new responsibilities that came with this role. All other states—including Russia, Britain, and France—can and do behave as ordinary states, emphasizing their own narrow interests and leaving the resulting problems to the Americans.

However, the United States has acted inconsistently, prevaricating and delaying, while WMD programs went from early research to advanced development and testing. In confronting Iraq, the United States has consistently sought the backing of an international coalition—a strategy that has distinct advantages but with costs generally underestimated in Washington.

As Eliot Cohen has noted, other countries in the world depend on America's willingness to act "as a global empire, rather than as one of two rival superpowers, or a normal state." However, the radical reduction in U.S. military capabilities and frequent cycle of threats and concessions have severely reduced American credibility in acting to enforce the Iraqi cease-fire requirements and in other areas. As Cohen notes, these changes have "steadily but noticeably eroded morale and equipment readiness."[18]

When the United States acts like an ordinary state in the Middle East, looking for allies before responding to the growing threats from Iraq and Iran, this is inconsistent. Cohen diagnoses the problem precisely, observing

> When, as in Bosnia, it is prepared to act, its allies usually go along; when, as in the recent confrontation with Saddam Hussein, the United States wavers, friendly states retreat into passivity.

When, on some occasions, the United States has demonstrated an ability to act powerfully (although only after a long period of deliberation and preparation), it has not shown the staying power necessary to deal with the persistent threats posed by countries such as Iraq, with a well-entrenched WMD infrastructure. To cite Cohen, "U.S. planners would prefer to prepare for quick, unconstrained, knock-down fights with easily identified opponents." However, in the Middle East, the long haul is what finally counts.[19]

The Continuing Alliance.

Although Israel must retain the capability of responding independently of the United States in the face of threats posed from states in the region (as demonstrated in the case of Iraq), the strategic relationship with the United States will continue to be of primary importance to Israeli security. As Cohen, *et. al.*, note,

> Israel's strategic dependence on its patron will grow in coming years. Developing an effective defense against missiles and nonconventional weapons will require a high level of technological cooperation... Israel is likely in a future war to require some form of direct U.S. assistance....[20]

As result, as Israeli leaders consider the options and their implications, it will be important to maintain and intensify the strategic dialogue with the American government, and to seek coordination and agreement to the extent possible. (Between 1992 and 1996, under the Labor Government, Israel considered a number of possible formulae to formalize the defense relationship with the United States. In 1996, following the assassination of Prime Minister Rabin, his successor, Shimon Peres, raised the possibility of a formal defense treaty in the context of a possible agreement with Syria and withdrawal from the Golan Heights.) Israeli leaders will have to put increasingly greater efforts into convincing the American government that its own (i.e., the United States) interests are served by intervention in the region, and by military action, when necessary.

At the same time, if Israel detects a steady weakening of Washington's capability to intervene in the region, or of its resolve, the alternative is greater emphasis on unilateral action.

FINDING THE RIGHT MIX

To the extent possible, Israeli leaders should and would prefer to pursue all available options. However, the high cost of defense and stable deterrence has placed some limits on their simultaneous pursuit. The acquisition and operation of the *Dolphin* submarines, the *Ofeq* reconnaissance satellites, the F-15 strike aircraft, and the *Homa* BMD system, are each extremely costly, even with substantial assistance from the United States.

As was demonstrated during the Cold War, the maintenance of a reliable second strike deterrent in a dynamic situation is costly, requiring constant improvements in response to external developments. Although, eventually, it is possible that the nations of the Middle East will realize their common interest in verifiable arms limitation agreements, this is still a long way off, and in the interim, the costs will remain very high.

At the same time, the Israeli defense budget has been declining steadily over the past decade, reflecting sharp reductions in government spending in order to allow for economic growth, and also a change in priorities and increased emphasis on social programs, including health, education, and welfare. Efforts by the Defense Ministers and the Israel Defense Forces (IDF) Chief of Staff to reverse this trend have failed to date.

Furthermore, as critics note, the bulk of the available resources for weapons and technology are still allocated to the acquisition of conventional platforms (fighter aircraft, helicopters, and tanks), and in the current 5-year plan, $5 billion are earmarked for these weapons. With the additional local costs of the *Homa* BMD and *Ofeq*, and for operation of other major systems, the economy cannot provide much more for research and development or the acquisition of such systems. It will prove difficult to maintain and modernize widespread missile defense systems and an advanced second strike deterrent, and consistent priorities will have to be assigned to guide decisionmaking at all levels.

In a broader sense, it is clear that the strategic balance in the trans-Mediterranean and Middle East is changing rapidly, with constantly shifting weapons, technologies, and alliances. In this context, Israel, like other states confronted with this situation, must be prepared to adjust its strategic policies and doctrine accordingly. Budgets, weapons acquisitions, research and development, manpower policies, training, tactics, and operations must all be adjusted and made consistent with these changing requirements. The difficulties should not be underestimated, given the massive bureaucratic inertia of any military organization, as well as the vested interests in the status quo and the need to maintain a formidable operational capability, while also introducing basic changes in each of these areas. However, in the Middle East, and in the Israeli environment, in particular, a static response to a dynamic environment is doomed to failure.

ENDNOTES - CHAPTER 14

1. Ze'ev Schiff, "Former U.N. Arms Inspector Charges: 'Iraq Now Has Three Virtually Complete Nuclear Bombs'," *Ha'aretz*, September 9, 1998, p. 1A.

2. This study is focused on the "top of the strategic pyramid"—the response to the threats from weapons of mass destruction and ballistic missiles. In parallel, major changes in Israel's conventional force doctrine and strategy are taking place, in the broader context of the "revolution in military affairs" (RMA) including the introduction of counter-offensive operations using a wide range of precision guided munitions, the transition from an army based on universal conscription to a smaller high-tech based military, and organizational changes to maximize the efficiency of these changes. For a detailed discussion of these issues, see, for example, Eliot A. Cohen, Michael J. Eisenstadt, and Andrew J. Bacevich, *Knives, Tanks and Missiles: Israel's Security Revolution*, Washington, DC: Washington Institute for Near East Policy, 1998; and Ze'ev Bonen and Eliot Cohen, *Advanced Technology and Future Warfare*, Security and Policy Studies No. 28, Ramat Gan, Israel: BESA Center for Strategic Studies, Bar Ilan University, 1996.

3. Gerald M. Steinberg, "Israeli Responses to the Threat of Chemical Warfare," *Armed Forces and Society*, Vol. 20., No. 1, Fall 1993, pp. 85-101. For an analysis of Arab perceptions of the Israeli nuclear deterrent, see Ariel Levite and Emily Landau, *Israel's Nuclear Image: Arab Perceptions of Israel's Nuclear Posture*, Tel Aviv: Papyrus, 1994 (Hebrew).

4. Michal Yudelman, "Peres Gives Sign of Nuclear Capability," *Jerusalem Post*, July 14, 1998.

5. *Ha'aretz*, January 12, 1995.

6. Gideon Alon, "Netanyahu Warns Iran: 'Israel Will Defend Itself,'" *Ha'aretz*, August 5 1998, http://www3.haaretz.co.il/eng/scripts/show_katava.asp?id=25328&mador=1&datee=8/5/98.

7. Amnon Barzilai, "Military Reviews Nuclear Policy, As Israel Called 'Vulnerable' To Missile Attack," *Haaretz*, August 25, 1998, citing *Defense News*.

8. See Gerald M. Steinberg, *Dual Use Aspects of Commercial High-Resolution Imaging Satellites*, Security and Policy Series Paper No. 17, Ramat Gan: BESA Center for Strategic Studies, Bar Ilan University, 1998; Gerald Steinberg, "Middle East Space Race Gathers Pace," *International Defense Review*, October 1995, Vol. 28.

9. In an interview with Reuters, former minister Yuval Ne'eman revealed that during 1973, the Israelis deployed Jericho missiles in an open area to insure that they would be visible to Soviet satellites, with the objective of deterring Soviet deployment of nuclear weapons in Egypt. According to Neeman, these missiles were not armed with nuclear warheads. Reuters, "Israel Deployed Nuke-Capable Missiles in 1973 War," September 26, 1998.

10. Amnon Barzilai, "Israel developing cruise missile?"*Ha'aretz*, July 30, 1998; Douglas Davis, "Report: Israel to Get Subs with Nuclear Strike Capability," Jerusalem Post, July 3, 1998; Martin Sieff, "Israel Buying 3 Submarines to Carry Nuclear Missiles," *The Washington Times*, July 1, 1998.

11. Davis; Sieff.

12. See, for example, Gerald M. Steinberg, "Israeli Responses to the Threat of Chemical Warfare," pp. 85-101.

13. Interview with Lieutenant General Lester L. Lyles in the *Israel Air Force Journal* and cited by Amnon Barzilai, "Military Reviews

Nuclear Policy, as Israel Called 'Vulnerable' to Missile Attack," citing "One on One," *Defense News*, August 17, 1998, p. 22.

14. Steve Rodan, "Return to Sender," *Jerusalem Post*, July 19, 1998.

15. Counteroffensive measures, aimed at destroying mobile and fixed-site launchers, are also under consideration, and Israeli analysts have sought to improve on the American failure to destroy Iraqi *SCUD* launchers during the 1991 Gulf War. See Cohen, Eisenstadt, and Bacevich.

16. *The Proliferation Primer, A Majority Report of the Subcommittee on International Security, Proliferation and Federal Services*, Washington, DC: Committee on Government Affairs, U.S. Senate, January 1998, p. 1.

17. Scott Ritter, "The Final Straw," *Wall Street Journal*, September 3, 1998 (via *Iraq News)*, and "Uncovering Iraq's Weapons of Mass Destruction: Past Achievements, Current Challenges," *Policywatch 338*, summary of presentation by Scott Ritter before the Washington Institute for Near East Policy, September 8, 1998.

18. Eliot A. Cohen, "Calling Mr. X," *The New Republic*, January 19, 1998.

19. *Ibid*.

20. Cohen, Eisenstadt, and Bracevich, p. xvii.

CHAPTER 15

AMERICAN POLICY TOWARD THE MIDDLE EAST IN CLINTON'S SECOND TERM

Robert O. Freedman

INTRODUCTION*

While U.S. President Bill Clinton achieved a number of successes in his Middle East policy during his first term in office—most noticeably the Oslo peace agreement between Israel and the PLO that was signed on the White House lawn in September 1993—during his second term U.S. Middle East policy has proved much more problematic.[1] Not only has the Oslo peace process run into serious difficulty, but the U.S. "dual containment" policy toward Iran and Iraq, which he inherited from the Bush administration and then intensified during his first term, had come close to collapse. The United States has also encountered problems in peripheral areas of the region, such as Cyprus, while also becoming beset by the problem of terrorism. Compounding the President's difficulties was a Republican-dominated Congress which became increasingly assertive as President Clinton became bogged down in the Lewinsky affair which, after January 1998, began to seriously threaten his presidency. This chapter will examine U.S. policy toward the Middle East in the first 2 years of Clinton's second term, looking first at what American goals were at the time President Clinton was reelected in November 1996 and then assessing the administration's success or failure in meeting these goals by January 1999, with a concentration on the U.S. role in the

---

*I am indebted to Dr. Robert Lieber of Georgetown University and to Dr. Steven David of Johns Hopkins University for their comments on the first draft of this paper.

Arab-Israeli peace process and U.S. policy toward Iraq and Iran.

THE ARAB-ISRAELI PEACE PROCESS

U.S. goals for the Middle East in the period just before the 1996 U.S. presidential election were clearly and concisely spelled out by then U.S. Assistant Secretary of State for Near Eastern Affairs Robert H. Pelletrau in a speech before the Fifth Annual Southwest Asia symposium of the U.S. Central Command (CENTO).

> Securing a just, lasting and comprehensive peace between Israel and its neighbors remains a cornerstone of our overall foreign policy. A successful peace process will enhance regional stability, remove a rallying point for fanaticism, and enhance prospects for political and economic development. The United States is engaged in several fronts to advance peace negotiations, an engagement which in turn helps achieve our other objectives in the Middle East. These include preserving Israel's security and well-being; maintaining security arrangements to preserve stability in the Persian Gulf and commercial access to its resources; combating terrorism and weapons proliferation; assisting U.S. businesses, and promoting political and economic reform.[2]

Pelletrau's emphasis on the peace process as the key to overall U.S. policy in the Middle East reflected a realization that had become concretized in U.S. policy over the past two decades: that it was very difficult for the United States to simultaneously maintain good relations with Israel and with friendly Arab states—especially the oil producers of the Persian Gulf—unless Washington was working both assiduously and successfully to bring about a peace agreement between Israel and its Arab neighbors. While much of the Arab world, seeing a direct threat from Iraq, did rally around U.S. efforts to repel Iraqi aggression against Kuwait in the August 1990-March 1991 period, at a time when the Arab-Israeli peace process was making little progress; during Clinton's second term, the United States was to have a great deal of difficulty rallying Arab support against Iraqi violations of United Nations (U.N.) Security Council Resolutions in November 1997 and January/February 1998, at least in part because of the near collapse of the Arab-Israeli peace process. Conversely, once the United States got the peace process back on track with the Wye Agreement in October 1998, Clinton got far more support from the Arab states during the mid-November 1998 confrontation with Iraq, although as Wye faltered in December 1998, this was to negatively affect popular opinion in parts of the Arab world when the United States finally decided to bomb Iraq.

A year before the U.S. presidential election of 1996, the Arab-Israeli peace process had suffered its first blow when an Israeli religious fanatic, Yigal Amir, assassinated Israeli Prime Minister Yitzhak Rabin who had pioneered the effort to reach peace with the Palestinians. In 1993 Rabin and Palestine Liberation Organization (PLO) leader Yasser Arafat had signed the Oslo I "Declaration of Principles" on the White House lawn, a ceremony which underlined the U.S. backing of the peace agreement which, however, had been forged by direct negotiations between Israelis and Palestinians. A year later, with President Clinton also present, Rabin and King Hussein ibn Talal of Jordan signed a peace treaty, which transformed the unofficial peaceful relationship between Israel and Jordan into a public one. In September 1995, despite a series of Hamas and Islamic Jihad terrorist attacks against Israeli civilians, Rabin and Arafat signed the Oslo II agreement that turned over the major Palestinian cities of the West Bank (except for Hebron) to Palestinian rule, a process that was completed by January 1996 and accompanied by elections for a Palestinian Parliament and Palestinian Executive, the latter won, to no one's surprise, by Arafat.

As the peace process developed between 1993 and 1995, the United States took the lead in fostering multilateral working groups bringing representatives from Israel and 13 Arab countries, along with 30 countries from outside the Arab world, to deal with problems that cut across the region as a whole, such as water, the environment, the refugee issue, and arms control and security.[3] The highlights of these multilateral meetings were the economic summits that took place in Arab capitals such as Amman, Cairo, and Casablanca and brought together Arab and Israeli businessmen to discuss possible business deals.

Following the assassination of Rabin, however, the peace process began to deteriorate—in spite of the best efforts of his successor, Shimon Peres, to hold it together. In February and March 1996 Hamas terrorist bombings in the heart of Jerusalem and Tel Aviv helped create an atmosphere that led to the election of anti-Oslo Israeli politician Benjamin Netanyahu as Israeli Prime Minister in May 1996, despite the attempts of the United States to rally support for Peres by organizing an anti-terrorism summit at the Egyptian town of Sharm el-Sheikh in March 1996.

Following the election of Netanyahu, one of the first things the Israeli leader did, once he put together his governing coalition, was to journey to Washington. Besides meeting President Clinton, he also addressed the American Congress, and in his speech made assertions that were clearly aimed at winning over the Republican-dominated body, such as announcing his plans to privatize state-owned Israeli companies, deregulate the Israeli economy and eliminate U.S. foreign aid to Israel. The alliances Netanyahu was to reinforce with key Republican leaders (he had been a frequent visitor to Congress when he was the Likud opposition leader from 1993-96) were to greatly aid him when he came into conflict with Clinton over the peace process, something he was soon to do. Indeed, while in his inaugural speech in the Israeli Knesset, Netanyahu offered peace to both the Palestinians (in return for "maximum security for Israel in the face of terror and war")[4] and to Israel's Arab neighbors, his policy of expanding Jewish settlements on the West Bank angered the Arabs. Israeli-Palestinian relations hit a crisis in late September 1996 when, after unilaterally ordering the opening of the Hasmonean tunnel near the Temple Mount which was holy both to Moslems and Jews, fighting erupted between Israelis and Palestinians, causing the deaths of 70 people. President Clinton, in an effort to defuse the crisis which took place little more than a month before the presidential election, invited Netanyahu, Arafat, King Hussein, and Hosni Mubarak to Washington (Mubarak refused to go, a sign of the chilling of U.S.-Egyptian relations). While the emergency summit achieved little in substance, the crisis was eased. Nonetheless, the degree of trust between Arafat and Netanyahu, never very high to start with, all but evaporated, and it was to be the United States that was forced to get intensively involved in the peace process (unlike the situation in the Oslo I and Oslo II negotiations) in order to broker an agreement for the partial (80 percent) Israeli withdrawal from the city of Hebron in January 1997. The agreement also stipulated that Israel would undertake three additional troop redeployments over the next 18 months.

Just a month later, however, Israeli-Palestinian relations received a major blow. Prime Minister Netanyahu, possibly reacting to pressure from the right wing of his governing coalition, which had been strongly opposed to the Hebron agreement, announced on February 26 that Israel would build a new Jewish neighborhood, which he called Har Homa, of 6,500 housing units in traditionally Arab East Jerusalem. When he announced days later that the next Israeli troop redeployment would turn over only 2.7 percent of Israeli-controlled West Bank territory to the Palestinian Authority, the peace process came to a halt. Arafat then not only broke off talks with Netanyahu, he also sharply diminished the security cooperation between the Palestinian police and the Israeli army stipulated by the Oslo II agreement, leading Israelis to charge that he was encouraging terrorism. Terrorism in fact did resume, with a bomb in a Tel Aviv cafe in March set off by Hamas, killing 3 Israelis, and additional bombs in Jerusalem on July 30 and September 4, killing a total of 21 Israelis and wounding hundreds more. Netanyahu reacted to the bombings by imposing a border closure that prevented Palestinians on the West Bank and Gaza from working in Israel (a tactic also periodically used by Rabin), by withholding tax payments previously collected from Palestinians working in Israel and owed to the Palestinian Authority, and by threatening to send Israeli forces into Palestinian areas to root out the terrorists.

In September 1997, after appearing to withdraw from the Middle East peace effort, the United States again intervened, this time with the peace process on the verge of total collapse after the two Hamas bombings. The new U.S. Secretary of State Madeline Albright, who had been sworn in on January 23, 1997, but had not yet made an official visit to the Middle East, came to Israel in an effort to jump-start the stalled peace process. She appealed to Arafat to take unilateral action to root out the terrorist infrastructure, and called on Netanyahu for a "time-out" in settlement construction in the occupied territories, a plea Netanyahu rejected. The peace process continued to stagnate until November when the Israeli cabinet voted in principle in favor of another troop withdrawal but specified neither its extent nor its timing. Meanwhile, Clinton had grown exasperated with what his administration perceived as stalling by Netanyahu and publicly snubbed the Israeli Prime Minister during Netanyahu's November 1997 visit to the United States to talk to Jewish organizations. Netanyahu's ties to the Republicans in Congress and to their allies on the religious right of the American political spectrum (such as Jerry Falwell whose Liberty University students regularly make pilgrimages to Israel)[5] helped insulate the Israeli leader from U.S. pressure, a process that would continue into 1998 as a weakened Clinton got bogged down in the Lewinsky scandal.

Despite his growing weakness, Clinton, acting through his Secretary of State Madeline Albright, again sought in May 1998 to salvage the peace process whose apparent demise was badly damaging the U.S. position in the Middle East. Arab friends of the United States, as well as its Arab enemies, increased their complaints about a U.S. "double standard" in the region of pressuring Iraq (see below) while not pressuring Israel. Albright, in an effort to reverse this situation, following meetings with Netanyahu and Arafat in London, issued an ultimatum for Israel to accept a 13 percent withdrawal. This, however, failed due to the support Netanyahu received from Republicans in the U.S. Congress, the pro-Israeli lobby in the United States led by the American-Israel Public Affairs Committee (AIPAC), and the Christian Religious Right.[6] Interestingly enough, however, American Jewry was badly split over Netanyahu's policy, with Reform and Conservative Jews, already angry at Netanyahu for his favoritism to Israel's orthodox Jews, calling for Netanyahu to more energetically engage in the peace process while Orthodox Jews (a clear minority in the American Jewish community) tended to support the Israeli Prime Minister.

Albright continued her efforts during the summer, however, reportedly calling Netanyahu seven times between July 5 and 8.[7] On July 10, after Albright's meeting with two senior Palestinian negotiators—Saeb Uraqat and Nabil Sha'th—U.S. White House spokesman Mike McCurry stated that there was "a limit to the degree in which we participate in a process that doesn't have utility,"[8] and on July 13, State Department spokesman James Rubin pointedly noted:

> the ball is not in the Palestinian court; the ball is in the court of the Israelis to try to work with the Palestinians and work with us to come to a second 'yes'. We have a 'yes' from the Palestinians, and we are looking to get ourselves in a position where the Israelis can say 'yes' as well.[9]

During the summer of 1998 the U.S. effort took on a new focus—seeking to get Israeli approval by linking the Israeli withdrawal in stages, to Palestinian action to combat terrorism and assure Israeli security. Meanwhile a new element had been added to the Israeli-Palestinian conflict, Yasser Arafat's threat to unilaterally declare a Palestinian state upon the expiration of the Oslo I agreement on May 4, 1999. While Netanyahu issued a counter-threat of a unilateral Israeli response, which many interpreted as annexation of large parts of the West Bank if Arafat went ahead to declare a state, the Palestinian leader's threat may have been enough to get Netanyahu to agree to meet Arafat in late September 1998 in Washington when both leaders would be in the United States to address the U.N. At his first meeting with Arafat in a year, Netanyahu finally agreed in the presence of Clinton to the 13 percent withdrawal figure stipulated by the United States, but only on condition that 3 percent of the area would be a "nature reserve" on which the Palestinians would be prohibited from building, a condition to which Arafat agreed.[10] The 13 percent figure was a considerable concession for Arafat who had initially demanded a 30 percent withdrawal, and the Palestinian leader also toned down his speech at the U.N. where he refrained from threatening to declare a state on May 4, 1999. But other issues continued to raise questions about the ultimate success of the negotiations even as Netanyahu and Arafat agreed to return to Washington in mid-October. First and foremost were the security agreements which Israel demanded in return for its phased 13 percent withdrawal. These included the specifics of Palestinian action to dismantle terrorist cells, extradite prisoners, confiscate excess guns, and stop what the Israelis called "incitement" of citizens through anti-Israeli speeches, sermons, and propaganda.[11] Other issues included the opening of an airport in Gaza, safe passage for Palestinian officials traveling between the West Bank and Gaza, and a clear repudiation by the PLO of its charter calling for the destruction of Israel. Then, of course, there were "final status" issues such as Jerusalem, borders, water, refugees, and the future of Israeli settlements that were supposed to be negotiated by May 4, 1999. Clinton met with Arafat separately the next day to urge him to work effectively to combat terrorism, although the ultimate success of the U.S. President's efforts remained to be seen. Nonetheless, the Central Intelligence Agency (CIA), an organization with the confidence of both Israelis and the Palestinian Authority, was proposed as a compromise institution to monitor Palestinian efforts to curb terrorism. Indeed, as far back as March 1998, the Hamas spokesman Ibrahim Ghawsah, had noted the effectiveness of the CIA when he complained that "military operations" against Israel had "become difficult" because of security cooperation between Arafat's Palestinian Authority and Israel, "especially after the CIA joined in this coordination."[12]

However, beside the security questions involved in a Palestinian-Israeli agreement, there were real concerns whether Clinton was strong enough to broker an agreement, given the Lewinsky affair. Natan Sharansky, Minister of Industry and Trade in Netanyahu's government and a close confidant of the Israeli Prime Minister, openly wondered "America is weak, so Arafat must wonder whether they can deliver and that affects their role here."[13] On the Palestinian side, Ziad Amir Amr, a Palestinian lawmaker stated:

> Before the scandal, at least, [Clinton] had some credibility. He could send an envoy or secretary of state and people would take it seriously. I don't think he can be taken seriously. He has no ability to do anything about the peace process. Its not even a realistic option.[14]

If this situation were not bad enough, the United States faced another dilemma, the illness of King Hussein whose country, Jordan, was now not only Israel's closest Arab friend (at least on the elite level) but also, after some disruptions during the Gulf War when the King supported Saddam Hussein, was again a major U.S. ally in the Arab world. Should Hussein die, not only could Israeli-Palestinian relations be further strained, but the entire Middle East peace process could be jeopardized.

Despite the skepticism of both Israeli and Palestinian parliamentarians and the illness of King Hussein, Clinton was able to move the peace process several steps forward in mid-October as Netanyahu, Arafat, and King Hussein (who left the Mayo Clinic to play an important mediating role) gathered with U.S. officials at the Conference Center of the Wye Plantation on Maryland's Eastern Shore. After 8 days of intense bargaining which involved the threat of a walkout by Netanyahu and Clinton's postponement of a trip to California to aid the reelection campaign of the embattled Senator Barbara Boxer, a modest agreement was achieved between Netanyahu and Arafat. The agreement involved Israel withdrawing in three stages from 13.1 percent of West Bank land (3 percent of which would become a nature preserve), transferring an additional 14.2 percent of land jointly controlled to sole Palestinian control, releasing 750 prisoners, and agreeing to the opening of a Palestinian airport in Gaza, of two corridors of safe passage between Gaza and the West Bank, and of an industrial zone between Israel and Gaza. In return, Arafat agreed to changing the Palestine National Charter to clearly eliminate the 26 articles calling for Israel's destruction, although the manner in which the change was to take place was a bit vague (reference was made to an assembly of Palestinian notables). Clinton's promise to be present during the Palestinian action, however, would serve to dramatize the event. Arafat also agreed to issue a decree prohibiting all forms of incitement to violence, to cut the number of Palestinian police to 30,000 (from 40,000), to arrest and confine 30 terrorism suspects wanted by Israel, to collect illegal weapons and suppress terrorism, with the CIA attesting to the fact that the Palestinian Authority was making every effort to crack down on terrorism.[15] The two sides also agreed to resume negotiations on final status issues.[16]

Given the issues still to be resolved between Israel and the Palestinians, the achievements at Wye were quite modest, and the modicum of trust between Arafat and Netanyahu that had been achieved at Wye seemed to evaporate following their return home, as each issued bellicose statements while terrorist acts orchestrated by Hamas threatened the process of the planned three-stage

Israeli withdrawal.[17] Nonetheless, Clinton had achieved several important things as a result of the Wye Agreement. First, by demonstrating that he was still a leader with international influence, he helped dispel the weakened image of the American presidency caused by the Monica Lewinsky affair. Second, by getting the peace process back on track, he demonstrated to the Arabs that the United States was not following a double standard *vis-à-vis* Iraq and Israel. Indeed, in the subsequent confrontation with Iraq in mid-November 1998, this development was to help the United States isolate Iraq in much of the Arab world. Third, Clinton's political position *vis-à-vis* Netanyahu was strengthened. The Israeli Prime Minister's unwise raising of the Jonathan Pollard affair in the latter stage of the negotiations alienated some of Netanyahu's Republican supporters. Netanyahu suffered a second political blow as a result of Republican losses in the House of Representatives in the U.S. mid-term elections that took place less than 2 weeks after the Wye summit, and which were widely seen as a repudiation of Republican efforts to impeach Clinton. Speaker of the U.S. House of Representatives Newt Gingrich, perhaps Netanyahu's closest ally in the Republican-dominated Congress, was forced to resign as a result of the Republican defeat (Gingrich had predicted gains of 35-40 Republican seats), to be replaced (albeit only temporarily due to his own sex scandal) by Robert Livingston, who was considerably more cool to Israel.[18] While the House of Representatives, in a highly partisan independent process, went on to vote two articles of impeachment against Clinton, the President's standing in American public opinion polls soared, and the impeachment vote did not serve to weaken him politically. Whether Clinton could use his restored political position to bring added pressure on Netanyahu to move the peace process forward soon became a moot point, however, as the Israeli Prime Minister, beset by defections from his own government, moved to call for new elections. In the process, implementation of the Wye Agreement, which had been suspended by Netanyahu in early December 1998, was frozen.

Initially, the Wye Agreement appeared to restore a modicum of confidence between Arafat and Netanyahu. Israeli troops, in the first stage of the agreement, withdrew from 2 percent of the occupied West Bank; Israel released 250 Palestinian prisoners, and allowed the opening of the Palestinian airport in Gaza. However, the momentum for peace was quickly reversed. Palestinians, complaining that the prisoners who were released were only "car thieves," not the political detainees they wanted, carried on violent protest activities.[19] These protests, together with a series of Palestinian terrorist attacks against Israelis, including the attempt by a Hamas suicide bomber to ram a bus filled with Israeli school children in Gaza, an attempt to set off a bomb in the Mahane Yehudah market in Jerusalem, and an attack on an Israeli soldier in Rainallah (actions which Arafat proved unwilling or unable to prevent), led Netanyahu, under heavy pressure from right-wing elements in his governing coalition. to freeze additional troop withdrawals on December 2. The Israeli Prime Minister conditioned the resumption of the withdrawals to Arafat, halting what he called a campaign of incitement against Israel, foregoing his intention to declare a Palestinian state on May 4, 1999, and acceding to Israel's selection of the prisoners who were to be released.[20]

For its part, the Clinton administration, despite the ongoing impeachment process, was making major efforts to keep the peace process going. On November 29, speaking at a Palestinian donor conference he had convened in Washington, President Clinton pledged $400 million in additional aid to the Palestinians, on top of the $500 million he had pledged in 1993. All told, some $3 billion in aid was pledged to the Palestinians, an amount that would greatly help the beleaguered Palestinian economy, although questions were raised at the conference about corrupt Palestinian officials siphoning off previous aid for their own personal use.[21] The United States also sought to downplay the conditions Netanyahu had placed on further Israeli troop withdrawals under the Wye Agreement, with State Department spokesman James P. Rubin stating on December 2, 1998, "The agreement should be implemented as signed. We do not believe it is appropriate to add new conditions to implementation of the agreement."[22] The most important effort to restore momentum to the Israeli-Palestinian peace process was taken by Clinton himself when he journeyed to Gaza in mid-December to witness the Palestinians formally abrogate the clauses in the Palestine National Charter calling for Israel's destruction, an action which the Netanyahu government had long demanded. While Clinton was on hand to witness the vote that he, too, had urged on Arafat, the end result of his visit was a warming of relations between the United States and the Palestinian Authority, which received increased international legitimacy as a result of the U.S. President's visit—an outcome which Israeli critics of Netanyahu blamed on Netanyahu. As Bar-Ilan University professor Shmuel Sandler noted, "Netanyahu boxed himself in, wanting to survive politically and believing he can have his cake and eat it [too]. He will have to pay a price as Washington opens up to the Palestinians."[23]

While U.S.-Palestinian relations, at least on the level of the Palestinian "street," were to suffer a serious blow when the United States bombed Iraq 2 days after Clinton's visit to the Palestinian Authority,[24] Clinton's personal relationship with Arafat was to remain strong, as Arafat was to meet Clinton and Albright in Washington in early February. In any case, Clinton's summit with Arafat and Netanyahu following the visit to Gaza proved unsuccessful despite the U.S. president's claims of reviving the stalled Middle East peace talks, as Netanyahu held fast to his position that no further withdrawals would take place until the Palestinians met his conditions.[25] This position, however, proved the death knell for his coalition government, as members from within Netanyahu's ruling Likud party, led by Defense Minister Yitzhak Mordechai, threatened to pull out of the government because of Netanyahu's obdurate position on the peace process. Suffering a major political blow when his Finance Minister Ya'acov Ne'eman resigned, Netanyahu moved to call for new elections before his government would fall on a non-confidence vote.[26] With elections scheduled for May 17, 1999, the peace process was in effect frozen, leaving the United States somewhat nervously on the diplomatic sidelines, hoping that Arafat would not prematurely declare a Palestinian state, and thus strengthen the chances for Netanyahu's reelection.

At the same time, American leaders had to be concerned about the sudden succession process in Jordan. Kina Hussein, who was suffering a relapse of his cancer, left the United States where he was undegoing cancer treatment to fly back to Jordan. There the King replaced his brother, Hassan, as Crown Prince, with Hussein's eldest son Abdullah. Given the fact that Hassan, who had been Crown Prince for more than 30 years, was a strong supporter of the peace process and that Abdullah, a general in the Jordanian army, was politically inexperienced, U.S. officials had to be concerned. While Secretary of State Albright quickly visited the Crown Prince to offer U.S. support, and President Clinton offered $300 million in additional aid, the death of King Hussein, which came soon after his selection of Abdullah as Crown Prince, added a new challenge to the U.S. leadership because it removed a moderating influence from the often volatile Palestinian-Israeli relationship, and King Hussein, who had been so valuable at Wye, would be sorely missed.[27]

THE RISE AND FALL OF DUAL CONTAINMENT: U.S. POLICY TOWARD IRAQ AND IRAN

If President Clinton was encountering difficulty in fostering peace between Israel and the Palestinians, his efforts at containing both Iraq and Iran, a policy he actively pursued during his first term in office, had all but collapsed in the 2 years following his reelection in November 1996. For dual containment to be effective, the United States had to be willing not only to support large U.S. military forces in the Persian Gulf, but also to have the will to use them if either Iran or Iraq got out of line, rather than use one to check the other as the United States had done in the 1970s and 1980s. Two states also had to be kept isolated from countries in their immediate region and be prevented from receiving support from outside countries.[28] Iran, with which the European Union countries followed a policy of "constructive engagement," never really faced such isolation, while Iraq, a pariah in most of the Arab world because of its invasion of Kuwait in 1990, by 1997 began to acquire increased support from Arab countries such as Egypt and Syria, while having received support from Russia as far back as 1993. In addition, U.S. policy toward Iran had clearly shifted by June 1998 from containment to an effort at a rapprochement, in large part because of the election of a reform-minded Iranian cleric, Mohammed Khatami, as President of Iran.

U.S. Policy Toward Iraq.

During his first term, Clinton had been challenged by Iraqi leader Saddam Hussein on a number of occasions. In June 1993, following an abortive Iraqi attempt to assassinate former U.S. President George Bush who was visiting Kuwait, the United States bombed an intelligence center in Baghdad. In October 1994, Saddam Hussein moved his army toward Kuwait, and the United States responded by airlifting military forces to Kuwait and warning Iraq not to invade, a threat that achieved its purpose. The United States was less successful in late August 1996, however, when Iraqi troops, in cooperation with the KDP (the Masud Barzani faction of the Kurdish opposition), attacked the rival PUK faction of Jallal Talabani which had been aided by Iran, and drove it from Irbil, thus severely damaging U.S. efforts to forge a united opposition to the Iraqi regime. The United States responded by expanding its "no-fly" zone in the south of Iraq to the 33rd parallel, and by bombarding Iraqi air defense installations, although France, which had hitherto cooperated with the United States in maintaining the "no-fly" zone, did not in the newly extended part of the zone.[29] The Arab opposition may have also been caused by their view of limited U.S. cruise missile attacks as worse than useless, stirring up of Arab popular anger while not threatening the bases of Saddam Hussein's power.

The major Iraqi challenges to the United States were to come in the fall of 1997 and the winter of 1998 and were to result in a weakening of the U.S. containment effort, something that was to be the result both of a sharp erosion in President Clinton's domestic political stature, and in support for his anti-Iraqi policies in the Arab world. Making matters more difficult for the United States was the active diplomacy of Russia which was seeking to rebuild its position in the Middle East.

There were three main reasons for Russian leader Boris Yeltsin's support of Iraq. First, to demonstrate to the world and to an often hostile Duma (Parliament) that Russia remained an important factor in the world, both willing and able to oppose the United States. Second, to obtain repayment for the $7 billion owed Russia's predecessor, the Soviet Union—something that will not happen until after the lifting of sanctions on Iraq. Third, Russian arms manufacturers and oil and gas companies seek contracts in Iraq, even though they cannot actually begin operations until sanctions are lifted. With these interests in mind, it is easy to explain Russian behavior in both the October-November 1997 and January-February 1998 crises, although Russian policy was far more coherent in the October-November crisis.[30]

In the fall of 1997, U.S. weapons inspectors, who were in Iraq as part of the U.N. inspection team (UNSCOM) checking on Iraq's development of weapons of mass destruction (WMD), were prohibited by Iraq from carrying out their mission and left the country, followed by the other U.N. inspectors. The United States threatened military action against Iraq and began to mobilize its forces. At the peak of the crisis, Russian Foreign Minister Yevgeny Primakov called Secretary of State Madeline Albright back from a visit to India and met with her and other members of the U.N. Security Council at 2:00 a.m. in Geneva on November 20, 1997. With the help of France, which was also pursuing lucrative arms and business deals in Iraq, Primakov put together an agreement under which the weapons inspectors would be let back into Iraq in return for a vague promise about lifting the sanctions.

The agreement proved short-lived, however, and in January Saddam Hussein, claiming that the U.S. sanctions were starving the Iraqi people, began backtracking on the agreement by prohibiting inspections of his "presidential palaces," which were suspected as weapons depositories. This led to the United States and Great Britain massing their forces in the Persian Gulf, and it appeared as if a conflict was imminent.

Several factors, however, prevented the outbreak of war. First, Clinton was now beset by the Monica Lewinsky affair, which became public in late January and which eroded his political position. Second, domestic support for an attack on Iraq proved not as strong as the Clinton administration had hoped, as on February 18, 1998, Secretary of State Albright and some of her administration colleagues encountered a hostile reception during a Town Hall meeting at Ohio State University on U.S. policy toward Iraq that was broadcast worldwide by CNN.[31] A third factor was a clear lack of support from America's Arab allies who appeared to be moved by Saddam's portrayal of his suffering people. In November 1997, at the height of the first crisis with Iraq, many of America's major Arab allies, including Saudi Arabia, Morocco, and Egypt, boycotted the U.S.-sponsored regional Arab-Israeli economic conference held in Doha, Qatar. As the Egyptian newspaper *Al-Ahram*, which usually reflects government opinion, noted—despite the U.S. support for the "oil for food" agreement that allowed Iraq to import substantial amounts of food and medicine—"The American position toward Iraq cannot be described as anything but coercive, aggressive, unwise, and uncaring about the lives of Iraqis, who are unnecessarily subject to sanctions and humiliations."[32] The Arab leaders also made clear their dissatisfaction with the United States for not pressing the Netanyahu government to move ahead with the peace process, complaining that the United States had a double standard in the Middle East, pressuring Iraq but not Israel.

Arab criticism of the United States continued into the February crisis when Saudi Arabia would not permit the United States to use bases on its soil to attack Iraq, reportedly because of U.S. "inability to push forward the quest for a broader peace between the Arabs and Israelis."[33] The Arab opposition may also have been caused by their view that limited U.S. cruise missile strikes would be worse than useless, stirring up the anger of the "Arab street," while not threatening the bases of Saddam Hussein's power.

In the face of these constraints as well as opposition from Russia and France to a U.S. military attack, President Clinton chose a diplomatic way out of the impasse, this time with the help of U.N. Secretary General Kofi Annan, who extracted the promise from Saddam Hussein that the Iraqi leader would not interfere with UNSCOM inspections. The agreement, however, was strongly criticized by Republican leaders in Congress such as Trent Lott, Jesse Helms, and John McCain, who, as Clinton weakened politically, became increasingly assertive spokesmen on U.S. foreign policy.[34] Their clamor became louder in late August when the chief U.S. inspector on the UNSCOM team, Scott Ritter, resigned in protest at what he said were deliberate U.S. efforts led by Secretary of State Madeline Albright to derail inspections in order to avoid another military confrontation with Iraq.[35] The resignation occurred on August 26, 3 weeks after Saddam Hussein on August 5, barred surprise inspections and said he would only allow remote monitoring and repeat visits to known sites. Since the Iraqi leader had long had a policy of trying to hide evidence of Iraq's efforts to construct

WMD, and UNSCOM, with Ritter often in the lead, had been successful in ferreting out the WMD information primarily by surprise inspections (although the information released by Iraq after the defection in 1995 of Saddam's son-in-law, Hussein Kamil, was also helpful). Saddam's barring of surprise inspections meant the effective end of U.N. monitoring of Iraq's weapons programs; and the U.S. failure to react to the Iraqi move, which Ritter (and many others) saw was in direct contravention of UNSC Resolution 687, precipitated his resignation. While the United States was subsequently to get a unanimous U.N. Security Council condemnation of the Iraqi leader's action (following Saddam's decision to interfere with routine UNSCOM monitoring)[36] along with a deferment of any Security Council decision on lifting sanctions,[37] it appeared that Iraq was now relatively free to engage in a crash program to build WMD, although the continuation of the sanctions on his regime appeared to limit Saddam's ability to do so.

Following Ritter's resignation, Congressional Republicans held hearings on what they called a reversal of U.S. policy toward Iraq, with House Speaker Newt Gingrich saying that what was involved suggested a "secret shift from confrontation to appeasement" that was in direct conflict with the government's public rhetoric. Gingrich[38] further attacked Clinton by stating that, if Ritter's accusations were true, "Your administration's tough rhetoric on Iraq has been a deception, masking a real policy of weakness and concession."[39] In response, Secretary of State Albright, citing the unanimous U.N. Security Council vote against Iraq, asserted that the administration's policy would be more effective in curbing Saddam Hussein than that of Scott Ritter,[40] although few Republicans appeared convinced. The administration did score a success in its Iraq policy, albeit perhaps only a small one, in mid-September when it persuaded the Kurdish factions of Masud Barzani and Jallal Talabani, whose internecine conflict had facilitated the capture of Irbil by Saddam Hussein's forces 2 years earlier, to work together and share power in Northern

Iraq.[41] Whether the agreement would hold, however, remained to be seen. Meanwhile, Senate Majority Leader Trent Lott and House International Relations Committee Chairman Benjamin Gillman introduced a bill at the end of September 1998 that authorized the Clinton administration to select one or more Iraqi opposition groups that would receive up to $97 million in U.S. Defense Department equipment and military training "to seek to remove the regime headed by Saddam Hussein in Iraq and promote the emergence of a democratic government."[42] While the Clinton administration initially opposed the bill (although Clinton was later to sign it) because it limited its flexibility of action over Iraq, it appeared that the congressional Republicans, unhappy with Clinton's handling of Iraq, were thrusting forward an alternative policy.

Fortunately for Clinton, Saddam Hussein again overreached himself and allowed the American President, albeit for only a very short time, to seize the initiative against the Iraqi leader. On October 31, 1998, Saddam Hussein ended all Iraqi cooperation with UNSCOM, precipitating yet another unanimous Security Council vote condemning Iraq and demanding that the ban on cooperation with UNSCOM be ended.[43] When Iraq refused to change its policy, the UNSCOM inspectors left Iraq, and Clinton again began to mobilize U.S. forces for a possible strike against the Iraqi leader. But the political situation in November 1998 was far different from what it had been during the November 1997 and February 1998 crises. In the first place, Clinton was greatly strengthened by the U.S. mid-term elections which were seen, as noted above, as a public repudiation of Republican attempts to impeach him. Second, after Clinton concluded the Wye Agreement, which involved a further Israeli withdrawal from occupied territory, the Arab world was far less hostile to U.S. pressure against Iraq. Indeed, the Arab Gulf coalition that fought against Iraq—Egypt, Syria, and the Gulf

Cooperation Council—issued a strongly worded warning to Iraq on November 12, stating:

> Iraq must heed U.N. Security Council resolutions and abide by them to avoid military confrontation... The Iraqi government will be solely responsible for all repercussions resulting from its decision to block UNSCOM from carrying out its inspections...[44]

A third problem which had hampered U.S. action against Iraq in the previous two crises, Russian opposition, had all but dissipated by November 1998. Beset by a monumental economic crisis, having defaulted on its foreign loans, and now having to virtually beg the United States and Europe for food to get through the winter, Russia was in no position to try to block a U.S. military strike on Iraq.[45]

In this strengthened political position, Clinton decided to launch a major military attack against Iraq, only to call it back at the very last minute after receiving information that Iraq, under the imminent threat of attack, had agreed to allow the UNSCOM inspectors to resume their work.[46] While Clinton claimed the Iraqis had "backed down" and threatened to initiate attacks if Iraq failed to fully cooperate with UNSCOM,[47] many commentators thought Clinton had lost a golden opportunity, now that he had both the Arab world and a united Security Council behind him, to destroy the bases of Saddam's power, including the Republican Guard, the suspected sites of WMD, and Iraq's remaining military capability. While in his November 15 news conference Clinton asserted that,

> the return of the inspectors, if they can operate in an unfettered way, is the best outcome, because they have been and remain the most effective tool to uncover, destroy and prevent Iraq from rebuilding its weapons of mass destruction,[48]

Clinton's critics asserted that it was only a matter of time before Saddam Hussein again interfered with the UNSCOM inspectors, and at that time Clinton might not have the favorable domestic and diplomatic situations to enable him to launch a major military attack against Iraq. Indeed, this was to be the case 1 month later when a politically weakened Clinton decided, in cooperation with the British, finally to launch a military attack against Iraq.

By mid-December 1998, Clinton's position had weakened on two fronts. In the Middle East, Israeli Prime Minister Netanyahu, as noted above, had suspended Israeli participation in the Wye River Agreement, and Clinton had not been able to reverse the decision. At home in the United States, the Republican-dominated House Judiciary Committee, in what was generally seen as a highly partisan action, had pushed through, on a party-line vote, a four-count impeachment indictment against Clinton, and the resolution was awaiting action by the full House of Representatives. It was precisely at this point that Clinton, citing UNSCOM Chairman Richard Butler's report that the Iraqis had again seriously interfered with the activities of the inspectors, and concerned that, with the Islamic holy month of Ramadan coming in a few days, the United States would have had to postpone the attack for more than a month, giving Saddam time to hide his WMD equipment, launched the attack. In the words of President Clinton:

> The conclusions [of UNSCOM chairman, Richard Butler's report] are stark, sobering, and profoundly disturbing . . . In short, the inspectors are saying that, even if they could stay in Iraq, their work would be a sham. Saddam's deception has defeated their effectiveness. Instead of the inspectors disarming Saddam, Saddam has disarmed the inspectors.
>
> This situation presents a clear and present danger to the stability of the Persian Gulf and the safety of people everywhere. The international community gave Saddam one last chance to resume cooperation with the weapons inspectors. Saddam has failed to seize the chance.
>
> And so we had to act and to act now. Let me explain why: First, without a strong inspection system, Iraq would be free to retain and begin to rebuild its chemical, biological, and nuclear

weapons programs in months, not years. Second, if Saddam can cripple the weapons inspection system and get away with it, he would conclude that the international community, led by the United States, had simply lost its will. He will surmise that he has free rein to rebuild his arsenal of destruction. And some day, make no mistake, he will use it again as he has in the past. Third, in halting our air strikes in November, I gave Saddam a chance, not a licence. If we turn our backs on his defiance, the credibility of U.S. power as a check against Saddam will be destroyed.

That is why on the unanimous recommendation of my national security team, including the vice president, the secretary of defense, the chairman of the Joint Chiefs of Staff, the secretary of state and the national security adviser, I have ordered a strong sustained series of air strikes against Iraq. The are designed to degrade Saddam's capacity to develop and deliver weapons of mass destruction and to degrade his ability to threaten his neighbors.[49]

The attack on Iraq, coming on the eve of the impeachment vote, gave rise to strong criticism both in the United States and abroad. While many Republicans such as outgoing House Majority Leader Newt Gingrich and Senator John McCain of Arizona supported the attack, Senate Majority Leader Trent Lott, who heretofore had urged Clinton to take a tougher stand on Iraq, stated, "I cannot support this military action in the Persian Gulf at this time. Both the timing and the policy are subject to question."[50] While Lott later backed away from the statement, the political damage had been done, and was reinforced by Republican Representative Gerald Solomon, the Chairman of the House Rules Committee, who asserted, "Never underestimate a desperate President."[51]

Even before the United States launched the attack, National Security Adviser Samuel Berger, in a speech at Stanford University on December 8, had articulated in a more detailed way than ever before, the administration's strategy toward Iraq. He noted that the United States would be working "step-by-step, in a practical and effective way" to undermine and eventually oust Saddam Hussein, and he linked that goal with a pledge "to use effective force if necessary." Berger's statement was coupled with incentives for people in the center of power in Baghdad to overthrow Saddam, as the U.S. official promised "to ease economic sanctions" against a new Iraqi regime and also "work to relieve Iraq's massive economic debts."[52]

In this light, an analysis of the military attack itself, which lasted 70 hours, reveals that it was not only aimed at weakening Saddam's capacity to make WMD and threaten Iraq's neighbors, but also to weaken the very basis of his regime. Chairman of the U.S. Joint Chiefs of Staff Harry Shelton estimated that between 600 and 1,600 members of the Iraqi Republican Guard, a main prop of the Iraqi government, had been killed in the U.S. attacks, which also targeted the headquarters of Iraqi military intelligence, the special Republican Guard, and the special security organization, while leaving regular army units alone.[53] The U.S. strategy in doing so seemed aimed at encouraging a future coup, on the assumption that regular army officers were less likely to support Saddam than the Republican Guard, the special Republican Guard, or the special security organization. The United States also claimed success in degrading Saddam's WMD capability even though "dual use" facilities such as pharmaceutical plants were not targeted, to avoid civilian casualties. The U.S. commander in the Persian Gulf, General Anthony Zinni, stated that, as a result of the attacks, Iraq's missile development might have been set back 2 years.[54] The United States also hit an oil refinery near Basra that Saddam was using to refine oil to be smuggled out through the Persian Gulf in violation of U.N. sanctions. Zinni asserted that the 300 ship-launched cruise missiles were particularly effective, hitting more than 85 percent of their targets; while overall, 75 percent of the strikes were rated "fully successful."[55]

Following the end of the bombing campaign, Berger again articulated U.S. policy toward Iraq, this time in a speech to the National Press Club. He noted that there were only two possible outcomes to U.S. policy toward Iraq—total

Iraqi compliance with U.N. Security Council demands, which he stated was "unlikely"; or the downfall of Saddam Hussein, which he said was "inevitable." Berger noted that the United States opposed a return to the pre-attack situation in which Saddam could instigate crises whenever he wanted by promising to give UNSCOM unfettered access and then obstructing the inspectors' work. He also stated that the United States now had an open-ended commitment to use military force to block the rebuilding of the WMD and communications equipment destroyed by the U.S. and British attacks. In addition, Berger asserted that the United States was prepared to devote resources to "practical and effective" efforts to build an opposition to Saddam.[56] However, Berger also stated that the United States was not willing to ensure Saddam's immediate departure through the commitment of the hundreds of thousands of U.S. troops which would be needed for the task.[57]

While the U.S. was evaluating the impact of the missile and air strikes, and working to undermine Saddam's position within Iraq, it was coming under strong criticism for its actions from Russia, France, and China. The Russians, who had long sought to lift the embargo against Iraq, seized on the U.S.-British attack not only to severely criticize the United States, but also to push for the lifting of the embargo. A sick Yeltsin, under attack from communists in his Parliament who sought to impeach him, used the U.S. attack to try to demonstrate Russia's continuing importance in the world, despite its serious economic problems. He denounced the attack and withdrew, albeit only for a short time, the Russian ambassadors from the United States and Great Britain. Russian ambassador to NATO Sergei Kiseljack went so far as to accuse the United States of launching the strikes just to test its newest weapons.[58] In addition Moscow sought the ouster of UNSCOM Chairman Richard Bulter, whom Russia's deputy UNSC representative, Yuri Fedotov, said, "We just don't trust."[59] Yeltsin also sought to increase the role of U.N. Secretary General Kofi Annan in dealing with the post-attack political situation in which Saddam Hussein refused to readmit the UNSCOM inspectors.

France, which also denounced the attack and also wished to secure economic benefits in Iraq, sought to capture the diplomatic initiative by tying the lifting of the oil and petroleum embargo against Iraq to the establishment of a new "independent and professional control commission under the authority of the Security Council," while continuing the ban on forbidden weapons into Iraq.[60] While Russia supported the French plan, the United States opposed it, demanding that UNSCOM remain the U.N. inspection arm, although in an effort to demonstrate it was not opposed to the welfare of the Iraqi people, the United States offered to allow Iraq both to sell more oil and to import spare parts for its oil industry.[61] Meanwhile, someone in the office of the U.N. Security Council leaked the information that UNSCOM investigators had collected eavesdropping intelligence, and given it to the United States to help it undermine the Saddam Hussein regime.[62] Both the United States and Butler denied the charge, and Kofi Annan himself stated, through a spokesman, that he had "no evidence of any kind that UNSCOM had assisted U.S. intelligence."[63] The leaking of the story, however, timed as it was, appeared to be an effort to undermine the credibility of UNSCOM in general, and Butler in particular, and was utilized not only by Iraq, but by Russia and France as well, to demand the end to UNSCOM.

While the inconclusive discussions at the U.N. were proceedmg, Saddam Hussein was seeking to recapture the initiative in the Gulf, although once again his heavy-handed actions appeared to backfire. Thus, after offering virtually no resistance to the joint U.S.-British attacks, at the end of December Saddam declared the U.S. no-fly zones "null and void" and began to launch attacks against U.S. and British planes patrolling the zones. The end result of the process was the further weakening of Iraq's defense capability as, by the end of January, the United States claimed to have destroyed an estimated 20 percent of Iraqi air defense installations, while suffering no losses of its own.[64] Meanwhile, on the Arab diplomatic front, Saddam was also suffering losses. Frustrated because of a lack of Arab support during the U.S. and British attacks, Saddam called for an Arab summit, only to pull out his delegation when the Arab delegations present demanded that Iraq renounce "provocations" against its neighbors and that it comply with all U.N. resolutions before economic sanctions could be lifted.[65] Before the meeting, Saddam had called for the Arab masses to overthrow their leaders, and had directed particular criticism against the Egyptian regime of Hosni Mubarak. Speaking on Iraqi television, Saddam urged the Arabs to "revolt and unseat those stooges, collaborators, throne dwarfs, and cowards! Revolt against injustice. Surely we will remain forever as revolutionaries against them."[66] Such statements were not calculated to win the support of Arab leaders, and, by the end of January, Iraq was even more isolated in the Arab world than it had been before the U.S.-British attacks.

As Iraq remained isolated in the Arab world and weakened militarily by its ongoing military conflict with the United States, there was yet another attempt to forge a U.N. Security Council consensus on action toward Iraq. At the end of January, the Security Council agreed to a Canadian proposal for a three-part review of the Iraqi situation under which there would be a review of (1) Iraq's disarmament situation, (2) the condition of the Iraqi population living under sanctions, and (3) an accounting of missing Kuwaitis and others during Iraq's occupation of Kuwait from August 2, 1990 to March 1, 1991.[67] While Iraq turned down the U.S. proposal, demanding that the U.N. Security Council condemn the U.S. and British air strikes and immediately lift the embargo, at a minimum the Security Council was again cooperating on Iraq, albeit on at a rather minimal level.

As the U.N. was again grappling with the Iraqi situation, the United States was stepping up its efforts to overthrow

Saddam Hussein's regime. On January 21, Secretary of State Albright appointed Frank Ricciardone to the post of special representative to the opposition groups working to overthrow Saddam. Earlier she had announced the Iraqi opposition groups eligible for the $97 million in U.S. aid under the Iraq Liberation Act (the Iraqi National Congress, the Iraqi National Accord, the Islamic Movement of Iraqi Kurdistan, the Movement for the Constitutional Monarchy, the Kurdistan Democratic Party and the Patriotic Union of Kurdistan).[68] Given the differences among the six groups (a seventh group, the Iranian-backed Supreme Council for Islamic Revolution in Iraq, rejected U.S. help), the United States faced a formidable task in coordinating an effort to overthrow Saddam. This point was made abundantly clear—albeit in a rather nondiplomatic way—by General Zinni who, in testimony to the Senate Armed Services Committee, stated that none of the Iraqi opposition groups "had the viability to overthrow Saddam at this point," and he warned that, if the opposition did prove successful, the end result could be "a disintegrated, fragmented Iraq ... and the last thing we need is another rogue state."[69] While the administration sought to put the best face on General Zinni's remarks, with State Department spokesman James Foley noting that he agreed with Zinni's conclusion that "this is not going to be an easy or short term effort,"[70] there was some question whether U.S. policy on Iraq was fully coordinated. In any case, while Saddam had been effectively isolated in the Arab world—mostly through his own mistaken diplomacy—and his military power had been considerably weakened, the United States still appeared to have a long way to go before the Clinton administration's new policy toward Iraq, the overthrow of the Saddam Hussein regime, was realized.

Iran.

While even during Clinton's first term there were voices in Washington calling for an improvement in relations with Iran, the memories of the hostage crisis of 1979-80 and of the ill-fated Iran-Contra Affair of the 1980s, coupled with Iran's death sentence on the writer Salman Rushdie, its conduct of terrorism abroad, its efforts to obtain WMD, and its opposition to the Arab-Israeli peace process, which took the form of military aid to such anti-Israeli terrorist groups as Islamic Jihad, helped prevent any policy change, as did the Republican sweep of Congress in the 1994 elections. Indeed, Iranian-American relations actually deteriorated further during Clinton's first term[71] as the United States refused to permit the U.S. airplane manufacturer Boeing to sell passenger aircraft to Iran. Similarly, the United States pressured Azerbaizhan to drop Iran from an international consortium developing one of Azerbaizhan's off-shore oil fields, and in 1995 President Clinton signed a Presidential order banning U.S. companies from investing in Iran's oil industry, thereby forcing U.S. oil firm Conoco to cancel a $1 billion agreement to develop two Iranian off-shore oil fields. In 1996, Clinton went further and signed the Republican-inspired Iran-Libya Sanctions Act (ILSA) which imposed a number of sanctions against foreign firms investing more than $40 million in Iran's oil and gas industry. Yet another blow to U.S.-Iranian relations in 1996 was the terrorist attack against the Khobar Towers residence of U.S. airmen in Saudi Arabia, which killed 19 U.S. airmen. At the time, the terrorist attack was widely attributed to Iran which made no secret of its opposition to U.S. forces in the Persian Gulf, although more recently suspicion has shifted to Osama Bin Laden.

While the United States was endeavoring to isolate Iran, it did not receive much help from its NATO allies. The French firm, Total, signed the off-shore oil deal that Conoco had been forced to cancel, and Turkey, which faced a rapidly growing demand for natural gas, signed a 20-year, $20 billion dollar agreement to import gas from Iran. Energy-related issues also divided the United States from its allies on the question of the preferred export route for Caspian Sea oil and natural gas. Many Europeans who depend more on energy imports than the United States, preferred the shorter, less expensive, and more secure route from the Caspian through Iran to the Persian Gulf. The United States backed the more expensive, longer, and much more insecure route from Azerbaizhan through Georgia and Turkey to the Mediterranean (the Baku-Ceyhan route). The United States also clashed repeatedly with Russia over Iran because Russia was Iran's major supplier of sophisticated military equipment, such as aircraft and submarines, and was also selling nuclear reactors and missile technology to Iran.

The hostility between the United States and Iran, so evident during Clinton's first term, began to diminish during the early part of his second term. The precipitating factor was the unexpected and overwhelming (70 percent of the vote) election of Mohammed Khatami as Iran's President in May 1997. The moderate Iranian leader, although challenged by hardliners in the Iranian regime including Iran's religious leader, Ayatollah Khameini, who controlled important levers of power such as the army, police, and Pasdaran, sought to increase cultural and personal freedom in Iran, while also improving relations with Iran's Gulf neighbors, Europe, and, to a lesser degree, with the United States.

Khatami's efforts to improve Iran's regional position began with the dispatch of the new Iranian Foreign Minister, Kamal Kharazzi, on a tour of Arab capitals with a message that Iran wanted peaceful and cooperative relations with the Arab world.[72] Next came the Organization of Islamic Countries (OIC) Summit held in Teheran in December 1997, where Khatami was unanimously elected as chairman of the OIC for the next 3 years. At the summit, Khatami moderated Iran's position on the Arab-Israeli peace process, stating Iran would accept any solution which the Palestinians accepted, and Iran got the support of the other Islamic countries in opposing U.S. sanctions.[73] The rapprochement between Iran and its neighbors continued in March 1998 with the visit of former Iranian President Hashemi Rafsanjani, himself a moderate, to Saudi Arabia, where the two sides discussed, *inter alia*, the drop in oil prices to below $13 a barrel, a development that hurt both countries. Saudi Arabia and Iran were subsequently to agree to an oil production cutback.[74] Iran also sent out feelers to Iraq, and the hard-pressed regime of Saddam Hussein, looking to escape its own isolated position, responded positively although the two countries remained at odds over unsettled issues from their 1980-88 war. By mid 1998, the only issue of consequence remaining in Iranian-Gulf Arab relations was the dispute over the three islands in the Persian Gulf (Big Tunb, Little Tunb, and Abu Musa) which are claimed both by Iran and the United Arab Emirates but are currently occupied by Iran—an occupation that dates back to the time of the Shah. In the new mood of Gulf Cooperation Council (GCC)-Iran cooperation, however, the islands issue now appears to be far less of an area of contention that it was in the past.

As Iran was improving its ties with the Gulf Arabs, it was stepping up its relations with Russia and France, two of its leading trade partners. Russia, which was Iran's leading supplier of military equipment as well as nuclear reactors, saw Iran as a useful ally in a number of Caucasian and Central Asian trouble spots from Chechnya to the Tajik civil war to Afghanistan, as well as a major market for Russian military and civilian exports.[75] For its part, France also rejected U.S. efforts to isolate Iran economically, and in 1997 Total joined with Russian and Malaysian energy companies in an agreement to develop Iran's South Pars natural gas field—a direct challenge to U.S. efforts to limit Iranian energy development.

The challenge, however, was not met by the United States because Iran's efforts at improving its ties with foreign countries by 1998 now also included the United States, which was to reply in kind. What could be called a limited rapprochement began in December 1997 when, in a news conference, President Khatami stated, "I first of all pay my respects to the great people and nation of

America."[76] Three weeks later, in a CNN interview, he proposed to the United States the idea of an exchange of "professionals, writers, scholars, artists, journalists, and tourists." President Clinton responded in kind at the end of January when he broke the U.S. public stereotype of Iran as a hostage-holding terrorist nation by calling Iran "an important country with a rich and ancient cultural heritage of which Iranians are justifiably proud" and asserted that the current differences between Iran and the United States were not "insurmountable."[77]

The first tangible results of the new atmosphere between the two countries came in February 1998 when a group of American wrestlers were triumphantly received by Iranian wrestling fans during the Takhiti Cup tournament in Teheran.[78] During the spring, the United States took two further actions to build up momentum for a rapprochement. In May Clinton waived sanctions against the French, Russian, and Malaysian companies planning to develop Iran's South Pars gas field,[79] and in June Secretary of State Madeline Albright, in a speech to the Asia Society in New York, after noting that the United States had implemented a more streamlined procedure for issuing visas to Iranians, offered to "develop, with the Islamic Republic when it is ready, a road map leading to normal relations."[80]

During the summer and early fall, however, the road to normal relations developed a few potholes. Under pressure from the Republicans in the U.S. Congress, the United States extended the mandate of Radio Free Europe and Radio Liberty to broadcast into Iran to "promote democracy."[81] In addition, Iran's testing of a medium range missile, the Shahab 3, in July raised concerns in the United States that Iran was making unexpectedly rapid progress on its way to developing WMD, a concern shared by Israel and its lobby in the United States. Despite these events, there was a great deal of expectation of a further thaw in U.S.-Iranian relations when Khatami and his Foreign Minister Kamal Kharazzi journeyed to New York for the opening of the fall session of the U.N. In his U.N. speech,

Khatami continued his theme of dialogue, calling on the U.N. to declare the year 2001 the "year of dialogue among civilizations." However, he took a sharply anti-Israeli tone, stating that peace and security would come to the Middle East only when all Palestinians had the right to "exercise sovereignty over their ancestral homeland," and that "Palestine is the homeland of Moslems, Christians, and Jews, not the laboratory for the violent whims of Zionists." The Iranian leader, nine of whose diplomats had been killed by the Taliban in Afghanistan and whose army now maneuvered menacingly on the border of that country, also called for a broad-based government in Afghanistan, representing all ethnic groups and communities.[82] The next day, Khatami also took a critical stance toward the United States in a news conference in which he rejected the idea of government-to-government talks between the United States and Iran, although he did welcome what he termed a "change in speech" by the United States. He complained, however, about a number of American actions, including the U.S. economic embargo against Iran and U.S. opposition to pipelines carrying Caspian Sea oil through Iran. He also protested the failure of the United States to return the Iranian assets it had frozen, and for allocating money to Radio Free Europe and Radio Liberty for Persian-language broadcasts that would "hurt the government of Iran." In an effort to diffuse criticism of Iran's human rights position, however, Khatami seemed to lift the Iranian death threat against the author Salman Rushdie by stating, "We should consider the Salman Rushdie issue as completely finished . . . The Iranian government has officially announced that, in practice, it has made no decision to act on this matter"—an assertion which, while welcome in the West (Great Britain immediately upgraded diplomatic relations with Iran), provoked a firestorm of criticism among Khatami's hard-line opponents in Iran.[83] The Iranian President also met with a group of Iranians living in the United States and Canada and asked them to invest in Iran as he set out to develop a dialogue with the Iranian exile community.[84]

The official response to Secretary of State Albright's appeal for a road map to improve relations came in Foreign Minister Kharazzi's speech to the Asia Society on September 28, and it was filled with criticism of the United States, emphasizing a number of the points already stated by Khatami in his news conference several days earlier. These included attacking the United States because of its imposition of sanctions against Iran, U.S. efforts to "sabotage" Iran's efforts to play a role in promoting regional stability, the U.S. propaganda war against Iran because of its Persian-language broadcasts on Radio Free Europe, and America's "retarding economic prosperity of Iran and the region" by its obstruction of the building of a pipeline through Iran to ship oil and gas from Central Asia and the Caucasus.[85] Iran also chose not to exploit the opportunity for person-to-person diplomacy on the Afghan issue, an area of common interest with the United States. The Clinton administration also opposed the Taliban and had just bombed Osama Bin-Laden's terrorist bases located in Afghanistan. Nonetheless Kharazzi decided, reportedly on the orders of Khameini, not to participate in a U.N.-sponsored meeting on Afghanistan at which Secretary of State Madeline Albright was present.[86]

In analyzing the hard-line positions of both Khatami and Kharazzi, it appears that the central factor affecting their behavior was the strong conservative counterattack against Khatami in Iran during the summer. The mayor of Teheran, Gholanhossen Karabaschi, an ally of Khatami, was sentenced to 5 years in prison on alleged corruption charges in July. Former Interior Minister Abdollah Nouri lost his post in June and in early September was physically attacked, along with Ayatollah Mahajerani, another Khatami ally who was the Minister of Culture and Islamic Guidance, by thugs apparently sent by hard-line conservative forces.[87] Making matters worse, Iran's supreme religious leader, Ayatollah Khameini, launched an attack against the Iranian media which had been acting with considerably more freedom following Khatami's election. Khameini charged that sections of the media had abused their freedom, and that action would be taken against their "creeping excesses."[88] Soon afterwards, the popular Iranian newspaper *Tous* was closed, and its managing director and two of its staff members were jailed. Then the weekly magazine *New Way* was also closed, two senior editors at the state-owned Islamic Republic news agency were jailed, and two-thirds of the Iranian parliament (180 of 270) called for journalists who wrote against "Islamic principles" to be tried for threatening national security.[89] The situation got so bad that an Iranian judge was quoted as saying that the jailed journalists could face the death penalty for "fighting God."[90]

It appeared that the Iranian conservatives were using the war scare with Afghanistan to fight back against Khatami's policies of domestic and foreign moderation, and by mid October, it was an open question as to which side would emerge victorious. In any case, following the Khatami visit to the United States, it appeared that U.S.-Iranian relations had come to a crossroads. In both countries there was opposition to moving ahead with the rapprochement. In the United States, it was primarily the Republicans in Congress, linked to anti-Iranian elements in the Israeli lobby.[91] They remain suspicious of Iran, arguing that Khatami can't really control the radicals in Iran, even if he wanted to, and they openly wonder whether Khatami's "charm offensive" is nothing more than a tactic to put Iran's enemies off guard, while Iran was acquiring WMD. Khameini's strong criticism of the Wye Agreement served to reinforce their opposition. On the Iranian side, Khatami's conservative opponents, still smarting over his election victory, have opposed not only his domestic reforms but also his moderate foreign policy approach to the United States. With President Khatami now under onslaught from Iranian conservatives, it is not at all clear as to whether the rapprochement can continue, unless the United States is forthcoming with a major concession such as the release of frozen Iranian assets, permission for U.S. companies to invest in Iran's oil and gas infrastructure, or removal of U.S. opposition to foreign investment in Iranian oil pipelines. Whether Clinton, despite his improved political position following the Wye Agreement and the midterm elections, is strong enough to take such steps is very much in doubt.

CONCLUSIONS

In assessing U.S. policy toward the Middle East in the first 2 years of the second term of President Clinton, several conclusions can be drawn. First, the clear-cut policy direction evident in his first term of office has now fallen into disarray. Second, while Clinton secured a number of Middle East policy successes during his first term, his second term has been marked by some significant failures. In the Arab-Israeli conflict, Clinton's effort to promote the peace process has run into serious problems as negotiations between Israel and the PLO virtually ended between February 1997 and September 1998, and the limited progress he achieved in the fall of 1998 in the Wye Agreement, which quickly ran into trouble, pales into insignificance when compared to the issues that still need to be negotiated between Israelis and Palestinians. In Clinton's first term, Israelis and both Palestinians and Jordanians did most of the negotiating themselves, with the United States essentially standing on the sidelines as a cheerleader. During the American leader's second term, the lack of trust between Arafat and Netanyahu necessitated a much more active role for the United States. Yet the American effort, at least at the top level (President and Secretary of State) seemed disjointed. Newly appointed Secretary of State Madeline Albright did not even make a visit to the Middle East until 8 months into her term and then only after a series of terrorist bombings. For his part, President Clinton, apparently exasperated by Netanyahu's policies, publicly snubbed the Israeli leader during his November 1997 visit to the United States and then—through Albright—gave an ultimatum to Netanyahu 6 months later, only to prove unable to enforce it. Given the history of high level U.S. activity in the Arab-Israeli conflict, something regional leaders have come to expect, Clinton's policy of apparent benign neglect followed by frenetic activity raised serious questions about U.S. policy, and the freezing of the implementation of the Wye Agreement by Netanyahu in December 1998, despite Clinton's protestations, could only raise further doubts about U.S. policy capability.

If Clinton's policies toward the Arab-Israeli conflict have had, at best, limited success, during the first 2 years of his second term, U.S. policy toward Iraq has been even more problematic, and the degree of success the United States achieved in its zero-sum game conflict with Iraq was, in large part, due to Saddam Hussein's mistakes. During this period, U.S. strategy evolved from supporting UNSCOM, despite numerous infractions of U.N. resolutions by Saddam Hussein who sought in every way possible to impede the UNSCOM inspectors, to a policy of working with Iraqi opposition groups under the Iraq Liberation Act to overthrow Saddam, a policy that was stepped up following Clinton's decision in December 1998 to belatedly bomb Iraq. This action, while it was aimed both a weakening Iraq's WMD capability and striking at the major supports of Saddam's regime like the Republican Guard, also led the Iraqis to prohibit the return of UNSCOM inspectors. In an effort to demonstrate to the Arab world that the United States was only opposed to the regime of Saddam Hussein, not to the Iraqi people, the United States also pioneered the "food for oil" agreement, although the impact on the "Arab street" of this measure did not seem significant. Meanwhile, beginning in the summer of 1998, the Republican-led Congress began to urge Clinton to take ever stronger measures against Iraq, although several of these Republican hawks, like Senator Lott, did not choose to support Clinton when he finally attacked Iraq in December 1998—on the eve of the House impeachment vote. Fortunately for Clinton, however, Saddam's heavy-handed attempts to overthrow opposing Arab regimes led to his isolation in the Arab world, while his efforts to belatedly challenge the U.S. and British planes in the no-fly zones of northern and southern Iraq led to the further degradation of his military capacity. Finally, his main ally on the U.N. Security Council, Russia, was far too weak economically and politically, let along militarily, to take action to protect him.

In the case of Iran, U.S. policy has had more of a mixed result. The old policy of dual containment pursued so strongly during Clinton's first term seems now to have been jettisoned, with the United States now seeking to improve relations with Iran while keeping Iraq isolated. The United States embarked on a policy of rapprochement with Iran following the election of Mohamed Khatami as Iran's President in May 1997. Yet the policy of limited rapprochement, replete with positive oratory and symbolic actions by both sides, seems to have run its course, and it remains to be seen if U.S. and Iranian leaders, each of whom is beset by domestic opposition to the limited rapprochement, can push the process much farther.

In looking to the reasons for the U.S. policy disarray and Clinton's relative lack of success in his Middle East policies during his second term, several factors appear paramount. First is the Republican Congress which provided support for hard-line Israeli Prime Minister Binyamin Netanyahu in his efforts to slow the peace process and rebuff Clinton's pressure, and which challenged Clinton's policies on Iraq and Iran as well. While Clinton cannot personally be held responsible for the election of Netanyahu which, along with the Hamas terrorism that Arafat proved unwilling or unable to suppress, proved to be a major obstacle to U.S. efforts to forge a Middle East peace, he can certainly be held responsible for the Monica Lewinsky affair which breathed new life into the Ken Starr special counsel investigation of his presidency and led to the beginning of an impeachment process. This process strengthened the role of Congress in U.S. foreign policy and enabled foreign leaders like Netanyahu and Saddam Hussein to resist U.S. pressure.

The Lewinsky crisis undermined Clinton's efforts to build a coalition against Saddam Hussein in February 1998, as much of the world's perception (whether true or not is besides the point) was that the crisis stemmed, not from Saddam's defiance of the U.N. inspectors, but from Clinton's efforts to divert attention from the Monica Lewinsky affair. Similar criticism was leveled against Clinton when he finally decided to launch a major attack on Iraq in mid-December 1998, just as the House of Representatives was preparing to vote articles of impeachment against him. Indeed, one of the weaknesses of U.S. policy toward Iraq has been Clinton's unwillingness to use force when the political situation favored it, and poor timing when he belatedly chose to use significant force. There are times in international crises when force must be used, and it is not clear that Clinton fully understands this.

Finally, the weakness of his presidency appears to limit how far Clinton can go in building on the opportunity provided by the election of a moderate to the presidency of Iran. With the administration's dual containment strategy now a matter of history, the chance to build a new relationship with Iran is the first genuine opportunity for the United States to change direction on Iran in two decades and to improve the American position in the Persian Gulf as a result. Yet the weakness of the Clinton administration seems to preclude the steps needed to move the U.S.-Iranian rapprochement on to the next stage, although the domestic opposition faced by Khatami is certainly a major factor as well.

In sum, despite some small and perhaps transitory successes like the Wye Agreement, American policy toward the Middle East during the first 2 years of President Clinton's second term has been a highly problematic one. Whether the United States can be more successful in pursuing its policy goals in the region during the remainder of Clinton's term is a very open question.

ENDNOTES - CHAPTER 15

1. For an overview of U.S. policy toward the Middle East in Clinton's first term, see Don Peretz, "U.S. Middle East Policy in the 1990's," in Robert O. Freedman, ed., *The Middle East and the Peace Process*, Gainesville: University Press of Florida, 1998, pp. 347-364.

2. Robert H. Pelletrau, *American Objectives in the Middle East*, Occasional Paper Series No. 7, US-GCC Corporate Cooperation Committee, Washington, DC, 1996, pp. 2-3.

3. *Ibid.*, pp. 6-7.

4. The text of Netanyahu's speech can be found in *Collier's International Yearbook*, New York: Collier-Newfeld, 1997, p. 116.

5. David Coven, "Liberty U. to send 3,000 students on a study tour of Israel," *Chronicle of Higher Education*, September 25, 1995, p. 51.

6. For an analysis critical of U.S. strategy at this time, see Robert Satloff, "Shifting Sands: The U.S.'s Disturbing New Israel Policy," *New Republic*, June 1, 1998.

7. Cited in Donald Neff, "American Impatience Grows," *Middle East International*, No. 579, July 17, 1998, pp. 10-11.

8. *Ibid.*, p. 11.

9. *Ibid.*

10. Martin Sief, "Arafat Accepts Israeli Land Deal for West Bank," *Washington Times*, September 30, 1998.

11. Steven Erlanger, "U.S., Israel and Arafat Inch Toward Pact," *New York Times*, September 29, 1998.

12. Vernon Loeb, "CIA Emerges to Resolve Middle East Disputes," *The Washington Post*, September 30, 1998.

13. Deborah Sontag, "Patch of Desert Key to Mid East Talks Next Step," *New York Times*, September 9, 1998.

14. Lee Hockstader, *The Washington Post*, September 18, 1998.

15. Eric Schmitt, "The CIA: New Role as Umpire May Bring More Risk," *New York Times*, October 24, 1998. For an article strongly

criticizing this new role for the CIA, see Edward G. Shirley, "CIA Needs Reform, Not New Missions," *Wall Street Journal*, November 19, 1998.

16. For a description of the Wye Agreement, see Barton Gellman, "Netanyahu, Arafat Sign Accord," *The Washington Post*, October 24, 1998.

17. Nonetheless, despite strong opposition from the right wing of the Israeli political spectrum, the Israeli cabinet approved the Wye Accord by a vote of 8 to 4, with 5 abstentions. The cabinet's conditions for so agreeing, however, which included a required Palestinian vote to repeal the 26 offending articles of the Palestine National Charter (an issue fudged at Wye) may presage future problems. See Lee Hockstader, "Israel Puts Pact in Doubt: Cabinet Votes Approval but Adds Conditions," *The Washington Post*, November 12, 1998. The Wye Agreement supported by Labor, Meretz, and the Arab parties, was passed overwhelmingly in the Israeli Knesset by a vote of 75 to 19, with 9 abstentions. (See Nina Gilbert and Danna Harman, "Knesset approves Wye," *Jerusalem Post*, November 18, 1998.)

18. See William A. Orme, Jr., "Paying for Mideast Plan, U.S. Walks Tightrope," *New York Times*, November 19, 1998; and Seth Gitell, "Fall of Gingrich Leaves Netanyahu Bereft of Key Ally in Congress," *Forward*, November 13, 1998.

19. Lee Hockstader, "Attacks Kill Arab; Injure 3 Israelis," *The Washington Post*, December 3, 1998.

20. Ann LeLordo, "Israel Issues Ultimatum, Halts West Bank Pull-out," *Baltimore Sun*, December 3, 1998.

21. Philip Shenon, "U.S. and Other Nations Plan More Aid for Palestinians," *New York Times*, December 1, 1998; and Martin Sieff, "Palestinians Get More U.S. Aid," *Washington Times*, December 1, 1998.

22. Hockstader, "Attacks Kill Arab, Injure 3 Israelis."

23. Judy Dempsey, "Palestinians Turn the Tables on Israelis: Arafat Poses as Clinton's Friend as Netanyahu Sulks," *Financial Times*, December 16, 1998.

24. Toni Marshall, "Clinton Goes from Cheers to Jeers in Two Days," *Washington Times*, December 18, 1998.

25. Stephen Fidler and Judy Dempsey, "U.S. Claims It Has Put Peace Process Back on Track," *Financial Times*, December 16, 1998.

26. Judy Dempsey, "Deep Freeze in Jerusalem," *Financial Times*, December 23, 1998.

27. Philip Shenon, "Wary U.S. Broods on a Peace Process Minus King Hussein, *New York Times*, January 31, 1998.

28. For a background on the dual containment policy, see Peretz, pp. 353-355. For a recent debate on the continued utility of the policy, see *The Middle East Institute Newsletter*, Vol. 49, No. 5, September 1998, pp. 1, 6. For a highly negative view of dual containment, see Hisham Melham, "Dual Containment: The Demise of a Fallacy," Washington, DC: Center for Contemporary Arab Studies, 1997.

29. For an analysis of these events, see Phebe Marr, "Iraq After the Gulf War: The Fallen Idol," *The Middle East and the Peace Process*, p. 232.

30. Russia's motivations and policy are discussed in Robert O. Freedman, "Russia's Middle East Ambitions," *Middle East Quarterly*, September 1998, pp. 31-40.

31. The ill-fated Town Hall meeting is described by Sam Husseini, "Short Circuiting the Media/Policy Machine," *Middle East Research and Information Project*, No. 208, Fall 1998, p. 33.

32. R. K. Ramazani, "The Emerging Arab-Iranian Rapprochement: Towards an Integrated U.S. Policy in the Middle East," *Middle East Policy*, Vol. 6, No. 1, June 1998, p. 51.

33. *Ibid.*, p. 52.

34. Stephen Zunes, "Confrontation with Iraq: A Bankrupt U.S. Policy," *Middle East Policy*, Vol. 6, No. 1, June 1998, p. 100.

35. The text of Ritter's resignation statement can be found in *Washington Times*, August 28, 1998.

36. Barbara Crosette, "Chief U.N. Inspector Reports More Interference by Iraq," *New York Times*, September 4, 1998.

37. Robert S. Greenberger, "Security Council Suspends Iraq Review Pending an Agreement Over Inspection," *Wall Street Journal*, September 10, 1998.

38. Barton Gillman, "Gingrich Opens Fire on White House Iraq Policy," *The Washington Post*, August 29, 1998.

39. Judith Miller, "Gingrich Questions U.S. Policy on Iraqi Arms Inspections," *New York Times*, August 29, 1998.

40. Thomas Lippman, "Albright Defends Handling of Iraq," *The Washington Post*, September 10, 1998.

41. Philip Shenon, "Two Kurd groups unite against Baghdad in pact brokered by U.S.," *New York Times*, September 18, 1998.

42. Walter Pincus, "Bill Attempts to Shift U.S. Policy on Iraq," *The Washington Post*, October 1, 1998. See also Sean Scully, "House Strongly Backs Anti-Saddam Activities," *Washington Times*, October 6, 1998; and Philip Shenon, "House Votes $100 Million to Aid Foes of Baghdad," *New York Times*, October 7, 1998. The bill passed the House of Representatives by a vote of 360-38.

43. Barbara Crosette, "U.N. Avoiding Talk of Force, Criticizes Iraq on Arms Team," *New York Times,* November 6, 1998.

44. Thomas Lippman and Bradley Graham, "Support for U.S. Stance on Iraq Grows," *The Washington Post*, November 13, 1998, and Howard Schneider, "Baghdad Stiffens as U.S. Air Armada Assembles Nearby," *The Washington Post*, November 13, 1998.

45. Michael R. Gordon, "Food Crisis Forces Russia to Swallow Its Pride," *New York Times*, November 7, 1998.

46. For an analysis of this decision, see Bradley Graham, "White House Advisers Split on Halting Attack," *The Washington Post,* November 16, 1998.

47. In his news conference, Clinton laid out five conditions for Iraq to meet: First, Iraq must resolve all outstanding issues raised by UNSCOM and the IAEA; second, it must give inspectors unfettered access to inspect and monitor all sites they choose, with no restrictions or qualifications, consistent with the memorandum of understanding Iraq itself signed with U.N. Secretary General Annan in February; third, it must turn over all relevant documents; fourth, it must accept all weapons of mass destruction related resolutions; and, fifth, it must not interfere with the independence or the professional expertise of the weapons inspectors. *The Washington Post*, November 16, 1998.

48. *Ibid.*

49. *Washington Post*, December 17, 1998.

50. David Rosenblum, "Despite Earlier Statement, Senator Lott Says He Supports U.S. Strikes Against Iraq," *The Washington Post*, December 18, 1998.

51. Gerald Baker, "Cynical View from Clinton Opponents," *Financial Times*, December 17, 1998.

52. Barton Gellman, "U.S. Committed to Change in Baghdad, Berger Says," *The Washington Post*, December 9, 1998.

53. Steven Fidler, "U.S. General Claims up to 1,600 Iraqi Troops Killed," *Financial Times*, January 9, 1999. See also Bradley Graham, "The Big Military Question: What's Next?," *The Washington Post*, December 21, 1998.

54. *Ibid*.

55. Dana Priest, "U.S. Commander Unsure of How Long Iraq Will Need to Rebuild," *The Washington Post*, December 22, 1998.

56. Thomas Lippman, "Two Options for U.S. Policy," *The Washington Post*, December 24, 1998.

57. Rowan Scarborough, "Ground Troops Not Part of Plan," *Washington Times*, December 24, 1998.

58. David Buchan, "Europeans Rally to Allies' Cause," *Financial Times*, December 19, 1998.

59. Barbara Crosette, "U.S. Is Urged to Ease Call to Inspect Atomic Arms," *New York Times*, December 22, 1998.

60. Herbert Vedrine (the French Foreign Minister), "Way Out of the Impasse," *Financial Times*, January 18, 1999.

61. Associated Press, "Clinton Eases Curbs on Sale of Spare Parts for Iraq's Oil Industry," *Wall Street Journal*, January 18, 1999.

62. The information was leaked to *The Washington Post*. See Barton Gellman, "Annan suspicious of UNSCOM Role," *The Washington Post*, January 6, 1999.

63. Michael Littlejohns, "U.N. Rejects Claims that Iraq Arms Inspectors Spied for the U.S.," *Financial Times*, January 7, 1999.

64. Steven Lee Myers, "U.S. Presses Air Attacks on Iraq in a Low-Level War of Attrition," *New York Times*, February 3, 1999.

65. Douglas Jehl, "As Arab League Urges Iraqis to Obey the U.N., They Walk Out of Meeting," *New York Times*, January 25, 1999.

66. Douglas Jehl, "Iraq's Angry Call for Revolt Splits Arab Nation," *New York Times*, January 6, 1999.

67. Reuters, "Baghdad Slams U.N. Plan to Review Relations," *The Washington Post*, February 1, 1999.

68. Vernon Loeb, "U.S. Names New Representative for Iraqi Anti-Saddam Groups," *The Washington Post*, January 22, 1999.

69. Vernon Loeb, "General Wary of Plan to Arm Groups in Iraq," *The Washington Post*, January 29, 1999.

70. Associated Press, "Clinton's Plan to Oust Saddam Faulty, Zinni Tells Senate Panel," *The Washington Post*, January 29, 1999.

71. For a review of U.S. policy toward Iran in Clinton's first term, see Shaul Bakhash, "Iran Since the Gulf War," in *The Middle East and the Peace Process*, pp. 248-250. See also Kenneth Katzman, "Beyond Dual Containment: Revisited," *Middle East Insight*, September-October 1998, pp. 4-5.

72. Ramazani, p. 56.

73. *Ibid.*, p. 55.

74. *Ibid.*, p. 57.

75. For a study of Russian-Iranian relations, see Robert O. Freedman, "Russia and Iran: A Tactical Alliance," *SAIS Review*, Summer-Fall 1997, pp. 93-109.

76. Ramazani, p. 58.

77. *Ibid.*

78. John Marks, "Wrestling Diplomacy," *Middle East Insight*, September-October 1998, pp. 47-48. Marks is the president of "Search for Common Ground," an organization dedicated to bringing together countries that are at odds with each other. The author of this chapter is also a member of that organization.

79. Robert S. Greenberger, "U.S. Sees Limits to Economic Sanctions," *Wall Street Journal*, September 9, 1998.

80. The text of Albright's speech is found in *Middle East Insight*, September-October 1998, pp. 45-46.

81. See Thomas A. Dine, "Broadcasting to Iran," *Middle East Insight*, September-October 1998, p. 51.

82. Elaine Sciolino, "Iranian President Paints a Picture of Peace and Moderation," *New York Times*, September 22, 1998.

83. Elaine Sciolino, "Iranian Dismisses all hope now for a political thaw," *New York Times*, September 23, 1998. For an explanation of the role of the Persian language service of RFE/RL by its director, Steve Fairbanks, see *Gulf 2,000 List*, November 18, 1998.

84. Howard Schneider, "Iranians Hope to End Rogue Status," *The Washington Post*, September 23, 1998; and "Khatami Urges Iranians to Invest in Their Country," *Financial Times*, September 21, 1998.

85. Elaine Sciolino, "Top Iranian Official Rejects U.S. Overtures on New Ties," *New York Times*, September 29, 1998.

86. Betsy Pisik, "U.S. Iran Officials Meet on Afghanistan Problem," *Washington Times*, September 22, 1998; and author's interview with an Iranian scholar, Washington, DC, October 16, 1998, who asserted that Khameini did so to reassert his primacy in Iranian foreign policy as he was doing in domestic policy.

87. Mark Huband, "Pressure on Iran Media Grows," *Financial Times*, September 24, 1998.

88. Douglas Jehl, "Iran Shuts Popular Newspaper that Questioned Hard Line on Taliban and Arrests Top Editors," *New York Times*, September 18, 1998.

89. Howard Schneider, "Guessing Wrong What News Was Fit to Print," *The Washington Post*, September 28, 1998; "Iran Suspends Several Moderate Magazines," *The Washington Post*, September 20, 1998; and "Iranian Journalists Targeted by Parliament," *The Washington Post*, September 24, 1998.

90. "Iranian Judge Threatens Journalists," *The Washington Post*, September 22, 1998.

91. See James Morrison, "Embassy Row: Iran Still 'Outlaw'," *Washington Times*, September 16, 1998. See also "Next Steps with Iran: A debate with Patrick Clawson, Geoffrey Kemp, Edward Shirley and Kenneth Timmerman," *Middle East Quarterly*, June 1998, pp. 63-77.

CHAPTER 16

EUROPE, THE MEDITERRANEAN AND THE MIDDLE EAST

Rodolfo Ragionieri

Introduction.

The records of European policies with respect to the Mediterranean and the Middle East are mixed and perplexing. On one side you have the attention permanently devoted to the region by all the Southern and most Western European countries. Moreover, more than one attempt was started in the past to develop a common Western European approach to the relations with countries of the Southern and Eastern shore of the Mediterranean Sea, and particularly Arab countries, since the Euro-Arab dialogue of the 1970s up to the Barcelona process of the 1990s. Nevertheless, the burden of past legacies, the pursuit of national policies and, last but not least, the overwhelming presence of the United States in the area have often (if not in most cases) weakened these efforts.

This is especially apparent as far as the hottest issues in the area, such as the Israeli-Palestinian peace process or the ongoing conflict in Algeria, are concerned. For example, in 1993 the late Alex Langer, in a question at the European Parliament, openly stated what is a widespread view concerning the European role in the peace process in the Middle East: "I have the impression that Norway has done a great deal more in real terms than the European Union, and I am rather sad about that."[1]

Does this impression correspond to reality? There is certainly a part of truth: if you look at publications on the history of the Arab-Israeli conflict, the role of European states (with the exception of Norway) and of the European

Community (EC) in the last decades is one of neglect, and in the Israeli and Palestinian press, the interest given to Europe is much less prominent than that granted to the United States.

Generally speaking, many questions can be put forward and should be answered. First, are national policies of major European countries totally at odds with each other, or is it possible to observe in some respect an even unwillingly emerging European consensus? Second, can we speak in some respect of a foreign policy of the European Union (EU) in the area (if we can speak about that at all)? Third, what are the possible obstructions to this policy?

In order to give an answer, first an overview of general European interests and perceptions of the area will be given. After that, an outline of different national policies in the area will be developed. Before coming to some conclusion, the role of the EU in the peace process in the Middle East will be discussed.[2]

General Perceptions: From Threat to Risk.

It is important to stress the importance of the whole area and of all of its problems and conflicts for European security. It is not unusual to listen to people (especially American scholars or officials) maintaining that, for Europe, Mediterranean policy is important only as a tool to prevent massive immigration. It is a curious view that the United States (thousands of miles away from the Middle East) would be more involved in Middle Eastern security than the EU and single European countries. It would be equivalent to the statement that the United States is interested in Latin American politics with the only purpose being to put under control the immigration from the southern part of the Americas.

There are basically four reasons for European interest: dependence on energy raw materials (and, generally speaking, economic relations), geographic proximity, migration, and Islam as both a domestic and foreign policy issue (this must be taken into consideration separately from migration issues).

Economic relations. Energy supplies from Middle East and North Africa (MENA) are more critical to Europe than to the United States (obviously excluding European oil producers, like the United Kingdom and Norway). For example, in 1995 Western Europe imported 9.6 million oil barrels/day; of these, 5.5 million from countries of MENA. During the same year, the United States imported 8.8 million oil barrels/day; of these, 1.8 from the same region.

Import and export between the EU and these countries is moreover much more relevant than between the region and the United States: European exports to developing countries represent 18 percent of the total, against a U.S. percentage of 8.8 percent; imports are 15 percent, against 6 percent.

Geographic proximity. First of all, any crisis in MENA threatens Europe by means of horizontal escalation. Europe is the natural geographic rear of any military operations in the area, as it was during the Gulf War. Thus, concerns about proliferation of weapons of mass destruction are related to immediate security concerns and not only to wider fears regarding conflicts and stability in the international system.

Migrations. Large numbers of immigrants from Mediterranean countries are hosted by most EU countries. Among them there are older immigration countries like France and Germany, and more recently ones like Italy and Spain. Thus, migrations are a concern of domestic policies, inner European policy, and foreign policies. The presence in Western Europe of millions of immigrants from the whole region—from Morocco to Iran—makes European concerns about stability a very concrete issue. In case of crises in the region, an influx of refugees could increase the already consistent flow, as, for example, the case of Kosovo or Kurdistan.

Islam. The presence in most Western European countries of substantial and often increasing Muslim minorities makes Islam both a domestic and foreign policy issue. This is related not only to immigration, because large permanent Muslim communities are present in France and Germany.[3]

It is quite clear that the perception of the situation evolved from a picture of threat that characterized the Cold War era, to a more subtle awareness of latent risks. This is, nevertheless, enough to define very basic security perceptions and interests even in a very rough realist framework. Moreover, there are historical ties to Israel and Arab countries which cannot be described only in terms of "national interests as power." These historical ties and heritages are obviously different for different countries.

Europe: Unity and Diversity.

Almost any European country has its own specific problems with respect to the Mediterranean. Spain has enclaves in Ceuta and Melilla. France has major maghrebi communities and its historical ties, especially to Algeria. Germany has the difficult problem concerning political relations with Israel, without damaging the relations with Muslim countries, and the relevant permanent Turkish and Kurdish communities.

While dealing with the tensions between the contradiction of a common European foreign and security policy and national policies, one has to consider two main complexes, which could be roughly defined as the "objective" and the "subjective" variables. The first set is formed by what are sometimes called "geopolitical variables." The second set is composed by inherited traditions, perceptions, and, generally speaking, the foreign policy identity of countries. These factors make, for example, two countries of comparable size in population and gross national product like Italy and France[4] completely different in the self-representation of their international role, and thus in their foreign policies. Starting from certain given conditions, the elites of different European countries have been constructing their different Mediterranean policies.

Even though foreign policies are often constructed and formulated in terms of national interests, perceptions of threat and the search for relative or absolute gains are shaped into foreign policies by so-called national traditions. Inherited perceptions and prevalent ideas on national identity and their relative places and roles in international society shape the action of political, diplomatic and military personnel in each country.[5]

In this outline the main features of policies of major EU countries are reviewed. Greece and Turkey are excluded for two reasons. First, because their respective policies are considered elsewhere. Second, because they are entangled in a conflict making them at the same time actors and an issue in European policies.

Italy. Italian policy with respect to the Mediterranean has been characterized by a permanence, i.e., the existence of an Arab policy, since the 1950s. It would perhaps be more precise to speak about a Mediterranean policy, or of an attention with respect to Arab countries and actors, because many scholars argue that these policies have been often contradictory and pursued by different actors in the Italian political and economic arena.[6]

These policies have not only been ideological and Third-World-ist, as Italy's critics claim, but have also corresponded to a certain construction of Italian national interests. They were defined in the 1950s by a part of the Christian Democrats, and by the national agency for energy (ENI, Ente nazionale idrocarburi, i.e., literally National Agency for Hydrocarbons), and its director, Mattei. Moreover, during the 1970s and after, there was a substantial agreement between most of government parties and the leftist opposition (i.e., the Italian Communist Party) with respect to Middle Eastern policy. At the beginning of that decade the Christian Democrat Aldo Moro, foreign minister in the last two Rumour cabinets, was among the promoters of the Euro-Arab dialogue.[7]

It is remarkable that during the 1980s, a period of highest confrontation (at least in declaratory policies) within the government and particularly between the Socialist Party and its leader, Bettino Craxi, and the Communist Party and its leaders, among them Enrico Berlinguer, there was substantial agreement on the relations with Arab countries and on the possible solutions of the Israeli-Arab conflict.[8] This was made stronger by the personal ties of Giulio Andreotti, Bettino Craxi, and Enrico Berlinguer with many Arab leaders, first among them Yasir Arafat. The orientation of the Italian foreign policy was made evident by the Sigonella affair (December 1985), when a confrontation between *Carabinieri* and the Seals took place during the *Achille Lauro* hijacking.

A potential discontinuity in this policy was declared by Antonio Martino, the Foreign Minister of the center-right Berlusconi government (May-December 1994). Just after the formation of the cabinet, during a visit to the United States, he declared that "the Berlusconi government will pursue the most pro-Israeli policy in the last twenty years, although without taking distances from the Palestine Liberation Organization (PLO)" and that in Middle Eastern affairs Italy would not be ideologically pro-Arab.[9] Nevertheless, he had to make a considerable effort to convince the Israeli diplomacy of the democratic conversion of the post-fascist party Alleanza Nazionale (National Alliance). Moreover, he was the first European minister visiting Gaza after the establishment of the Palestinian National Authority.[10]

This general attitude is reflected by the active role of Italian governments and nongovernment organizations (NGOs) cooperating in the economic development of Palestinian territories. Some Israeli perception notwithstanding, Italian public opinion is not hostile to the Jewish state. According to a poll published by the journal

Limes,[11] for the majority of Italians (81.7 percent) the condition for the existence of a Palestinian state is provided by its full acknowledgment of the state of Israel. On the other side, the majority (58.8 percent) of Italians refuse to take a partisan position, declaring to prefer both Israelis and Palestinians.[12] Moreover, it should not be forgotten that the Italian delegation at the United Nations (U.N.) was instrumental in the cancellation of the (in)famous Zionism equals to racism resolution of the General Assembly. According to the Italian columnist Arrigo Levi, this poll reflected the fact that in Italy the roots of anti-semitism are not deep, and that the connection between Israel and the Jews plays a positive role.[13]

Just because of its ties to Middle Eastern countries and/or personalities, sometimes Italy acted as a forerunner to European and even Western policies, as happened in March 1997 when Italian Minister for Foreign Affairs Lamberto Dini went to Teheran few days after Rafsanjani's visit to ar-Riadh, during a phase of mutual opening in foreign policies between Iran and western countries. One year later, Italy was the first Western country to be visited by an Iranian president, Khatami, after the Islamic revolution.

Another factor making a difference in Italian foreign political and economic relations has been Libya. Italian companies of different dimensions have an interest in cooperation with Libya, and this country is a traditional important supplier of oil for Italy. Economic interests mix with a traditional propension to dialogue, confirmed, for example, in the last years by former Prime Minister Romano Prodi.[14]

France. France is the only European state which has an ambition to play openly the role of a global medium-sized power. This is especially true as far as Arab, and generally speaking Mediterranean, countries are concerned. Since Algeria's independence, de Gaulle declared and pursued a French Arab policy. After the years marked by the end of bipolar confrontation and the Second Gulf War, there was a transformation from an Arab policy to a Mediterranean policy.[15] This is reflected in an interview the French foreign minister released to the French quarterly journal, *Politique internationale*, where he declared:

> I think that the expression "Arab Policy" can give rise to confusion. If the matter is on one side to have active relations with "Arab countries" and, on the other, to take into consideration the Arab dimension of global problems, then this policy is pertinent for France. But if you mean that France should have one Arab policy, global and undifferentiated, and support all Arab points of view, the expression is neither justified nor convenient.[16]

In the Mediterranean area, this role is played in different theaters: the Maghreb, the Levant, the Balkans, and the Gulf, if you take into consideration the enlarged Mediterranean. In each of these theaters, France can claim both contemporary interests and a historical tradition. For example, Algeria represents a special interest for France, and the special relationship has been characterized by bilateral relations since the independence.[17] It is unthinkable that any French president or government would give up a national policy with respect to Algeria. At the same time, French politicians cannot pursue an interventionist course in Algerian politics, since that could be charged with "colonial attitudes." Moreover, other difficulties have been provoked by diverging, or simply different, views within the French leadership. A first dividing issue was provided by the Sant'Egidio initiative, when the external leadership of the Front Islamique de Salut, (FIS, Islamic Front of Salvation) met with the Front of National Liberation, the Front of Socialist Forces, and other minor groups in Rome, at the Sant'Egidio community. At that time there was a difference between Prime Minister Balladour, very cautious with respect to any interference into Algerian affairs and support to the Sant'Egidio initiative, and Defence Minister Leotard, who openly supported a political arrangement between the Algerian government and the Islamic armed opposition. A similar difference surfaced later, in the socialist government: at the beginning of 1998, where Prime Minister Jospin expressed his opinion that the Algerian government bore some responsibility for the violence occurring in the country, Foreign Minister Vedrine declared he had no doubt about the official version. These differences do not conceal a substantial support of the Algerian government, but they do not make it easier for the EU to articulate its own position on this issue.

In the Gulf, French policy has (or had) been marked by good relations with Iraq. The former French defense minister Chévenement went so far as to declare, in February 1990, that the development of the Hussein missile was a factor enhancing stability in the region of the Gulf. This position has not been officially repudiated: Védrine remarked that there is a difference between Iraq in the 1970s and the 1980s, and the same country in the 1990s, and that the change in French foreign policy was caused by the occupation of Kuwait in August 1990.

As far as the Israeli-Palestinian peace process is concerned, it was apparent during Chirac's visit to the Palestinian Territories in the Fall of 1996 that he wanted his country to play a more visible role in the diplomatic process in the Middle East. When Chirac took the floor in front of the Palestinian Legislative Council and Yasir Arafat, he spoke as though he were speaking to the representatives of a fully sovereign and democratic country.[18] In his speech he accepted most of the Palestinian positions, and underlined the importance of the development of Palestinian institutions and of the creation of a Palestinian state. These outspoken statements were certainly not contradictory with the declaratory policy of the EU, but the decision to take such a clear stand was in contrast with the low profile adopted at that moment by the EU.

Spain. In the Euro-Mediterranean context, the role of Spain has been conditioned by its interest in the Maghreb, both political and economic. Spanish-Moroccan relations have been always shadowed by the question of the enclaves of Ceuta and Melilla, and by the objective concurrence between Spanish and Moroccan agricultural products. Nevertheless "Spain's long-term interest did not necessarily coincide with the short-term interest of the producers. In short, one could not reduce Hispano-Moroccan relations simply to a discussion about tomatoes."[19]

The importance for Spain of a Mediterranean policy has always been reflected, since Franco's death and her access into the EC, by Spanish activism to implement a European framework for the Mediterranean.

Britain. British foreign policy has been oscillating in the last few years. The problem of the identity of British foreign policy in this area is as old as the decision to retreat east of Suez. This decision implied giving up a direct independent role in the Near East and the Gulf. Often in this area influence was exerted by means or in cooperation with American power, and sometimes by means of international organizations. However, conservative prime ministers always appraised the preferential relationship with Washington more valuable than any kind of independent initiative in the area or European cooperation. This has changed, at least in declarations, with the Blair government and the appointment of Cook as foreign minister. This is particularly clear if you compare the reaction of Jeremy Rifkin, foreign minister in the Major cabinet, to the visit to Israel and the Palestinian Territories of the French President Chirac, and the initiatives of Robin Cook in the spring of 1998. It is well-known that Rifkin evaluated Chirac's initiative during his visit as "romantic," and added that "it endangers the American role in the peace process."[20] In this connection it must be noted that he considered a Palestinian state as a viable option, and this could be considered as an evolution in British foreign policy, which was perhaps brought about by a kind of "European drag."

The Labor foreign minister Robin Cook took a much tougher stance, especially with respect to the issue of settlements, and in particular the settlement of Jebel Abu Ghneim/Har Homa.[21] During his visit, he confirmed that his concern over Israeli settlement policy was shared by the EU members. Robin Cook's attitude was obviously a consequence of the European role he was performing, but also apparently reflected a break with respect to his predecessor Rifkin's positions.

Nevertheless, as far as the Gulf is concerned, British governments have so far been very close to U.S. statements and actions. The question is whether this can be considered contradictory with a British *nouvelle vague* aimed at creating an increasing European integration in the area of security and foreign policy.

Germany. The German[22] approach to the Middle East and to the relation with Arab countries has been determined since the foundation of the republic by different and sometimes conflicting factors.[23] On one side the historical guilt with respect to the Jewish people has made German-Israeli relations distinctive. They were marked at the beginning by the question of reparations due to Israel as the representative of the Jewish people. This made the traditionally good relations with Arab countries tense, and Arab countries played a peripheral role in German foreign policy, even though they grew more important as energy raw materials suppliers.

Nevertheless, after the substantial failure of German Middle East policy and the change in government in the Federal Republic of Germany (FRG) in the 1960s, the Palestinian question played a more relevant role. The new policy was defined as characterized by *Ausgewogenheit* (balance).

From this point of view, self-determination, which was requested for the Germans, could not be denied to the Palestinians. The expression "right of the Palestinian people for self-determination" was for the first time endorsed by the FRG in 1974, at a General Assembly of the U.N. (vote for a declaration). It is interesting that the German position was charged with unilaterality—before 1969 in favor of Israel, and in the 1970s and later in favor of the Palestinians.

Things did not change much with the end of the Cold War, the Gulf War, and the beginning of the peace process.[24] Germany follows a two-track policy, German and European. Whereas there can be reasonable doubts about the European character of the foreign policy of Bonn in some areas, like the Balkans, it is undoubtable that in the Middle East a fairly integrated approach is taken. In many respects there is both a domestic and a foreign policy focus, both in subregional and functional issues.

Another serious issue contributing to the determination of German policies is the presence of relevant Turkish and Kurdish communities of immigrants in Germany. The German government must always keep a delicate and sometimes precarious balance. This was clear during the crisis triggered by the arrival of the Kurdish leader Abdallah Ocalan in Italy and his arrest. The German government did not ask for extradition, even though the German magistracy had called for his arrest. The trial of Ocalan in Germany would have implied a confrontation between the Kurdish and Turkish communities in Germany, with relevant consequences on domestic policy, from the point of view of order and security, and foreign policy (German-Turkish relations). This combination of domestic and foreign policy is the primary reason for the German approach to the issues of Islam, fundamentalism and a relevant permanent Muslim community in Germany.

The EC and the Middle East.

At the beginning of this chapter it is important to note how European positions with respect to the conflict evolved, until the Venice Declaration and its further specifications. The start of change can be located in the oil crisis after the

October (Kippur/Ramadan) War in 1973, and the increasing differentiation of European and American interests.

In a declaration released just after the war (November 6, 1973), EC states agreed that a just peace had to take into account the legitimate rights of the Palestinians, that it was not admissible that territories are taken by force, and that Israel should terminate the military occupation of the territories taken during the Six-Day War. Together with these statements, EC states always stressed the necessity of a global approach to peace in the Middle East, and consequently they expressed doubts with respect to the Camp David process. Nevertheless, EC states did not intend to transform the differences between themselves and the United States into a full-fledged transatlantic crisis.

The ensuing Euro-Arab dialogue substantially failed, mainly because Europe was basically interested in oil supplies, and Arab countries in a dramatic change in the European attitude with respect to the Palestinian problem. More precisely, one of the main obstacles was the acknowledgement of the PLO.

The process of evolution of European positions and of differentiation of European and American interests and views led in the following decade to the Venice declaration that was issued by the European Council after a 2-day conference in Venice on June 13, 1980:

> The time has come to promote the recognition and implementation of the two principles universally accepted by the international community: the right to existence and to security of all the states in the region, including Israel, and justice for all the peoples, which implies the recognition of the legitimate rights of the Palestinian people.
>
> A just solution must finally be found to the Palestinian problem, which is not simply one of refugees. The Palestinian people, which is conscious of existing as such, must be placed in a condition, by an appropriate process defined in the framework of the comprehensive peace settlement, to exercise fully its right to self-determination. These principles apply to

all parties concerned, and thus to the Palestinian people, and to the PLO, which have to be associated with the negotiations.

Other points which would mark the European attitude in the following years were the call for the end of the occupation of Palestinian territories, and a firm stance against unilateral initiatives in Jerusalem and settlement policy. The position of the EC and of the European Political Cooperation did not change in the years following the Venice declaration, and was possibly strengthened after the failures of the Israeli attempts to create a leadership alternative to the PLO and the beginning of the intifada.

In Madrid, Hans van der Broek, Minister of Foreign Affairs of the Netherlands and acting President of the Council of Ministers, confirmed the Community's views on the peace process in the Middle East:

> ... The Twelve consider it of the utmost importance that the parties have committed themselves to the road map of this conference: direct negotiations on the basis of resolutions 242 and 338 ... The political negotiations are to be underpinned by multilateral negotiations on regional cooperation in fields of mutual interests. We look forward and expect to be working closely with all the parties to ensure progress along these lines ... The Twelve's guiding principles throughout the negotiating process are those which have since long governed our position. They remain unchanged. These principles are Security Council resolution 242 and 338, the principle of land for peace, the right of all states in the region, including Israel, to live within secure and recognized boundaries and the proper expression of the right to self-determination of the Palestinian people.

In van der Broek's speech you can find a functionalist and rationalist attitude that was partially successful in the process of European integration, and the illusion that a process modelled on the Conference for Security and Cooperation in Europe could be started in Madrid. As we see below, the same functionalist attitude characterized the approach to multilateral talks. Unfortunately, these illusions have been so far doomed because of the many difficulties in the Palestinian and in the Syrian track.

Between Madrid, Oslo and Barcelona.

After the peace conference was convened in Madrid at the end of October 1991, two processes started: the better known bilateral talks, and the multilateral track.[25] As is well-known, bilateral talks brought about peace between Israel and Jordan, whereas the present course of the Israeli-Palestinian process took other paths after the success of the left-wing coalition in the Israeli election of May 1992 and secret contacts between PLO and Israel in Scandinavia just before the elections.

The multilateral track was structured into five working groups, respectively on arms control and regional security, water, environment, refugees, and economic development. Other multilateral processes developed in the area, like the Middle East and North Africa economic summits, and after 1995 the Barcelona process. It makes sense to ask whether this multitude of multilateral processes has been an advantage or a hindrance.

The idea of the multilateral track is grounded in a functionalist conception of international cooperation, that is, presumed to start from "technical" issue areas. The cooperation in those issue areas would induce the states to put aside or to solve their "high politics" problems. The dynamics and explication and denomination of the processes of cooperation is variable according to the various schools of thought of functionalism and neo-functionalism. However, the expectation is that the advantages of cooperation and the mutual learning and understanding in "lower politics" or technical issue areas would create the climate for agreements in security.

The multilateral talks had basically two aims. The first was obviously to try to start cooperation in sensitive, but in some cases "technical," areas such as water resources and to extend it to more sensitive and "political" ones. This first objective reflected the above quoted "functionalist" mentality. The other aim was drawing the international community, and particularly the EU, into the process with a consolation prize, but excluding the EU from the more relevant—both from the political and mediatic point of view—bilateral talks, *chausse gardé* of the United States.

The EU had to run the Regional Economic Development (RED) Group. Meetings of this group took place in Brussels in May 1992, in Paris in October 1992, in Rome in May 1993, in Copenhagen in October 1993, and in Rabat and in Bonn in January 1994. After the Declaration of Principles in the Copenhagen round, every part agreed on the necessity to intensify the work of the RED Group to ensure it would not be marginalized. The EU tried to encourage the various delegations about long-term economic relations and about possible institutional mechanisms, processes, and frameworks to support the efforts towards regional cooperation. After Rabat, a monitoring committee was established, and after that a secretariat, which had to be based in Amman. After the 1996 Israeli elections, the multilateral track (and the RED Group) virtually ceased their activities, and it is difficult to point out any single important issue where an achievement can be found. But that was linked to progress in bilateral talks.

In the diplomatic process following the Madrid conference, functionalist dynamics have not been able to work (even approximately) because security problems have so far been of the existential type (or are perceived to be so) for all actors, and especially for those at the core of the problem, i.e., Israelis and Palestinians.

The European Role after the Establishment of the National Palestinian Authority.

After the establishment of the Palestinian National Authority (PNA) the activity of the EU and of EU states was marked by economic aid and (sometimes un-)diplomatic missions. If you look at the political and diplomatic activity in this period of time (at least until the appointment of Moratinos in October 1996), there is not much new: many visits of Euro-troikas to the Middle East and statements confirming the usual position of the EU. Some of them, like those concerning settlement policy and Jerusalem, were not particularly agreeable for Israeli governments. However, condemnation of terrorist acts has always been uncompromising, Arafat was often requested to fight terrorism more effectively, and calls for the end of the boycott to Israel were a must in most European declarations.

European economic role, on the contrary, has been so far relevant: 45 percent of the aid to the Palestinian Territories comes from the EU as such (not from member countries). For example, in the years 1990-91, 60 millions of Ecu (mecu) were supplied by the EU as development aid. In the year 1991, 43 percent of the total aid to the United Nations Relief and Works Agency for Palestine Refugees (UNRWA) in the Middle East was provided by the EU. In 1993, 15 Palestinian universities and five administrations received 75 mecu. For the years 1994-98, 500 mecu were deliberated in 1993, and that sum was later increased. In April 1994 the Council decided to support the establishment of the Palestinian police with a sum of 10 mecu, though this decision was characterized by formal problems in the decisionmaking process between Council, Commission, and the Parliament. After the Taba/Washington agreement the European role in Palestinian elections was absolutely essential, with financial (14 mecu) and political support given by the presence of 300 observers, 30 of whom were members of the European Parliament.

The economic support of the EU can be considered as an effect and a cause—at the same time—of the European concern for the peace process. On one side there is a wide agreement that economic development in the Palestinian territories is an important factor of stabilization. On the other side, any stalemate in the process puts Palestinian economy under stress for closures of the Palestinian areas or any kind of constraint, and this makes European continuing aid (and financial burden) necessary.

At the same time (especially with the Rabin/Peres government) there were bilateral agreements signed by the EU and Israel, such as the agreement of November 11, 1995, for a political dialogue on a regular basis, economic cooperation and the establishment of a free trade area (according to the Barcelona spirit), and agreement on telecommunications.

This economic role notwithstanding, the EU has not so far been able to develop an adequate political role in the process. The reasons for this diminished role are manifold. They can be traced back to three main factors: the attitude decided in Barcelona with respect to existing frameworks, the U.S. purpose to maintain leadership in the process, and the Israeli and (to a lesser extent) Arab perceptions of the European role.

As is well-known, the European approach to existing frameworks for conflict resolution has been not to interfere with already existing diplomatic processes. This has caused the noninterference with the Oslo process, which started in a sense even before Labor success in 1992 elections.[26] This European attitude was reinforced by the American will not to share the leadership in areas perceived as absolutely vital to U.S. interests. Moreover, U.S. administrations have often perceived European perspectives as different in many respects, particularly as far as the attitude towards alleged terrorist organizations or pariah states is concerned. For example, many European governments and the EC had relations with the PLO, even when the United States considered it officially as a terrorist organization, and the differences with respect to Iran or Libya are well-known.

The problem of Israeli perception is not related only to the Venice declaration and "Arab policies" of some European countries and the EU.[27] The historical collective memory of the Jewish people represents Europe as the continent of anti-semitism, pogroms, and the Shoah. Moreover, European reactions to the intifada were perceived by Israelis (and sometimes were really) as absolutely disproportioned. In European media the use of words such as genocide and extermination tended to equate Israeli behavior with respect to Palestinians with the Nazi treatment of Jews. The Israeli public opinion, on the other side, tended to generalize European exaggerations and "bad taste" (to make use of understatement), and often attributed to Europeans the will to "normalize" the Jews and so get rid of any guilt feeling.

These perceptions have been made stronger by a behavior which is perceived as a double standard, i.e., the fact that heavier human rights violations in Arab countries (and later, sometimes, in the Palestinian territories) have not been criticized with the same eagerness marking criticisms against Israel. Obviously these perceptions do not make it easier for the Israelis to overcome the thought that all this is a modern variety of the old—even though of different types—European anti-semitism.

As is the case for the behavior of the British administration during the mandate, Arab and Palestinian perceptions are in a sense the mirror image of Israeli ones.[28] First, often, especially in the public opinion, there is little—yet increasing—awareness of differences between European countries and the United States, and complaints are made against "the West" as a whole. Moreover, even those making a difference object to Europeans that there is no coherence between statements and actions, since declarations would imply a tougher stance, and possibly economic sanctions against Israel, which has always been rejected by European states and the EU. In this respect, the Arabs charge Western countries with a double standard, because, for example, Iraq is much more heavily punished than Israel for not complying with U.N. Security Council resolutions.

A frequent criticism is the lack of a real common European foreign policy. This criticism is stronger when divergent attitudes emerge, as in the case of the Chirac-Rifkind controversy.

In order to overcome the political and perceptional difficulties in the implementation of a European role, the Council appointed Miguel Angel Moratinos as a "special envoy" to the Middle East on October 28, 1996. His mandate is to have contacts with all the interested parties—the countries of the region, the United States, and the international organizations—observe the evolution, and contribute to the implementation of the agreements.

The reactions to Moratinos' appointment were diverse. The Americans did not fully agree. The U.S. special envoy disagreed, stating in a quintessential diplomatic style:

> I think that it is important when you are in a delicate stage of a negotiating process for all those who want to be helpful to find the best ways to be supportive. Right now, I think that it is generally agreed, not only by the party, but by others, that the effort that we are making is the one they support.[29]

On the Palestinian side, PLO representative in Brussels Leyla Shaheed declared:

> The U.S. and Europe have different opinions about how to develop and support the peace process. The European position concerning the Palestinian issue and other matters in the region is far more advanced than that of America... There are European countries which... call clearly for a Palestinian state... Israel prefers to deal with the Arabs through the Americans and therefore, does not want a European role, because the European position toward peace is similar to the Arab and Palestinian one.[30]

The record of Moratinos' activity is generally positive, but it has been marked by low profile. Even his interviews often reflect this; for example, a recent interview to a Palestinian weekly is a masterpiece of diplomatic low profile. This does not mean that his activity has been judged as insignificant. On the contrary, his mediation has in many situations contributed to keep channels of communications alive. Israeli attitudes, which were at the beginning cautious, became later more favorable.

Nevertheless, the usual problems remain on the table. For example, in March 1999 the usual question concerning Jerusalem was raised again by a note of the Israeli foreign minister Ariel Sharon concerning the Orient House in East Jerusalem, expressing the Israeli view that European representatives cannot visit it because PNA institutions are not allowed in Jerusalem. The European position, confirmed in the occasion by the German ambassador, is that the Orient House is a PLO, and not a PNA, institution, and that East Jerusalem is by no means a part of Israel. This only makes clear that even sharp differences have not so far been overcome.

Final Considerations.

At the conclusion of the chapter I must give an answer—at least tentative—to the questions posed at its beginning. First, there is not much difference with respect to perceived threats to security and objectives of foreign and security policy. A difference can be made for the Gulf, but this has more to do with transatlantic relations than with real perceptions of threat. Second, a consensus is emerging, at least with respect to some important issues, such as the Middle East peace process. As far as problems like Algeria, the divisions between different schools of thought seem to be rather transnational than national in character.

The obstructions are provided more by nationally located bureaucratic interests than by clear and well-founded national interests: diplomacies do not want to share their decisionmaking processes, military personnel do not want to be reduced or submitted to different chains of command, and so on. Moreover, the coordination of different national traditions is not easy, especially when some actors want always to stand in the first rows.

Whereas, as written above, a consensus is emerging in the area of the Israeli-Palestinian peace process and, generally speaking, of Israeli-Arab relations, things are more difficult with respect to the Gulf and Algeria.

In the first case, the U.S. policy of double containment is not shared by all Europeans. Differences within the EU became apparent during the Anglo-American attack of Iraq in December 1998, when Blair was almost totally isolated from the Continent (with the exception of the Spanish leader, Aznar). In this case the problem is related to three main factors. First, Britain's attempt to maintain both its traditional relation with the United States and its effort to foster a more coordinated European foreign policy. This double track is probably perceived by Blair and his foreign minister Cook as not contradictory. Maybe it is not in the short run, at least formally, but it cannot be sustained in the long run. Second, the fact that the Gulf is outside the geographical scope of any common enterprise of the EU; it is in the Middle East, but outside the range of Barcelona. Third, the most important factor is probably the stagnation of CFSP, which will be the subject of the concluding remarks.

As far as Algeria is concerned, the difficulties French governments have so far met in dealing with this conflict are magnified in the European case.[31] Obviously all EU states are torn between the possible charge of neo-colonialist interference on one side, and, on the other, the humanitarian horror of slaughters, and the more political and security related concern for the possible spread of unrest and terrorism to Europe. Troikas and delegations of the Parliament carried out missions in Algeria, and met the President and members of the government and of the Parliament. Nevertheless all the institutional instances of the EU have so far refrained from any role of mediation between the parties. This is the picture emerging, for example, from the meeting of the EU foreign ministers in Luxembourg in November 1997,[32] or from the visit of the delegation of the European Parliament to Algeria (February 8-12, 1998).[33]

In this context, it is not possible even to outline the possible causes of what has been called "Europaralis," i.e., the stagnating process of a CFSP.[34] Certainly one problem of the EU is that it had to cope just after the Maastricht summit with its worst nightmare, i.e., the war in former Yugoslavia. However, the lack of unity with respect to the Gulf and the pretense of national bureaucracies or individual personalities to play their own role, or to go their own way in single issues or conflicts, are all elements that make European policies less credible. Moreover, the perspective reduction of the Barcelona process to agreements for economic openings does not generate the momentum necessary for a strengthened role in the Mediterranean and the Middle East.

ENDNOTES - CHAPTER 16

1. Question 693/93 by Alex Langer, *et al.*, at the European Parliament.

2. The Barcelona process is only referred to in this paper, as it is discussed in Roberto Aliboni's contribution to this publication.

3. This could or should be an increasing factor even in U.S. domestic policy, but the impact of the Muslim community in the United States is still negligible with respect to its size.

4. In 1993 France had a GNP of U.S.$1,289,054,000 (U.S.$22,360 per capita), whereas Italy had a GNP of U.S.$1,134,800,000,000 (U.S.$19,620 per capita).

5. See Jutta Weldes, "Constructing National Interest," *European Journal of International Relations, Vol. 2, No. 3, Autumn 1996*, p. 275.

6. See Antonio Varsori, *L'Italia nelle relazioni internazionali dal 1943 al 1992 (Italy in International Relations from 1943 to 1992)*, Roma: Laterza, 1998.

7. See Piero Craveri, *La Repubblica dal 1958 al 1992 (The Republic from 1958 to 1992)*, Torino: UTET, 1995.

8. A difference was made by some erratic references, on the socialist side, to a Palestinian-Jordanian confederation.

9. See Ennio Caretto, "Martino: saremo piu filo-israeliani" ("Martino: we shall be more pro-Israeli") *Il Corriere della sera*, Vol. 25, No. 5., 1994, p. 7.

10. See Lorenzo Cremonesi, *Il Corriere della sera*, October 19, 1994, p. 7.

11. See "Le sabbie mobili e la regina di Saba" ("Mobile Sands and the Queen of Sheba"), *Limes*, Vol. 4, No. 1.

12. 5.2 percent preferred the Israelis, 8.9 percent the Palestinians, 14.6 none of them.

13. See Arrigo Levi, "Il tricolore in Terra Santa?" ("The Tri-color in the Holy Land?"), *Il corriere della sera*, March 4, 1997, p. 8. Levi's opinions concerning Jewish-Italian and Israeli-Italian relations are not shared by all observers, especially in the Italian Jewish community.

14. See Franco Venturini, "Sì al dialogo con Irak e Libia" ("Yes to Dialogue with Iraq and Libya"), *Il corriere della sera*, July 17, 1997, p. 13.

15. See Hayète Chérigui, *La politique méditerranéenne de la France: entre diplomatie collective et leadership*, L'Harmattan, Paris 1997, pp. 13-15.

16. "De l'utilité de la France" ("On the Utility of France," interview with Hubert Védrine, French Minister for Foreign Affairs), *Politique internationale*, No. 78, Winter 1997-98, p. 44.

17. See Ulla Holm, "Algeria: France's Untenable Engagement," *Mediterranean Politics*, Vol. 3, No. 2, Autumn 1998, p. 104; Paul-Marie de La Gorce, "La France et le Maghreb" ("France and the Maghreb"), *Politique Étrangère*, Vol. 60, No. 4, Winter 1995/96, p. 927.

18. See "Voyage au Proche-Orient—Discours prononcé par le président de la République, devant le Conseil législatif palestinien" ("Journey to the Near East, Speech given by the President of the Republic in front of the Palestinian Legislative Council"), *La politique Étrangere de la France*, 1996, p. 245-247.

19. Richard Gillespie, "Spanish Protagonismo and the Euro-Med Partnership Initiative," in Richard Gillespie, ed., *The Euro-Mediterranean Partnership. Political and Economoic Perspective*, London: Frank Cass, 1997, p. 42.

20. See Mohammed Shaker Ahmed, "Chirac the Romantic," *The Jerusalem Times*, Vol. 3, No. 143, November 1, 1996, p. 5.; Vol. 5, No. 215, March 20, 1998, p. 1.

21. See Elias M. Zananiri, "Cook condemns Israel's settlement policy,"*The Jerusalem Times*, Vol. 5, No. 215, March 20, 1998, p. 1.

22. I deal here only with the FRG, even though triangular relations between FRG, GDR, and third countries played a role, especially during the Adenauer and Erhardt era, i.e., the 1950s and the 1960s.

23. See Friedemann Büttner and Peter Hünseler, "Die politischen Beziehungen zwischen der Bundesrepublik Deutschlands und den Arabischen Staaten," in Karl Kaiser and Udo Steinbach, eds., *Deutsch-Arabische Beziehungen*, München: Oldenbourg, 1981, pp. 111-152.

24. See Udo Steinbach, "Interesse und Handlungsmöglichkeiten. Deutschland in Nahen und Mittleren Osten," in Karl Kaiser, Hanns W. Maull, and Joachim Krause, eds., *Deutschlands neue Aussenpolitik. Bd 3 Interessen und Strategien*, München: Oldenbourg, 1996, pp. 189-194.

25. On the multilateral track, see Joel Peters, "The Barcelona Process and Arab-Israeli Multilatral Talks: Competition or Convergence?," conference paper, Workshop of the Bertelsmann Foundation, "The Political Role of the EU in the Middle East," Frankfurt, October 26-28, 1997.

26. See Mahmud Abbas (Abu Mazen), *Through Secret Channels*, Reading: Garnet Publishing, 1995.

27. See Shlomo Ben Ami, "Europa y el conflicto de oriente Próximo" ("Europe and the Middle East Conflict"), *Política Exterior*, Vol. 66, No. 12, November/December 1998, pp. 97-111; Joseph Alpher, "The Political Role of the EU in the Middle East: Israeli Aspirations," conference paper, Workshop of the Bertelsmann Foundation, "The Political Role of the EU in the Middle East," Frankfurt, October 26-28, 1997.

28. See, for example, Abdel Monem Said Aly, "The Political Role of the EU in the Middle East: An Arab Perspective," conference paper, Workshop of the Bertelsmann Foundation, "The Political Role of the EU in the Middle East," Frankfurt, October 26-28, 1997.

29. See *The Jerusalem Times*, Vol. 3, No. 142, October 25, 1996.

30. *Ibid.*

31. See for example, Claire Spencer, "Algeria: France's Disarray and Europe's Conundrum," in Barbara A. Robertson, ed., *The Middle East and Europe. The Power Deficit*, London: Routledge, 1998, pp. 170-183.

32. See Andrea Bonanni, "L'Europa cerca il modo per 'aiutare l'Algeria'" ("Europe Looks For a Way to Help Algeria"), *Il corriere della sera*, October 26, 1997.

33. See DOC\CR\346\346221, PE 226.130, March 3, 1998.

34. A whole literature on the subject is flourishing. See, for example, Jan Zielonka, *Europaralisis*, Basingstoke: Macmillan, 1998.

CHAPTER 17

THE SPIRIT OF ETERNAL NEGATION: RUSSIA'S HOUR IN THE MIDDLE EAST

Stephen J. Blank

After the Cold War many believed that the United States could act more unilaterally and more deeply in the Middle East to resolve existing conflicts without running the great risks stemming from superpower competition.[1] Today that hope is in danger of frustration. One reason is that super or great power competition has returned to the area. Since 1994, Russia has shown increasing determination to regain something like its traditional regional role. Certainly the Middle East's inherent proclivities for conflict have facilitated Russia's return to the area and frustrated U.S. policy. But Russia's overall international situation and perception of it, as well as the structure of Russian domestic politics, present even more compelling motives for Moscow's revived policy. Russian Middle East policy results from the intersection of global, regional, and domestic forces, an interaction that must be analyzed to make sense of Moscow's policies.

Historically the non-European region most penetrated by foreign intervention, the Middle East's internal cleavages still lead foreign governments into repeated involvement in its affairs and rivalries, for two main reasons. First, this foreign intervention certifies the interveners' international role, status, and power. That certification is as much a weapon in those governments' domestic policies as it is in their foreign policy. By enhancing their foreign standing, governments obtain greater leverage with which to maneuver amid shifting domestic coalitions as well as abroad. Often those coalitions add a strong foreign policy component to their basic domestic orientation.[2]

The second reason has often been to use the status gained by being seen as a credible regional player to overturn the local and "global" status quos and realize thereby a government's local, regional, and global strategic interests. The Middle East remains an area where a state, aspiring to a higher status because it is blocked elsewhere, can act with reasonable impunity to upset the status quo when a crisis emerges and force its way into the counsels of the mighty. The Middle East now enjoys the role the Balkans played in world politics before 1914 and remains the true seat of today's "Eastern Question" in international politics.

But today's Middle East is not that of the Cold War. Many analysts now accept that the linkages between the former Soviet republics of the Transcaucasus and Central Asia with the classical Middle East are reshaping the Middle East's definition. Today, Middle Eastern players, notably Israel, Turkey, and Iran, act resolutely throughout Central Asia and Transcaucasia, thereby erasing the former dividing lines between them.[3]

Consequently, Russia's Middle Eastern policy emerges out of numerous opportunities and dangers, if not threats, emanating from the region, from world politics in general, and from domestic sources. Even as Russia's regional policy and its new diplomatic offensives realize these two purposes of foreign intervention, they are also responses to this combination of threat and opportunity. Undoubtedly Moscow will continue to seek to enlarge its role in the area, especially under the new government led by Yevgeny Primakov. Earlier, as Foreign Minister, Primakov pulled off notable diplomatic victories with regard to Iraq, mainly due to U.S. incompetence and ineptitude rather than Russian power. The U.S. fiasco in the crises over U.N. inspections of Iraq's weapons of mass destruction (WMD) capabilities to prevent their reappearance in 1997-98 seemingly highlighted Moscow's role as a potential equal or aspirant to that role vis-à-vis Washington in the Middle East. As a result, the sanctions regime will come under constant pressure and might even collapse after 1999, even though U.S. intelligence maintains that Iraq could restore a credible WMD and missile capability in the region within 1-3 years after that.[4] While Russia surely won great temporary victories in 1997-98, the lasting strategic benefits are harder to discern.

The Forces Behind Russian Policy.

Moscow's regional policies constitute part of a broader quest to enlarge its domestic room for maneuver and international status. Primakov has often proclaimed that Russia must have a global role and policy. As President Boris Yeltsin's 1996 action policy stated, Russia should conduct a global, i.e., "multivector," foreign policy, leading to a situation where its word would be decisive in world affairs, and no major decision in international affairs could be reached without Russia. Primakov even asserts that Russia's return to global prominence is "as a natural desire in the multipolar world."[5] In pursuit of these objectives, Russia has intervened diplomatically and shipped military systems in Cyprus, in the Arab-Israeli peace process, in the sanctions regime against Iraq, and in support of Iran's political ambitions. It has asserted itself regionally and globally to force Washington and skeptical local governments, e.g., Israel, to take it seriously as an equal to the United States. In the Gulf it also seeks to fracture the U.S.-built alliance system and leverage the congruence between its and France's Middle Eastern policies to affect the European and global chessboard. As *Le Nouvel Observateur* reported, one of French President Jacques Chirac's confidants stated that if France wants to play an international role, it benefits from the existence of a strong Russia which helps it reaffirm itself as a major power "free from any complex and ready to play the card of stability." Translated into clear English (or French in the original) this means that:

In the Middle East both countries want to reactivate old friendships and offer Arab and Israeli leaders a chance to talk to someone else than Washington. France can only do this by acting as the EU's political driving force, and Russia has been helping it to gain this status. As for Russia, it can only achieve this goal by making sure it does not appear to be scheming against Western interests, a risk it can avoid through consultation with France.[6]

The implicit, and sometimes explicit, threat is always that Moscow might then exploit its formidable capabilities for disrupting the Middle Eastern and even European status quo to make life uncomfortable for its opposite numbers.

Moscow must invoke the specter of its trouble-making capabilities and even on occasion actually deploy them because it operates in a highly unfavorable climate in the Middle East and more generally on the world stage. The most profound, overarching, and inescapable threat, and one that grips Moscow on a daily basis, is that Russia is and for some time has been a failing state. As of August 1998, one may even say it became a failed state. This failure would include the total breakdown of the center's ability to raise taxes, disburse funds, enforce laws, govern the outlying provinces, and maintain a monopoly on the legitimate use of force throughout the state.[7] By whatever standard of state failure one measures, Russia is uncomfortably close to a perfect correspondence with those standards.[8] The specter of state disintegration due to those factors constantly weighs upon the calculations of Russia's policymakers and political community.[9] Thus while we in the United States might argue that the post-Soviet picture was the most benign threat environment in recorded Russian history, prominent Russian analysts concluded by 1993 that threats abounded everywhere and the situation was steadily worsening.[10] Hence the security issue or dilemma that drives policy towards the new Middle East is now as much inside Russia's borders as it is an external threat.

Concurrently, Russia also discerns multiple external risks that shape its policy. The primary foreign threat that Yeltsin and Primakov, not to mention others, invoke is to Russia's integrity.[11] One reason why Russia's integrity is at risk is because Russia's deimperialization and democratization remain incomplete. Prominent politicians still argue that the former Soviet republics will return to some form of complete integration with Moscow on Moscow's terms.[12] Therefore Moscow still cannot fully accept either the new borders of the Commonwealth of Independent States (CIS) or of the Baltic states, as well as the notion that the "successor states" have or should have the same sovereignty as other states. A Brezhnev doctrine for the former Soviet Union still haunts the Kremlin's imagination. One major reason for continuing to pursue the goal of integration—the priority in foreign policy—is precisely to prevent any further internal separatism within Russia.[13] This is a classic attribute of an imperial policy to divert attention from internal weakness. Yet it takes place where Russia's military and economic policy instruments are relatively useless.

Therefore, Russian policy or strategy towards the Middle East is essentially negative. It is haunted by the prospect of any foreign power getting a lasting foothold there, and from there into the CIS. Like Goethe's *Mephistopheles*, it incarnates the spirit of eternal negation. Russia until now has been able occasionally to obstruct or frustrate foreign policies of other governments, but it has failed spectacularly to create anything of a positive lasting nature abroad. For Moscow, the CIS and the adjacent Middle East cannot be allowed to come under foreign influence. We can characterize the Kremlin's policy as strategic denial across the board, in economics, diplomacy, and military policy. Moscow discerns threats of varying intensity, but always of substance from *any* consolidated Western presence in the CIS or in the Middle East which would open the way to that presence in the CIS. Sergei Arutinov, a renowned ethnologist in Moscow argues that,

A Turco-Israeli close cooperation is a positive fact from the world-wide point of view. But generally it would worsen Russian-Turkish and Russian-Israeli relations. It may also provoke the reemerging of anti-Semitism in Russia. It will evoke much anxiety in Armenia too. First, a mutually acceptable solution about Karabakh must be found and only then a Turkish-Israeli cooperation may start to be realized in the Near East and the former USSR states. Otherwise, it may trigger Russian-Iraqi, Russian Iranian, Armenian-Iranian rapprochements, push Armenian extremists in the world to a cooperation with Palestinian extremists.[14]

Moscow often employed a similar argument against NATO enlargement. However, the assertion that any foreign advance will undo Russia's friendship towards and identification with the West only reflects how shallow that friendship and identification are. Likewise, in the Middle East, Moscow's policy presents a similar negativity. For example, Primakov has repeatedly complained about Russia being marginalized in the peace process between Israel and the Arabs. Instead, he argues that the U.S. monopoly should give way to greater participation by Russia and the European Union (EU). Yet, at the same time, Moscow makes wholly unrealistic demands that the peace process be a comprehensive and simultaneous affair, with peace being made with all the remaining belligerents at once and is busy arming all of Israel's enemies, Iran, Syria, and even covertly Iraq. Naturally, Israel rejects Russia's participation on this basis. Meanwhile Primakov went so far as to boast, when the peace process appeared to be dead, that he was content not to share the U.S. failure.[15] This attitude of simultaneous complaint, yet refusal to participate constructively and offer useful ideas, typifies Moscow's overall policy.

This program of strategic denial becomes particularly clear when Moscow confronts not just Israel's or Turkey's presence in the Transcaucasus and Central Asia, but also Washington's and NATO's appearance there. The presence of huge deposits of oil and gas in Kazakstan, Turkmenistan, and Azerbaijan has lured American and Western investors, and now their governments, into the Transcaucasus and Central Asia in such a way as to make these areas increasing hotbeds of competition with Russia and to pose what Moscow sees as a mortal threat to its vital interests in integration and internal stability.[16] Would-be geopoliticians like Zbigniew Brzezinski argue that it is a vital U.S. interest to so firmly implant itself in these states as to exclude Russian influence there.[17] Whether or not this is the proper U.S. objective, Washington is following through on this policy, thus arousing Moscow's deepest fears.[18]

Yet precisely because Moscow views these areas' full sovereignty and its consolidation as a threat to its survival as a state, this Western presence, whether American, Turkish, or Israeli, is unsettling at best and a major threat at worst. This only shows the continuing hold of zero-sum thinking over Russian policy. If Russia's neighbors are fully secure and cannot be threatened by Russia, due to other states' strong interest in them and their own internal stability, then Russia itself is threatened. As U.S. analyst Alvin Rubinstein observed,

> Clearly, any strategic vision worthy of critical examination must be rooted in historical context. With respect to Central Asia, this means a view of the region as a vast borderland between Russia and the Middle East. Any policy that contributes to the viability of the new republics and ensures their non-threatening character to Russia must, by virtue of consolidating this strategic buffer zone, redound to the long-term security of Turkey, Iran, and the Arab states of the Persian Gulf region.[19]

The U.S. regional policies are closely tied to NATO's enlargement and the dual containment of Iran and Iraq. U.S. writers increasingly call the CIS part of the "greater Middle East" and the "strategic fulcrum of the future" or the "strategic high ground," due to its energy resources.[20] Robert Blackwill and Michael Stuermer claim that "no Western power has been safe without some measure of influence or control over the southern and eastern shores of the Mediterranean."[21] This area now includes the Transcaspian, since Washington and Ankara want the terminus of Transcaspian oil and gas to be Ceyhan on the Southeastern Mediterranean. Nor do U.S. officials shrink from spelling out their grander visions of the future.

Ambassador Matthew Nimetz postulates the growing importance of the Mediterranean region as a whole. Therefore, a clear U.S. commitment to remaining a military power here will markedly enhance regional security. This is true for the major NATO powers as well: France, Germany, Italy, Great Britain, Spain, Greece, and Turkey.[22] To maintain regional security, NATO must not only integrate the entire region into the Western economy and foster the development of "pluralistic institutions," NATO must also grasp the military nettle.

> The Pax NATO is the only logical regime to maintain security in the traditional sense. As NATO maintains its dominant role in the Mediterranean, it must recognize a need for the expansion of its stabilizing influence in adjacent areas, particularly in Southeastern Europe, the Black Sea region (in concert, of course, with the regional powers, primarily Russia, Ukraine, Romania, Bulgaria, and Turkey) and in the Arabian/Persian Gulf. The United States must continue to play the major role in this security system. The Sixth Fleet will be the vehicle to implement this commitment for years to come, although this is something that might be reviewed some time down the road.[23]

Supposedly, Russia's views either do not count or Russia will blithely accept this outcome.

Given the centrality of energy to Russia's economy and to the West, what conclusion about NATO's future activities in the CIS and Middle East should a Russian planner or policymaker adopt when analyzing Nimetz' words or the following statement by former Secretary of State Warren Christopher and former Secretary of Defense William Perry?

> The alliance needs to adapt its military strategy to today's reality: the danger to the security of its members is not

primarily potential aggression to their collective territory, but threats to their collective interests beyond their territory. Shifting the alliance's emphasis from defense of members' territory to defense of common interests is the strategic imperative. These threats include the proliferation of weapons of mass destruction, disruption of the flow of oil, terrorism, genocidal violence, and wars of aggression in other regions that threaten to cause great disruption. To deal with such threats alliance members need to have a way to rapidly form military coalitions that can accomplish goals beyond NATO territory.[24]

Thus Russian elites, and not Primakov alone, constantly profess that they face linked challenges in Europe, the CIS, and the Middle East due to the American hegemonic drive. And from the point of view of Realpolitik, they have much justification for seeing things in this way. The problem for Primakov and his colleagues is that they apparently see the world exclusively in terms of a zero-sum game, often with the open threat of force.[25] U.S. leaders, on the other hand, see things in an entirely different and Wilsonian, or what Walter MacDougall calls a global meliorist light, so while we do not have a clash of ideologies in the old sense, fundamental approaches to international relations and politics are embroiled here in the Russo-American confrontation in the Middle East.[26]

Nor are these the only threats that Moscow faces. Russian analysts and officials habitually worry that Russia may be excluded from European and Middle Eastern decisionmaking as Washington and NATO move closer to its border. Russia may also be consigned to an economic role as a provider of raw materials and deprived of the opportunity to partake of the contemporary technological and post-industrial revolution. This would leave it as a perpetually inferior power.[27] They also worry about any form of Muslim self-assertion, whether national or religious, as a threat and often associate either of these phenomena under the terms, Wahhabism, Pan-Turkism, or Pan-Islamism, without regard for the scholarly distinctions among these phenomena.[28]

As the Afghan crisis sparked by the Taliban's victories indicates, Russia fears any spillover of any of these phenomena into Central Asia, the advent of massive refugee problems, and the involvement of its troops in containing these threats from Afghanistan. Furthermore, there is the persistent danger that some analogous kind of movement might commence in Russia itself, detach the affected area from Russian control, and spread throughout Russia, reviving fears of the state's disintegration. More dangerous, yet, is the possibility that outside sponsors like Turkey or Iran may actively encourage and support such movements.[29] Precisely because Iran could easily undertake such a policy, Russia, already in February 1992, indicated its continuing willingness to supply Iran with conventional and dual-use arms and technology sales.[30]

However, aiding Iran thusly brings Russia face to face with the prospect of such an internal threat being combined with an external threat from a Muslim regime. This could range from upheaval caused by some form of Muslim self-assertion, either religious or national, to conventional support from abroad for that group in rebellion. Or the level of threat could escalate further. If proliferation to Russia's south is allowed to go unchecked, then weapons of mass destruction could figure either as deterrents of one or both sides or as active weapons in the conflict.[31]

The following analysis captures the diversity of many of the regional threats as seen from Moscow (and not only from there).

> *Geopolitically*, the black hole of Central Asia now constitutes an expanded part of the new Middle East. *Geoculturally*, few other regions entail a nation-state border system of such potential transparency, where common and cross-border religious, ethnic, linguistic, and collective memories could act individually or jointly as destabilizing or integrating factors. From Kazakhstan to Egypt (and one could substitute Tajikistan to Algeria and Sudan-SB) dynamics of anticolonial feeling [old or new], economic underdevelopment, uneven development,

religious revivalism, arms proliferation, artificial borders, and ethnoterritorially driven conflicts are characteristic.[32]

These regional threats are complicated by the role played by the United States in its own right and as leader of several global alliances, e.g., its alliance with NATO, Israel and Turkey, all of whom are seen as encroaching on Russia's vital interests. Russian analysts take for granted that the United States wants to oust Russia from its traditional vital interests and destroy it as a great power.[33] Naturally that threat is intolerable. It is all the more intolerable because Russia harbors dreams of equality with the United States, a dream voiced by Yeltsin many times.[34] Sergei Rogov, director of the USA Institute and an advisor to the government and Foreign Ministry, has written that,

> First of all, Moscow should seek to preserve the special character of Russian-American relations. Washington should recognize the exceptional status of the Russian Federation in the formation of a new system of international relations, a role different from that which Germany, Japan, or China or any other center of power plays in the global arena.[35]

As Dmitri Trenin of the Carnegie Endowment observes, Russian analysts argue that current difficulties are transient but Russia is *entitled* to this "presidium seat" in Europe, the Middle East, Asia, and on global issues.[36] Yet any realistic analysis knows this aspiration is a dangerous illusion given Russia's weaknesses. Thus Moscow's negative policies must be calibrated so as to prevent Washington from slamming the door on Russia even as it works to frustrate U.S. policies.

However, Moscow also discerns opportunities which are seen as offsetting or that allow it to keep those threats at a distance. Within the Middle East itself, the internal ethnic rivalries within states, e.g., Kurds vs. Turkey, Palestinians vs. Israel, offer both neighbors of those states and interested outside players opportunities to interfere with and offset the host states' policies. Thus Moscow has aided the Kurds on numerous occasions, just as it has consistently supported minorities in the Transcaucasus against Baku and Tbilisi.[37] Moscow has also tried to broker a truce between rival Kurdish factions in Iraq, to bolster Saddam Hussein's regime in Baghdad, and to discomfit Ankara which regards any unified Kurdish political stance, even one across the border in Iraq, with unfeigned alarm and suspicion.[38]

A second cleavage in the Middle East is the linked series of inter-state rivalries. Iran vs. Arabs, Israel vs. Arabs, Iran vs. Israel, inter-Arab strife, now most notably in the Gulf, but also in Lebanon, for example. These regional "contradictions," to use the Soviet term, show little sign of disappearing. Few, if any, regional governments have adopted the thinking of U.S. professors with regard to international politics nor do they accept the new liberal dispensation. Security is still conceived largely in military terms. Strategic territory is still vital, zero-sum thinking and proliferation of WMD are pervasive. Uncooperative behavior is rampant and so on.[39] Naturally such behavior not only obstructs the search for resolution of regional conflicts, it also impedes U.S. efforts in its search for peace and raises the constant specter of American military engagement, as in Iraq. These contradictions facilitate the entry of a power who seeks to exploit them, through arms sales, diplomatic support, covert support for breakaway movements, and the like, for grander strategic objectives.

Further contradictions derive from the fact that Washington very much wants Russia to join with U.S. global initiatives and has shown an exceptional forbearance to Russia in the face of a lot of provocation and bad temper. Unfortunately, this forbearance, whatever else it has gained, also has reaped more "tantrums" and protests at U.S. policy. While they only further poison the bilateral well; they offer many Russian elites the consoling illusion of standing up to Washington even as Russia falls apart.

Other contradictions apply as well to America's allies, especially France. Russia and France both view each other as states which must be cultivated in order to enhance their respective standing *vis-à-vis* Washington, so that Washington will offer them more benefits in order to keep them on its side and pay more attention to their interests in pursuing its own goals.[40] Thus the cultivation of France and support for its opposition to American policies in the Gulf and the Israel-Palestine conflict translates into a search for global leverage *vis-à-vis* the United States, especially in Europe.[41] France, too, seeks to enhance its standing *vis-à-vis* Moscow and Washington as well as in the Middle East by its calculated display of distance from American policy.[42]

Therefore Primakov's diplomacy and policy seek leverage by trying to create regional and/or strategic partnerships with states who are willing to some degree to align their goals with Moscow's in different areas of the globe.[43] Primakov's approach very much follows the tradition of Alexander II's Foreign Minister Prince Gorchakov who, after the defeat in the Crimean War, sought to minimize threats to Russia and enhance her status by precisely the same search for regional partnerships and the exploitation of contradictions in areas where Russia could advance. Primakov has explicitly invoked this aspect of his predecessor's policies and is clearly inspired by it.[44] As an article in the Foreign Ministry's journal, *International Affairs*, stated,

> For Russia, the transition to a multi-polar world will create the possibility of diversifying the directions of foreign policy and of developing constructive strategic relations immediately with some influential partners. This increases the possibility of a maneuver necessary for ensuring the country's security under the conditions of a resource deficit and of the transition period in the development of our country which is attended by difficulties.[45]

Primakov's successor as Foreign Minister, Igor Ivanov, echoed this sentiment when he noted that Russian foreign policy now demanded the skill of seeking compromises considering different states' interests, and of seeking allies, "not for life but for a specific given instance."[46]

Russia's Approach to the Middle East.

Moscow's Middle Eastern policies have fully crystallized under Primakov's intellectual and political leadership. As Primakov has become Prime Minister, they are likely to continue along those same lines. This approach also quite clearly enjoys the support of President Boris Yeltsin and Russian elite opinion. It comprises a doctrine that is called multipolarity but which stems from traditional geopolitics, a doctrine having dangerous implications for Russia.[47]

The emphasis on geopolitics implies that Russia's claim to be a great, even global, power is guaranteed by virtue of its size and location irrespective of its internal state of affairs and the qualities of its domestic, economic, and military performance.[48] Primakov and Yeltsin have argued that Russia has global interests and its potential, not its reality, is what counts.[49] The doctrine of multipolarity postulates that Russia increasingly lives in a multipolar world where any one power or bloc, i.e., the United States, cannot be allowed to dominate in a hegemonic fashion anywhere, e.g., the Middle East. Russia, as a great power due to its potential, if not yet its reality, must play a global role, not just a regional one, and be seated at the "presidium table" of all international affairs.[50] Or as Leonid Brezhnev and his Foreign Minister Andrei Gromyko stated, no international issue can be decided without Russian participation. A consensus exists that Russia, in Yeltsin's words, "deserves to be a great power." Unfortunately employing this formulation means that Russia is not a great power. Russia claims a status beyond its real capacities, but one that encourages any other party who is dissatisfied with the status quo. Primakov, in the face of much earlier reformist doctrine to the fact that Russia is now only a regional power, has said Russia is a global actor and conducts an avowedly global policy and has adopted the Brezhnev line.[51] And that globalism, despite rhetoric to the contrary, often directly challenges U.S. policies, not just rhetorically, but through tangible political actions.

As expressed by Russian analysts, this globalism derives from two axioms which are held with almost religious certainty across the Russian political spectrum. As General Makhmut A. Gareev, one of Russia's most respected military theorists, writes,

> The main idea of contemporary Russia is that it can, must, and will be reborn and develop as a great power. This is not determined by someone's wishes, but by fundamental objective factors: historical traditions, geopolitical situation in the world, real economic, political, and spiritual needs, which would always manifest themselves and are impossible to 'cancel.' We must be ready to defend this idea.[52]

Key security figures, like former Deputy Defense Minister and Security Council Secretary Andrei Kokoshin, have espoused comparable views.[53] Logically, therefore, Russia's future status, if not present weakness, should entail its seat at the "presidium table" of world politics.

This outlook resonates across Russia's political spectrum and is expressed in the term *Derzhavnost'*, an inherent, objectively given great power status. This legacy goes back to the Tsars and is perhaps one of the greatest fetters upon Russia's ability to maneuver in contemporary international affairs. Because Russia's elite instinctively believes that Russia's potential and size makes it automatically a great power, these elites have sacrificed Russia's economic welfare to the paraphernalia of securing great power status. Hence Russia lacks a solid foundation for maintaining that status. Moscow has consistently striven to attain an international and now global position, based mainly on military factors that its economy and society could not sustain. This striving has also consistently precluded or inhibited efforts at democratic reform and arouses international suspicion about Russia's ultimate aims.

Today's globalism is also based on the second axiom that Russian national interest dictates a policy of countering the United States in all the key regions, Europe, the Middle

East, CIS, and Far East in order to safeguard Russian national interest and great power status as Washington's equal.[54] One advocate of "limited globalism," Oleg V. Davydov, describes it as a policy of accepting that Russia is fated to be a global power and one of the key centers of multipolarity as it develops. But it must also pursue a pragmatic line of engagement where and when its vital interests are joined. Other comparable analyses argue along similar lines.[55] The logical corollary of this belief, dating back beyond the Bolsheviks to the Tsars, is that any Western influence near Russia's "sphere of influence" automatically is hostile and a threat that must be countered.[56]

First and foremost, this policy line aims to appease Russian domestic policy, and it has allowed Primakov to use the doctrine of *Derzhavnost'* to increase domestic support for foreign policy and remove it as an issue in the domestic struggle for power. Instead, as Ivanov stressed, there is now a basic consensus with the Duma and across the elite on foreign policy deriving from the mystique of "*Derzhavnost.*"[57] Second, by acting along the line of national interest apart from and against the United States, Primakov has followed a policy that commanded Yeltsin's support, without which he could not function. Third, Primakov has also wrested control of foreign policy away from many of the rivals that his predecessor, Andrei Kozyrev, faced unsuccessfully. Fourth, Primakov has also benefited from the tough negotiations and agreement he won on NATO enlargement that is universally regarded as the best deal Russia could get, and his brilliant exploitation of the inept U.S. policy toward Iraq during 1997-98. These successes have allowed Primakov to conduct a policy of cultivating allies or partners with whom to prevent American hegemony in each regional domain. In the Middle East these partners are Iran, Iraq, Syria, Cyprus, Libya, and Sudan. Moscow cultivates them using all the tools of the trade, diplomatic support through the U.N. and inter-state relations, commercial trade, shared interests in energy issues, sales of weapons and nuclear technology, and perhaps most importantly, the cultivation of a common approach to the Middle East and its security issues.

Primakov has long argued that it is essential for Russia and the Middle East that the United States not play the sole role of regional hegemon.[58] Russia must constitute an equal and opposing presence. In 1991, on a mission to the area to save the Soviet Union's regional position, he said that Middle Eastern leaders, "consider it necessary that a united economic and military-strategic area of the USSR be preserved."

> They wanted a USSR presence in the Middle East because this would preserve the balance of power. Nobody wants some power to maintain a monopoly position there. These states understand that our country creates an area of stability in this region with its new policy of non-confrontation with anyone, a policy oriented toward searching for ways of making interests coincide with those of other countries.[59]

There is no reason to believe that he has changed his views which clearly constitute the foundation of Moscow's regional policy.

And indeed, there is much truth to this perception. Egypt's President Hosni Mubarak and Yasser Arafat, among others, have publicly urged Moscow to return to an active role in the Middle East. Syria announced in March 1998 that, while it had not previously exerted much effort to develop ties with Russia, it was now doing so at the highest level. Iraq and Iran also welcome Russia's greater regional presence.[60] Consequently, Primakov's policies enjoy regional and domestic support.

Indeed, from the start of his tenure as Foreign Minister, Primakov and Yeltsin insisted that Russia would demand an increasing role in the Middle East to counter America's monopoly of the peace process.[61] Primakov also then observed that the previous policies were misguided.

> We explain our inadequate activity in the Near East by the fact that our efforts were aimed at evening our relations with the former cold war adversaries. But this was done without an understanding of the fact that, by not surrendering our positions in the region and even strengthening them, we would have paved the way to the normalization of relations a shorter and more direct way.[62]

Unquestionably this policy has discomfited the United States. It surprised Secretary Christopher in 1996 when he first encountered it, and it certainly has helped undermine the foundations of our erratic policy in the Gulf.[63] But more tellingly, it also has struck at the U.S. increasingly visible regional unilateralism.

This became clear very soon after Primakov came to power in 1996. Another Lebanese crisis broke out, and he attempted to mediate between Israel, the Lebanese guerrillas, and Syria. He offered his good offices based on his contacts with Syria, Iran, and these guerrillas, but at the same time blamed the Peres government in Jerusalem for the crisis. Not surprisingly, Israel and the United States rejected his overtures and criticism and his mission failed. But he used it to begin cementing Russian relations with France as well as with the broader Arab world in order to obtain his larger goals. Indeed, Primakov apparently viewed Peres' electoral defeat by Benyamin Netanyahu shortly afterwards with considerable satisfaction. On the one hand, Russia felt that Shimon Peres' Israeli government had been insufficiently warm to it, while Netanyahu had called for improved relations with Moscow. On the other hand, he correctly believed that Netanyahu would slow implementation of the Oslo peace plan and process to the point where serious strains would arise between Israel and the Arabs, and between Washington and the Arabs, and this slowdown of the peace process would offer Moscow numerous opportunities for improving its regional position. Moscow's former ambassador to Israel, Aleksandr' Bovin, actually observed that Primakov was not particularly friendly to Israel. Certainly Primakov publicly stated his happiness to saddle the United States with failure to achieve progress between Israel and the Palestinians in 1998.[64]

And this constitutes the danger in Russian policy. The problem is not just its confrontational posture toward Washington, Jerusalem, and Ankara. Rather, the problem is that Russia fuels regional tensions that Moscow can neither control nor avoid and which may rebound against Russia's own strategic interests. The great powers in the Middle East are as often as not unable to control their clients and instead have to follow up their play, leading them into dangerous, if not failed, policies.[65] Also, there has been no public sign of Russian ideas to advance the peace process. In view of the fact that a slowdown of the peace process and the implicit corollary of renewed Israeli-Arab tension are believed to be in Russia's national interests, one cannot credibly envision Russia as a valuable interlocutor or equal player in the peace process. So its demand for an equal seat at the table appears to be based ultimately on nothing more than a policy of eternal negation of American initiatives and Israeli policy. Yet this stance risks perpetuating and solidifying the high degree of regional tension that already exists. And arms supplies to one side or another do even more to poison that well and frustrate American policies in the peace process and in the Gulf. Certainly Russia's perceptions appear to be at least to some degree behind Syria's, Iraq's, and perhaps even Arafat's calculations. They fear that without Moscow they lack a credible source of counter-pressure to Washington and Jerusalem and want to force Israel to retreat to Oslo or perhaps 1967. Unfortunately, Russia's policies render it incapable of gaining Israel's trust as a guarantor of its security or of inspiring the trust needed to bring all sides closer to peace. Moreover, because Russia is Iraq's main support against sanctions and Iran's nuclear sponsor, Moscow's policies have injured possibilities for regional peace.

This is hardly surprising in one sense, given Russia's utter economic prostration. After all, a state that boasts that it did not spend one Kopek on the peace process hardly deserves a seat at the peace process table.[66] But the actual policy being conducted seems to have more to do with pacifying domestic elites and evoking memories of a status that Russia cannot maintain than with progress towards true domestic reform, reconstruction, and a true enhancement of Russia's foreign standing. This is because the insistence on empire and *Derzhavnost* have always been the rock upon which reform efforts have foundered. These aspects of Russian policy are evident in the four cases of policy towards Iraq, Iran, Cyprus, and the peace process. And they clearly involve playing to the domestic galleries, especially insofar as the issues of energy and proliferation are concerned.

Indeed, the domestic galleries are crucial because the failure to create a viable state and coherent national security policy process or mechanisms has given those galleries a disproportionate role in the formulation and conduct of policy. As Nikolai Sokov observes,

> The ability of the government to develop and implement policy will be strongly limited by the influence of politically relevant domestic actors, each of whom will hold a virtual right of veto over specific aspects of policy. Unlike in pluralist systems, [the government] will have only a limited ability to manipulate domestic coalitions for the simple reason that the coalition will be nearly all-encompassing and very stable.[67]

Furthermore, because these coalitions are so stable, only if some shock to the system (perhaps Primakov's accession to power and subsequent new economic policies) occurs will the dominant coalitions be unseated and new departures in policy take place.[68] And in such a system, government will try to incorporate all interests into foreign policy because their influence is so pervasive and stable.[69] The fact that not a single defense industry has been closed for bankruptcy until now, despite the utterly useless nature of much of their production, indicates the force of this lobby that can defend anti-national interests and value-subtracting firms and its ability to bend the state to its will.[70] Therefore it is easier and cheaper politically to incorporate these lobbies into the policy process early in the game and legitimate their presence through all of its stages. Therefore, as Sokov again notes, policy does not correspond to anything like the rational-actor model. Sectoral or partial interests are exalted and pursued at the expense of any coherent national interest. The failure of the state leads to the privatization of the state and the policy process.[71] In Russia's Middle Eastern policy, the energy and defense industry lobbies provide particularly telling examples of how this process occurs in actual policymaking.

Russia and the Gulf: Energy and Weapons.

Since 1991, the Gulf has become the main focus of Russia's Middle Eastern policy. This attests both to Russia's shrunken reach, the rise of the peace process after 1991, and Iran's enhanced strategic importance *vis-à-vis* the CIS and Russia. But it also reflects the rising importance of the struggle for energy shares in the CIS, a struggle that will probably determine the geopolitical fate of the Transcaspian states.[72] Russian support for Iraq and Iran is almost overdetermined, since these two states' support for Russia not only anchors its position in the Gulf, but also materially helps it in the struggle for energy.

The turn to Iran reinforces the existing partnership between the two states. It makes sense, given the U.S. blockade or embargo on Iran that drives Tehran to find other partners and both sides' need to establish an arrangement or regime, to sort out Central Asian and Caucasian conflicts and energy issues. Not surprisingly, the two states conducting policies that have isolated them to some degree from the international community came together. At a 1995 Irano-Russian roundtable,

The speakers alluded to the quest by Iran and Russia for an identity and to Russia's political determination to prevent any country from dominating the region [Central Asia and the Caucasus]. It was stressed that Iran and Russia are natural allies with distinctive natural resources and the predominance of any third power should be prevented. This is related to the manner in which the two sides define their strategic objectives. It was also stated that Russia's influence in Central Asia and the Caucasus should be treated with respect and if domination is not the objective, cooperation is possible.[73]

This was hardly the first time this conclusion was stated. It had already achieved the force of policy well before 1995. In 1992 Russian authorities already understood that they needed to continue providing Iran with conventional weapons (if not more dangerous dual-use technology) lest Iran make trouble for Moscow in Central Asia and the Caucasus, a perception that continues until now.[74] At the same time, this strategic partnership also belies or at least neutralizes Iran as the avatar of the Islamic threat used in the Russian media and by Russian elites to justify everything from Chechnya to Tajikistan. Iran is simply not regarded as a threat in actuality, no matter what might be said about fundamentalism in general. Perhaps this is due to the U.S. isolation of Iran that pushes it against Washington and towards Moscow, or it comes from Iran's highly circumspect policy in the CIS, or from the Russian weapon and technology transfers. Or perhaps all three of these factors help limit Iran's interests in the CIS. In fact, many policymakers recommend dealing with Muslim societies, specifically Iran, in order to engage this phenomenon and turn it away from threatening Russia, a solution that Primakov has espoused in the past.[75] Yeltsin's advisor, Andranik Migranyan, who calls for Russian hegemony in the CIS, stated that,

> In many areas Iran can be a good and strategic ally of Russia at [the] global level to check the hegemony of third parties and keep the balance of power. . . . Russia will try to further cooperate with Iran as a big regional power. We will not let the West dictate to Russia how far it can go in its relations. Of

course, we will try at the same time not to damage our relations with the West.[76]

Russia also clearly wants to "internationalize" the issue of Gulf security, obtain a role as a recognized guarantor of the area, either through the U.N. or through a regional alignment, and displace the U.S. primacy there, even as it recognizes the latter's strong regional interests.[77] Accordingly, Primakov supports the removal of foreign U.S. troops from the Gulf. Hence one goal of Russia's support for Iraq may be to achieve just this objective.[78] Iranian officials' statements also indicated an overt desire to arrive at a "division of responsibilities with Russia in regard to regional conflicts and energy issues."[79]

Therefore they are openly very critical of any Russian backsliding on energy issues in the Caspian.[80] That backsliding, as in Russia's recent deal with Kazakstan on the nature of the Caspian Sea that reflected Russia's waning ability to dictate to Kazakstan, led to sharp Iranian criticism and to a hurried visit by Deputy Foreign Minister Boris Pastukhov to reassure everyone that all was well.[81] Accordingly, until and unless Washington relaxes its efforts to isolate Iran from oil deals in Central Asia and the Caucasus, trade abroad and nuclear power deals, coupled with Russian resentment at U.S. policies, will provide excellent grounds for a durable marriage of convenience. Energy issues dictate much of these grounds for this marriage. The struggle for energy has made the entire Transcaspian area an arena for geopolitical conflict.

Unfortunately, the logic of the evolution of the U.S. policy of a full-scale, coordinated economic-military-political program to integrate the entire area firmly into the West has much to answer for in this connection.[82] While there are solid reasons for so acting and certainly this prospect offers the region much more than being tied to Moscow's corpse, it nonetheless extends U.S. power into what formerly was a Russian preserve.

As long as the Transcaspian basin is alleged to be larger than the Ghawar field in Saudi Arabia, the largest oil field in the world, a stake of this magnitude justifies Washington's compelling interest in the Transcaspian.[83] However, Russia, too, has compelling strategic interests in solidifying its position with Iraq and Iran due to the local energy situation. Energy revenues are crucial to every state in the region, including Russia, for reasons connected to their own internal political economy. All these states are rentier states whose main revenue comes from oil and gas sales, an external royalty or rent, the production of which is largely unrelated to the rest of the domestic economy. The concept of the rentier state originated with regard to Iran under Shah Mohammad Pahlavi (1941-79) but has grown to include other oil producing Arab states, e.g., Kuwait or Qatar. Some analysts substitute the term allocative state, but both refer to the same phenomenon.[84]

The establishment of rentier states in the CIS means that their stability depends on a continuing flow of energy revenues. To the degree that those revenues are interrupted or interdicted, these states' internal and external stability comes into question. It is not enough for these states to obtain foreign investment and diplomatic-military support, they must use those newly acquired advantages wisely over a long time to develop and stabilize.

Because they are rentier states, the Transcaspian states and Russia compete for the same export markets for energy. Russia's energy interests are vital to the survival of the government and state in their present form. The struggle between the particular interest of the energy companies, who seek more and more profits, from participating in the regional energy bonanza, and the Foreign Ministry that seeks to uphold a national state interest and close the region's prospects down altogether, has bedeviled Russian foreign policy and confirms Sokov's observations about the nature of the policy process.[85] This does not mean that Russia's survival as such is necessarily endangered by a failure to attain those interests and close the door on future energy competition. But Yeltsin's system is jeopardized by such a failure because of its incoherent national security policy process and weakness *vis-à-vis* the world economy.

Russia's energy interests are more extensive than those of its neighbors. Therefore Russian policy, as determined by the energy companies, and/or by the Foreign Ministry, fights to retain control over the CIS energy network. Oil and natural gas, which constitute the very foundations of the Russian economy and account for more than half the country's entire export earnings, are at stake. One might also contend that since the allocation of the oil rent is the key relationship between the ruler and the ruled, it is the basis of the government's legitimacy, something that was confirmed when the oilmen and bankers forced the collapse of the Kiriyenko government in 1998 when it tried to raise their taxes. And since foreign policy in such states consists largely of creating an environment conducive to the expansion and allocation of those rents, and the stability of the ruler's position, a hegemonic aspect is likewise intrinsic to their foreign policy.[86] Certainly this is the case for Russia, although we may see prolonged struggles between Primakov's government and the energy lobby on domestic issues in the months ahead.

As one of the world's leading producers and exporters of hydrocarbons, Russia cannot ignore Central Asia and Azerbaijan's intention to increase the extraction and export of oil and natural gas. The emergence of major new producers could reconfigure the global energy markets and profoundly affect price dynamics with immediate and severe consequences for Russia's economy. Coordinating Moscow's energy strategy with plans to increase the production and export of oil and gas in the CIS constitutes a primary national interest for Russia. Therefore Russia reacts negatively toward any external "meddling" in CIS energy affairs.[87]

Russia's efforts to take over the Caspian energy economy became visible in 1994, but its most recent formal policy was outlined in 1996 when the Security Council and the Ministry of Fuel and Energy proclaimed energy a major factor in safeguarding Russia's security. The fuel economy faces internal threats from the low level of energy efficiency in Russia, the non-payments crisis where debtors do not pay their bills for goods and services, and the lack of foreign investments. The solution to the internal economic failure is economic imperialism, i.e., "access to internal markets of neighboring countries," preserving and expanding "reliable external marketing outlets, and thus ensuring the transit through Russia energy carriers."[88]

Russia's "fuel diplomacy" should focus on establishing a common CIS system of energy security, including shared property, common development, integrated production companies, and free access to markets and resources. CIS states should view Russia as their major partner and collaborations with other countries as "economically inexpedient." Moscow would encourage Russia's oil giants, Gazprom, Lukoil (the premier gas and oil companies), and Transneft (the main pipeline company) to reach out into Kazakstan and Turkmenistan to preserve Russia's dominance over those states' economies and perpetuate a closed, exclusive sphere of influence there.[89]

As the largest exporter and refiner of oil and gas who controls the shipment of all petroleum products through its "steel umbilical cord" across the CIS, Russia has compelling reasons for this policy. On economic grounds alone, it has every reason to oppose any expansion of its rivals' market share should they be able to sell freely abroad. Therefore, it wages unceasing economic warfare against them and demands a cut from all of their projects, to explore or ship oil and gas. Russia has repeatedly blackmailed Kazakstan, Turkmenistan, and Azerbaijan into admitting Russia, often on concessionary terms, to their energy projects.[90]

Meanwhile Russia's own productive capacity in both oil and gas has steadily declined, and its energy industries are entangled in numerous dysfunctional economic and political relationships for all their apparent riches and profitability. Serious competition for Russia's current markets, especially from modernized producers using foreign capital, technology, and infrastructure, and enjoying Western political support, would undo Russia's domestic and foreign economic position. Moreover, the economic collapse ignited by the Asian crisis in late 1997 has already forced Russia to export more oil to obtain scarce foreign capital and squeeze domestic producers who will be under more domestic pressure to pay taxes. So energy producers face strong internal pressures to export more and restrict competition.

Since Russia's main source of foreign exchange derives from its energy exports, if those exports declined substantially, Russia's ability to earn foreign exchange and meet its large and growing international debts and its ability to sustain itself at home through access to foreign capital markets and international economic agencies would fall, too. Indeed, many Russian observers worry greatly that Russia might remain consigned for years to come to a semi-peripheral state in the world economy as an exporter of raw materials like oil and gas, and be unable to attain modern levels and forms of economic, industrial, and technological development. They fear a lasting economic-technological, and hence military, backwardness, leaving Russia at the mercy of the United States or other foreign coalitions.[91] Unhappily for them, there seems no way out unless Russia can convert its foreign earnings into development and internal investment capital. Until then, Russia must rely mainly on its energy economy for foreign exchange and seek to drive out competition as befits a true aspirant to monopoly status. But Russia's political economy promotes rent-seeking, not investment, and recycles economic-political pathologies throughout the system.

Complicating matters for Russia is its declining capacity to produce energy products. Its infrastructure is dilapidated and worsening, and its new sources of energy face formidable costs to explore and ship because of their location in the inhospitable Siberian north and east, and because there has been precious little investment from abroad or internally for over a decade. Furthermore, the present Russian economic climate does not favor external or even internal energy investment, and foreign firms are leaving in frustration and disgust. If anything, this situation will worsen, given the continuing inhospitable climate for foreign investment, one that may even worsen before it improves.

Meanwhile, Russia and the CIS states remain extremely wasteful consumers of energy, dependent on subsidized consumption at below market prices and on the big oil and gas firms' subsidization of housing, social welfare functions, etc. Without foreign income, because CIS and Russian purchases are way down since 1991, this whole rickety structure could come apart. Indeed, when the government started pressing Gazprom to pay more taxes in mid-1998 as a major financial crisis hit it, Gazprom predictably began demanding more payment from its foreign customers in the CIS.[92]

Gazprom's situation exemplifies the precariousness of this house of cards. Gazprom receives only 5-15 percent of its receipts for its goods and services in cash. Its exports, therefore, must subsidize its domestic operations which are in any case endangered as the infrastructure declines. It exploits this situation to justify its monopoly position and enormous tax arrears by citing its willingness to continue subsidizing customers who do not pay in cash—a category that includes most of Russia's city governments. Gazprom effectively has replaced the failing state and taken its payment for services rendered in the taxes that it does not pay. Yet its profits and those of other energy companies from exports do not return to the economy either as taxes or investments or even to cover current costs.[93]

Thus, if Gazprom's exports decline while other states provide cheaper gas and more of it through better pipelines and with foreign backing, its ability to subsidize the collapsing domestic economy and to avoid taxes declines with it. But worse, much of the municipal sector's economy declines with Gazprom for lack of gas and with that sector banks, housing, and others are all severely endangered. The dependence of key sectors of Russia's economy on Gazprom, the firm that was former Prime Minister Viktor Chernomyrdin's former employer, exemplifies the pathology of the rentier state. And the skewed dependence upon state protection, tax breaks, and non-cash payments underscores the extent to which Russia has failed to make the economic transition to a genuine market economy.[94] Certainly such dangers and the benefits of state protection that accrue to firms like Gazprom can explain the purely economic motives of Russia's energy barons and government when facing the prospect of enhanced rivalry from former satrapies whose independence Moscow still cannot accept.

The foregoing analysis explains why Gazprom has obstructed any Turkmen penetration of the Russian market, pipelines or access to customers outside Russia. It also explains the economic motives behind Russia's efforts to curtail the emergence of the Transcaspian states' energy economies. At the same time, Russia has consistently advanced a geopolitical rationale for reintegrating the whole area around itself as the main task of all state agencies.[95] However, the interests of the energy companies do not necessarily comport either with this geopolitical rationale or with Russia's own best interests. Gazprom's energy war against Turkmenistan, abetted by Moscow, drove Ashkhabad to Iran, Turkey, Germany, and the United States for financial, economic, and political support and weakened Moscow's future ability to leverage the situation in Turkmenistan. Neither Russian consumers, nor the economy, nor Russian national interests benefit from such policies, but Gazprom does. And its unassailable connections display how the privatization of Russian foreign policy undermines regional stability and development. But it also explains the economic-strategic motivation for Russia's policies towards Iraq and Iran.

Foreign observers like the International Institute for Strategic Studies in London (IISS) deride the U.S. claim concerning the size of regional oil and gas deposits which would make the entire region's holding larger than Prudhoe Bay, the East Texas fields, and the Ghawar field combined. Other energy industry figures and the calculations of specialists like Robert Ebel of the Washington-based Center for Strategic and International Studies argue that official U.S. estimates are far too high and claim that Caspian holdings will amount to no more than about 3-4 percent of global energy reserves.[96] Furthermore, the IISS argues that the cost of moving equipment into the area, the expense of construction and the transit fees that must be paid make Caspian investment of marginal utility at the low end of current oil prices. As oil prices have fallen further to their lowest point in a decade since the IISS went to press, investment will probably be affected and could become unviable. Oil and gas companies would probably then return to the Middle East because of the preexisting infrastructure and business arrangements.[97]

But that outcome would undermine the whole thrust of U.S. policy that seeks to minimize the need for Gulf oil and gas and to look elsewhere. As the IISS remarked, due to the cheaper cost involved in transporting Iraqi oil and gas, opening those products up to international markets and repealing the sanctions regime—an increasingly likely denouement—represents a major challenge to further development of Caspian energy holdings.[98] This is one major explanation of why Russia pushes so hard to end the sanctions on Iraq, an outcome that can only be seen as a major U.S. defeat and an equal setback to the Transcaspian states.[99]

And that consideration underlines the strategic linkages tying this region to the Middle East. To the extent that the Caspian region can be stabilized, the United States can afford to further diminish its need for Middle Eastern gas and oil and reduce Iran's, Iraq's, and Russia's potential to play decisive roles in the Western and American energy economy.[100] The diversification of supplies to avoid excessive reliance on unstable and volatile areas constitutes a major U.S. objective. But, at the macro or geostrategic level, U.S. policy strikes at Russia's main regional objectives as well as Iran and Iraq's hopes for a way out of their current strategic and economic impasses.

Local U.S. diplomats and the administration now regard the Transcaspian area as a "backup" to or substitute for dependence upon the Middle East if that region's oil supplies become problematic.[101] Russia's Iraq policy also combines many of the same motives, especially the desire for markets and an economic foot in the door and the desire for political leverage. There are undoubtedly, as well, many Russian political figures who loudly advocate breaking the U.N. sanctions on Iraq or overturning them so that Iraq and Russia could establish friendship, pay off Baghdad's $7 billion debt to Russia through oil sales and become a market for Russian business, especially in energy sectors. To the degree that Iraq breaks out of the sanctions regime, it can then not only pay off its debts to Russia, it can bring in Russian technology and capital to major investment deals and bypass the Transcaspian states, keeping them from becoming independent market rivals of Russia. It also will staunchly stand against any return of U.S. power to the Gulf. Likewise, Russian officials reiterate their desire to sustain the large Soviet economic investment in Iraq and develop it further.

Russia's political motives are equally important *vis-à-vis* Iraq. When Russia mediated the crisis in November 1994 that looked like a resumption of the war with Kuwait, it won much credit in Baghdad because it showed the erosion of the united front in the Security Council. The U.S.-led forces appeared to be in disarray. Russia's actions were rightly seen as a declaration of Russia's independence in the Gulf and assertion of the equal importance of its interests to

Washington's.[102] As Vladimir Tytarenko, then Deputy Chief of Mission in Baghdad observed, Russia's policy will be based on reinforcing strategic interests, and Russian interests in Iraq and the Middle East are no less important than America's interests. Stressing that local events have great repercussions in Russia, he played up trade rivalry with Washington, not ideological rivalry.[103] Viktor Posvalyuk, the Foreign Ministry's roving ambassador to the region, used that crisis to reiterate Russia's demand for an all-inclusive Gulf security system that it would help bring into being.[104] Primakov's tremendous diplomatic victory in 1997-98, when he twice brokered deals that forced America to back away from enforcing inspections of Iraq's WMD program, dramatically enhanced the perception of Russian return and American disarray in the area. But it built on previous achievements.

It now appears that the sanctions regime will come under continuing pressure and contention as Iraq struggles to escape from "the box" that U.S. officials foolishly maintained they put Saddam Hussein in.[105] In fact past U.S. policy toward Iraq, as revealed in mid-summer 1998, looked both duplicitous and weak, a deadly combination.[106] While the most recent crisis of November 1998 ended in Iraq's retreat and reacceptance of United Nations Special Commission on Iraq (UNSCOM) inspections, it will not be the last crisis triggered by Iraq's determination to overthrow the sanctions regime. Accordingly, we can expect that the other main reason for Russian domestic lobbies' support for Iraq—the desire of the oil, gas, and defense industry and the Ministry of Atomic Energy (Minatom) to sell their wares in Iraq—will come even more to the fore in the Gulf and throughout the Middle East than before.

Proliferation Policy.

As in energy, Russia's proliferation policy in the Middle East and elsewhere links domestic policy groups and factors with foreign policy interests. Russia's proliferation policy is a decidedly complicated affair. Formally speaking, Russia has a very sophisticated set of rules, laws, and decrees that have taken shape since 1992. These enactments have established a detailed and heavily bureaucratic regime governing customs controls, exports of dual-use, and military technology to the point where many Russian commentators flatly assert that no weapons or dual-use technologies can be sold or exported without the government knowing about it or against its wishes.[107] Those rules also attest to Russia's continuing desire to be taken seriously as a Western "liberal" state that supports non-proliferation.[108] Hence Russian writers maintain that, even if Russia is not a formal member of various international export control bodies, its regulations and laws are written with an eye towards conformity with international procedures.[109]

Although there have been many statements claiming that Russia opposes nuclear or other WMD proliferation, official reports consistently deny that Russia is now threatened by proliferation. The Duma, too, does not consider proliferation of WMD to be a threat to Russian security even if neighbors get these weapons.[110] And, in any case, it is the U.N.'s job to identify states who are contemplating proliferation. Russia opposes any export controls other than those imposed by the U.N. and IAEA, and insists that Iran and Iraq are nowhere near the achievement of a nuclear capability. Therefore the Iraqi "nuclear file" should be closed, and inspections ceased. Likewise, Russia refuses to participate in U.S. sanctions or blacklists against Iran, claiming that the IAEA reports Iran to be in full compliance with international standards and procedures.[111] And Primakov has repeatedly denied that Russia sells dual-use or nuclear weapons' capabilities to Iran. Therefore, attempts by outside actors like the United States to target states who otherwise are listed as complying with the IAEA, e.g., Iran, are unwarranted and merely an effort to undermine Iran's and Russia's presence in the marketplace for weapons where the competition is intense.[112] Russian reports and statements also constantly shun terms like rogue states. Instead, Russia espouses a policy of engagement with these states to deal with potential issues of proliferation while pursuing its own interests.[113] In fact,

> Rules to exclude "violator-participants" are not envisioned in the context of multilateral agreements. The nations take the recommended lists and guiding principles [of international conventions and agreements] as a foundation when considering the possibility of making specific foreign and economic deals, *but these principles are interpreted by each country proceeding from its own national interests. The imposition of sanctions also depends on national legislation. The regimes under analysis are in fact an aggregate of parallel and coordinated systems of export controls of all nations that adhere to the basic rules of export control.*[114] (italics author)

Furthermore, Russia's political establishment views American policy as hypocritical in that it seeks to bar Russian exports of the same kind of reactor to Iran that Washington has exported to North Korea. Russian analysts argue that,

> It is highly likely that a flexible policy in relation to North Korea could prove to be more sensible for strengthening the international non-proliferation regime under certain circumstances. But the opinion prevails among the Russian leadership that an uncompromising policy towards a number of other nations is not effective either. Whether Russia, in entering into agreements on technical collaboration, will be able to have a positive influence on the policy of such partners as Iran is another matter.[115]

The official rationale for proliferation policy emerged in Primakov's 1995 report as head of Russian Foreign Intelligence, the SVR. This report stated that Russian authorities strongly oppose nuclear proliferation precisely because Russia is especially vulnerable to the threats posed by proliferation, as a state close to many of the regions where would-be proliferators, who are already at odds with their neighbors, including potentially Russia, are active. The report stated that:

> For Russia the specific fate of the NPT (Non-Proliferation Treaty) will not only inevitably affect its strategic course for enduring security, but will also have a major impact on national security interests. The appearance of new nuclear countries on RF (Russian Federation) borders would create a real threat, destabilize the situation in the "near abroad" zone, and force it to revise the guidelines of Russian defense policy, including in terms of its nuclear component.[116]

Hence the main threat to the nonproliferation regime is countries like Israel, Pakistan, and India who are de facto nuclear powers but remain outside the treaty. Their capability is dangerous in itself and can spread, e.g., Pakistan's transfer of know-how to Iran and North Korea's export of missile technology to Pakistan. Since these states stand outside the Non-Proliferation Treaty, they cannot rely on the international community to provide "real levers" to stop their potential enemies from going nuclear. Accordingly, their exclusion from the NPT regime is a regionally destabilizing factor. That exclusion stimulates their enemies to follow suit. Surely Iran fulfills this designation. That fact alone logically should lead Moscow to resist any further nuclearization of the Middle East.[117] And Moscow still claims it follows this logic and this policy.

Furthermore, the SVR report categorically stated that Russia cannot support states pursuing a double standard toward "unofficial" nuclear countries or states, like Iran, who are on the nuclear threshold or seeking to acquire weapons. Because such tactics allow these threshold states to nuclearize further and triggers arms races among them and their enemies, supporting them is a highly dangerous policy.[118] At the same time, this policy comports with Russia's broader and oft-stated justification for exporting conventional weapons abroad.

Russian authorities state that national interest is the main factor determining foreign military-technical cooperation. This cooperation occurs within the frameworks of Russia's treaty and political obligations to the world community regarding the arms trade and of expanded transparency in such weapons transfers. These obligations include treaties like the NPT and other agreements to prevent the proliferation of WMD and missile technologies. Moscow further adjusts the volume of its sales to the capabilities of foreign states to provide them with a reasonable degree of training and proficiency that suffices for defense. But those trade balances preclude support for the excessive militarization of the recipient's economy and the ensuing aggravation of internal socio-economic and external regional tensions that undermine peace and development. Russia limits "to a maximum degree" the export of weapons to countries who violate international agreements with Russia or who are engaged in conflicts. Sometimes Russia forbids exports of certain systems, and it will not export weapons and combat equipment to states who may use them against Russian citizens, property, interests, and installations.[119] Many Russian writers on arms sales also now contend, as noted above, that the state has very strong controls over arms sales. And due to these extensive bureaucratic controls, it is unthinkable that any producer along with myriad sub-contractors could get away with secret, covert arms sales abroad.[120]

Moreover, with respect to Iran, Moscow has argued that there is absolutely no state policy of transferring WMD technology or know-how to Iran and that, in any case, Iran does comply with IAEA requirements and inspections.[121] Likewise, Primakov and others assert that Iran is not close to having a nuclear weapon and hence does not represent a threat to Russia.[122]

Obviously, if this is the policy, it is a highly responsible one even as it advances Russian economic, military, and political interests. But if this be the case, then Russian authorities and analysts cannot simultaneously claim, as they and their sympathizers within the administration regularly do, that they cannot control the export of conventional or WMD systems, technologies, and weapons.[123] Indeed, some Russian writers, notably Andrei Kortunov and Andrei Shumikhin, deny the whole claim of rigorous controls. They observed that Russian policy is distinguished by the absence of coherence and consistency due to the struggle among the "multipolar" interests and opinions at the policymaking level and the government's utter disorganization.[124] In this struggle, powerful factions in and around Russia's government strive to monopolize as much as possible of the policy processes that concern them. In highly technical issues like arms sales, it is easier for these interests to gain their goals.[125] Thus,

> In the area of WMD (and especially BM-ballistic missiles) proliferation, it is the narrow interest groups representing producers of some types of exportable hardware and materials that are especially eager to obtain "absolute" authority in laying out and implementing policies benefiting primarily their own positions. As traditionally was done in the former Soviet Union, additional practical means of achieving such a monopoly position are setting up a heavy veil of secrecy and acting under the guise of "overriding national security expediency."[126]

Since arms sales are so profitable, they have been repeatedly acknowledged to be a source of endless corruption and one in which powerful political figures get involved to enrich themselves or to provide funds for their political war chests.[127] In fact, the former head of Russia's domestic intelligence service, the Federal Security Service (FSB), General Nikolai Kovalev conceded, however opaquely, that many businessmen have little regard for Russia's proliferation interests and sell weapons or technology illegally or covertly.[128] Many analysts believe that such criminality is indeed possible, and even pervasive, for at least some classes of weapons. Therefore, these claims of strict controls point at two opposing but compatible conclusions.[129] If those claims of strict control are mendacious and Russia cannot control arms sales, then

Russia has lost state control of policies in support of a vital national interest.

If, on the other hand, the claims of strict control are true, the reports of corruption mean that it takes place with the active knowledge and participation of the Russian authorities. Inasmuch as we have repeated evidence of corruption admitted by those selfsame authorities or Russian journalists, this loss of control over policy seems obvious, but Russia cannot and will not admit it. But, at the same time, since this corruption is pervasive up to the very top of the government ladder, it is also clear that much of the corruption and mendacity is state sponsored. In other words, the fine words of the SVR report and other official statements of rectitude regarding proliferation are just that, words. The reality blends pervasive corruption, private aggrandizement, active official participation in and connivance with that corruption, and strict paper controls. Claims that Moscow cannot stop this trade or that its regulations preclude it strain credulity. The rhetoric of nonproliferation conceals a policy that abets proliferation.

The Reality of Russian Proliferation.

That reality, as revealed over the last several years, is then quite alarming. Russian and Western press reports indicate that Russia has become a conscious, willing, and major proliferator of WMD, including biological warfare capabilities. Iran's difficulties have forced it to let Russia take over its Bushehr reactor project as a turnkey operation. But even before that, U.S. and Israeli intelligence reported that Iran is now within 1 year of a nuclear missile capability, even if Russia now desists from helping it.[130] Since Russian authorities have acknowledged that Israel has presented a more comprehensive view of Iranian-Russian collaboration than did the United States, and Israeli intelligence throughout has been on the mark regarding Iran, there seems no reason to dispute this assessment.[131] These and other sources also cite Iran's great strides in ballistic missiles with Chinese, DPRK, and potentially Russian help.[132] Recent Russian reports detail the conscious participation and coordination of Russia's FSB, the high-level state commissions on non-proliferation, Ministry of Foreign Affairs, and probably the Ministry of Defense in projects to send Russian scientists to Iran to transfer nuclear know-how as Iran aims at intermediate range and then intercontinental ballistic missile capability (IRBMs and ICBMs, respectively). Furthermore, in 1996, Deputy Prime Minister and Minister of External Economic Relations Oleg Davydov revealed that Russia would sell Iran over $4 billion of machinery and equipment, including military equipment over the next 10 years, and that military hardware and complete sets of equipment for Iranian enterprises now constitute 85 percent of the total volume of deliveries to Tehran and could grow. In late 1995, the Iranian government also expressed an interest in raising the level of purchases of hardware, machinery, and equipment to $1 billion a year for the next 2 years, 1996-97. Should Iran pay off its debts to Russia by 2005, Russia could be exporting $4.5-5 billion annually.[133]

The known technology transfers of WMD to Iran involve SS-4 technology and the reactor at Bushehr as well as exchange of scientific know-how with Iranian scientists and training in Russia for them. The Bushehr reactor comprises four reactors plus turbines that Russia is now expected to provide, along with more military technology and weapons since Ukraine dropped out under American pressure. And all this assistance occurs even though Russian officials know full well and publicly profess that Iran intends to build nuclear weapons with this assistance![134]

Russia is also helping Iran develop a national communications satellite that will have an earth monitoring capability. The firm doing this work, the Spurt Science and Production Center, is known for its work on classified space programs. The space apparatus itself is being developed by the Reutov Mashinostroyenie Science and Production Association, which used to develop ballistic and cruise missiles and most important military space systems. The Izhevsk Radio Plant and the Aksion Joint Stock Company also regularly participated in Soviet space programs. Russia clearly knows this is a dual-use system, that Iran will have exclusive control over once it is designed, and that it will take 2-3 years from signing the contracts to finish the satellite.[135] More recently, it was reported that Russia is about to demonstrate gas centrifuges that are vital to the construction of atomic bombs to Iran, and sell it tritium (heavy water) as well.[136] These demonstrations and sales clearly violate President Yeltsin's 1995 agreement with President Clinton to terminate nuclear sales to Iran. The transfer of missile technology openly violates the membership rules for the Missile Technology Control Regime (MTCR) where Russia is a member and also automatically makes it subject to sanctions. And none of this includes the sizable and ongoing conventional weapons sales program to Iran which also flouts past promises that it would stop.

Yet Iran is a state whose nuclearization was listed in 1995 as a clear potential threat to Russia. Selling your potential enemies the atomic rope with which to hang you should not make good policy. Yet Russia persists and has ready answers to those who question the logic of its policy. Already in 1992 officials argued that Russia must sell arms to prevent Iranian support for Islam in the southern CIS and Russia, and that it is best to influence Iranian progress by these sales to limit the threat.[137] That rationale still operates today.

Other political considerations also are present. The SVR report says:

> Russian-Iranian cooperation could be a unique testing ground where the possibility and need for a member state of the "nuclear club" to fulfill its obligations under Article IV of the NPT whereby the participants in the Treaty must promote equitable, nondiscriminatory cooperation in the field of peaceful atomic power engineering but must, in doing so, prevent conditions for the proliferation of nuclear weapons [and this]

would be meaningfully examined. Cooperation in the cause of replacing the North Korean gas-graphite reactors with light water ones can also be the same kind of example.[138]

Russia seems to feel it must provide these technologies in order to prove its bona fides to Tehran. Clearly the issue here is an Irano-Russian security partnership on issues of common concern: Azerbaijan's westward turn, control of Caspian Sea oil and gas flows, stabilizing Central Asia, especially Tajikistan and Afghanistan, and Transcaucasia. Russia's search for Iranian cooperation and entry into the Gulf parallels its search for a point of entry into the Korean peace process by seeking access to the consortium to provide North Korea with reactors, gaining leverage in Korea and Asia. Thus nuclear sales are a large part of the entry price into the Gulf, Central Asian, and Korean political sweepstakes. North Korea's recurrent blackmail of the United States, Japan, and South Korea through threats to go nuclear if it does not receive sufficient funding indicates how that regional game is played.

Therefore in the Middle East, Russia also supports the withdrawal of U.S. forces from the Gulf, and aims to create a bloc of pro-Russian forces against U.S. and Israeli interests to compel Washington to admit Russia as an equal player with a veto into the peace process and Gulf security.[139] That ambition resurrects much of the previous Soviet policy of a bloc or entente among the former "rejectionist front" of the late 1970s to support Moscow's efforts to jeopardize the peace process against Israel and the U.S. monopoly of it. This is also the geostrategic factor driving support for Iran's, Iraq's, Libya's, Sudan's, and Syria's conventional and WMD rearmament. Iraqi buyers have toured Russian factories, bought gyroscopes from discarded SLBMs, and had these gyroscopes certified by the Russians. When Jordan intercepted the shipment, a rare table used to test guidance instruments was found. Although the Russians claim the gyroscopes were scrap metal, the table clearly was not, and its sale constitutes another violation of the Missile Technology Control Regime that Russia has apparently frequently violated with impunity.[140] Since the CIA now believes that once Iraq escapes sanctions, as seems increasingly likely, it will rapidly redevelop its capability for using WMD, it seems quite possible that Russian firms will help Iraq achieve this goal.[141] Nor are these the only cases of arms transfers to the Middle East. Syria has been receiving Russian conventional weapons, yet there are constant reports of Syrian interest in Russian collaboration in upgrading Syria's chemical and biological weapons capabilities and missile technologies. And apparently new conventional arms deals are in the offing with Syria, Egypt, and even possibly Iraq.[142] Yemen is also coming to Russia to buy SU-27 fighters and trainers, and S-300 surface-to-air missiles. During the Cold War, the Soviet Union also exported freely to Yemen who for years was engaged in a civil war and conflicts with its neighbors. While that stopped for a while when the Cold War ended, Yemen has returned to negotiate these sales, apparently to counter a threat it perceives either from Saudi Arabia or Ethiopia.[143] And there are growing signs of a Libyan-Russian rapprochement that could lead to atomic technology transfers and arms sales.[144]

Nor can Moscow pretend any longer that Iran is not seeking to go nuclear. When Iran tested its Shihab-3 missile in 1998, it became clear that Iran had adapted a North Korean Nodong missile to a mobile launcher, making it virtually invulnerable to antimissile systems. This missile's range comprises virtually the entire Middle East and parts of Russia. And "Not a single expert has any doubts that this vehicle is capable of delivering nuclear weapons."[145]

Analyzing Russia's Motives.

However, diplomatic objectives are arguably not the only, or perhaps not even the dominating consideration for Russia's support for international proliferation. Certainly Russia, like the Soviet Union, talked one way and acted another. In the late Soviet period, Moscow also supported proliferators despite its opposition to proliferation. A dual policy is nothing new.[146] And indeed, the conditions leading Moscow to favor it are, if anything, more desperate today than before.

Apart from influence over friendly states' military and foreign policies, another critical motive for military and civilian transfers of conventional as well as nuclear weapons and technologies of mass destruction is to save Russian civilian and defense industry. Primakov recently listed that goal as one of the foundations and main goals of Russian foreign policy.[147] That announcement represented a major departure from previous policy. Until now, in Russia, as elsewhere, conventional arms sales were regarded as an essential and legitimate policy instrument with which to uphold national defense industries which face great pressure from cutbacks in the post-Cold War environment. Now Russia has apparently given up on getting capital for its civilian reconstruction from other civilian sources and will aggressively sell weapons anywhere to restore civilian and defense industry.

This tallies with the report given by Duma member and military expert Alexei Arbatov to a conference in California last year. Arbatov revealed that the Defense Ministry told producers it cannot buy their weapons until 2005 when it hopes the situation will be stabilized so that Russia can reenter the next round of conventional procurement. Until then, they are free to sell any and all conventional systems without government export controls. And indeed, they must do so to obtain the income needed for research and development (R&D) for 2005.[148] Since arms sales are now supposed to fund military reform as well as defense industry and political operations like election campaigns, the pressure to sell anything abroad, even state-of-the-art systems, will surely intensify. Russian arms sellers proudly point out that they do not attach political criteria to deals or refrain from selling their state-of-the-art production.[149] The implications are clear. A fight for markets and likely arms race will occur throughout all the regions where Russia is pushing weapons.

This rationale also conforms to statements by Minatom about its sales of centrifuges and other nuclear technology to Iran. These sales prevent the layoff of thousands of workers in Minatom's far-flung empire, gain scarce foreign capital, and demonstrate and extend the level of Russian production technologies and know-how.[150] Fear of Iranian nuclear weapons was dismissed as a cover for economic rivalry as America's main objective. And as a final example of the utter cynicism with which this proliferation policy is conducted, Moscow and Iran jointly issued a joint call for a non-nuclear Middle East.[151]

Since Russia is engaged in a global quest for markets, we can expect a bruising competition with Western and other producers. Especially in troubled areas like the Middle East, this competition can only help further militarize all security relationships for Iran, its neighbors (including Iraq and the other Gulf states), Syria, Turkey, and Israel. Arms and technology sales which are also a major domestic political money tree, have duly become now a major state priority and a factor in destabilizing critical areas. Apart from offering Syria weapons, Russia is selling SAMs (SA-10s) to Cyprus and Iran, and offering nuclear technology, weapons technology, and reactors to India, China, Pakistan, Cuba, Syria, Iraq, and Iran. There is talk of $5 billion in atomic reactor deals and even of 50-70 transfers of reactors for cash to China.[152]

The foregoing goes beyond arguing that arms sales are undertaken to rescue Russian defense industry or even civilian industry, and the atomic industry located in Minatom. Arguably we see the takeover of a key domain of foreign, defense, and economic policy by an interest group or groups, defense industry, and the atomic industry. They are intent on rescuing themselves at the expense of Russia's civilian reconstruction or its vital strategic long-range security interests. Moreover, because the arms and nuclear sales industry is a gold mine in terms of access to foreign currencies and markets, it has become a cash cow for politicians to milk for purposes of building their private war chests. This helps explain why the arms sales program has undergone constant reorganization and changes in its leadership almost from the start, and has always been the subject of a continuing struggle for control over its revenues among the highest levels of the Russian government. Essentially in arms sales, including nuclear and other WMD sales, the lust for private gain has overtaken the effort to devise and execute a coherent national interest and strategy.

This privatization of the state does not mean that weapons and technologies are *solely* sold abroad for private gains. But it does suggest that the leaders of the state cannot disentangle their private interests from those of Russia or of international security more broadly, and are engaged in wholesale subversion of their own laws and treaties they have signed. In the past, and perhaps even now, there have been many cases of covert arms and technology transfer abroad. Foreign pressure has repeatedly led to the promulgation of new decrees and programs of export controls of sensitive and dual-use systems, all seemingly to no avail. The Iranian and other cases described below show us repeatedly that the claims about strict bureaucratic controls are mocked by high-level officials like Primakov who loudly deny Russia's involvement in proliferation even as they are deeply engaged in subverting their own laws. This confluence of private with public interests and high officials' continuous subversion of the state's laws and interests graphically testify to Russia's raging crisis of statehood, and the absence of a coherent national interest. Indeed, at the same moment as Russia sells weapons that are most likely to be used against Israel, its defense industry pushes joint Israeli-Russian deals for sales abroad, e.g., to China![153]

Minatom exemplifies this fusion of private and national interests. Its responsibilities include not just its employees' jobs, but a ramified social welfare network that served them and their families as well as all of Russia's reactors and civilian nuclear installations. Its two ministers, Viktor Mikhailov and his successor, Yevgeny Adamov, believe they must mount an aggressive international marketing campaign to provide for its well-being and that of its employees. Therefore Minatom strongly pushes nuclear exports to China, Iran, India, and more recently Syria and Cuba, all ostensibly for civilian use.[154] Minatom claims it must market its reactors aggressively to survive and other arguments do not move it for good reason. More recently, Minatom stated the aim of becoming a global competitor, a second Gazprom.[155]

There is every reason to expect this state of affairs to continue, if not entrench itself further. Primakov's views are already known, but the factors cited above accurately reflect the ongoing strength of the defense industry lobby. Since 1992 the myth has grown that arms sales are the way to recovery. And today's desperation, plus the assiduity of Russia's arms sellers, has encouraged this fantasy and created important constituencies for supporting a policy of making defense exports the priority of industrial policy. The emphasis on defense production as the expected locomotive of recovery was first voiced in 1992 by Mikhail Malei, Yeltsin's advisor on these issues, and was no more realistic then than it is now.[156] But the fantasy retains great appeal and is strongly entrenched among members of the arms sales community, like Yevgeny Anan'ev, the director of Rosvooruzhenie—the state's official agency for arms sales abroad. Arms sales command popular support among the regional governors, as they fund factories and keep people working while bringing in some desperately needed foreign revenue. Indeed, whole factories are working only for export now and would otherwise shut down, despite the risks of selling abroad.[157]

And as central power collapses, the regional governors are becoming increasingly influential players who wish to preserve the current regime at Rosvooruzhenie and deplore the agency's previous condition as a political football. Apparently they have been able to prevail and help retain Anan'ev in power, because he is quite solicitous of their interests and remits monies to them.[158] Thus key economic and political lobbies made up of governors, defense industry, and its numerous patrons or dependents help sustain defense industry as yet another unproductive rent-seeking sector of the economy. Whenever any effort has been made to shut down defense plants, among the most unproductive in the entire economy, a vociferous lobbying campaign has arisen to prevent this. Therefore, of approximately 1700 factories producing defense goods, only 500 produce anything worthwhile, and the rest cannot even be sold off at bankruptcy auctions. Yet they continue on the books and remain value-subtracting industries and a major component of Russia's "virtual economy."[159]

Politicians have also bought into this mythology. At the same time, Primakov's Deputy Prime Minister Yuri Maslyukov has made no secret of his desire to take control over the entire defense industry and foreign arms sales in order to reconstitute something like the Soviet defense industrial structure. So clearly the arms trade in its entirety will remain a political football.[160] Primakov's support for expanded arms sales in order to revitalize not just defense industry but civilian industry as well reveals a desire to use state policy consciously to reverse the global trend whereby civilian discoveries generate advances in military production.[161] The current crisis can only intensify the drive to sell dual-use technologies and weapons abroad even though Russia well understands that the global market for weapons is currently shrinking and that it often requires foreign financing to produce products that are saleable abroad.

Russian arms sales leaders have long since renounced any efforts to sell on the grounds of ideological conviction. Rather, arms are sold for economic and political considerations—a fact that has not precluded frequent barter deals which make no sense.[162] They have also proclaimed their willingness to sell systems that the Russian armed forces do not yet have since they cannot afford to buy them, and it costs more to produce for the domestic than the foreign market! Anan'ev now maintains that,

> In essence, weapons are now the most high-tech Russian exports meeting world standards today. Weapons represent around 80 percent of all Russian industrial exports. This alone justifies the creation of all of the necessary conditions for successful export expansion in the defense sector of our economy.[163]

Anan'ev clearly is calling for continued efforts to recover all of Moscow's previous markets and implicitly for remilitarizing the economy to promote arms sales that bring so much to Russia. He claims that increased arms sales are also linked with the recovery of Moscow's voice on the international stage. Arms sales have followed Russia's reassertion of its national interests and contribute to the successful promotion of those interests abroad. As he concludes,

> Military-technical cooperation with foreign countries is still one of the highest priorities of state activity in Russia. It is the source of a high percentage of state budget receipts in hard currency, represents an important means of paying the state debt, secures the employment of a large segment of the adult population, and guarantees the continued existence of the Russian military-industrial complex, which now produces products in high demand in the international market, surpassed only by energy resources in their competitive potential. Russian military have good prospects, but progress in this field will require the utmost consolidation of the efforts of all the structures and agencies participating in military-technical cooperation and legislative bodies on all levels.[164]

Cyprus.

Many of Russia's ambitions and the risks it runs thereby emerge in its arms deals with Cyprus to provide it with

S-300 surface-to-air anti-aircraft missiles which could easily be reconfigured to attack Turkey proper. Both Cyprus and Greece intended these weapons to be bargaining chips to compel Ankara and perhaps Washington to pay attention to the situation on Cyprus and negotiate a settlement to the issue of Turkish forces there.[165]

Moscow saw things otherwise. Not only did it gain a new client for its defense industries and further extend its influence into Cyprus, a known haven for Russian money-laundering, Moscow also saw a golden opportunity to drive a deep division into NATO by aggravating Greco-Turkish competition. One of the hallmarks of Russian policy has been a renewed emphasis on fostering ties with Greece to check Turkish ambitions and NATO's presence in the Balkans. This is based on Serbia's and Greece's interest in keeping Albania and Macedonia quiet, and not allowing Kossovo to secede. The pursuit of the rapprochement with Athens has even led to regular Greco-Russian security discussions and more recently to arms deals.[166] Naturally, Russia was more than happy to comply with Cyprus' request and train the Cypriots in the use of the system.

But for Ankara, this was and is a major threat, and it announced that it would shoot down the missiles or board the ships carrying them through the Straits. Russian spokesmen retorted that Russia might react to such actions as if they were an act of war. Russia's opportunism now bid fair to embroil it in a European war against Turkey and implicitly NATO. While this sat well with the many members of the elite who regard Turkey as a threat due to its unconcealed ambitions to build a Trans-Caucasian barrier against Russian influence and wrest energy pipelines and terminals away from Russia, this would also strike at one of Russia's major trading partners and at some of the most flourishing trade relationships that Moscow currently enjoys. Furthermore, Turkey let it be known that it might bar Russia from its huge defense contracts. And

Russian arms manufacturers actually expect such an outcome and see little prospect for that market.[167]

In short, Russian opportunism and its strictly short-term horizon—raising ready cash from defense sales—threatened some of its most vital interests and security. As a sign of what Russia stood to lose from the deal, originally announced in late 1996, Pavel Felgengauer, Russia's leading defense correspondent, wrote that in December 1996 Turkish Prime Minister Tansu Ciller offered to prevent NATO enlargement from becoming a new dividing line in Europe or a threat against Russia.[168]

> But the Russian arms traders and the all-powerful banks that finance and control arms trade were not interested. They had something more important than enlargement on their minds—profits. The Cyprus deal is strictly a commercial one which will bring huge returns to middle-men. Arms shipments to Turkey, on the other hand, only cover previous Russian government debt. And such deals do not bring any substantial profits to traders. The Russian arms trade lobby wanted the Cyprus contract as soon as possible in order to secure government-guaranteed commercial credit to the arms industry.Lending rates are falling in Russia and the earlier a good loan can be clinched, the better.[169]

Although there is clearly a disposition to see Turkey as the enemy, as an expansionist power, and as a leader in the attempt to penetrate Transcaucasia and the Black Sea, Russia cannot directly confront it yet. But the Black Sea Fleet clearly views Turkey as a threat and seeks parity with it.[170]

Furthermore, the crisis became internationalized. Turkey and Israel became close military partners, and Israel trained Turkish pilots in attacks against these missiles. Britain and the United States became alarmed at the military and intelligence issues involved if Cyprus got Russian technicians to run its air defenses. Moscow also warned Israel to desist from involvement. Finally, Washington has now directly brought its pressure to bear in attempting to negotiate a settlement with Greece and Turkey. The pursuit of short-term and crass opportunism on Russia's part frightened Cyprus and Greece, neither of whom wants a conflict. Thus they decided to take delivery in November 1998 rather than July, ostensibly because they did not want to disrupt the tourist season.[171]

Since then, Russia has reiterated its intention to fulfill every part of the contract as far as training, installing, and operating those weapons until the Cypriots learn how to use them. Moreover, there are reports of a long-term defense accord, presumably entailing further sales to Cyprus and/or Greece.[172] At the time of this writing, the situation remains unclear. Russia may get its money, but it is not certain the weapons will be delivered or that there will be further contracts. On the other hand, the arms might indeed go to Cyprus with unforeseeable consequences. But what is already certain is that an arms race has begun in the Eastern Mediterranean with Turkey, Greece, and Cyprus all racing to modernize and reequip their armed forces. And this arms race takes place in an atmosphere of growing Turkish fears of being surrounded on all sides by Russian missiles in the hands of Moscow's partners and its enemies.[173] We abetted this by cascading surplus weapons in Europe to Greece and Turkey after the CFE treaty went into effect, and these new Russian sales add more fuel to the fire. In either case, one may ask what lasting long-term benefits will accrue to Russia from this adventure compared to the costs involved.

Russia and the Peace Process.

Although Moscow certainly does not want a new war in the area since another Arab-Israeli war will only intensify Washington's dominance in the area, its policies towards the peace process are hardly helpful. This does not mean Moscow is the main author of the reasons for its present crisis, but its policies are now inimical to the cause of peace. Israel does not trust it, hopes of a rapprochement with

Jerusalem have been dashed, and Moscow has no ideas to offer any of the parties.

It did not have to be this way. There were forces in the Russian government, namely the military, led in this case by former Defense Minister General Pavel Grachev and more recently by Security Council chairman Andrei Kokoshin, who sought a lasting strategic dialogue, if not partnership with Israel. They very much sought this dialogue on behalf of Russian defense industry which saw a big opportunity to work with Israel's highly regarded defense and high-tech industries to gain access to those systems, Western technology and know-how, and new markets. Israel is making a fortune on revamping old Soviet arms, and the Russian defense industry clearly wanted access to this process. Accordingly, Grachev signed an agreement with Israel in 1995.[174] Kokoshin, too, wanted to continue this partnership and strategic dialogue with Israel to benefit the Russian defense industry.[175]

However, Russian proliferation towards Iran and support for Iraq and Syria's rearmament has made it difficult, if not impossible, to continue this partnership, and Israel has suspended economic cooperation with Russia.[176] Kokoshin was fired from the Security Council when Primakov became Prime Minister, although this was apparently done for internal reasons connected with the struggle for power in Russia. Still, Primakov's policies have made it quite impossible for Jerusalem and Russia to effect a rapprochement, and this seems to have been Primakov's goal. For example, when Israel advanced a new proposal for leaving Southern Lebanon through direct bilateral negotiations with Beirut, he supported Syria's policy of quashing this attempt and retaining Damascus' protectorate over Lebanon; in other words, preserving a source of tension in the area.[177] Primakov also gratuitously stated that, once the Palestinian Authority proclaims statehood, Russia would recognize it. Furthermore, Russia quite clearly is trying to associate itself with the EU as leaders in the peace process. This gambit won no plaudits in

Israel which regards both Russia and the EU as prejudiced, and not impartial, bystanders.[178] These actions, coupled with the mendacious policy towards proliferation and Iran, led Israel to lobby the U.S. Congress to impose sanctions on Russia, a prospect that clearly antagonized Moscow and did not help it or Washington in their mutual relations. This became especially true when Iran tested its Shihab-3 missile made with Russian help and demonstrated its growing missile capabilities.

Here again Primakov sacrificed economic advantage since Israel is Moscow's largest trading partner in the area, and the possibility of aiding the defense establishment by this strategic partnership, in favor of a policy whose roots date back to Brezhnev of orchestrating an anti-American and anti-Israeli bloc among Syria, Iraq, and Iran. The evident purpose of this policy seems only to force Washington to let Russia back into the Middle East by raising the high degree of tension that already exists there. Bereft of constructive ideas about the peace process and unwilling to invest in confidence-building measures or policies, Russia seems intent on playing a spoiler's role in the area's potentially most dangerous conflict. Yet there is little chance of it successfully persuading Washington to admit it to the peace process in any meaningful way.

In October 1998 its weak position was exposed when Yasser Arafat called for Russia to participate in the October 15, 1998, negotiations with Israel and the United States at the Wye Plantation. Arafat, appealing to Russia as co-chair of the Madrid conference of 1991, the formal genesis of the peace process, clearly wanted Moscow's full support for his goals of increased autonomy and eventual statehood. But Moscow can only support him to a limited degree. Although there is clearly much sympathy for his position and the Palestinian cause in the Duma and the government, other considerations also apply.[179]

Moscow's utter prostration and need for foreign support limits the degree to which it can directly confront the United

States on a vital issue. Thus Ivanov was quoted as saying that the creation of an independent Palestinian state, "cannot contradict Israel's national interests, especially in the sphere of security."[180] Presumably this is not exactly what Arafat wanted to hear from Moscow. While Moscow stated a request to participate in the Wye Plantation negotiations, at the same time it clearly had no new ideas to offer to either side.[181] But while this stance may not cause problems with Washington over an issue where Moscow cannot really exercise much leverage, it does not seem calculated to win over the suspicious Israelis or to convince the Palestinians that Moscow can be relied upon. As in much of Russian foreign policy, we see here a defensive demand to be taken seriously, a plea which in itself betrays the fact that here, as in Kosovo for example, Moscow is "irrelevant" to vital U.S. decisions and policy-making mechanisms.

Conclusions.

Unquestionably Primakov and his policies have been lionized at home. But it is unclear to what degree they have made Russia more secure, although some elites now feel better about Russia. However, tangible economic and political gains have been sacrificed, and it is not clear that Primakov's victories have achieved more than to annoy the United States and Israel. He certainly owes much to what could be the most inept U.S. policy in the Gulf in several years. While he has maneuvered most ably on the Russian and world stage, he oversees a still ruined estate whose management did nothing in the time he gave it to improve conditions or exploit the gains he made.

Moreover, his policies have abetted some of the most dangerous trends in world politics, specifically the diffusion of nuclear and other military technologies. From a U.S. point of view, these policies threaten our allies and our strategy which places a premium on foreign presence. Conventional, not to say nuclear, or chemical, or biological, warheads in the hands of an enemy in the region immensely complicates any hope of using Middle Eastern lodgements as forward bases. And as missile capabilities spread, they will embrace Europe and North Africa, with similar results for us. But this not a reason for Moscow to rejoice either. Those capabilities also put more and more of Russia's land mass at risk. Although Primakov and Yeltsin have repeatedly denied that they would be crazy enough to permit these capabilities to spread to states like Iran, that is exactly what they have done. Here, too, ultimately Russian policy's strength lies essentially in its capacity for negation of American and local initiatives that would possibly bring peace to the region and help calm Russia's own troubled southern frontier. As in the past, Russia has chosen power and prestige over true security and lasting commercial benefit for itself and its peoples. However, the old game seems to offer little but future danger to Russia. After all, if the present trend towards maximizing the state's status and reputation abroad grows at the expense of its ability to provide for domestic security, Russia, too, could then be burned in the fire that its policies have helped to stoke.

ENDNOTES - CHAPTER 17

1. Graham E. Fuller, "Soviet-American Competition in the Middle East: The Changing Face of International Conflict" and Steven L. Spiegel, "Arab-Israeli Crises, 1945-1990: The Soviet-American Dimension," both in Steven L. Spiegel, ed., *Conflict Management in the Middle East*, Boulder, CO: Westview Press, 1992, pp. 23, 172, respectively.

2. Jack Snyder, *Myths of Empire: Domestic Politics and International Ambition*, Ithaca, NY: Cornell University Press, 1991; Helen V. Milner, *Interests, Institutions, and Information: Domestic Politics and International Relations*, Princeton, NJ: Princeton University Press, 1998.

3. Philip Robins, "The Middle East and Central Asia," Peter Ferdinand, ed., *The New States of Central Asia and Their Neighbors*, New York: Council on Foreign Relations Press, 1994, p. 57; Daniel Pipes, "The Event of Our Era: Former Soviet Muslim Republics Change the Middle East," in Michael Mandlebaum, ed., *Central Asia and the*

World, New York: Council on Foreign Relations Press, 1994, p. 85; Andrei Tchistiakov, "Changes in the Middle East and the Outside World," *International Affairs*, No. 11-12, November-December 1995, pp. 107, 111; Bulent Aras, "Israel's Strategy in Azerbaijan and Central Asia," *Middle East Policy*, Vol. V, No. 4, 1998, pp. 68-81; David Menashri, ed., *Central Asia Meets the Middle East*, London: Frank Cass Publishers, 1998. Even Robins, who is skeptical of efforts to assert this linkage, concedes that, if there is more interaction between Central Asia and the Middle East, they will draw nearer as geopolitical entities, Robins, pp. 55-74. But we must remember that for Russia, the Caucasus and Central Asia have been the only geographical roads to those areas.

4. John Donnelly, "CIA: Iraq Could Restart Doomsday Lines 'overnight'," *Defense News*, September 8, 1998, p. 1.

5. Moscow, *Diplomaticheskii Vestnik*, in Russian, No. 7, July, 1996, *Foreign Broadcast Information Service, Central Eurasia* (henceforth *FBIS-SOV*)-96-211, October 31, 1996; Coit D. Blacker, "Russia and the West," Michael Mandlebaum, ed., *The New Russian Foreign Policy*, New York: Council on Foreign Relations Press, 1998, p. 183; *Johnson's Russia List*, no. 2097, March 8, 1998, *davidjohnson@erols.com*.

6. Moscow, *Rossiyskaya Gazeta*, in Russian, September 27, 1997, *FBIS-SOV*-97-272, September 30, 1997; Paris, *Le Nouvel Observateur*, in French, August 8-16, 1996, *Foreign Broadcast Information Service Western Europe* (henceforth *FBIS-WEU*)-96-156, August 12, 1996, p. 10.

7. Stephen Blank, "State and Armed Forces in Russia; Toward an African Scenario," forthcoming in a book to be edited by Anthony Joes and published by Praeger Publishers.

8. Ralph Peters, "Spotting the Losers: Seven Signs of Non-competitive States," *Parameters*, Vol. XXVIII, No. 1, Spring 1998, pp. 36-42; Pauline Baker and John A. Ausink, "State Violence: Toward a Predictive Model," *Parameters*, Vol. XXVI, No. 3, Fall 1996, pp. 19-31; and Robert Dorff, "Democratization and Failed States: The Challenge of Ungovernability," *Parameters*, Vol. XXVI, No. 2, Summer 1996, pp. 20-23; Carnegie Commission On Preventing Deadly Conflict, *Preventing Deadly Conflict*, Final Report and Executive Summary, New York: Carnegie Corporation of New York, 1997, p. 44.

9. "Yeltsin Address to Diplomats," *Mezhdunarodnaya Zhizn'*, No. 6, June 1998, and *The Russian Weekly*, No. 6, July 24, 1998, *davidjohnson@erols.com* (henceforth Yeltsin Address). See also Moscow, *Vooruzhenie, Politika, Konversiya*, No. 2, February 1, 1997, *FBIS-SOV*, August 23, 1998, for an interview with Ivan Rybkin, then

Secretary of the Security Council; and "Russia's National Interests: *Johnson's Russia List*, August 15, 1997, *davidjohnson @erols.com*; Paul Goble, "Can Russian Diplomacy Hold Russia Together," *Radio Free Europe/Radio Liberty Newsline*, September 23, 1998; *The Monitor*, March 19, 1998 and September 23, 1998; Yevgeny Primakov, "Russia: Reforms and Foreign Policy," *International Affairs*, (Moscow), No. 4, 1998, pp. 3-6.

10. Leon Aron, "The Foreign Policy Doctrine of Postcommunist Russia and Its Domestic Context," Michael Mandlebaum, ed., *The New Russian Foreign Policy*, New York: Council on Foreign Relations Press, 1998, pp. 27-33.

11. See the sources cited in Endnote No. 9.

12. "Seleznev Calls Ukraine to Order," The Jamestown Foundation, *Prism*, October 2, 1998.

13. Moscow, *Rossiyskaya Gazeta*, in Russian, September 23, 1995, *FBIS-SOV*-95-188, September 28, 1995, pp. 19-22; The Jamestown Foundation, *Prism*, Part 1, "The Fortnight in Review," November 13, 1998.

14. Quoted in Aras, p. 72.

15. Jim Hoagland, "Primakov's Task," *Washington Post*, September 17, 1998, p. 21; Moscow, *Interfax*, in English, February 22, 1996, *FBIS-SOV*-96-037, February 23, 1996, p. 18; London, *Al-Hayah*, in Arabic, January 3, 1996; *FBIS-SOV*-96-003, January 4, 1996, p. 9; Moscow, *ITAR-TASS World Service*, in Russian, October 31, 1998; *FBIS-SOV*-97-304, November 4, 1997.

16. Stephen Blank, "Every Shark East of Suez: Great Power Interests, Policies, and Tactics in the Trans-Caspian Energy Wars," forthcoming in *Central Asian Survey*.

17. Zbigniew Brzezinski, *The Grand Chessboard: American Primacy and its Geostrategic Imperatives*, New York: Basic Books, 1997; and, "A Geostrategy for Eurasia," *Foreign Affairs*, Vol. LXXVI, No. 5, September-October 1997, pp. 50-64.

18. Blank, "Every Shark East of Suez," forthcoming.

19. Alvin Z. Rubinstein, "The Geopolitical Pull on Russia," *Orbis*, Vol. XXXVIII, No. 4, Fall 1994, pp. 579-80.

20. Geoffrey Kemp and Robert Harkavy, *Strategic Geography and the Changing Middle East*, Washington, DC: Carnegie Endowment for International Peace, 1997, "Introduction," p. xiii.

21. Robert D. Blackwill and Michael Stuermer, "Introduction," Robert D. Blackwill and Michael Stuermer, eds., *Allies Divided: Transatlantic Policies for the Greater Middle East*, Cambridge MA: MIT University Press, 1997, p. 2.

22. Ambassador Matthew Nimetz, "Mediterranean Security After the Cold War," *Mediterranean Quarterly*, Vol. VIII, No. 2, Spring 1997, p. 29.

23. *Ibid*.

24. Warren Christopher and William J. Perry, "NATO's True Mission," *New York Times*, October 21, 1997, p. 25.

25. David Kerr, "The New Eurasianism: The Rise of Geopolitics in Russia's Foreign Policy," *Europe-Asia Studies*, Vol. XLVII, No. 6, 1995, pp. 977-988; Nikolai Sokov, "A New Cold War? Reflections of a Russian Diplomat," *International Journal*, Vol. XLIX, No. 4, Autumn 1994, pp. 914-915.

26. Walter A. McDougall, *Promised Land, Crusader State: The American Encounter with the World Since 1776*, Boston: Houghton Mifflin, 1997, pp. 172-222.

27. "Russia's National Interests:, *Johnson's Russia List*, August 15, 1997, davidjohnson@erols.com.

28. Mohiaddin Mesbahi, "Russia and The Geopolitics of the Muslim South," in Mohiaddin Mesbahi, ed., *Central Asia and the Caucasus After the Soviet Union: Domestic and International Dynamics,* Gainesville, FL: University Press of Florida, 1994, p. 295.

29. See, for example, General-Major Evgeny G. Nikitenko, "Russia's Role, Allies, and Threats in the New Eurasian World," *Defense & Foreign Affairs Strategic Policy*, June 1998, p. 10; Dushanbe, *Biznes i Politika*, in Russian, September 11, 1998, *FBIS-SOV,* October 6, 1998, for an interview with Russia's ambassador to Tajikistan, Yevgeny Belov, who makes similar charges.

30. Stephen Blank, "Russia and Iran in a New Middle East," *Mediterranean Quarterly,* Vol. III, No. 4, Fall 1992, pp. 124-127.

31. Nikitenko, p. 10.

32. Mohiaddin Mesbahi, "Introduction: The Emerging 'Muslim' States of Central Asia and the Caucasus," in Mesbahi, ed., p. 2.

33. Henry Trofimenko, "'New World Order' and Russian-American Relations," Hafeez Malik, ed., *The Roles of the United States, Russia, and China in the New World Order*, New York: St. Martin's Press, 1997, pp. 51-53.

34. *Yeltsin Address, Reuters*, January 19, 1997.

35. Sergey M. Rogov, "Russia and NATO's Enlargement: The Search for a Compromise at the Helsinki Summit," Center for Naval Analyses, Alexandria, VA, CIM 513/May 1997, p. 10.

36. For Trenin's views and other such expressions, see E-mail Letter from Darrell Hammer, *Johnson's Russia List*, February 5, 1997; Dmitry Trenin, "Transformation of Russian Foreign Policy: NATO Expansion Can Have Negative Consequences for the West," *Nezavisimaya Gazeta*, February 5, 1997, E-Mail Transmission; J. Michael Waller, "Primakov's Imperial Line," *Perspective*, Vol. VII, No. 3, January-February 1997, pp. 2-6; "Primakov, Setting a New, Tougher Foreign Policy," *Current Digest of the Post-Soviet Press* (henceforth *CDPP*), Vol. XLIX, No. 2, February 12, 1997, pp. 4-7.

37. Indeed, as Dmitri Trenin points out, Moscow has been on all sides of all questions in the Caucasus. Dmitry Trenin, "Russia's Security Interests and Policies in the Caucasus Region," Bruno Coppieters, ed., *Contested Borders in the Caucasus*, Brussels: VUB University Press, 1996, p. 99.

38. London, *Al-Hayah*, in Arabic, April 18, 1998, *Foreign Broadcast Information Service Near East and South Asia*, (henceforth *FBIS-NES*)-98-111, April 23, 1998.

39. Spiegel, pp. 166-172; Zeev Maoz, "Regional Security in the Middle East: Past Trends, Present Realities, and Future Challenges, *Journal of Strategic Studies*, Vol. XX, No. 1, March 1997, pp. 1-45.

40. *FBIS-SOV*, September 30, 1997, *FBIS-WEU*, August 12, 1996.

41. *Ibid*.

42. *Ibid*.

43. *Ibid*.; Blacker, p. 183; Moscow, *Komsomolskaya Pravda*, in Russian, September 30, 1998, *FBIS-SOV*, September 30, 1998.

44. Ye. Primakov, "Russia and the Outside World," *International Affairs* (Moscow), No. 3, 1998, pp. 7-13.

45. V. Lukov, "Russia's Security Challenges," *International Affairs* (Moscow), No. 1, 1997, pp. 14-15.

46. *FBIS-SOV*, September 30, 1998.

47. *Yeltsin Address*, *The Monitor*, September 23, 1998.

48. Gerhard Simon, "Russia's Identity and International Politics," *Aussenpolitik,* English Language Edition, No. 3, 1997, pp. 245-256.

49. *Yeltsin Address.*

50. Trenin; Hammer.

51. *Yeltsin Address;* "Ivan Rybkin on Russia's Global Role, Johnson's Russia List,* July 8, 1997, *davidjohnson@erols.com.*; Moscow, *Izvestiya,* in Russian, January 21, 1998, *FBIS-SOV*-98-034, February 3, 1998; Mohiaddin Mesbahi, "Russian Foreign Policy and Security in Central Asia and the Caucasus," *Central Asian Survey*, Vol. XII, No. 2, 1993, p. 187, for Primakov's globalism and statement that history never nullifies geopolitical values.

52. Gareev is quoted in Mikhail Tsypkin, "Military Power in Russian National Security Policy," Sanford R. Lieberman, David E. Powell, Carol R. Saivetz, and Sarah M. Terry, eds., *The Soviet Empire Reconsidered: Essays in Honor of Adam B. Ulam,* Boulder, CO: Westview Press, 1995, p. 204.

53. Andrei A. Kokoshin, *Soviet Strategic Thought, 1917-91,* Cambridge, MA: MIT Press, CSIA Studies in International Security, 1998, p. 195.

54. Aron, pp. 23-63; and for an official Chinese view, see Beijing, *Renmin Ribao Overseas Edition*, in Chinese, February 10, 1998, *Foreign Broadcast Information Service China* (henceforth *FBIS-CHI*)-98-041, February 12, 1998.

55. Oleg V. Davydov, "Russia's Foreign Policy in Transition: Prospects and Challenges in the Asia-Pacific Region," *Asian Perspective,* Vol. XXII, No. 1, Spring 1998, pp. 53-69; Mikhail A. Alekseev, "Russia's Cold Peace Consensus: Transcending the Presidential Election," *Fletcher Forum of World Affairs,* Vol. XXI, No. 1, Winter-Spring 1997, pp. 33-51.

56. John P. LeDonne, *The Russian Empire and the World, 1700-1917*, New York: Oxford University Press, 1997.

57. Aron, pp. 23-63; Alekseev, pp. 33-51; Lally Weymouth, "What Ivanov Wants," *Washington Post*, October 6, 1998, p. 23.

58. Alvin Z. Rubinstein, "Moscow and Teheran: The Wary Accommodation," Alvin Z. Rubinstein and Oles M. Smolansky, eds., *Regional Power Rivalries in the New Eurasia: Russia, Turkey, and Iran*, Armonk, New York: M.E. Sharpe, Inc. and Co., 1994, p. 31.

59. *Ibid.*, pp. 31-32.

60. Moscow, *ITAR-TASS*, in English, October 9, 1998, *FBIS-SOV*, October 9, 1998, for Arafat's proposal that Russia join what was then the upcoming summit at the Wye Plantation; for Mubarak, see Moscow, *Nezavisimaya Gazeta*, in Russian, September 23, 1997, *FBIS-SOV*-97-266, September 24, 1997; for Syria, see London, *Al-Hawadith*, in Arabic, March 13, 1998, *FBIS-SOV*-98-111, April 23, 1998.

61. Moscow, *Komsomolskaya Pravda*, in Russian, March 21, 1996, *FBIS-SOV*-96-056, March 21, 1996, p. 16; *The Jamestown Monitor*, March 14, 1996.

62. *Ibid.*

63. Moscow, *Izvestiya*, in Russian, June 8, 1996, *FBIS-SOV*-96-112, pp. 24-25.

64. Hoagland, p. 21; Moscow, *ITAR-TASS*, in English, April 23, 1996, *FBIS-SOV*-96-080, April 24, 1996, p. 24; Moscow, *Interfax*, in English, *Ibid.*, pp. 22-23. For an account by the Russian state newspaper, *Izvestiya*, which is rather critical of Primakov's undiplomatic tactics, see Moscow, *Izvestiya*, in Russian, April 26, 1996, *FBIS-SOV*-96-082, April 26, 1996, pp. 23-24; William Drozdiak, "Israel Says U.S. Should Broker Peace," *Washington Post*, April 22, 1996, p. A10; and Moscow, *ITAR-TASS*, in English, April 22, 1996, *FBIS-SOV*-96-079, April 23, 1996, p. 27.

65. This is hardly a recent trend. For an outstanding demonstration of this trend for the 1950s, see Fawaz A. Gerges, *The Superpowers and the Middle East: Regional and International Politics, 1955-1967*, William Quandt, "Foreword," Boulder, CO: Westview Press, 1994; and, more recently, Haim Shemesh, *Soviet Iraqi Relations 1968-1988: In the Shadow of the Iraq-Iran Conflict*, Boulder, CO: Lynne Rienner, 1992; Oles Smolansky with Bettie M. Smolansky, *The USSR and Iraq: The*

Soviet Quest for Influence, Durham, NC: Duke University Press, 1991; and Moshe Efrat and Jacob Bercovitch, eds., *Superpowers and Client States in the Middle East*, London and New York: Routledge, 1991.

66. Moscow, *ITAR-TASS*, in English, March 23, 1995, *FBIS-SOV*-95-060, March 29, 1995, p. 11.

67. Nikolai Sokov, *Domestic Structure, Economic Growth, and Russian Foreign Policy*, Program on New Approaches to Russian Security, Davis Center for Russian Studies, Harvard University, Cambridge, MA, Policy Memo Series, No. 23, 1997, pp. 1-3.

68. *Ibid.*

69. *Ibid.*

70. Clifford G. Gaddy and Barry W. Ickes, "Russia's Virtual Economy," *Foreign Affairs*, Vol. LXXVII, No. 5, September-October 1998, pp. 53-67.

71. Sokov, pp. 1-3; Stephen Blank, "Who's Minding the State?: The Failure of Russian Security Policy," *Problems of Post-Communism*," Vol. XLV, No. 2, March-April 1998, pp. 3-11.

72. Stephen Blank, *Energy, Economics and Security in Central Asia*, Carlisle Barracks, PA: Strategic Studies Institute, U.S. Army War College, May 1995.

73. Tehran, *Abrar* in Persian, March 7, 1995, *FBIS-NES*-95-052, March 17, 1995, pp. 71-72.

74. Blank, "Russia and Iran," pp. 124-127.

75. Moscow, *Mirovaya Ekonomika i Mezhdunarodnye Otnosheniya*, No. 1, January, 1995 (World Economy and International Relations), *FBIS-SOV*-95-056-S, March 23, 1995, pp. 11-16.

76. Tehran, *Irna*, in English, March 8, 1995, *FBIS-NES*-95-045, March 8, 1995, p. 51.

77. Tehran, *Abrar,* in Persian, March 7, 1995, *FBIS-NES*-95-052, March 17, 1995, pp. 71-72; Paris *AFP*, in English, March 21, 1995, *FBIS-NES*-95-056, March 23, 1995, pp. 47-48; Judith Perera, "Russia: Stepping Into the Gulf," *Middle East International*, March 20, 1995, p. 13; Moscow, *Interfax*, in English, December 5, 1995, *FBIS-SOV*-95-234, December 6, 1995, p. 25.

78. Stephen Grummon, "Introduction" in "Russian Ambitions in the Persian Gulf," *Middle East Quarterly*, Vol. II, No. 1, March, 1995, pp. 87-92; Alexei Vassiliev, *Russian Foreign Policy in the Middle East: From Messianism to Pragmatism*, Reading: Ithaca Press, 1993, p. 360.

79. Tehran, *IRNA* in English, May 30, 1995, *FBIS-NES*-95-104, May 31, 1995, pp. 65-66.

80. Tehran, *IRNA*, in English, July 20, 1998, *FBIS-NES*-98-201, July 21, 1998.

81. *Ibid.*

82. Blank, "Every Shark East of Suez."

83. International Institute of Strategic Studies, *Strategic Survey 1997/98*, London: Oxford University Press, 1998, pp. 22-29.

84. Jill Crystal, *Oil and Politics in the Gulf: Rulers and Merchants in Kuwait and Qatar*, Cambridge: Cambridge University Press, 1990; Giacomo Luciani, "The Oil Rent, the Fiscal Crisis of the State and Democratization," Ghassan Salame, ed., *Democracy Without Democrats: The Renewal of Politics in the Muslim World*, London: I.B. Tauris Publishers, 1994, pp. 130-155; Jacques Delacroix, "The Distributive State in the World System," *Studies in Comparative International Development*, Vol. XV, No. 3, Fall 1980, pp. 3-21; Hazem Bebalwi, and Giacomo Luciani, eds., *The Rentier State*, Vol. II, London: Croon Helm, 1990; H. Mahdawy, "The Problems and Patterns of Economic Development in Rentier States: The Case of Iran," M.A. Cook, ed., *Studies in the Economic History of the Middle East*, London: Oxford University Press, 1970, pp. 428-467.

85. Sokov, pp. 1-3.

86. Johannes Reisner, "Europe, the United States, and the Persian Gulf," in Blackwill and Sturmer, pp. 126-127.

87. Blank, "Every Shark East of Suez."

88. Elaine Holoboff, "Russia's Strategic Pipelines." *Brassey's Defence Yearbook*, 1997, London: Brassey's, 1997, pp. 119-120.

89. *Ibid.*

90. Blank, "Energy, Economics, and Security in Central Asia."

91. *Reuters*, December 17, 1997; *The Jamestown Monitor* and *Radio Free Europe/Radio Liberty Daily Digest*, December 19, 1997.

92. Sebastian Allison, "Gazprom Threats Seen as Empty," *Moscow Times*, June 16, 1998.

93. *The Jamestown Monitor*, December 23, 1997.

94. Gaddy and Ickes, pp. 53-69, which shows that Gazprom's situation is hardly unique.

95. *FBIS-SOV*, September 28, 1995.

96. Robert Ebel, *Energy Choices in the Near Abroad: The Haves and Have-Nots Face the Future*, Washington: Center for Strategic and International Studies, 1997, pp. 11-12; *Strategic Survey*, pp. 22-29.

97. *Ibid*.

98. *Ibid*.

99. *Ibid*.

100. *Ibid*.

101. R. Jeffrey Smith, "U.S. Leads Peacekeeping Drill in Kazakstan," *Washington Post*, September 15, 1997, p. 17.

102. M. A. Smith, *Russia and the Middle East*, Conflict Studies Research Centre, RMA Sandhurst, 1994, pp. 3-4; Perera, p. 13.

103. Baghdad, *Al-Jumhuriyah*, in Arabic, January 25, 1995, *FBIS-NES*-95-071, April 13, 1995, p. 39.

104. M. A. Smith, pp. 3-5.

105. This is widely expected even after Saddam retreated in the face of superior U.S. force in November 1998.

106. Barton Gellman, "U.S. Fought Surprise Iraqi Inspections," *Washington Post*, August 14, 1998, p. 1.

107. Pavel Felgengauer, "An Uneasy Partnership: Sino-Russian Defense Cooperation and Arms Sales," Andrew J. Pierre and Dmitri V. Trenin, eds., *Russia in the World Arms Trade*, Washington, DC: Carnegie Endowment for International Peace, 1997, pp. 87-105.

108. Michael Beck, "Russia's Rationale for Developing Export Controls," Gary K. Bertsch and Suzette R. Grillot, Editors, *Arms on the Market: Reducing the Risk of Proliferation in the Former Soviet Union*, Foreword by Sam Nunn, New York: Routledge, 1998, pp. 37-38, 49.

109. *Ibid*.

110. *Ibid.*

111. *Ibid.*, "The Non-Proliferation Treaty Must Be Prolonged," *Moscow News*, April 21-27, 1995, p. 13, is one of the first in this continuing series of arguments that have not changed through 1998. For example, Moscow, *Russkiy Telegraf*, in Russian, May 20, 1998, *FBIS-SOV*-98-140, May 21, 1998; and on Iraq, see Moscow, *Interfax*, in English, July 31, 1998, *FBIS-SOV*-98-216, August 6, 1998.

112. Beck, pp. 37-38.

113. Moscow, *Mirovaya Ekonomika i Mezhdunarodnye Otnosheniya*, in Russian, No. 7, July 1998, pp. 50-60, *FBIS-SOV*, August 28, 1998.

114. *Ibid.*

115. *Ibid.*

116. *Joint Publications Research Service, Arms Control*, (henceforth *JPRS-TAC*)-95-009-L, April 6, 1995, p. 1.

117. *Ibid*, pp. 5-7.

118. *Ibid.*

119. Admiral Valentin Yegorovich Selivanov (Chief of Staff of the Navy), "A Navy's Job," *Naval Forces*, Vol. XV, No. 2, 1994, p. 31.

120. Pavel Felgengauer, "An Uneasy Partnership: Sino-Russian Defense Cooperation and Arms Sales," Andrew J. Pierre and Dmitri V. Trenin, eds., *Russia in the World Arms Trade*, Washington, DC: Carnegie Endowment for International Peace, 1997, pp. 87-105.

121. *JPRS TAC*-95-009-L, April 6, 1995, pp. 5-7.

122. "The Non-Proliferation Treaty Must Be Prolonged," *Moscow News*, April 21-27, 1995, p. 13, is one of the first in this continuing series of arguments that have not changed through 1998.

123. David S. Cloud, "Warheadache," *The New Republic*, April 20, 1998, pp. 11-12.

124. Andrei Kortunov and Andrei Shumikhin, "Russia: Changing Attitudes Toward Proliferation of Missiles and Weapons of Mass Destruction," *Comparative Strategy*, Vol. XV, No. 2, April, 1996, p. 163.

125. *Ibid.*, pp. 163-164.

126. *Ibid.*, p. 164.

127. Stephen Blank, "Dreams of a Salesman: Russia and the Proliferation of Weapons of Mass Destruction," *The World & I*, October 1998, pp. 302-19.

128. Moscow, *ITAR-TASS World Service*, in Russian, July 13, 1998, *FBIS-SOV*-98-194, July 15, 1998.

129. Graham H. Turbiville, Jr., "Weapons Proliferation and Organized Crime: The Russian Military and Security Forces Dimension," Occasional Papers of the Institute for National Security Studies, No. 10, Colorado Springs, CO: U.S. Air Force Academy, June 1996.

130. Steve Rodan, "Secret Israeli Data Reveals Iran Can Make Missile in Year," *Defense News*, October 6-12, 1997, pp. 4, 28; Donnelly, p. 1.

131. Moscow, *Nezavisimaya Gazeta* in Russian, August 11, 1998, *FBIS-SOV*-98-223, August 17, 1998; Moscow, *Novye Izvestiya*, in Russian, August 14, 1998, *FBIS-SOV*-98-229, August 18, 1998.

132. *Ibid.*

133. "Middle East: Iran," *CDPP*, Vol. XLVIII, No. 48, December 25, 1996, p. 22; Moscow, *Novaya Gazeta Ponedelnik*, in Russian, March 16-22, 1998, *FBIS-TAC*-98-076, March 17, 1998; Moscow, *ITAR-TASS World Service*, in Russian, March 16, 1998, *Foreign Broadcast Information Service, Military Affairs*, (henceforth *FBIS-UMA)*-98-075; Executive Summary of the Report of the Commission to Assess the Ballistic Missile Threat to the United States, July 15, 1998, Pursuant to Public Law 201, 104th Congress, (henceforth Executive Summary), Moscow, *Russkiy Telegraf*, in Russian, June 6, 1998, *FBIS-TAC*-98-160, June 10, 1998.

134. Moscow, *Radiostantsiya Ekho Moskvy*, in Russian, May 11, 1998, *FBIS SOV*, May 13, 1998; *FBIS-UMA*, March 17, 1998, *FBIS-TAC*-98-076, March 17, 1998.

135. Moscow, *Russkiy Telegraf*, in Russian, February 25, 1998, *FBIS-SOV*-98-056, March 2, 1998.

136. Moscow, *Izvestiya*, in Russian, February 27, 1998, *FBIS-TAC*-98-057, March 2, 1998.

137. London, *The Guardian*, May 31, 1995, *FBIS-SOV*-95-105, June 1, 1995, p. 16, 137; Blank, "Russia and Iran, pp. 124-127. In 1994 Foreign Minister Andrei Kozyrev confirmed that the sale of weapons and nuclear components occurred on condition that Iran renounced the possession of nuclear weapons and support for the expansion of Islamic fundamentalism "of the extremist sort" into Central Asia. Moscow, *Mirovaya Ekonomika i Mezhdunarodnye Otnosheniya*, in Russian, No. 4, April, 1994, *Joint Publication Research Service, Military Affairs*, (henceforth *JPRS-UMA)*-94-029, July 8, 1994, p. 41.

138. *JPRS-TAC*, April 6, 1995, p. 7.

139. Stephen Blank, "Russia's Return to Mideast Diplomacy," *Orbis*, Vol. XL, No. 4, Fall 1996, pp. 517-535.

140. William C. Potter, "The Case That Russia Forgot," *New York Times*, April 3, 1998, p. A-25.

141. Donnelly, p. 1.

142. Moscow, *ITAR-TASS*, in English, November 15, 1998, *FBIS-SOV*, November 15, 1998; Moscow, *Novye Izvestiya*, in Russian, June 26, 1998, *FBIS-TAC*-98-177, June 29, 1998; Steve Rodan, "Debt Issue Fails to Derail Russia-Syria Talks on S-300," *Defense News*, June 1-7, 1998, p. 54; Moscow, *Segodnya*, in Russian, February 17, 1999, *FBIS-SOV*, February 17, 1999; and Moscow, *Izvestiya*, in Russian, February 19, 1999, *FBIS-SOV*, February 18, 1999.

143. Ed Blanche, "Yemen in Secret Talks to Buy SU-27 Aircraft," *Jane's Defence Weekly*, September 30, 1998, p. 20; Moscow, *Russkiy Telegraf*, in Russian, July 22, 1998, *FBIS-TAC*-98-208, July 28, 1998.

144. *Radio Free Europe/Radio Liberty Newsline*, October 13, 1998; Moscow, *Interfax*, in English, March 28, 1996, *FBIS-SOV*-96-061, March 28, 1996, p. 14; Moscow, *Interfax*, in English, March 28, 1996, *FBIS-SOV*-96-062, March 29, 1996, p. 15; Moscow, *Izvestiya*, in Russian, *FBIS-SOV*-96-063, April 1, 1996, pp. 21-22.

145. Moscow, *Segodnya*, in Russian, July 25, 1998, *FBIS-TAC*-98-208, July 27, 1998.

146. William C. Potter, "The New Suppliers," *Orbis*, Vol. XXXVI, No. 2, Spring 1992, pp. 206-209.

147. Moscow, *Nezavisimaya Gazeta*, in Russian, *FBIS-SOV*-98-077, March 18, 1998.

148. Arbatov made his remarks to the V Annual Conference on Russian Defense Decisionmaking sponsored by the U.S. Naval Postgraduate School, Monterey, CA, March 25-27, 1998.

149. Moscow, *Segodnya*, in Russian, December 14, 1995, *FBIS-SOV*-96-028-S, May 1, 1996.

150. Moscow, *RIA*, in English, July 6, 1998, *FBIS-SOV*-98-188, July 8, 1998; Matthew Brzezinski, "U.S. Frets Over Plan to Complete Reactor in Cuba," *Wall Street Journal*, April 1, 1998, pp. 14; *Chennai Dinamani* (Internet Version) in Tamil, March 25, 1998, *Foreign Broadcast Information Service Near East and South Asia* (henceforth *FBIS-NEA*)-98-084, March 27, 1998; Moscow, *Moskovskiye Novosti*, in Russian, March 8-15, 1998, *FBIS-SOV*-98-070, March 12, 1998; Moscow, *Interfax*, in English, March 17, 1998, *FBIS-SOV*-98-076, March 18, 1998; Moscow, *Nezavisimaya Gazeta* in Russian, March 17, 1998, *FBIS-SOV*-98-077, March 19, 1998; and most recently Russia has announced plans to build still another "research" reactor in Iran and will not stop selling one to India, "Russia Plans New Reactor in Iran, Official Says," *Washington Post Foreign Service*, April 7, 1998, p. 18, *RFE/RL Newsline*, May 19, 1998.

151. Tehran, *IRNA*, in English, July 17, 1998, *FBIS-TAC*-98-198, July 20, 1998.

152. See Endnote 150.

153. "Arms Trade," *CDPP*, Vol. XLIX, No. 25, July 23, 1997, p. 28.

154. See Endnote 150.

155. Moscow, *Rossiyskaya Gazeta*, in Russian, June 5, 1998, *FBIS-SOV*-98-160, June 10, 1998.

156. Stephen Blank, *Challenging the New World Order: The Arms Transfer Policies of the Russian Republic*, Carlisle Barracks, PA: Strategic Studies Institute, U.S. Army War College, 1993, pp. 6, 16-17.

157. Kent E. Calder, *Pacific Defense: Arms, Energy, and America's Future in Asia*, New York: William Morrow & Company, Inc., 1996, pp. 38-39, 46.

158. Moscow, *Russkiy Telegraf*, in Russian, July 14, 1998, *FBIS-SOV*-98-195, July 15, 1998.

159. Ickes and Gaddy, pp. 53-67.

160. For Maslyukov's views, see his articles, "Voenno-Promyshlennyi Kompleks: Poka Degredatsiia eshche Obratima," *Pravda*, March 6-13, 1998, pp. 32-35, and "Oboronnomu Kompleks Nado Pomoshch'," *VTS*, January 19-25, 1998, pp. 32-36, both made available to the author by Dr. Igor Khripunov of the University of Georgia.

161. *FBIS-SOV*, March 18, 1998.

162. Moscow, *Segodnya*, in Russian, December 14, 1995, *FBIS-SOV*-96-028-S, May 1, 1996.

163. Moscow, *Izvestiya*, in Russian, December 24, 1996, *FBIS-SOV*-96-248, December 26, 1996; Moscow, *Nezavisimaya Gazeta*, in Russian, (Electronic Version), July 22, 1998, *FBIS-SOV*-98-222, August 13, 1998.

164. *Ibid*.

165. Athens, *I Katheimerini*, in English, September 1, 1998, *FBIS-SOV*, September 1, 1998.

166. Moscow, *Interfax*, in English, October 2, 1998, *FBIS-SOV*, October 2, 1998.

167. See the remarks of Aleksei Arbatov in Cyprus, Nicosia, *Cyprus News Agency* in English, September 27, 1998, *FBIS-SOV*, September 27, 1998; and Moscow, *Novye Izvestiya* in Russian, July 1, 1998, *FBIS-SOV*-98-183, July 6, 1998; Simon Saradzhiyan, "Russians Are Skeptical of Turkish Accord," *Defense News*, June 1-7, 1998, p. 62. It is worth noting that Dmitri Trenin characterizes Russia's Turkey policy as "schizophrenic." Dmitri Trenin, "Russia and Turkey: A Cure for Schizophrenia," *Perspectives*, Vol. II, No. 2, June-August 1997, pp. 57-65.

168. Pavel Felgengauer, "Cyprus Arms Sales for Profit," *St. Petersburg Times*, January 26-February 2, 1997. Incidentally, Felgengauer is one of the strongest advocates of the view that arms sales

are fully controlled by the bureaucracy, a view at odds with this article, but a contradiction that remains unreconciled.

169. *Ibid.*

170. Nikitenko, p. 10; Umit Eginsoy, "Turkish Moves in the Caucasus, Balkans, Irk Rivals in Region," *Defense News*, August 3-9, 1998, p. 12; Istanbul, *Milliyet*, July 31, 1997, *FBIS-WEU*-97-212, August 1, 1997.

171. Istanbul, *Cumhurriyet*, in Turkish, March 11, 1997, *FBIS-WEU*-97-072, March 15, 1997; *Ibid.*, pp. 97-240, August 28, 1997; Tel Aviv, *Ma'ariv*, in Hebrew, April 16, 1998, *FBIS-TAC*-98-106, April 17, 1998; Nicosia, *I Makhi* in Greek, August 11, 1998, *Foreign Broadcast Information Service Western Europe* (henceforth *FBIS-WEU*)-98-223, August 17, 1998.

172. Nicosia, *O Filevtheros*, in Greek, September 30, 1998, *FBIS-SOV*, September 30, 1998.

173. Andrew Borowiec, "Turkey, Foes Engage in Race to Buy Arms," *Washington Times*, October 14, 1998, p. 13; *FBIS-WEU,* March 15, 1997, August 28, 1997.

174. Eugene Kogan, "Clandestine Liaisons: Israeli-Russian Defence Co-Operation," *Jane's Intelligence Review*, May 1996, pp. 218-219; Moscow, *NTV*, in Russian, December 1, 1995, *FBIS-SOV*-95-232, December 4, 1995, p. 23; Moscow, *Radio Rossii Network*, in Russian, December 5, 1995, *FBIS-SOV*-95-234, December 6, 1995, p. 25; Moscow, *Interfax*, in English, December 9, 1995, *FBIS-SOV*-95-237, December 11, 1995, p. 30; Moscow, *Krasnaya Zvezda*, in Russian, December 5, 1995, *FBIS-SOV*-95-233, December 5, 1995, pp. 20-21.

175. Tel Aviv, *Ha'aretz* in English (Internet Version), August 10, 1998, *FBIS-NES*-98-222, August 13, 1998; *The Jamestown Monitor*, August 12, 1998, August 13, 1998, *FBIS-SOV*, August 17, 1998; *FBIS-SOV*-98-229, August 18, 1998.

176. Ed Blanche, "Israel Stops Gas Deal in Russia-Iran Missile Row," *Jane's Defence Weekly*, September 17, 1997, p. 3.

177. Moscow, *ITAR-TASS*, in English, March 30, 1998, *FBIS-SOV*-98-089, March 31, 1998.

178. London, *Al-Hayah*, in Arabic, June 4, 1998, *FBIS-SOV*-98-159, June 9, 1998.

179. Jamestown, *Prism*, October 16, 1998, Part I, "The Fortnight in Review," p. 3.

180. Moscow, *Interfax*, in English, October 9, 1998, *FBIS-SOV*, October 9, 1998.

181. Jamestown, *Prism*, October 16, 1998, p. 3.

ABOUT THE AUTHORS

DR. ROBERTO ALIBONI is Director of Studies at the Institute of International Affairs, Rome.

DR. STEFANO BIANCHINI is Director of the Center for Studies on East-Central and Balkan Europe, University of Bologna.

DR. STEPHEN J. BLANK is Research Professor of Russian/Soviet Affairs at the Strategic Studies Institute, U.S. Army War College.

DR. STEVEN L. BURG is Professor of Politics, Brandeis University.

DR. STEPHEN C. CALLEYA is Deputy Director and Lecturer in International Relations, Mediterranean Academy of Diplomatic Studies, University of Malta, and International Representative of the International Office, University of Warwick.

DR. THEODORE A. COULOUMBIS is Professor of International Relations, University of Athens, and Vice President of the Hellenic Foundation for European and Foreign Policy.

DR. ROBERT O. FREEDMAN is President of Baltimore Hebrew University.

DR. SAMI G. HAJJAR is Director, Middle East Studies, Department of National Security and Strategy, U.S. Army War College.

DR. R. CRAIG NATION is the Elihu Root Professor of Military Studies, U.S. Army War College.

DR. ALESSANDRO POLITI is at the Ministry of Defense, Rome.

DR. RODOLFO RAGIONIERI is at the Department of Political and Social Science, Center for the Study of War and Peace, Florence.

COLONEL VALERI RATCHEV is Deputy Director of the Center for Strategic Studies of the Ministry of Defense of Bulgaria.

DR. MOHAMMAD EL-SAYED SELIM is Professor of Political Science, Faculty of Economics and Political Science, Cairo University.

DR. DUYGU BAZOGLU SEZER is Professor of International Relations at Bilkent University, Ankara, Turkey.

DR. GERALD M. STEINBERG is Associate Professor of Political Studies at Bar Ilan University; and Director of Conflict Management and Resolution, and Senior Research Associate at the Begin-Sadat Center for Strategic Studies.

DR. MARIO ZUCCONI is at the University of Urbino, Urbino, Italy.